ENGAGEMENTS WITH RHETORIC

A PATH TO ACADEMIC WRITING
AT THE UNIVERSITY OF MARYLAND

Taken from:

Envision: Writing and Researching Arguments, Second Edition
by Christine L. Alfano and Alyssa J. O'Brien

Style: Lessons in Clarity and Grace, Ninth Edition
by Joseph M. Williams

Rhetorical Grammar: Grammatical Choices, Rhetorical Effects, Fifth Edition
by Martha Kolln

Having Your Say: Reading and Writing Public Arguments
by Davida H. Charney and Christine M. Neuwirth with David S. Kaufer and Cheryl Geisler

Writing: A Guide for College and Beyond
by Lester Faigley

From Inquiry to Argument
by Linda McMeniman

Learning Solutions

New York   Boston   San Francisco
London   Toronto   Sydney   Tokyo   Singapore   Madrid
Mexico City   Munich   Paris   Cape Town   Hong Kong   Montreal

Cover Art: Cover image courtesy of the University of Maryland

Taken from:

Envision: Writing and Researching Arguments,
Second Edition
by Christine L. Alfano and Alyssa J. O'Brien
Copyright © 2008 by Pearson Education, Inc.
Published by Longman
New York, New York 10036

Style: Lessons in Clarity and Grace, Ninth Edition
by Joseph M. Williams
Copyright © 2007 by Pearson Education, Inc.
Published by Longman

Having Your Say: Reading and Writing
Public Arguments
by David H. Charney and Christine M. Neuwirth
with David S. Kaufer and Cheryl Geisler
Copyright © 2006 by Pearson Education, Inc.
Published by Longman

Writing: A Guide for College and Beyond
by Lester Faigley
Copyright © 2007 by Pearson Education, Inc.
Published by Longman

Rhetorical Grammar: Grammatical Choices,
Rhetorical Effects, Fifth Edition
by Martha Kolln
Copyright © 2007 by Pearson Education, Inc.
Published by Longman

From Inquiry to Argument
by Linda McMeniman
Copyright © 1999 by Allyn & Bacon
A Pearson Education company
Boston, Massachusetts 02116

Pearson Learning Solutions, 501 Boylston Street, Suite 900, Boston, MA 02116
A Pearson Education Company
www.pearsoned.com

Printed in the United States of America

1 2 3 4 5 6 7 8 9 10   V011   15 14 13 12 11 10

000200010270593726

JL/CA

ISBN 10: 0-558-75233-0
ISBN 13: 978-0-558-75233-0

CONTENTS

The current curriculum used in English 101 at the University of Maryland, College Park, is based on a curriculum created by Prof. Jeanne Fahnestock and used first at UMCP in 1992. From materials Prof. Fahnestock wrote for the course, a custom publication, titled *The Introduction to Academic Writing*, was created several years later. Under the direction of Prof. Linda Coleman, materials created by a wide variety of English 101 instructors, based on the materials and curriculum established by Prof. Fahnestock, were collected into that first text. The *IAW*, as it was commonly called, was revised several times and used for over a decade in the program. The material in this new textbook has, in turn, been developed from those materials. This path to development demonstrates the ways that writing is social and communal, and harkens back to the rhetorical foundations of the course, for materials used in the teaching of rhetoric from the classical era through the twentieth century were repeatedly reinscribed, revised, and adjusted for their particular times and audiences. This book, then, continues that tradition of being based on classical foundations and revised by teachers striving to make the material fresh and applicable for their students.

Many people deserve acknowledgment for this text, from Prof. Jeanne Fahnestock and Prof. Linda Coleman, to the instructors who contributed materials or helped to revise various versions of the *IAW*, to current instructors in the program who worked as an editorial team on this text. In many ways, it's no longer a simple matter to say who authored a particular page in this book. Thus I want to acknowledge both groups.

Several pages in this current volume were explicitly adapted from materials from *The Introduction to Academic Writing*, and those pages were written or revised in various editions of the *IAW* by many the following former English 101 instructors, many of whom have gone on to become professors at various institutions of higher education across the country: Allison Brovey, Ryan Claycomb, Frank DeBernardo, Jeana Delrosso-Freeman, Kate Dobson, Rob Doggett, Magdelyn Hammond, Jaime Osterman, Donna Packer-Kinlaw, Meg Pearson, Patricia Franks Porcarelli, Alisse Portnoy, Rachel Portnoy, Erin Sadlack, and Vera Tobin.

An editorial team that included Rebekah Benson, Michelle Boswell, Heather Brown, Alyson E. Doulos, Stephanie Graham, Nabila Hijazi, Mark Hoffman, Tyler Mills, Thomas Moretti, Jason Payton, Kelli Skinner, and Jana Wilson discussed and offered advice about the current text, suggesting and selecting materials to be included in the book. On their advice, the Freshman Writing Program team of myself, Beth Colson, Dr. Wendy Hayden, and Thomas "Jody" Lawton selected, wrote, edited, and revised materials in the text. Lisa Sibbett shared with us the exemplary efforts of her student, Scott DeMuth, and he agreed to have his "Considering the Other Side" paper on recycling included here; similarly, one of my former students, Nene Fofana, agreed to have a draft of her "Experience and Other Evidence" paper included. Scott Eklund, the Program's Administrative Coordinator, in addition to authoring several sections of this volume, also performed many of the tasks of literally putting the book together, by researching, scanning, printing, typing, and mailing the documents that make up this text.

Our colleagues at Allyn Bacon Longman at Pearson Education, Jerry Higgins and Chip Noonan, were always encouraging, helpful and excited about this project.

Just as this book stands on the shoulders of its predecessor, I will borrow the dedication which my predecessor, Prof. Linda Coleman, wrote there: "those whose [names] are listed are by no means the only people whose contributions are represented here. The fact is, nearly everything in this text is the result of the work, ideas, comments, and suggestions of the teachers and administrators of the Freshman Writing Program. Those who teach English 101 are a thoughtful, energetic, and committed group of people. The curriculum would not be possible without them; the course would not be possible without them; and, accordingly, it is to them and their students that this effort is dedicated."

Linda C. Macri, Phd.
Director, Freshman Writing Program
June 2007

Welcome to Introduction to Academic Writing, commonly known as English 101. This semester, you'll do a great deal of writing, editing, rewriting, reading, and research. English 101 is a required course at Maryland, one of three "fundamental studies" requirements that all students have to fulfill. Of these three courses, two are writing requirements, which indicates the importance of writing to not only your college career but the life you are preparing for.

In English 101 this semester, you will learn the conventions of academic inquiry and research and how to construct an argument from that process. Universities such as UMCP are often referred to as "research universities" because the work that goes on here centers on research. But that research doesn't just matter on this campus or on university campuses in general. As Dr. Mel Bernstein, Vice President for Research at UMCP, notes, "Academically-based research is a critical contributor to graduate and undergraduate education programs, to local and national economic development and to advancing peoples' health, security and general well being, both in the US and internationally." So learning how to produce and analyze academic writing, making and understanding arguments based on sound research, will be a skill you will use not only in college but also beyond, in your work life and your life as a member of a community.

English 101 is an introduction, and that's a significant distinction. You'll find that you'll be asked to write many different types of assignments over the next four years, but in this course you won't practice every kind of assignment that might be asked of you during your undergraduate career. Instead, English 101 will prepare you to ask questions and analyze the situations of writing so that you will be able to enter the discourse in other fields, figure out the kinds of questions that matter, and understand how to proceed with inquiry and writing.

The title of this book refers to what we emphasize in the course. The title suggests that you'll be engaging in rhetoric, so first, let's consider that term. We often hear the term *rhetoric* used pejoratively, in phrases such as "mere rhetoric" or "that's just rhetoric." Although *rhetoric* is often used to indicate ornamentation or empty words, the term refers to a classical concept. Rhetoric was the cornerstone of education for centuries. For Aristotle, a teacher of rhetoric in classical Greece, rhetoric was "finding the available means of persuasion," while for Quintilian, a teacher from classical Rome, it was "a good man speaking well." In English 101, when we speak of rhetoric, or persuasion or argument, terms often used interchangeably, we mean something beyond confrontation and controversy. Instead, we emphasize understanding the appeals that you can make to create a common ground with your audience, a conceptualization that echoes back to Aristotle's definition of finding the avenues that will be persuasive, as well as Quintilian's idea that rhetoric is not just about arguing and winning but being ethical in one's practices as well.

The word *engagement* clearly comes to play in this sense. In rhetoric, you are engaging your audience, asking that they see things as you do, join with you in your position, your opinion, or perhaps even your call to action. To engage is a familiar term for us; it means to occupy someone's attention or efforts, as when we engage someone in conversation. It also means to secure, attach, attract, or obtain something, as in "I've engaged the room for our party" or "try and engage his attention." We say we are "engaged in a pursuit" when we become involved in something. It implies something of a pledge, and sometimes a confrontation (as when we engage in battle). And perhaps many of you will recognize the popular culture reference that Capt. Jean-Luc Picard ordered "Engage!" when he was ready to take the *Enterprise* onto its next mission. All these definitions come to play in what you'll do this semester when you have an engagement with rhetoric.

For English 101, the term engagement also resonates because of our focus on *civic engagement.* In your course, you'll explore what that term means, but we can start here by asking you what the term might mean. Considering all those meanings of "engage," and given that "civic" is an adjective that means pertaining to the citizen, *civic engagement* refers to something secured, attracted to, pledged by the citizen. You are the citizen here—a citizen of a nation, a community, a university, a classroom. In English 101, you'll be asked to consider that role and how you will perform it.

Throughout this book, you will learn more about rhetoric and civic engagement. By the end of the semester, you will have had repeated engagements with rhetoric, engagements that you will take on to your other classes here at Maryland and to your experiences beyond. Hinting at perhaps the most common use of the term, I hope that your engagement with rhetoric this semester is full of joy but also full of thoughtful reflection on the life the two of you will lead in the future. Best wishes!

Linda C. Macri, Phd.
Director, Freshman Writing Program
University of Maryland, College Park

I

STARTING POINTS

Have you ever had the experience of sitting with a blank sheet of paper (or a blank computer screen) before you and being unable to make any progress on a writing task that you are trying to accomplish? Does it seem that there are just too many things to think about? That you don't know where to start? As surprising as it might sound, even experienced writers feel this way sometimes. There's no shame in admitting it: writing is hard work. Effectively putting thoughts down on paper requires great effort and careful consideration; you must think about what you want to say, what order you want to say it in, what wording or style you want to use. It can often seem overwhelming.

Classical rhetoricians, who wanted to systematize the process of writing speeches, developed a pattern for steps in the writing process, so that speech writers could proceed in an organized fashion and consider everything necessary for composing a good speech. This pattern became known as the "parts" or **canons** of rhetoric. One influential version of this pattern included five canons: invention, arrangement, style, memory, and delivery. This structure can also be adapted to other types of composition besides speeches, as long as we keep in mind the distinctions between composing oral speeches and composing typewritten papers.

INVENTION: GENERATING ARGUMENTS

Of all the steps in the writing process, invention is probably the hardest—and the most important. Invention is the crucial first step of determining what to put in your paper. One reason it can be so hard to figure out what we want to say is that we often take for granted that good writing has to be "original" in the sense of saying something the likes of which has never been said before. When taken to an extreme, this notion almost makes it seem as if good writing appears magically out of thin air. In reality, good writing can indeed be original, but classical rhetoricians recognized that real originality has less to do with trying to produce something from nothing, and more to do with working with what you already have and making it better. After all, when entrepreneurs "invent" a new tool or labor-saving device, they work with materials that are already available; they don't just magically create something from nothing. Similarly, classical rhetoricians imagined "invention" as a process of "finding" ideas that already exist—appropriately enough, since the word "invent" really means "come upon" or "find." Thinking about writing in this way can make the writing process less intimidating, since you're no longer under pressure to come up with something absolutely new. It doesn't mean that there's no room for originality or creativity. On the contrary, some of the most original and creative writing owes a great deal to ideas and writings that came before it.

So how exactly do you go about "inventing" an argument? There are several options available. You may already be familiar with the method called **brainstorming**, in which you jot down a list of words, phrases, or ideas on a sheet of paper as they come to you, not worrying (at least at first) whether everything fits together neatly; this process can give you a place to start. There's also the technique known as **freewriting**, in which you try to write continuously for a set period of time, not worrying about things like grammar and sentence structure. Using methods such as these, you may come up with some things that you may eventually choose not to include in the final draft of your paper, but the more material that you can generate using invention exercises, the more potential material you will have to choose from when you are deciding what belongs and what doesn't.

ARRANGEMENT: ORGANIZING ARGUMENTS

So you've figured out what you want to say. Does it matter what order you say it in? With respect to argumentative writing, we can definitely say yes. The order in which you present your material can have a significant impact on the success or failure of your writing. To take one example, let's say you have three main points, two of which the audience might find strongly convincing, but one of which is weaker and less convincing. Should you save the best for last, and therefore present the weakest point first? That might cause your audience to lose interest early on, thinking that all your points will be as ineffective as the first one. Or do you leave the weakest point for last? That might be problematic too, since the last point is often the one most likely to be remembered by the reader, and you don't want the reader to walk away dwelling on your weakest point. In such a situation, many experts recommend a sort of "sandwich" structure in which the weakest point comes in between the two stronger ones. The point is that when you write your own papers, you must make decisions about how best to organize your material, keeping in mind the audience and purpose of your writing.

In addition to thinking about how to present your main points, it's also necessary to consider how to begin and end the paper, as well as what other structural features your paper might need. Papers that jump right into their main points with no background or context are generally not successful or even interesting to readers, since readers need to know why the topic is important before they can make sense of what a writer is arguing about that topic. The same goes for papers that end too suddenly. For this reason, a very basic pattern of writing arrangement consists of an introduction, body (where the main points are explained in detail), and conclusion. For longer papers (such as the final paper that you will write this semester), you will learn about an expanded version of the basic arrangement pattern. This version, called the "parts of a full argument," is especially helpful when you have more than a few sentences of background information, and when you must think about how to organize both your own supporting points and your refutation of opposing points. In the end, it's important to keep in mind that usually there is no single correct way to set up a paper. Instead, a different range of options is available in each case, and you as the writer must decide which option is best for the audience you are trying to reach and the purpose you are trying to achieve.

STYLE: EXPRESSING ARGUMENTS

How you say something can be as important as what you say. Language can be a tricky thing, because it presents us with a seemingly endless range of potential problems. Some words have more than one meaning, and you want your readers to be clear about what meaning you intend. Different words can have the same meaning; or, more likely, they have meanings that are very similar but with slightly different connotations, and you will need to think carefully about which is the right one to use in a given situation.

To add to the complexity, no single variety of any language can be used in all possible situations. The language appropriate to a formal event would be inappropriate in a more casual context. The style a writer uses on a particular occasion may be influenced by things like dialect, slang, jargon, and colloquialisms, or it may be carefully crafted to be as neutral as possible. We have all probably wished at one time or another that language were simple, that there were only one single, correct word for each object or idea, so that there would never be any confusion or ambiguity. It might seem as if that would make writing (and indeed, all communication) much easier.

Looked at another way, however, the complexity of language presents us with a great opportunity. Different forms of language exist both because people themselves are different and because the same people can use different forms of language depending on the situation. Thus, the complexities inherent in language are best seen from a rhetorical perspective as possibilities available for a given audience and situation. The study of style, the consideration of how best to express one's own ideas to a specific audience in a particular situation, is empowering because it gives us the chance to make choices for ourselves, to choose our words just as we choose our method of organization. How formal should you be? What tone do you want to express in your writing? Will your audience understand jargon if you use it? Does your audience expect conciseness, or does the complexity of your content require you to present some information in two or three different ways?

To help you think about these and other stylistic issues, a number of language skills are built into the writing curriculum. Practicing these skills can help you develop your own written style, enabling you to make choices about emphasizing ideas in different ways, using figures of speech to create patterns and support your arguments, and combining sentences so that your writing flows more smoothly. In essence, style is about learning what options are available, so that you can use your own creativity to make the most effective choices in your writing.

MEMORY: STORING ARGUMENTS

Since classical rhetoricians were concerned primarily with composing speeches that would be delivered before an audience (and in an era without teleprompters), they devoted a considerable amount of thought to techniques that would help speakers memorize their points and arguments so that they could deliver them without having to look at notes. Such techniques often included mnemonic devices and "tricks" to aid memorization. For the composition of typewritten papers, memorization for oral delivery usually does not play a prominent role, but memory—in the sense of where typewritten arguments are *stored*—is still important. Think of what we mean when we talk about a computer's "memory," for example. Today, a number of technologies are available that allow us to store documents with ease, and it is to our advantage to make use of them. It goes without saying that you should save a copy of a paper that you are working on. But it pays to save *multiple* copies of really important documents (including ones that will be turned in for a grade), since accidents happen—files can be corrupted, disks can get erased, hard drives can crash, flash drives can get lost, and so on. To be on the safe side, you may even want to take the precaution of saving your paper to an email attachment that is stored in your email system; that way, even if your own hardware fails at some point, you still have a version of your paper on email that you can access. You may also find it helpful to deliberately save multiple versions of a single paper. For example, it's difficult to undo a major change to your draft if you don't have an earlier version saved. So you should consider at least saving a file copy of your rough draft and a separate copy of your final draft, so that you can access both versions electronically if you decide that it's useful to do so. Not only can using these labor-saving techniques help you out of potentially disastrous computer malfunctions, but they can also make the overall writing process flow more smoothly.

DELIVERY: PUBLISHING AND FORMATTING ARGUMENTS

"Delivery" originally referred to the act of delivering speeches orally before a live audience. Being an effective speaker usually means speaking loudly enough and at the right speed so that the audience can easily hear and follow the speech, enunciating clearly and according to the audience's standards for public speech, and perhaps using gestures to emphasize a point. But even in writing, delivery is important. For writing, we can think of delivery in two aspects: how an argument is transmitted to an audience, and how a typewritten argument is formatted.

When a speech is delivered orally before a live audience, the audience simply hears it as the speaker delivers it. But if your argument is typewritten, how would your audience physically receive it? For example, if you imagined writing your paper to "every citizen of the United States," how would you ensure that every citizen in the country could read your argument? It's obviously impractical to imagine mailing a copy of your argument to everyone in the country. Could you have it published in a venue in which everyone could read it? You might imagine having it published in a widely-read newspaper or magazine, but realistically, there's no newspaper or magazine that is read by *every* person in the country. How about publishing it online? Even then, it is worth considering that some American citizens don't have access to the internet.

In many cases, thinking about issues like these can prompt you to reconsider your audience, to narrow it down in order to make your argument more effective. For example, even if you are writing about an issue with a national scope—say, what to do about illegal immigration—that doesn't mean that your argument should be written to every citizen of the U.S. Your argument is more likely to be successful if you focus. For example, if you decide that you want to focus on the effect of the immigration debate on American presidential campaigns, then you could write your paper to scholars of government and politics, and emphasize the aspects of the issue that are most interesting to them. Since they are experts in political science, they would be able to put your argument to better use in advancing the national debate on immigration and politics than the "average" American citizen would; many of the latter might not only disagree with what you're arguing, they might even lack interest in the political side of the issue. By choosing to deliver your argument by having it published in a political science journal (such as *The Journal of Politics*), or even by imagining that you would distribute copies to your instructor and fellow students in the Government and Politics course that you're taking this semester, you can use the concept of delivery to narrow your audience and be more confident that the audience will be interested in your scholarly approach to the topic.

Thinking about where you would publish your argument is helpful for conceptualizing your audience, but within the context of ENGL 101, you will be designing your papers so that a special set of overhearers—your instructor and (in draft workshops) your fellow students—can read it. Thus, your paper must be formatted so that these readers can understand your argument. Formatting requirements that might seem minor are really a matter of audience expectation. For example, consider how your experience of reading a textbook, such as this one, would change if it were printed in tiny type, in a strange script or Old English style font, or, worse, if it were handwritten. Would you bother to read it? Would you even be able to read it? This is why most teachers have standard requirements for what papers should look like. For example, double-spacing your papers and leaving one-inch margins allows your teacher to make comments on your paper that will help you understand both what you did well and what you could improve on. Page numbers help readers find their way around the paper. And using a clear, standard format for citing your sources helps readers track down additional information and helps you establish yourself as a valid participant in a public or scholarly debate.

Other seemingly minor issues with potentially substantial impact also relate to delivery and format. Printing problems can happen to anybody, but when a writer turns in a paper with printing that obviously hasn't been aligned correctly, or that is far too light because of ink problems, it makes the paper—and the writer—look bad. If you submitted such a document to an audience other than your teacher (if, for example, you submitted a resume with that problem to potential employers), your readers wouldn't be inclined to take it seriously, and there is no reason why your teacher is obligated to do so, either. That's why you should print out your paper ahead of time so that you can correct any printing problems that may arise. And don't fall into the habit of handing in your paper as a jumble of loose sheets; you should staple your paper together (or at the very least paper-clip it) so that your teacher doesn't have to keep track of loose paper. Finally, perhaps the most important part of delivery is turning in your paper when it's due. Even the most brilliant argument cannot achieve its intended purpose if it's not delivered at the right time.

For these reasons, you will be expected to follow formatting guidelines in your papers. Your teacher will include information about formatting requirements on his or her course policies.

SEEING THE PARTS OF RHETORIC AS A WHOLE

This five-part pattern is a useful tool, but it should be used with flexibility. Ideally, an orderly writing process would treat invention first, then arrangement, then style, then memory, and finally delivery. But in reality, good writers keep all of them in mind throughout the composing process. In the middle of considering arrangement, you may discover that your paper seems unbalanced and that you need to add another main point, which sends you back to the invention process to find more material. Also, the parts can overlap; arrangement and style can be closely related, especially when you consider the layout of sentences within a paragraph. The parts of rhetoric, then, are not meant to be rigid and inhibiting. Instead, they are simply terms and concepts for things that writers need to think about under any circumstances. They give you a way of structuring the process of writing; just keep in mind that this structure can be adaptable and open-ended.

INVENTION—GENERATING IDEAS WITH STASIS THEORY

One way to invent something to say is to think about the kinds of questions people might ask about a subject. Just as classical rhetorical theory offers a system for the process of writing, it also offers a system for inventing or analyzing what's at issue in any debate. This system is called **stasis theory**. Stasis theory can help you come up with ways to argue and it can help you understand the ways others are arguing. The term *stasis* comes from a Greek term that means "a stand," as in "taking a stand." For the Greeks, who literally pictured their arguments, the arguer envisioned where "to stand" in a particular debate. The best translation here might be "issue," as in understanding what is "at issue" in a controversy. That's a phrase you might hear in a news report covering a topic; the reporter, having introduced the topic and offered some information, might begin to delineate "what's at issue" in the topic by saying what various participants or factions in the debate think and what kinds of questions come up in the matter. When you are thinking about a topic for a composition, it can be useful to imagine yourself as a reporter looking at some problem and beginning to think about what's at issue, where the controversies are, where you may take a stand.

Stasis theory presents us with categories or questions to pose in understanding a debate or understanding where there is debate or disagreement in an issue. There are many theories about how many categories of the stases there are; some theorists use slightly different categories than the ones we have included here. In general, the stases and the questions they pose are these:

Stasis	Questions
Conjecture (or fact/definition, or essence/existence)	Did it happen? Does it exist? What is it? How is it defined?
Cause/Effect	How did it get this way? What caused this to happen? What are/will be the effects of this?
Value	Is it a good or bad thing? Is it right or wrong, honorable or dishonorable? Is it better or worse, more or less desirable than any alternatives? Should it be sought out or avoided?
Action	What should we do about this? What actions are possible? What proposals shall we make about it?
Jurisdiction	Who should handle this matter? Who has the right to decide this matter?

STAKING A CLAIM WITH STASIS THEORY

Perhaps you want to write about an experience you had with the police last year. One day, you were driving home from a friend's house, and you saw police lights flashing in your rearview mirror. You were pulled over, and the white police officer looked at you suspiciously and asked to see your license. Too afraid to ask what this was about, you just complied. Later that night, you heard that a crime had been committed not far from where you were stopped, and the suspect was vaguely described as a young African American man. You too are a young African American man. When you tell the story to some friends, they say that you were stopped for DWB—driving while black.

How can you begin inquiry into this experience? There's no doubt that it occurred—you were definitely stopped. But what other possible questions arise here. Think about stasis theory. What can you call what happened to you—was it routine police work? racial profiling? Why did it happen? Was it a good or bad thing it happened? Was it reasonable or unreasonable? Should you do something about it? What could be done about it? Is it up to you as an individual to do something about it, or should you look to others to respond? If you use these questions from stasis theory, you can find what about the issue interests you and focus on that in your inquiry.

Or perhaps one of the experiences you cherish most from your childhood was listening to stories from your grandmother. She told stories about everything—about when she was a small girl on a farm during the Great Depression, about when your dad was born, stories she made up, stories she heard herself as a young girl. But how can you write about this in terms of an argument of inquiry? Again, you might use the questions from stasis theory to help you think about whether there are any issues to consider here. Again, there's no disputing that this happened, but you can again think about definitions—were the stories your grandmother told you just stories, or could they be considered folklore? Why do we tell stories? Is it to pass along values, or just for entertainment? What effect did these stories have on you? What effect does storytelling have on children (or cultures) in general? Is hearing stories a good thing? Is it better for children to hear stories from family than, say, to watch television or see movies? Should we encourage the telling of stories among families? How should we encourage storytelling? Who should do such encouraging, if we agree it should be done?

EXERCISE

Think of a favorite memory from your childhood. Write a brief paragraph about the memory, and then share these paragraphs in small groups of three or four classmates. Talk about each in turn. Is there recognizable controversy in any of these memories? If not, can you turn the ideas from these memories into topics for inquiry? As a group, try to come up with a question that relates to the memory from each stasis. After you have several questions, discuss which of these might be the best choice for more inquiry, and think about what academic discipline might investigate such a question.

WHAT IS "EXIGENCE," AND WHY DO I NEED TO KNOW?

How many times have you written something—or read something—that just didn't seem to have much of a reason for being (aside, perhaps, from getting a grade in a class)? Although this problem certainly arises outside the classroom, it plagues the writing most students do in school. Perhaps your research paper leaves the impression of being unrelated to anyone or anything in the "real world," or your essay just doesn't seem to go anywhere or do anything important. We can probably all think of times when a reader's most honest response to our writing would reasonably have been "So what? Why should I care about this?"

Writing that fails to answer the "so what?" question lacks what is known as **exigence**. That is, it fails to convey the urgency, importance, usefulness, timeliness, or interest of its subject for its particular audience. Readers are likely to become bored because they find the writing pointless. Isn't that the last thing we want our readers, including our professors, to think? On the other hand, writing that establishes exigence gives its readers a genuine reason to keep reading.

Kairos and *Chronos* and Exigence

In Ancient Greece, there were two different concepts of time. *Chronos* expressed quantifiable, linear, time; it's the source of our word "chronological," for example. But they also conceived a term that expressed a sense of circumstance or situation. That word, *kairos*, is more akin to a sense of quality of time rather than quantity of time. We might think of it more in the sense of "the right time" or a "window of opportunity." And it is to this sense of *kairos* that exigence refers. When something has exigence, it is taking advantage of the right time, the right place, of a sense of urgency or advantage or appropriateness.

Intrinsic and Extrinsic Exigence

Writers must always be conscious of exigence as they compose, but because exigence is related to the audience and the situation, it often seems to exist outside of the writer's control. There are, in other words, situations that seem to have an **extrinsic** sense of exigence; the situation itself presents all the urgency and appropriateness, seeming to demand a response. For example, if there is a terrible natural catastrophe in, say, California, we expect the President to make some remarks about it. In that case, it seems to be the situation that calls for a response. Not only does it call for a response, but it calls for a certain kind of response. We can imagine what we would deem appropriate or inappropriate for the President to say in such a situation. In the workplace, assigned work provides the exigence for writing a report or a memo. In these cases, the exigence comes from the situation; so long as you attend to the subject at hand, you will have established the exigence for your discourse for that audience. (While this kind of situation might seem to "naturally" demand a response, the idea that a situation in endowed with essential exigence is thought by many to be questionable; instead, they suggest that there are social or situational reasons why we expect certain responses, why some things seem to "be" news and others are not).

In contrast to situations with a strong sense of extrinsic exigence, other situations seem to need to have exigence created for them. That will be the case with most of your writing. While indeed you are responding to a situation outside of your own making—that is, you are responding to a requirement set up by the instructor of your course—beyond that exigence you should also consider creating a sense of urgency and need for your writing. We refer to the author creating the exigence as a situation of **intrinsic** exigence; that is, the exigence is created within the composition rather than in the situation outside of the writing. How do you fashion such an opening, such a sense of urgency or demand for your argument? By showing your readers that a problem exists, that there is a situation that demands their attention, that you will discuss something they will find interesting and applicable to their lives.

Can You Give Me an Example?

Let's start with a typical example from *The Washington Post*. When the paper runs a story evaluating twenty brands of bottled water, the writer of the article may begin by explaining, "Since last week, when the federal government released studies showing that tap water in forty states is polluted, there has been a run on bottled water. What are the better brands?" Why does a story about bottled water begin this way? With his lead-in, the writer has shown the audience that his story addresses a problem that may affect them: much tap water is polluted, so they are probably changing to bottled water right now—shouldn't they know which is the best buy? Thus, the writer creates exigence for his story.

In academic writing, a writer might begin by referencing past works written on a topic, or with a review of the literature, or a review of what past scholars have said, on a given topic. The writer does this to establish exigence in the scholarly debate on the topic: people in the field are talking about it, and the writer is adding a new dimension to the conversation. An article in *College Composition and Communication* on using technology in the classroom aimed at an audience of writing teachers and scholars, for example, might begin by referring to recent articles on the topic published in journals of the field. The writer might then show what his article adds to the conversation about teaching with technology. Or, a writer might show that no one else has talked about a topic, and create exigence that shows how this new view adds to the field. For example, an article in a history journal on a lesser-known historical figure might begin by showing how this figure has been ignored in past scholarship and then by establishing the importance of this figure to understanding a particular point in history. Writers publishing in scholarly journals provide exigence that shows how their work is adding to the academic conversations in the field.

Now let's look back at the opening paragraphs of this discussion of exigence. You will find that we began by identifying a need or problem that affects our audience: students. We assumed that as students, you would find this problem pressing enough to read about our proposed solution. If you felt that this discussion was worth reading, for a reason other than passing a quiz, perhaps we have proven our point?

In these cases, the writers have taken steps to create an impression of exigence *for their readers,* even though the writers themselves naturally believe that the problems they are addressing are obviously both real and pressing. The point is that writers must begin with language that leads readers to believe that they should care.

When Do I Establish Exigence? Do I Just Need a Catchy Introduction?

Exigence should be apparent throughout a paper, and the first place it would appear is the introduction. When a reader finds that she has something at stake in a particular argument, issue, or decision, she will read on. In the first several sentences, it is essential to pull your reader in with a brief and clear picture of how your topic is relevant to her experience or self-interest.

Since you only have a few moments to catch a reader's attention, you should try to establish exigence early on. But readers may continue asking "So what?" as they read; if your writing continues to provide an answer to this question, they will continue reading. Thus, establishing exigence goes beyond writing a clever or captivating introduction. Solid exigence should reside behind your thesis statement, and every other statement in your text, because it keeps your readers' needs in mind. It is a factor guiding your selection of information to include and information to discard. It is a factor determining the order in which information is disclosed, and the way your writing is introduced and concluded. Exigence tells the writer and the reader what the importance behind the work is, providing focus and giving a sense of force or drive behind the words.

Let's consider the possible differences between a catchy introduction and the establishment of exigence. An introduction to a paper arguing for research funds for cystic fibrosis could be a sad story about a child with cystic fibrosis. The story could be a pathetic appeal to readers which could provide the "hook" that encourages them to continue reading past the first paragraph or two. In fact, the story could be an important supporting argument for your thesis. But it may not be enough to convince readers that they have a stake in the issue. What would be enough? Maybe the articulation of a problem marked by an urgency: thousands of children each year are born with this debilitating disease.

This brings us to a very important distinction in persuasive writing. There is a subtle difference between compelling your readers to read and persuading your readers to hold a position or to change their minds or to act for change. For the writing you do in this class, then, think of your interesting introduction and your established exigence as two separate things that work together. But remember that your argument needs both an interesting introduction to engage readers and established exigence to convince them that they have a stake in the issue about which you are writing.

SOURCES OF ARGUMENT: THE COMMON TOPICS

In most times and places, the medium for public discourse has been speech, not writing. In ancient Athens, for example, litigants argued their cases orally in front of juries of 251 or 501 people. Unlike today there was no obligation to let the other side know what you were going to do in advance, so speakers needed to be able to speak eloquently and persuasively and to respond fluently and effectively to opposing arguments as soon as they were uttered. The ability to craft a persuasive argument on the spot requires not only a very good memory but also some devices to generate effective arguments without getting lost in the details. One such device is what we call the **common topics**.

The common topics are sources of argument that can be used in just about any situation. Many arguments are based on one of these four categories:

- **definition**
- **cause and consequence**
- **comparison**, sometimes referred to as **analogy**
- **testimony and authority**.

These sources of argument are invention techniques for supporting a thesis.

How do they work? One way to understand them is to consider the metaphor underlying the expression *common topic*. *Topic*, in this technical sense, does not mean subject or content of a piece of writing. It comes from the Greek word *topos* (plural *topoi*), meaning 'place' or 'location' (think of terms like *topographical*). *Topic* in the specialized rhetorical sense simply means "a (metaphorical) place where you look for an argument." Common topics, then, are sources of argument that work for just about every argument—it's difficult to imagine any discussion in which you couldn't use some kind of comparison.

A topic, then, is a technique or line of argument. When writers try to persuade someone, they are always looking for *topoi*, or topics, in our technical sense, that their audience will recognize. The common topics are used in nearly every type of persuasive writing because many people accept these as methods of argument.

How Are the Common Topics Used?

1. Definition

The Department of Transportation begins an advertising campaign to cut down on aggressive driving with the slogan:

Driving is not a game.

This little slogan contains an argument from **definition**. It claims that there is a category, "game"—which we associate with playfulness, recklessness, immaturity, and a lack of harsh consequences—whose characteristics should not apply to driving.

An argument from definition, or "the nature of things," names or labels a group, a class, a kind, or a category. Once a subject is placed in that class or sits under that label, an audience's beliefs about the category transfer to the subject. If, on the other hand, we can show that a subject does not belong in an expected category, we can begin to undo an audience's expectations about the subject.

For example, if Stephen King's novels belong to a special literary genre (category) called "horror," then they will probably be compared or judged only with other novels in that genre. Or if we believe there is a category of person called the "visual learner," then we believe that by nature a person in this category has an inherent "visual learning" quality. It's not something he does; it's something he is. Similarly, if there is a special kind of criminal (itself a category) called the "chronic offender," by nature different from other criminals, then once a person is labeled "chronic offender," institutions may feel justified in treating that individual differently from criminals in other categories.

Definition arguments can be easily overlooked because they can be very subtle. If an author labels an act "political," for example, she believes, and wants readers to believe, that there is a category of "political acts" that this particular act belongs to. Sometimes a writer relies on an audience accepting a categorization or label readily in this way; in other situations, the arguer anticipates resistance and argues for categorization.

Arguers can spend a significant portion of an argument putting subjects into or taking subjects out of classes, groups, and categories. They may even adopt the strategy of creating a new class or category.

2. Cause and Consequence

A city planner supports a proposal for increasing park space and public seating in city centers by predicting that such a change will improve the economic condition of a city. The support here comes from envisioning positive **consequences**, the good effects that will follow from the proposal. Predicting consequences (good, bad, or mixed) is a common strategy in arguments that evaluate or propose action.

Giving a plausible account of the causes that precede instead of the consequences that follow can also support a variety of positions. For example, if an audience can be convinced that global warming was caused by a particular dominant factor, that factor will be the focal point of proposals for change. If consumers can be convinced that drinking a particular beverage will help them lose weight, weight loss or health will be the theme of the advertisement. Politicians often use **cause and consequence** arguments when they argue that current problems are caused by the policies of their opponents; any future improvement will be the consequence of their election.

Causal arguments can also back up definitions, particularly definitions of actions characterized by their motives. Thus we label acts differently depending on our beliefs about the doer's motivation; the law, for instance, makes a significant distinction between premeditated and unpremeditated murder.

3. Comparison (Likenesses and Differences, Similarities and Contrasts)

When writers of travel brochures call San Antonio the "Venice of Texas," they are hoping to transfer the notions readers associate with the city on the Adriatic (canals, fine cuisine, great tourist attractions) to the city on the San Antonio River. They argue by **comparison**.

Comparisons, claims about likenesses and differences, support arguments by

- clarifying definitions: *A polysemous word is a word with several meanings like a song with several different renditions.*
- explaining causes: *The smell of vanilla works like soft music to calm hospital patients.*
- supporting predictions: *This new writer will become the next J.K. Rowling.*

But comparisons are most useful for transferring attitudes and values. When one line of conduct toward Saddam Hussein before the first Iraq war in 1991 was compared to Neville Chamberlain's appeasement of Hitler before World War II, the rhetor was arguing for more than a historical comparison. Think about the values and attitudes transferred from one situation to another when nineteenth-century American suffragists argued that prohibiting women from voting was a repetition of the tyranny that inspired the American Revolution. Now think about the comparison used by anti-suffragists: protecting women from the burden of the vote was like protecting the home from barbarism.

Comparisons can be extended into elaborate parallel cases for supporting recommendations. For example, rhetors often compare the Iraq war to the Vietnam War. At the opposite end of the scale, argumentative comparisons can occur in a single word or brief phrase. When a critic writes of a movie's "Hitchcockian suspense," that critic pushes toward a positive evaluation by comparison since Hitchcock's movies are conventionally admired for their suspense.

4. Testimony and Authority

A radio ad encouraging you to spend your vacation in Paris talks about:

Six days in the most popular city in Europe.

The appeal here is based on **testimony**, the witness of the many tourists whose visits have made it "the most popular," and on our assumption that what most people choose or do has merit. Other appeals based on testimony use the opinions of a specially qualified group (e.g., "most conservationists believe . . .") or the opinion of a single authority either selected from a qualified group or somehow uniquely endowed (e.g., "Former Vice President Al Gore predicted . . ."). Some academic disciplines rely heavily on the perspectives and judgments of authorities, and arguers frequently borrow the voices of authorities by quoting.

In the same way that the opinions of "most people" or of special groups or of qualified authorities have persuasive value, so do certain institutions and publications. When you read phrases like "according to a government report . . .", or "the University's policy states . . .", or "Federal policy requires . . .", you are constructing an argument based on authority (one that could probably be backed by consequence). Certain publications also carry authority by convention, that is, by the agreement of many users and uses over time. So, for example, an arguer who wants to validate current facts about a nation's military power will cite *Jane's Defence Quarterly.* The *Oxford English Dictionary* authorizes historical definitions; the *Congressional Record* substantiates motions made in the House of Representatives. Finally, different groups hold certain books and persons so authoritative in matters of faith and morals that they become holy.

How "Common" Are the "Common Topics"

Go through a paper you have written in the past. You will most likely find that you used at least one (if not all) of the common topics to support your argument.

ARGUMENT PARAGRAPHS: CLAIMS, EVIDENCE, AND ANALYSIS

By now, you understand that in order to persuade your audience of the merit of your thesis, you must support that thesis with a number of well-proven arguments. The rhetorical strategies you have learned thus far will help you develop sound persuasive arguments. But how can you present those arguments so that they support your thesis effectively? How should you use your evidence so that it is clear how your argument works? Where should you include the analysis of your evidence so that your audience fully understands your point?

Adhering to an effective argumentative paragraph structure will help you in all these areas. Good argumentative paragraphs are composed of three main elements: **claims**, **evidence**, and **analysis**. Each paragraph should combine these elements to prove *one* clear point, which in turn supports your thesis. Just as your evidence should work together to prove a claim, your claims should work together to prove your thesis, and analysis should make these connections explicit and clear.

Ordinarily, your audience will expect to see your **claim**, which is a kind of topic sentence, within the first two sentences of a paragraph. The claim is an assertion expressing the argument you want to make within this individual paragraph; it helps your audience understand exactly what it is you are trying to prove in this section of your paper.

After your claim, typically you will want to present the **evidence** that supports your claim. Use concrete, vivid, and specific evidence to illustrate and develop your claim. This evidence may be statistics, logic, testimony, or examples—anything that supports your reasoning. Use your rhetorical strategies to develop the best evidence for your audience.

It is not enough, however, to simply present your evidence and assume that your audience will make the connection between your claim and your evidence. You must follow up with your own **analysis** of the evidence you presented. You need to show your readers why the evidence proves your point, why the evidence is interesting or relevant or important, and how the evidence relates to your overall argument.

When all of these conditions are met, you will have developed a sound argument that supports your overall thesis.

COMMON PITFALLS TO AVOID

Too many claims in one paragraph: Keep your paragraphs focused on proving a single, specific idea. If you try to present a number of arguments in one paragraph, you won't have room for enough evidence to support them all. An argument needs proof; your audience will rarely accept your argument on the strength of your word alone. Thus, without evidence and analysis to support your claims, your claims are wasted. Additionally, a reader's eye is automatically drawn to the white space at the start of a new paragraph; use that space rhetorically to call attention to a new idea. If you bury your claim inside a paragraph, your reader may not realize that you are presenting a new idea at all.

Too much evidence in one paragraph: If one piece of evidence is good, two pieces are better, and three are better yet, right? Not always. You need to consider your evidence carefully, choosing the ideas most likely to persuade your audience.

Not enough analysis: Analysis is the heart of your paper: it is where you bring your own creative ideas into the argument, where you blend your own reasoning with the facts and evidence already present in the debate. As such, it's worth spending time here to show how your argument works. By providing detailed, in-depth analysis of the connections between your evidence and your claims, you persuade your reader of both your mastery of the subject matter and the validity of your argument.

CLAIMS, EVIDENCE, AND ANALYSIS IN PRACTICE

The paragraph below illustrates how claims, evidence, and analysis work together to create a convincing argument. Not only is the paragraph well developed, but it also provides examples of a clearly stated claim (marked in **bold**), effective evidence (in *italics*), and thoroughly developed analysis (underlined) linking the evidence and claim together in an interesting and thoughtful way.

One of the most notable aspects of the show is the way it treats the concept of race in America. The *Cosby Show* approaches this issue in many ways, and one of them is the way in which the show presents relationships between people. All of the main characters have friends and constant interaction with people from a wide range of backgrounds such as Cubans, Africans, Asians, and many other ethnicities. *One interesting example comes from an episode when Theo invites his teacher, Professor Grayson, over to the house to help him convince his parents to allow him to go to Egypt. Theo and his friends jokingly convince his father that he cannot figure out Professor Grayson's background. In a humorous scene, Cliff guesses but is terribly wrong. Professor Grayson is Irish, Native American, and African American, and the most positive thing about her revelation is that no one is shocked by her mixed race.* This is a significant moment because, in this episode, the show purposely brings the issue of race to the forefront and the added humor sends the message that race can bring people together rather than tear them apart. In addition, this scene depicts the beauty of race and shows that it is all right to be different. In a world where people of mixed races exist but are often looked down upon, the fact that the "Cosby Show" is presenting a situation where people of all races are moving beyond the boundaries of race is especially noteworthy.

Note

We are indebted to Cliff Williams for permission to reproduce a paragraph from his English 101 paper: "*The Cosby Show*—Changing America Thirty Minutes at a Time" (University of Maryland, Fall 2002).

For every piece of writing that is composed, there is an *author*, a *purpose*, and an *audience*. This is true whether the document is a grocery list that we write to remind ourselves what items we need to pick up at the store, a grant proposal whose merits will be evaluated by an independent committee of scholars, or a call to action seeking our neighbors to join a neighborhood watch. Based upon who makes up the audience, we—as writers—have a greater or lesser responsibility to generate interest in the subject, to justify our position, and to include specific details.

Take, for example, the following essay assignment:

At the 1893 World's Fair, Aunt Jemima Pancake Mix was introduced; Nancy Green, an African American servant, was hired to portray the slave chef Aunt Jemima. Quaker Oats still owns the rights to the name and the product today. In the 1920s, advertisements by N.C. Wyeth showed the slave chef serving pancakes to Confederate soldiers—including General Robert E. Lee. Many African Americans and civil rights activists still find the name association and the history of the image of Aunt Jemima Pancake Mix problematic. Write an argument convincing Quaker Oats to take one of the following courses of action: change the logo (the picture of Aunt Jemima); change the name of the product entirely; or keep the name and the image the same.

How much does a change in who we address affect how we write the argument? Let's say, for the example above, that we were writing the CEO of Quaker Oats. Would we choose a casual or formal style? Should we include slang words for effect or would that make it more likely that the CEO of Quaker Oats would dismiss our petition?

In 2001, Quaker Oats merged with Pepsico, Inc. Therefore, if we directed our argument to the CEO of Pepsico, Inc., it might begin as follows:

Dear Indra K. Nooyi, CEO:

I am writing this letter as a third generation customer of Quaker Oats products to ask that you consider changing the name of Aunt Jemima Pancake Mix. I am an African American. Although my daughter, age five, is unaware of why the name on the box or the current image on the box is problematic for me, she picks up on the fact that I flinch every time she asks me to buy a box of her favorite pancake mix. How do I explain to her that the reason why I flinch is not what the current image represents but rather what previous incarnations of Aunt Jemima Pancake mix depicted: notably Aunt Jemima serving Confederate soldiers who were seeking to continue the enslavement of my African American ancestors?

Sincerely,
X Y

Now, imagine that we are the same person writing an argument with the same position to Oprah Winfrey: to be read aloud in an episode of *Oprah*. How would our argument change?

> Oprah, I am sick and tired of being reminded every time I take my five year-old daughter grocery shopping that she is too young to understand why I am not happy when she begs me for "Aunt Jemima Pancake Mix, Mommy!" Can't Quaker Oats understand that no mother wants to explain to her pre-K daughter that that name and that image has a history chock full of slavery, inequality, and degradation? Our children are smart. They know if we are troubled, and they become troubled themselves seeing us as such. Why should my daughter suffer because I feel the horrible legacy of Aunt Jemima's Pancake mix? Changing the image on the box is not enough. The name of the product must also change.
>
> Sincerely,
> X Y

Why is the second argument successful for its audience but a disaster if it were accidentally submitted to the CEO of Pepsi instead? It has to do with the way the writer tailors her argument to the specific context in which the argument will be heard. On *Oprah*, there is an established precedent for communicating one's anger and doing so in a way that other viewers of Winfrey's show will relate to and identify with. However, the CEO of Pepsi would likely take offense both to X Y's language and to the way in which she suggests that being offended by the product is a foregone conclusion.

Is either the CEO of Pepsi or the viewers of *Oprah* an **academic audience**? Why or why not? Many of the assignments you submit in college will be for an academic audience, an audience whose goal is not necessarily to effect change or to sympathize with the plight of one party or another but to study the issue in even more depth.

YOUR OWN INTENDED AUDIENCE, SECONDARY AUDIENCES, AND OVERHEARERS

For all of your formal papers this semester, you will be asked to construct an *intended audience*. This group of readers will be the exact group that your composition is trying to inform or persuade. You may identify this group by their age, their education, their familiarity with your topic, their gender, their ethnicity or nationality, their religion, their orientation, their opposition or support of your position, and/or a host of other characteristics.

You may also choose to identify a *secondary audience* that might stumble across your argument. If you do so, you will also be responsible for convincing this group of readers but not in such a way that you risk losing the support of your primary audience.

A secondary audience is one type of example of a group that we call *overhearers*. Overhearers may or may not be members of an originally specified audience. These individuals might instead be interested in how the primary group of readers, the *intended audience*, or a secondary group of readers, would receive the argument. For example, when you as an employee of (let us say) a software company write a letter to a subcontractor, your *intended audience* will be the individual to whom you are writing, but the letter may have many overhearers, including perhaps your boss, your company's legal office, and the board of the subcontractor's company. When you are composing the letter, you might have in mind that the board of the subcontractor's company would eventually weigh in on your proposal. You might have even thought of the board members as a secondary audience. You are probably far less likely to factor into the composition of your letter your own boss and your company's legal office. However, this does not make either of those entities less important. As *overhearers*, they serve crucial functions.

In this class, you will have two sets of overhearers.

Your classmates: As often as time allows, you will share what you have written in class. This sharing may occur both in formal rough draft workshops and in peer review sessions. The job of your classmates will be to read your work both with your intended audience in mind and your teacher: the other overhearer. Your classmates should be able to give you an excellent idea as to whether your writing kept their interest, and they should be able to weigh in as to whether your composition achieves the aims of the assignment as they understand those aims.

Your teacher: Ultimately, the overhearer whose evaluation of your work will matter the most in terms of your grade is your instructor. He or she will be rendering a judgment as to how well your writing fulfills each individual assignment. An important part of satisfying each assignment will be capturing and maintaining the interest and attention of your instructor, who will be trying to put himself or herself into the position of a member of your intended audience. This does not mean, however, that you should specify an uneducated audience with the hopes that the instructor will not place as high a regard on grammar or style. He or she will be adhering to the grading criteria for what satisfies an A paper, a B paper, a C paper, a D paper, and an F paper regardless of what audience you choose. Think of your teacher as being the most important overhearer that you must convince. In this case, what you must convince him or her of is that you have persuaded your intended audience fully and met the criteria for an excellent submission.

WRITING THE AUDIENCE ANALYSIS

Preceding each formal paper that you write this semester, you will be asked to submit an **audience analysis**. In one paragraph or two, you will be asked to describe your intended audience in detail (education, gender, age, race, religion, familiarity with your topic, etc.) and identify the reasons why they support or oppose your position. You will also be asked to choose the context in which your argument will be read or heard, either by choosing a publication choice (such as a hypothetical journal titled *Civic Engagement Weekly*) or by selecting an arena in which your orated argument may be heard (such as being read on *Oprah*).

This class may be the only class you take in which your final drafts will be evaluated as to how well they convince an audience of your choosing of your position in a context that you select. This is a huge advantage, so long as your choices are ones that will lead you to write a more persuasive argument.

HOW WILL AN AUDIENCE ANALYSIS IMPROVE MY ARGUMENT?

First, knowing who constitutes your audience and what they value may assist your choices of arrangement and rhetorical strategies. In any paper, you have a limited amount of space; you must therefore be able to decide which pieces will be most likely to persuade your audience and what order will be most effective in accomplishing your overall goal.

Second, all readers have certain expectations, particularly with regard to style and tone. You must be able to adapt your writing style to the writing situation. Otherwise, you could alienate your readers by violating their expectations for persuasive writing, for example, by including jarring or inappropriate elements. In some cases, an unusual figure of speech or slang word will add interest; in others, it will offend your audience and detract from your argument. You are responsible for meeting the standards of both your intended audience and your instructor.

CHOOSE AN ACADEMIC AUDIENCE

Although you will be given significant say in specifying the level of education that your audience has and/or the level of expertise that your audience holds with regard to your chosen topic, our recommendation is that you choose an audience that is college enrolled or higher and an audience that is familiar with your choice of topic. Our rationale is that the audience analysis should be written before you write the formal assignment and, as such, it should set the bar for what you attempt to accomplish. If you choose an uneducated audience or an audience that is completely uninformed, your goals may be much lower and, subsequently, what you can achieve both in terms of content and in terms of style may be reduced.

WHAT HAPPENS SHOULD YOU ALSO CHOOSE AN ACADEMIC SETTING?

In this class you will be given more say than in almost any other as to the vessel in which your argument appears. Will your argument appear in an academic journal, a letter to the editor of a local newspaper, or as part of an in class presentation? The first and third contexts or settings in the previous list are academic ones, in which the target audience's purpose will be to receive the argument as part of a larger context of study and not as an invitation to take action themselves. To succeed in reaching an academic audience, you must—as in any other rhetorical situation—create exigence for your thesis. You must keep the audience's interest and persuade them that your carefully supported position is one that warrants further investigation and research as well as their philosophical support.

SHOULD YOU CHOOSE AN AUDIENCE THAT SUPPORTS OR OPPOSES YOUR POSITION?

In many cases, this may the one trait in terms of your audience analysis that you are not given a choice on. Your instructor may require that you write to an opposing audience or to a supportive audience. Regardless of whether you are allowed to make this choice, it is worthwhile to keep the opponents of your position in mind as you are conceiving and structuring your argument. It is a much loftier goal to attempt to convince the opponents of your position than it is to convince your allies.

WRITING THE AUDIENCE ANALYSIS

Now, we are at the stage in which you must actually construct the audience analysis. Your analysis will be judged based on how specific it is and whether it addresses all of the aspects of the writing situation. Included in these aspects are the thesis that you will be attempting to prove and the publication choice. After reading your audience analysis, your reader should be able to proceed directly to the argument understanding perfectly what his or her position is in relation to your thesis and your context for publication.

Here are some basic questions that you should consider in your audience analysis:

1. Who are my readers? What characterizes them socially and culturally? What is their level of education? What is their socioeconomic status? (class) What is their demographic? (their age range) Are they primarily of a particular race, gender, religious affiliation, or orientation?
2. What do they already know about my topic?
3. What attitudes or stances do my readers have toward my topic?
4. What does my audience have in common with me in terms of shared values or experiences?
5. If we are likely to disagree, what is the nature of that disagreement and what is their rationale for that disagreement?
6. What role do I want my readers to take on as they read? What am I trying to do or convince them of? Should I address them formally or casually and/or intimately? Should I appeal to my audience primarily through logic, through appealing to their emotions or values, or to their sense of ethics or credibility?
7. What form should my argument or appeal take? Where would it be published or heard?

Let us consider writing an audience analysis for X Y in her argument to convince the CEO and the Board of Directors of Pepsico, Inc. to change the product name of Aunt Jemima Pancake Mix. The first step X Y should take is to identify her thesis. The paragraph that follows is one possible audience analysis.

> This argument that Aunt Jemima Pancake Mix should be renamed is directed to Indra K. Nooyi, the CEO of Pepsico, Inc., which owns Quaker Oats, and Pepsico, Inc.'s Board of Directors. As such, my readers will be highly educated, possessing MBA degrees if not PhDs in Business Administration. Their age demographic might be between 32 and 60. Although the CEO of Pepsico, Inc. is female, it would not surprise me if the majority of the Board of Directors were male. I would also be surprised if any of my audience were African Americans. Therefore, my audience might be completely unfamiliar with the historical stigmas that have been attached both to the image of Aunt Jemima depicted on the box of Aunt Jemima's Pancake Mix and the character of Aunt Jemima herself. In this formal letter addressed to CEO Indra K. Noovi, I will attempt to explain how the legacy attached to Aunt Jemima's Pancake Mix haunts me even though there are no visible signs left on the box to call up that history for my five-year-old daughter. I will point out to my audience that I am a third generation customer of the pancake mix so that they will appreciate that there is an economic aspect to my appeal to change the name.

Notice how some traits that we could put in an audience analysis—religion, orientation—are not appropriate for this audience analysis. You will have to decide which traits are important. Also notice how, for X Y's audience analysis, we used first person voice for the audience analysis. This would also change based upon your publication choice and your purpose.

PEER REVIEW: AN INTRODUCTION

Since writing is always about reaching an audience, the best way to revise your writing is to show it to an actual audience. Often, we may think that we have expressed our views clearly to the reader, but, since we are the writer, we already know what we think. Therefore, we need a reader to give us her perspective on whether the views are expressed clearly.

Most writing is not produced in an isolated tower with the writer hiding from the rest of the world. Writing, in fact, is often a social act. The writer not only interacts with other texts, writers, and ideas within the text itself, but often also produces the writing in a more social setting. Writing groups are popular places for writers to gather and exchange ideas and drafts. Getting feedback at all stages of producing a text, including brainstorming, drafting, and revising, often results in a more clear and polished final draft.

Professional writers do not usually publish a first draft; similarly, you should never turn a first draft in to your teacher. Professional writers always get someone else to read their work before it is published. But, as students, you may find it harder to find readers for your work due to busy schedules. Therefore, English 101 sets aside class time for you to receive feedback on your writing from a reader.

But peer review not only benefits the writer of a paper; the editor, or reviewer, is also given a chance to sharpen her critical reading skills. Many peer editors have found that not only do they receive helpful feedback on their own writing, but that their own writing also benefits from looking critically at another's writing. For example, the editor might also find that she is pointing out issues in the paper that occur in her paper as well.

Think of peer review not as an opportunity to get your writing "fixed"; instead, see it as an opportunity to read more critically, to receive feedback from a reader's perspective, and to engage in a conversation on what this class is all about—writing.

But am I qualified to be a peer editor?

Of course you are. You are a peer of the writer. Through this course, you are learning critical reading skills and a vocabulary to talk about written communication and argumentation. Now, you can put these skills to use.

You don't have to be an "expert" on the topic or an "expert" on writing to be a good peer editor. You don't have to have perfect grammar skills to be a good peer editor. What you do need is to be able to respond to the writing as a reader. It's even better if you are not an expert. It helps the writer maker sure her writing is clear to a non-expert audience.

How can I be a good peer editor?
- Be positive. Always find the strengths of a piece of writing. We always appreciate knowing what we are doing well.
- Be critical. The writer wants to hear how her writing comes across to a reader and may not get anything useful out of "this is fine" all over the paper. We can be critical with-

out being mean. If you feel uncomfortable offering a certain critique, it can be helpful to phrase it with qualifiers ("I'm not sure about..." or "As a reader...")

- Provide detailed comments. Avoid saying, "This is a good example." Instead, say, "This example works if you do X and Y" or "This example would be more effective if you X."
- Phrase your comments as comments from a reader rather than as condemnations of the author. Avoid saying, "you are not making sense here" or "you are contradicting yourself." Instead, say, "I'm not sure I understand this part. Is it saying that we should or should not support the argument stated in the thesis? The part I have underlined seems to contradict the thesis." Use "I" statements instead of "you" statements.
- Attend to global concerns (content, argument, thesis, audience) before sentence-level concerns (grammar). After all, the writer might decide, based on your feedback, to revise a section of the argument to strengthen it and may end up eliminating parts that might be unclear. The commas you inserted might appear in a sentence that the writer ends up taking out.
- Engage with the ideas of the paper. Remember, a reviewer isn't just looking for something "wrong" with the paper. A reviewer is reading and thinking about the ideas put forth in the paper. We often get the most useful feedback when a reviewer is enthusiastic about our ideas and responds by simply talking about the topic and what it means to him or her.

You may find it helpful to read the paper as a whole first, without writing any comments on it. Then, write your impression of the paper as a whole. You can then attend to section-level revisions in your second reading of the paper, and sentence-level revisions on a third reading, if you have time.

What should I do to prepare my draft to be reviewed?

- Try to come as close to a final draft as possible. If it is possible, and time permits, bring the draft as you would hand it in to your teacher. Then, you will be able to get feedback on the more finalized ideas, rather than initial ideas that you want to change later.
- Bring all materials relating to the paper, including the audience analysis and bibliography. Bring your handbook for a quick reference. Also, if you have questions about how to cite a source, bring a copy of the source.
- Revise and edit before the workshop. Spell-check your draft. We all make mistakes. But the best feedback will come when the reader is engaged in the ideas and argument of the paper, rather than when the reader has to circle typos that spell-check could catch or that you could catch on your own.
- Come prepared with questions or concerns that you have about the paper that you would like feedback on. Readers always like reading with a specific purpose in mind.

But isn't taking advice from others a form of plagiarism?

If someone else writes or rewrites the paper for you, it is a form of plagiarism. But if you take suggestions to rework the draft, then it is acceptable. Most honor codes also differentiate between "unauthorized" and "authorized" assistance on papers. Peer review and help from The Writing Center are "authorized" forms of assistance; paying an editor is not.

It is a good practice to acknowledge the feedback of others in your final draft. You can do so by including a footnote with the title stating, "I thank _____ for her feedback on earlier versions of this paper. Any mistakes are mine."

During this semester, you'll often hear your instructor talk about "civic engagement" or say something like "In English 101, we focus on talking about civic engagement." But what does that term mean, and what does it mean in the context of your introductory writing class?

CIVIC ENGAGEMENT AT THE UNIVERSITY OF MARYLAND

The University of Maryland, College Park, has made civic engagement a part of the University's mission. Here is a mission statement from the campus committee charged to develop civic engagement across campus:

MISSION FOR CIVIC ENGAGEMENT AND LEADERSHIP AT THE UNIVERSITY OF MARYLAND

The mission for civic engagement and leadership at the University of Maryland is to develop civically engaged citizens, scholars, and leaders.

As University administrators, faculty, and staff, we strive to enable all students to develop their full potential as citizens with a heightened sense of responsibility to the multiple communities in which they are now and will be involved. We must prepare our students to be intentional, lifelong learners who, through the creation and application of knowledge, will address social issues and pressing community problems as they continue to emerge.

Effectiveness in civic engagement is dependent upon students developing leadership capacities to work well with others to accomplish change that benefits the common good. This socially responsible leadership approach includes being ethical, inclusive, and collaborative; knowing one's self; and recognizing one's interdependence with others.

Students must also have the ability to think in complex ways about moral and ethical issues, to understand and live by their values, and to help society shape its values. It is important that they realize how their choices impact individuals, communities, and social institutions locally and globally.

Students come to the University with different levels of understanding of and involvement in civic engagement and leadership. Thus, we must provide students with the appropriate balance of challenge and support that enables them to move to the next level.

In order to be an environment where student learning around civic engagement and leadership will flourish, the University should encourage the scholarship, teaching, and service of faculty, administrators, and staff whose work is grounded in the civic and social issues of the greater community.

The University of Maryland currently provides a rich array of educational experiences in the areas of civic engagement and leadership. Our mission is to increase,

enhance, and integrate these experiences to empower students to be civically engaged citizens, scholars, and leaders in communities on campus and in Maryland, the nation, and the world.

—*Report of the Team on Civic Engagement and Leadership, February 2004*

(available at *http://www.csl.umd.edu/CCEL/CCEL_Mission.htm*)

As this mission statement suggests, the University places a great deal of value on the idea of being civically engaged. How do they define civic engagement? Here's the definition offered by the same coalition:

Civic engagement is acting upon a heightened sense of responsibility to one's communities. That includes a wide range of activities, including developing civic sensitivity, participation in building civil society, and benefiting the common good. Civic engagement encompasses the notions of global citizenship and interdependence. Through civic engagement, individuals— as citizens of their communities, their nations, and the world—are empowered as agents of positive social change for a more democratic world. Civic engagement involves one or more of the following:

1. Learning from others, self, and environment to develop informed perspectives on social issues;
2. Recognizing and appreciating human diversity and commonality;
3. Behaving, and working through controversy, with civility;
4. Participating actively in public life, public problem solving, and community service;
5. Assuming leadership and membership roles in organizations;
6. Developing empathy, ethics, values, and sense of social responsibility;
7. Promoting social justice locally and globally.

—Civic Engagement and Leadership Team, 11/03; Steering Committee of the Coalition for Civic Engagement and Leadership, 6/04

That's a fairly broad definition. What is gained by making the definition so broad? How might students apply that definition to their own college years?

The University of Maryland has been recognized as a school committed to civic engagement by the Princeton Review, an organization you are probably familiar with in their work of providing students with information to help them select colleges. In 2005, Princeton Review published a book called *Colleges with a Conscience: 81 Great Schools with Outstanding Community Involvement*, and named UMCP as one of those 81 schools. On their website explaining how they selected the schools named, the authors say, "Colleges and universities have long been hubs for active and engaged citizens determined to make a contribution to their communities. Over the past two decades, these institutions of higher education have refocused on their civic mission by pioneering new strategies for creating more engaged citizens."

What might have caused institutions of higher learning to refocus their attention on their civic mission in the past couple of decades?

CIVIC ENGAGEMENT AND YOUR ENGLISH 101 COURSE

The current English 101 syllabus was inspired by classical rhetorical education, which had its origins in the public sphere of classical Greece and Rome. Then, students (who were all men of certain economic stature) were trained by teachers such as Aristotle for the purpose of becoming active citizens in the polis. The Freshman Writing Program here at College Park, like similar programs across the country, believes that students can learn a great deal about composing arguments from the theories put into practice back in those times. We also believe that such a rhetorical education can, in the 21st century, prepare students for civic engagement. But at the same time, we want you to understand civic engagement and think about what its role in higher education generally—and your education specifically—can and should be.

Included here are several documents that argue that education and civic engagement should be linked. Do you agree? What values are represented by these arguments? Who is the audience for these documents?

[links to *http://www.cived.net/tioce.html*—The Importance of Civic Education and *www.compact.org/ resources/declaration*—Presidents Declaration on the Civic Responsibility of Higher Education]

PRESIDENTS' DECLARATION ON THE CIVIC RESPONSIBILITY OF HIGHER EDUCATION

from Campus Compact*

As presidents of colleges and universities, both private and public, large and small, two-year and four-year, we challenge higher education to re-examine its public purposes and its commitments to the democratic ideal. We also challenge higher education to become engaged, through actions and teaching, with its communities. We have a fundamental task to renew our role as agents of our democracy. This task is both urgent and long-term. There is growing evidence of disengagement of many Americans from the communal life of our society in general, and from the responsibilities of democracy in particular. We share a special concern about the disengagement of college students from democratic participation. A chorus of studies reveals that students are not connected to the larger purposes and aspirations of the American democracy. Voter turnout is low. Feelings that political participation will not make any difference are high. Added to this, there is a profound sense of cynicism and lack of trust in the political process.

We are encouraged that more and more students are volunteering and participating in public and community service, and we have all encouraged them to do so through curricular and co-curricular activity. However, this service is not leading students to embrace the duties of active citizenship and civic participation. We do not blame these college students for their attitudes toward the democracy; rather, we take responsibility for helping them realize the values and skills of our democratic society and their need to claim ownership of it.

This country cannot afford to educate a generation that acquires knowledge without ever understanding how that knowledge can benefit society or how to influence democratic decision making. We must teach the skills and values of democracy, creating innumerable opportunities for our students to practice and reap the results of the real, hard work of citizenship.

Colleges and universities have long embraced a mission to educate students for citizenship. But now, with over two-thirds of recent high school graduates and ever-larger numbers of adults enrolling in post secondary studies, higher education has an unprecedented opportunity to influence the democratic knowledge, dispositions, and habits of the heart that graduates carry with them into the public square. Higher education is uniquely positioned to help Americans understand the histories and contours of our present challenges as a diverse democracy. It is also uniquely positioned to help both students and our communities to explore new ways of fulfilling the promise of justice and dignity for all, both in our own democracy and as part of the global community. We know that pluralism is a source of strength and vitality that will enrich our students' education and help them learn both to respect difference and to work together for the common good.

---

*http://www.compact.org/resources/declaration/Declaration_2007.pdf

We live in a time when every sector—corporate, government, and nonprofit—is being mobilized to address community needs and reinvigorate our democracy. We cannot be complacent in the face of a country where one out of five children sleeps in poverty and one in six central cities has an unemployment rate 50 percent or more above the national average, even as our economy shows unprecedented strength. Higher education—its leaders, students, faculty, staff, trustees, and alumni—remains a key institutional force in our culture that can respond, and can do so without a political agenda and with the intellectual and professional capacities today's challenges so desperately demand. Thus, for society's benefit and for the academy's, we need to do more. Only by demonstrating the democratic principles we espouse can higher education effectively educate our students to be good citizens.

How can we realize this vision of institutional public engagement? It will, of course, take as many forms as there are types of colleges and universities. And it will require our hard work, as a whole and within each of our institutions. We will know we are successful by the robust debate on our campuses, and by the civic behaviors of our students. We will know it by the civic engagement of our faculty. We will know it when our community partnerships improve the quality of community life and the quality of the education we provide.

To achieve these goals, our presidential leadership is essential but, by itself, it is not enough. Faculty, staff, trustees, and students must help craft and act upon our civic missions and responsibilities. We must seek reciprocal partnerships with community leaders, such as those responsible for elementary and secondary education. To achieve our goals we must define them in ways that inspire our institutional missions and help measure our success. We have suggested a Campus Assessment of Civic Responsibility that will help in this task (*www.compact. org/presidential*).

We ask other college presidents to join us in seeking recognition of civic responsibility in accreditation procedures, Carnegie classifications, and national rankings and to work with governors, state legislators, and state higher education offices on state expectations for civic engagement in public systems.

We believe that the challenge of the next millennium is the renewal of our own democratic life and reassertion of social stewardship. In celebrating the birth of our democracy, we can think of no nobler task than committing ourselves to helping catalyze and lead a national movement to reinvigorate the public purposes and civic mission of higher education. We believe that now and through the next century, our institutions must be vital agents and architects of a flourishing democracy.

We urge all of higher education to join us.

THE IMPORTANCE OF CIVIC EDUCATION

from National Alliance for Civic Education*

In 2000, the 32nd Annual Phi Delta Kappa/Gallup Poll found that Americans rank "preparing people to become responsible citizens" as the number-one purpose of the nation's schools. Over the thirty-two years of the poll, the public has not wavered in its conviction that schools and educators have a special responsibility to educate young people for citizenship. For similar reasons, over one-fourth of all state constitutions state that a system of public instruction is required because an informed and capable citizenry is vital to the preservation of a free and democratic government.[1] And in addition to schools, many other institutions—from religious congregations to scouting organizations to political parties—also profess commitments to civic education.

Despite this consensus, there is some disagreement about exactly what makes a "responsible citizen":

- Some stress the importance of knowing and respecting our nation's social and political history, founding documents such as the Declaration of Independence, the Federalist papers, and the Constitution, and the visions of freedom that our country was founded upon.
- Some prize a willingness and ability to think critically, to deliberate with others, and when necessary to challenge authority and to make society more just.
- Some see "responsible citizens" as people who provide direct, voluntary care for others in need.
- Some emphasize the need to create public goods through collaborative work and are especially interested in the civic and democratic potential of employment and professional practices.

Although there are interesting and even fruitful differences of emphasis among these models of citizenship, they are not mutually exclusive. Indeed, a citizen in the twenty-first century should be comfortable acting in *several different ways*—upholding laws or protesting, voting or forming new organizations—as the situation demands. Citizens need an overlapping set of knowledge and intellectual skills for all of these tasks.[2] They also need the participation skills that are necessary to monitor and influence civic life, such as the ability to work with others and express ideas.

Statistics and everyday experience show that people who know a great deal about government, politics, and public affairs also tend to vote and to join organizations, while those with low levels of knowledge do not participate.

- The correlation between education (i.e., years spent in school) and political engagement is "the best documented finding in American political behavior research."[3]
- In the 26 countries where 90,000 14-year-olds were recently surveyed by the IEA, civic knowledge was a major predictor of intentions to vote.

*http://www.cived.net/tioce.html

- Several surveys have shown that adults who know a great deal about politics and public affairs are likely to vote, no matter how interested they are in politics. But those with little knowledge generally believe that they are powerless-and abstain from politics.[4]
- Adults with high levels of political knowledge make consistent choices and stick to them over time. They assess leaders on the basis of policies and ideologies as well as character. But those with low levels of knowledge tend to make inconsistent decisions and judge public officials only on the basis of perceived personality. Commenting on some poorly informed voters who were polled by the *Washington Post* in 1996, political scientist Michael Delli Carpini said, "It was as if their vote was random."[5]
- Knowledge is also a necessary precondition for deliberating about public affairs. Even watching other people discuss politics can be difficult unless one understands some basic facts and vocabulary. Samuel Popkin and Michael Dimock have argued that people who lack information cannot tell the difference between a serious exchange of views and a squabble, so they tune politics out completely. As Richard Niemi and Jane Junn write, "One can live one's whole life without knowing that the president is the commander-in-chief of the armed forces or, for that matter, without knowing the name of the president. But how many political discussions and how many news reports would be incomprehensible without this information?"[6]
- Adults with high levels of political knowledge are likely to be socially tolerant, trustful, and engaged in community affairs.[7]
- Finally, citizens need certain kinds of information, experience, and skills before they can work with others to solve local problems or create things of public value. Thus, for example, students who participate in extracurricular activities during high school are most likely to join organizations later in life.[8]

There is alarming evidence that students are not getting the knowledge and skills they need to participate in civic, community, and political life. (Please see our page on "*What Young People Know*" for details). This lack of knowledge is probably one reason that less than one-third of Americans aged 18–24 voted in 1996. When asked why they do not participate in the electoral process, the two major reasons given by young people are that "they do not think that their vote makes a difference (26%) and that they don't have enough information (25%).[9]

In 1999 the National Association of Secretaries of State (NASS) conducted a nationwide study of American youth. Fifty-five percent of respondents agreed with the statement, "schools do not do a very good job of giving young people the information they need to vote." The survey also found that young people lack meaningful understanding of the democratic process and of citizenship, with many students unable to give any real thought to one's role as citizen.

To make matters worse, civic knowledge is not evenly distributed. Those who most need the power that comes with political skills and information are least likely to receive an effective civic education. For instance, two out of three of the poorest Americans cannot describe the political parties' attitudes toward government spending, whereas most wealthy Americans know exactly how the Democrats differ from the Republicans.[10] This information gap helps to explain the difference in voter participation between rich and poor, because it makes no sense to vote if you lack information about the issues.

In their preliminary report released in January 2001, the National Commission of the High School Senior Year states:

> If we go along as we have been, about half our people, perhaps twothirds, will flourish, well-educated, comfortable with ambiguity, and possessed of the self confidence that accompanies self-knowledge, they will be well-suited to participate in an increasingly global and multicultural world and to exercise the responsibilities of citizenship. The other one-third to one-half of our people are more likely to flounder. Poorly educated, worried about their place in a rapidly changing world, they may look on the complexities of an interdependent world as threatening and the demands of citizenship as a burden.

Such disengagement and lack of knowledge and skills is troubling for any democratic political system. Democratic values are not passed down through the genetic code; each generation of students is asked to recreate values and develop a vision for the future.

While many people are working to improve the quality of math, science and reading education, we believe that too little attention has been paid to civic education. A concerted effort is needed to place greater emphasis on civics requirements, in-school service learning, standards, curricula and teaching methods. Meanwhile, outside the classroom, private organizations, news media, political parties, and other institutions must rededicate themselves to creating the next generations of citizens.

—Amber Wichowsky (with Peter Levine)

NOTES

1. Center for Civic Education, University of Texas at Austin, 1999.
2. U.S. Department of Education, 2000?; William A. Galston, "Political Knowledge, Political Engagement, and Civic Education," *Annual Review of Political Science* (2001), 4, p. 218.
3. See Norman H. Nie, Jane Junn, and Kenneth Stehlik-Barry, *Education and Democratic Citizenship in America* (Chicago, 1996), p. 31
4. See Richard Morin, "Who's in Control? Many Don't Know or Care," *Washington Post*, January 29, 1996, pp. A1, A6. See also Michael Delli Carpini and Scott Keeter, *What Americans Know About Politics and Why it Matters* (New Haven, 1996), pp. 230–267; and League of Women Voters Press Release, August 26, 1996, "Survey Indicates Nonvoters Lack Information, Recognition of the Consequences of Elections" (poll conducted in March of 1996).
5. Delli Carpini and Keeter, pp. 232–38; Popkin and Dimock, pp. 125–7; Delli Carpini quoted by Morin.
6. Samuel L. Popkin and Michael Dimock, "Political Knowledge and Citizen Competence," in Stephen Elkin and Karol Soltan (eds.) Citizen Competence and Democratic Institutions (Penn State Press, 1999); Richard G. Niemi and Jane Junn, *Civic Education: What Makes Students Learn* (New Haven 1998), p. 11.
7. Delli Carpini and Keeter; Sidney Verba, Kay Lehman Schlozman, and Henry E. Brady, *Voice and Equality: Civic Voluntarism in American Politics* (Harvard, 1995).

8. The evidence from several studies is summarized in Judith Torney-Purta, Carole L. Hahn, and Jo-Ann Amadeo, "Principles of Subject-Specific Instruction in Education for Citizenship," Subject-Specific Instructional Methods and Activities, vol. 8, pp. 400–3.

9. National Association of Secretaries of State. "New Millennium Project–Part 1 American Youth Attitudes on Politics, Citizenship, Government and Voting." *Survey on Youth Attitudes.* The Tarrance Group. (Lexington, KY 1999).

10. Delli Carpini and Keeter, pp. 214–5

INQUIRY AND ARGUMENT

from *From Inquiry to Argument*

Read the following selection carefully, then respond as indicated below:

> Imagine that you enter a parlor. You come late. When you arrive, others have long preceded you, and they are engaged in a heated discussion, a discussion too heated for them to pause and tell you exactly what it is about. In fact, the discussion had already begun long before any of them got there, so that no one present is qualified to retrace for you all the steps that had gone before. You listen for a while until you decide that you have caught the tenor of the argument: then you put in your oar. Someone answers; you answer him; another comes to your defense; another aligns himself against you. . . . However, the discussion is interminable. The hour grows late, you must depart. And you do depart, with the discussion still in progress.
>
> —Kenneth Burke, *The Philosophy of Literary Form*

Writer's Journal

In your notebook, write informally to explain the meaning of the passage. Then describe its effects on you and express any other responses you may have. Strive for an entry of at least 150 words.

FROM INQUIRY . . .

Let's begin with the term *inquiry,* a simple word, one we all know how to use. If you examine the following uses of *inquiry* (and its relative, *to inquire*), some may strike you as more appropriate than others:

1. Sal inquired about the penalty for late payment of his gas bill.
2. Judith made an inquiry as to the location of the restroom.
3. The House of Representatives began an inquiry into the states' enforcement of highway traffic laws.
4. The counterman inquired what flavor ice cream I wanted.

If you discuss your responses with classmates, you might discover you agree—that in sentences 1 and 3 *inquiry* works well, but that in 2 and 4 it seems artificial or awkward. In these sentences, you may prefer *asked* as less grand, less affected. Or perhaps you disagree because you can envision a scene or context for sentences 2 and 4 that calls for a special, more elevated word than *ask*. You can agree, however, that the word *inquiry* and the act of *inquiring* are not about asking just any question; an inquiry is more self-conscious, more intentional.

A look in the dictionary reveals that the word *inquiry* shares the same Latin root as *question*: *quaerere*, meaning "to seek." The prefix *in* serves as an intensifier, so we might say that inquire is built from its roots to mean "to seek intensely." In the actual definition, an inquiry is said to be a "question or query" or "a close examination of some matter in a quest for information or truth."

I like this last definition because the phrase "quest for information or truth" reflects the deepest purpose of academic life, the discovery of explanations that will endure—at least until the next inquiry. And "close examination" implies study and research, processes that flow beneath and animate all the teaching and talking, paper writing and e-mailing, reading and note taking that form the day-to-day activities in higher education.

But this definition doesn't tell us much about the context of inquiry or about its inspiration. Why bother to inquire? What creates the need to know?

The Motives for Inquiry

Consider a time when you made an intensive search for knowledge. Make a list of such times. Do these occasions have anything in common? What motivated your need to know?

Often, the search for information or "truth" results from a problem, an impending decision, a conflict between possible choices, or some other controversial situation. The need may be immediate and practical. Perhaps someone whose father has developed cataracts wants information about eye disease in order to understand possible treatments.

Or the need may be to plan for the future. A student may be about to make the life-altering decision to attend college and so collects and studies many college catalogues in order to make the most appropriate choice. A county might study traffic patterns over the course of the workday and workweek so that future road improvements can be planned.

Or the necessary information may be more abstract: solving a societal problem such as a rise in high school dropout rates requires analyzing and perhaps conducting numerous studies of adolescent behavior, the educational system, family dynamics, and so forth.

So an inquiry implies certain things: a problem, dilemma, or controversial issue, first of all, and a community that has a stake in resolving that problem.

The Context of Inquiry

Such a community can be official, such as a township, a civic or professional group, or a university. But many communities or groups of people linked by a common interest or situation are informal and unofficial. Cliques in a high school, recreational groups such as golfers or quilters, and fans of the ballet or progressive jazz are examples. Any group that uses discourse—that is, any form of written or spoken communication—to maintain itself, articulate and solve group problems, and otherwise assist its own cohesiveness and identity is called a **discourse community**. Members of discourse communities—and we are all members of several—base their interactions with each other on the discourse expectations of the group. The discourse community is an active collaborator in any member's use of language, providing a vocabulary and expected styles of discussing and handling issues of concern and even limiting or defining acceptable topics. Such a community has conventions for discussing, analyzing, and proving ideas and for addressing conflicts.

A high school clique may evolve a trademark vocabulary that reaffirms its identity and may develop customary ways of discussing academic work, friendships, romances, and other topics. Inside jokes can be cued with a few words, and greeting or parting may involve signature phrases or gestures. To a certain extent, any member's behavior and talk, both subject and style, will be based on the group's expectations.

ACTIVITY 1

Identifying Discourse
Communities

A town-council meeting will also be characterized by a customary discourse. Some characteristics of its discourse will be common to town-council meetings throughout the United States, for local government officials and politically active citizens constitute an informal national discourse community. Most likely, the discussion will be sprinkled with technical terms or jargon derived from various professional domains: the law, real estate, health and public safety, and so on. The discourse will be generally polite and somewhat formal but probably will include informal segments in which humorous asides and little in-jokes lighten the mood. Discourse will follow an agenda, the shape of which may be mandated by law or determined by custom. Proceedings will follow parliamentary procedure to a greater or lesser extent. Decisions will be made by the head official or the council through voice vote, secret ballot, or consensus as local law requires or as is customary.

It is fair to say that any inquiry a person conducts occurs within the web of a discourse community, and it involves interaction with that community. Individual inquiries require dialogue, perhaps oral, perhaps written. How a problem is defined, how study and research are performed, and what counts as a result or solution are all determined by our linguistic and social environment. Discourse communities limit their members to the discourse formulations within them; but discourse communities also open pathways for members by providing conventions of wording and expression and patterns of thought out of which understanding is built.

ACTIVITY 2

Exploring Discourse
Communities

ACTIVITY 3

Recognizing
Discourse
Communities

As Gregory Clark writes, "Using language is necessarily an act of collaboration through which we create the meaning we share, a socially constructed meaning that is inherently incomplete".

The Civic and Academic Discourse Communities

Two broad discourse communities that encompass specialized and regional discourse communities are the academic and the civic discourse communities.

The Civic Discourse Community

The civic discourse community is the broad discourse community of U.S. public life and includes all of us who communicate with each other about the issues and topics of the day, either interpersonally or through reading newspapers and magazines, listening to radio or television news, and so on.

Strictly defined, *civic* means pertaining to citizenship, but in an expanded sense civic refers to everything affecting the community in which people live, including issues national, local, and international, and topics directly and indirectly governmental. The topics of the chitchat that hums around us—about the sensational murder trial, the latest crime statistics, shocking infant mortality rates, the search for effective treatments for AIDS and cancer—and the goings-on of our lawmakers in Congress all come under the banner of civic issues.

In a free society, discourse about issues is a part of the democratic process. As political science professor John Nelson writes, "The relationship of politics to rhetoric [effective language use] is especially intimate in the domestic policies of America and other representational democracies. . . . To ask about the legitimacy of governors, laws, and policies in a representational polity is largely to ask how well it communicates public opinions to public officials, how well the officials communicate public needs to citizens, and how well the citizens communicate among themselves about public problems." In a sense, democracy comes down to communication. As a result, orienting people to take an interest in and function well in the national and local civic discourse communities is an important goal of education.

Civic discourse also encompasses the information and ideas flowing to us via the mass media. But the civic discourse community is not a creation of the mass media; there was a civic discourse community before there was CNN or television or the *New York Times*. Civic discourse has always been assisted by the media, whether printed one-page broadsides sold for a penny on the streets of colonial Philadelphia or presidential debates broadcast by national networks or extremist diatribes uploaded to an Internet forum. But civic discourse goes on among individuals and in public arenas, in meetings of town councils and parent-teacher organizations, student councils and boards of trustees. This discourse community, although broad in its inclusiveness, does foster conventional, accepted ways of thinking, discussing, analyzing, and ultimately approving or discrediting ideas that affect everyone within it.

Several reading selections at the end of this chapter draw from and comment on the civic discourse community. John Leo, whose column appears regularly in the national weekly newsmagazine *U.S. News and World Report,* comments on the failure of our discourse community—at least as it is represented by call-in and talk radio—to be sufficiently argumentative. Josie Mazzaferro, whose opinion piece was published on the *Philadelphia Inquirer*'s op-ed page, writes to defend the civic-mindedness of her twenty-something generation, which has often been discounted as "slackers." Complaining that the civic discourse community is too often short-circuited by a knee-jerk hopelessness, Chris Satullo, a *Philadelphia Inquirer* editor, shows how the tone of discussion in our discourse community can affect the solving of such civic problems as graffiti, school discipline, and television violence.

The Academic Discourse Community

The academic discourse community is sometimes called "academia"; others refer to it, not so approvingly, as "the ivory tower." Sarcasm aside, the academic discourse community is a national, even international, one that shares many characteristics with the civic. But, in addition to discussion and analysis, the academic discourse community mandates research and the active or conscious creation of new perspectives, new connections between ideas, and new ways of looking at the world—that is, new knowledge.

The local academic discourse community that you, your classmates, professors, and other college staff members belong to has its own specific characteristics, many of which are shared by people at other colleges and universities around the country and even around the world. Within any academic institution, there are smaller discourse communities, the academic disciplines. Like the academic discourse community as a whole, your college's academic departments are local sites of larger discourse communities of each discipline. Within each, there will be customary types of problems and controversies and expectations about how inquiry is conducted and what form the outcomes of inquiry will take.

For example, you can imagine how different the research conducted by an English major on the topic "symbolism in Stephen Crane's novels" would be from that of a psychology major assigned to write about recent research on infants' reactions to sweet, salt, and bitter tastes. An education major preparing a case study of a dyslexic child would conduct a different inquiry and write quite a different paper than a biology major assigned to do a laboratory experiment and write a lab report. If you at are the beginning of your college experience, you are a member-in-training of academia, and you may be somewhat unsure of the language expectations this community has. This book focuses on the expectations of the broad academic community rather than the requirements of specific disciplines.

ACTIVITY 4

Exploring Academic Discourse

The academic discourse community has a somewhat stronger emphasis than the civic on the written word, in that texts in libraries have been the major medium of interaction among scholars within a field. Although today many researchers turn to the World Wide Web or the Internet for some of their research, the outcome is still printed text read privately. Oral and public discourse does occur in academia, of course, not only in the college lecture hall and discussion classroom but in disciplinary conferences, forums, public lectures, and, increasingly, online in electronic forums. Academia is and will likely remain a text-oriented culture in which writing is a fundamental aspect of issue discovery, problem solving, and knowledge creation. Understanding and using well the modes of inquiry and discussion common to the academic disciplines are necessary for success in college.

. . . TO ARGUMENT

Taken in its everyday sense, the word argument may imply a battle: my side versus your side, "us" against "them," often a fruitless banging of heads that can be ended only with an insult or a begrudging remark like "everyone's entitled to an opinion." Our day-to-day experience with argument is often strongly oppositional and intensely frustrating.

Within the academic and civic discourse communities, argument refers to the building and presenting of a developed case in support of a position on an issue or controversy. When people analyze and evaluate the results of their quests for truth and knowledge—their inquiries—and formulate a position convincingly for presentation to others, they engage in argument. We often become interested in a controversy in midstream, like a person entering the parlor where Burke's unending conversation is going on. Arguments are already flowing, and so our inquiry must begin with understanding the arguments that have already been made.

Disputes over ideas raise new questions and inspire new inquiries, resulting in a land-scape of understandings, possible truths, and perspectives. Arguments themselves weave in and out of the inquiry process and usually don't boil down to a simple pro and con or "us" against "them." In fact, the win-lose mind-set can cause people to overlook the range and complexity of viewpoints on an issue. Besides the form of argument that defends an opinion, our common discourse includes other argumentative forms in which negotiation or recon-ciliation between oppositional views is sought and in which inquiry and the posing of ques-tions are prominent.

Consulting the dictionary on argument is informative. There we learn that the root of the word is *arg*, meaning "to shine, white, or the shining or white metal, silver." The Latin word *arguere* based on this root means "to make clear, or demonstrate" ("Arg-"). Knowing about these related roots helps me get a feel for the goal of argument: to come up in clear water after diving in deep, to achieve some clarity about important issues.

Arguments can open minds, encourage complexity of opinions, and advance the appre-ciation of evidence, but they don't always change minds. As we shall see, many factors under-lie a person's choice of opinion, and not all of them are easily addressable in an argument. (Section 2 will address some of these factors.) If argument's goal is converting readers, then most arguments are failures. But when argument is seen as a mode of participation in our dis-course community, as a vehicle for personal and intellectual growth, and as a means to encour-age and validate new options, perspectives, and solutions, then argument can be a vital and exciting process.

With the discourse community in mind, we can put aside those images of raised voices and pounded tables and see argumentation in a more positive light: as a means of participation in the larger intellectual forum of our society. In addition, in its testing of our ideas, argument can provide personal growth and intellectual maturing that is lifelong and ever-complicating. Argument, then, is an honorable and pro-ductive activity that seasons our own perspective and makes a respon-sible contribution to our society.

ACTIVITY 5

Exploring Real-Life
Arguments

The Elements of Argument

Argument in the broadest sense is an ancient discipline—a form of discourse cultivated by the ancient Greeks and Romans and passed down through the centuries as a means of engaging and advancing ideas and activating support. The writings that have come down to us about argument, from Aristotle through Cicero and Quintilian, provide terminology and strategies about argumentation that are still in use today. This is so even though the ancient rhetoricians (that is, specialists in effective language use) concentrated on oral rather than written language because oratory was then the major component of civic discourse. The ancients associated argumentation with citizenship; it was considered a communal activity designed to promote good civic policy as well as a method for testing ideas, philosophical, ethical, political, or otherwise. As one scholar in the field puts it, the "Greeks and Romans invented and developed rhetoric . . . specifically for their politics."

Formal argumentation involves more than batting around ideas in a free-for-all. Rather, in argumentation, a person presents a position, also called a **claim**, **assertion**, or **proposition**. A claim can clarify facts, explain causes (of problems), promote a value, or advocate a solution, policy, or change. An argumentative claim asserts the most believable or best position to hold on an issue or policy. What is most believable or best will necessarily be determined by the standards of the discourse community in which the argument occurs—and even then a debate frequently occurs over which standards should hold sway. The argumentative writer's goal is to set out the claim in a manner most convincing to the members of the discourse community being addressed.

Argument today includes a broad field of methods, techniques, and perspectives on how meaning is attached to events and situations, how viewpoints are articulated, developed, and lent credence—that is, supportability. But many expectations about argumentative discourse hold true throughout academic and many civic discourse communities:

1. Ideas are valued on the basis of evidence.
2. Ideas build on the ideas and evidence of others, as acquired through research.
3. Arguers will be knowledgeable about the major relevant ideas on a subject of controversy.

Expectations about Evidence

In the civic and academic discourse communities, whether an idea has value or not is usually determined by whether it is supportable—that is, whether there is evidence for it. This may seem so obvious that it might go without saying, and it often does. But requiring ideas to be backed up in order to be valued is a basic assumption that is especially strong in the academic and, to some extent, the civic discourse communities.

In our culture, as a result of our Greek and Roman heritage, the test of whether a claim should be believed lies in the reasonableness of the analysis and evidence. Logic, explored in depth by the ancients, is one of the ways such credence is achieved. Factual information also comes into play in creating a reasonable claim. But there is no formula for reasonableness, no one definition or standard. Rather, reasonableness encompasses a broad spectrum of qualities, including logicality of ideas, depth and breadth of evidence, coherence with similar historical events or cases, practical concerns for fairness and effectiveness of consequences, and comprehensiveness. Philosopher Richard Rorty claims that reasonableness is a state of mind: "to be rational is simply to discuss any topic—religious, literary or scientific—in a way which [avoids] dogmatism, defensiveness and righteous indignation."

The term *evidence* may remind you of a court of law, and to some extent this image is appropriate. Evidence for an argument must be weighed and evaluated, just as in a courtroom.

Not all evidence is "created equal." There are different types, and not all types work to support every claim or work well in different discourse communities. Some evidence, for example, is factual. Facts include the results of scientific research and experimentation; data acquired by taking surveys of people's opinions or living conditions; details gathered by observation; information about events, people, and so forth recorded in public records, documents, or news reports. Examples, which are individual factual cases, also weigh in as evidence.

But only some claims call for facts as evidence. Sometimes explanations and analyses are offered as support for belief in a claim. In an argument against zoos, for example, a person might explain how different the behavior of a wild gorilla is from that of a captive, leading to the assertion that the educational value of watching a gorilla in a zoo is negligible.

Analytic evidence might take the form of discussions of causes and effects; comparisons or contrasts with similar situations, events, or issues in history, politics, culture, or nature; processes or procedures. And whether evidence is logically applied remains another concern.

People argue about what evidence should be acceptable to answer questions raised about civic and social issues. Should a dramatic or extraordinary example alter one's perspective? Does, for example, the televised trial of a scandalous murder case accurately inform us of the ways our justice system works most of the time? To what extent can statistics be relied on as a determinant of truth? If the SAT test scores of U.S. students have been declining since the 1960s, and television became almost universal in U.S. households in the 1950s, should television be blamed for the decline in student ability? Should SAT scores be accepted as a reliable measure or definition of how educated our students are?

As you can see from these questions, even the idea of what is reasonable is subject to inquiry and debate.

Expectations about Research

A second convention within both the civic and academic discourse communities is the expectation that ideas will build on other ideas. For most arguers of claims, supporting evidence comes through research in printed or multimedia sources and is borrowed from other analysts, experiments, or researchers. The discourse community assumes that research will be done accurately and thoroughly, that it will be focused and analytic, and that other thinkers and writers who contribute to the understanding gained will be acknowledged.

In our culture generally, ideas are perceived as "owned." People who formally present ideas to the discourse community—in print or via a recordable medium—are held accountable for them. When anyone refers to, discusses, or incorporates the ideas or articulated knowledge of another, it is conventional to acknowledge the original source. In civic discourse, such acknowledgment is usually informal, often just a mention of a commentator's or writer's name or an author's book title. In the academic discourse community, however, the procedures for acknowledgment of ideas are codified into formal documentation rules that members of each discipline are expected to follow.

When Al Gore appears on *Larry King Live* to talk about the environment, his discourse represents his distillation of everything he's read and heard about the subject; his book, *Earth in the Balance,* acknowledges his debts in notes. Gore's handling of sources reflects an academic seriousness and respect for others' ideas. When a student jots down Gore's televised words and quotes them in a paper, she will acknowledge her debt to Gore, but not to all the influences on his thinking.

Attributing ideas to their authors, either formally or informally, suggests ownership, but technically and in a legal sense ideas cannot be owned—that is, they cannot be copyrighted or registered with the federal government as the property of a particular person. Only the specific expression of ideas can be legally tied to a person through copyright. So a poem, a newspaper opinion piece, or a film review can be copyrighted. Reviewer Janet Maslin's opinion of the film

The English Patient cannot be copyrighted, but her review—the actual words—can be. But the convention of acknowledgment is more inclusive than legal copyright. Any idea or information borrowed from someone who has formally presented ideas, either in published words or "for the record" on electronic media, must be acknowledged as originating in that source.

Expectations about Coverage

Both the academic and civic discourse communities expect that arguers will, to some extent, possess a command of pertinent evidence and other relevant arguments on all sides of the issue in question. The civic discourse community is more lenient on this requirement, but, still, in most contexts, an informed arguer is a more believable one. Depending on the context, it may be important to be knowledgeable about the most recent discussions and evidence on the issue or about the well-known, controversial, or classic arguments about the topic, and most likely to show awareness of positions opposed to your own.

In the academic discourse community, arguers are expected to present a complete view of the issue—that is, to review and engage the important ideas and viewpoints about the topic. Many academic disciplines expect their full members—graduate students and professors—to "review the literature"—that is, to identify all the relevant claims and evidence on the topic—before going on to build their own arguments. It is expected that new understandings and interpretations will build on previous arguments and defend against possible objections by providing disqualifying reasoning or evidence.

Academic writers strive for complete, encyclopedic coverage of a controversy, but expectations for undergraduate students are not so stringent. In responding to college assignments, students should determine what the expectations of coverage are and then limit coverage of the controversy or issue accordingly. Time, if nothing else, should force you to both read selectively and present a relevant sampling of other writers' positions.

Classical argumentation provides for the consideration of alternate viewpoints in the refutation stage of an argument. Refutation is a catchall for a variety of ways of dealing with opposing claims. A writer might simply acknowledge the existence of differing points of view; maintain the priority or special relevance of his or her own view; briefly discount other views; accept a qualified or partial version of an opposing view; or identify and thoroughly critique flaws in opposing arguments. Some writers even structure or develop their own presentation of evidence through the refutation of differing views.

Beyond refutation, there are other ways of interacting with different viewpoints. Striving for a middle ground or writing to establish common ground is one technique for using arguments to advance solutions to current societal problems. Writing to foster negotiation between differing views or adopting a "Rogerian," or noncombative, stance are other ways people work with multiple viewpoints. And using an inquiry perspective, in which questions are identified instead of answered, can also be a constructive approach to competing claims.

The Subject of Argument

Not everything is fair game for argumentation. Statements or assertions of personal preferences and tastes, for example, are just that—personal. No one can argue with you about your love of Cherry Garcia ice cream or your enjoyment of *The X Files*. Such tastes are unarguable.

However, the healthfulness of a Cherry Garcia—based diet or the artistic merits of a television series are suitable topics for argument because such arguments involve establishing a common standard of value or merit and comparing the specific choice—Cherry Garcia or *The X Files*—to these standards. Personal tastes become arguable when objective criteria can be established. Wine lovers, for example, have a system of taste analysis that removes the subjectivity from wine tasting and provides a standard for discussion and debate.

Assertions that proclaim accepted facts are usually deemed unsuitable for argument. Consider the following claims:

Automobile seatbelts save lives.
Vitamin C is a requirement for good health.
Dyslexia can seriously affect a student's ability to learn.

At one time, all these claims were hypothetical, but as research was conducted, these assertions have come to be considered facts.

Sometimes "facts" may turn out to be less than proven, or they may be alleged to be less than certain. Hence, although most people accept as a fact that smoking is unhealthful, some in the cigarette industry mounted the argument that smoking has nothing to do with cancer and heart attacks and is not addicting. Likewise, it's hard to argue with the facts that show the dangers of motorcycling bareheaded, yet motorcyclists have risen up to contest these facts and have mobilized to get helmet laws changed.

Legitimate and well-positioned arguments against "facts" sometimes do occur. After all, at one time, it was considered a fact that the sun revolved around the earth, and someone had to contest this idea to establish the reality. Within the discourse community of particular academic disciplines, for example, arguments do occur over facts. In history and science, new discoveries or reinterpretations of existing evidence may cause an argument over whether to revise a "fact," or something previously thought to be true. New discoveries of fossils and bones cause frequent revisions of the facts about when and where and how humans developed.

In many academic fields, there are areas where the facts are constantly uncertain or where debate rages over what the facts are. "Is there life elsewhere in the universe?" is a factual question that remains open to debate because science just has not accumulated enough evidence. More down-to-earth facts can also be uncertain. The authorship of a book sometimes attributed to Mikhail Bakhtin is uncertain, for it was published under the name of Bakhtin's less important colleague, V.N. Voloshinov, at a time when Bakhtin was in danger of imprisonment for his ideas. *Marxism* is either a collaboration between Bakhtin and Voloshinov, wholly by Bakhtin, or by Voloshinov under Bakhtin's influence, depending on which Bakhtin scholar you read.

Finally, it is difficult to argue over assertions of belief that are based on faith, tradition, or membership. The disciplines of philosophy and religious studies have developed modes of inquiry and debate about such matters as whether God, devils, angels, and so forth exist, but outside such specialized study assertions about religious matters are nearly unarguable.

READINGS

THE UNMAKING OF CIVIC CULTURE

John Leo

John Leo is a regular columnist for the weekly newsmagazine U.S. News and World Report, *where this piece appeared on February 13, 1995. Copyright 1995 by U.S. News and World Report. Reprinted by permission.*

One night last summer, I was the substitute host on one of the popular late-night radio talk shows in New York. For four hours, the switchboard lit up with listeners eager to talk about the two hot-button topics of the evening: domestic violence and Afrocentrism. Calls rolled in from feminists, antifeminist women, abused women, abused men, blacks and whites discussing the fine points of ancient Egypt and the treatment of blacks by white historians. With one exception (a man who calls in regularly to disparage blacks), the callers conducted a very serious, informed debate with great civility.

Why doesn't this happen more often? On most talk radio, 75 percent of the listeners seem to phone in to echo what has just been said. Most others seem to be patrolling for group slights or to point out that the guest is full of beans.

So far, the political discussions on the online computer services haven't seemed much better. Last week in the *U.S. News* forum on CompuServe, an exasperated woman named Julie tapped out the message that "Reading some of the threads online is like listening to my two teens arguing over anything and everything: 'Did not . . . Did too . . . Did not . . . Did too . . . MOM!!' "

Many social critics have tried to explain the low level of political discussion and debate. Some think the increasingly truculent and ideological tone of American politics makes debate seem too wearing and pointless: Each side knows what the other will say, so why bother going through it again and again?

In his last book, *The Revolt of the Elites and the Betrayal of Democracy,* the late Christopher Lasch blamed the rise of television debate (which puts a premium on appearance and unflappability rather than on the substance of argument) and the rise of "commercial persuasion" (an increasingly cynical electorate comes to feel manipulated by PR people, lobbyists and advertising campaigns).

Instant Plebiscite

Jean Bethke Elshtain, in her new book, *Democracy on Trial,* makes a related point. Technology, she says, has brought us to the brink of a politics based on Instant plebiscite: With telepolling and interactive TV, politicians can respond to the majority's wishes (and whims) on any subject, "so there is no need for debate with one's fellow citizens on substantive questions. All that is required is a calculus of opinion."

This is a skewed form of democracy, that fits the current atomized state of American society. Politics can be based on the offhand views of mostly semi-informed individuals sitting alone in front of the TV, randomly pushing buttons. But as Elshtain says, "A compilation of opinions does not make a civic culture: such a culture emerges only from a deliberative process."

Lasch argued that a citizenry can't be informed unless it argues. He wrote that only an impassioned political argument makes the arguer look hard for evidence that will back up or tear down his position. Until we have to defend our opinions in public, he said, they remain half-formed convictions based on random impressions: "We come to know our own minds only by explaining ourselves to others."

Many critics argue that the rise of state bureaucracies, converting citizens into clients, has eliminated the local meetings that served as seedbeds of public political argument. So has the rise of politics based on litigation, which downgrades all political argument not conducted in front of a judge. This has gone hand in hand with the "rights" revolution. Once a desire is positioned as a right, by definition it can't be challenged. It's a trump card, beyond debate.

A great many of these offenses against ordinary democracy have been conducted by the left, but the right has been guilty too, chiefly of importing strongly held moral positions directly into politics as assertions rather than as matters of debate. A conviction may be personal or religious, but it has to be defended rationally against people with different principles, or there is no point in discussing it at all.

The hollowing out of our civic culture has many causes that help explain the decline of political debate. A crucial one is the rise of the therapeutic ethic. Starting in the 1960s, the nation's sense of itself has been deeply influenced by the rapid spread of therapies, encounter groups, self-help, the language of self-esteem and personal growth and an array of New Age notions, some of them quasi religions based on the primacy of the self.

This has created a vast Oprahized culture obsessed with feelings and subjective, private experiences. In some ways, this culture of therapy has positioned itself as the antidote for America's fragmentation and the decline of civic culture. It pushes young people into monitoring their own psyches and away from environments where they might learn civic and political skills. And it tends to kill any chance for political debate by framing values as mere matters of personal taste. You like vanilla. I like butter pecan.

It's important to reverse this process. We need a lot more emphasis on public discourse and common problems, and a lot less mooning about our individual psyches.

Questions for Inquiry

1. According to Leo, what is the problem that is "unmaking" our civic culture? What examples of this problem does he offer? According to him, what should be the goal of public discourse in a democracy?
2. What do the two authors, Lasch and Elshtain, contribute to Leo's analysis? What does the reference to these two authors suggest about the audience Leo expects for his column?
3. What causes of the "low level of political discussion and debate" does Leo identify?

II

RHETORICAL ANALYSIS

from *Envision*

Rhetoric's classic definition as the art of persuasion suggests a power. So much of what we receive from others—from family and friends to 30-second blurbs on TV—is intended to persuade. Recognizing how this is done gives greater power to choose.

—Victor Villanueva, Jr.

Everywhere around us, words and images try to persuade us to think about the world in certain ways. From "Got Milk?" ads to political campaign posters, words and images combine to move us, convince us to buy something, shape our opinions, or just make us laugh. Living in such a world requires us to pay attention and to think critically and analytically about all the texts we encounter every day. We can see this persuasive power especially in visual texts, such as the political cartoons and comics you might find on your favorite Weblog or in the campus newspaper.

Consider the political cartoon shown in Figure 1. How do the words and the images work together to persuade audiences to think, feel, or act a certain way?

Nick Anderson's cartoon conveys a powerful message about how steroid use has damaged the relationship between young fans and their baseball-star role models. Notice how when the athlete's steroid needle literally "pops" the child's balloon—and thus, implicitly, the child's admiration for the athlete—the written words "Oh, sorry kid" show a lack of true contrition; the font, selection, and arrangement of words make the player seem anything but sincere. Rather, the brightly colored muscular back takes over the entire space of the cartoon, showing the audience (baseball-loving fans) how steroids not only hurt the players but also hurt the game, the fans, and even perhaps our country's future by demoralizing children.

We can understand how this cartoon works by asking questions about its argument, audience, and author. When we ask questions like these, we are analyzing how texts can be **rhetorical,** how

they aim at persuading specific audiences through the careful choices made by the writer in composing the text.

We've chosen to focus on comics and political cartoons in this chapter; by studying these texts, you'll develop skills as both a reader and a writer, learn how to analyze rhetoric, and create powerful arguments about the texts you encounter every day. In the process, you'll come to appreciate how writing as we know it is changing, causing us to approach it with a new set of eyes and rhetorical tools.

Figure 1   Nick Anderson's cartoon from *The Courier-Journal* uses color and exaggerated form to argue that steroid-using baseball players are popping the dreams of young children. *Source:* Copyright 2004 Nick Anderson. All rights reserved. Reprinted with permission of Nick Anderson in conjunction with Washington Post Writers Group and the Cartoonist Group.

CHAPTER PREVIEW QUESTIONS

- How do we read and analyze texts rhetorically?
- How do we write about visual texts?
- How do thesis statements help us make arguments?
- How can we compose titles and draft analysis essays?

UNDERSTANDING TEXTS RHETORICALLY

To approach texts rhetorically means to ask questions about how the text conveys a persuasive message or *argument*, how the text addresses a specific *audience*, and how the writer operates within a *specific context* or *rhetorical situation*.

You encounter many kinds of texts every day, even in just walking across campus. Once you recognize how these texts function *rhetorically*, you'll see that, as rhetoric scholar Victor Villanueva writes, "So much of what we receive from others—from family and friends to 30-second blurbs on TV—is intended to persuade. Recognizing how this is done gives greater power to choose." In other words, once you see how texts try to shape your mind about the world, then you can decide whether or not to agree with the many messages you encounter on a regular basis.

To grasp this concept, let's follow one hypothetical student—we'll call her Alex—as she walks to class and note the rhetorical texts she sees along the way. First stop: the dorm room, your average institutional room, which Alex and her roommate have decorated with Altoids ads they've ripped from magazines. There's also a large poster for the women's basketball team on one wall and a small Snoopy comic taped above the computer screen. As Alex turns off her computer, we notice what's on the screen: the Website for Slate.com, complete with an animated ad for an online dating service and an annoying pop-up telling Alex she'll win $50 if she clicks now. But Alex doesn't click; she shuts the machine down, piles her glossy-covered textbooks in her backpack, and slams the door shut on her way out.

Alex walks down the hall, past the rooms of other students in the dorm who have photos and graffiti on their doors, pausing in the lounge where several of her friends are watching a rerun of Jon Stewart on a large flat-screen TV. She watches until the show breaks for a commercial for Nike shoes, then she continues, down the stairwell decorated with student event flyers—a charity dance for the victims of Hurricane Katrina, a rally against immigration laws, a dorm meeting to plan the ski trip—and she pushes her way out into the cool autumn air. She only has two minutes to get to class, so she walks briskly past the student union with its event bulletin boards and its large hand-painted sign, "Café, open 6 A.M.–midnight, best crisps on campus." Two students at a small card table have painted their faces blue, and they hand her a small blue card with the cartoon of a surfer on it. "Come to our Hawaiian luau at the fraternity Saturday night!" they call to her as she crosses the quad and heads toward the statue of the university founder on his horse.

Alex then walks over the school crest embedded in the center of the walkway and past a group of students congregated outside the administration building, waving signs that protest the conditions of university janitorial workers. She turns left, weaving along the back of a cluster of gleaming steel and brick buildings that constitute the engineering quad. To her right, she passes a thin metal sculpture called *Knowledge and Life* that guards the entrance to the library. Finally, she reaches her destination: the English department. As Alex jogs up the stone steps, she stops momentarily to pick up the campus newspaper and scan the photos and headlines on the front page before folding the newspaper under her arm. Down the hall and into the classroom she rushes, but she's late. The professor has started the PowerPoint lecture already. Alex picks up the day's handout from the TA and sits down in the back row.

Now that we've seen Alex safely to her seat, how many rhetorical texts did you notice along the way? Ads, posters, cartoons, Websites, textbooks, television shows, flyers, statues, signs, newspapers, PowerPoint slides, even architectural design: each can be seen as an example of rhetoric. Once you begin to look at the world rhetorically, you'll see that just about everywhere you are being persuaded to agree, act, buy, attend, or accept an argument: rhetoric permeates our cultural landscape. Recognizing the power of rhetoric to persuade is an important part of learning to engage in contemporary society. Learning how to read texts rhetorically is the first step in thinking critically about the world.

CREATIVE PRACTICE

The next time you walk to class, pay attention to the rhetoric that you find along the way; take notes as you walk to catalog the various types of persuasion you encounter. Then, write up your reflections on your observations into a *personal narrative essay*. Discuss which types of rhetoric were most evident, which were most subtle, and which you found the most persuasive.

UNDERSTANDING RHETORIC

In one of the earliest definitions, ancient Greek philosopher Aristotle characterized **rhetoric** as *the ability to discern the available means of persuasion in any given situation*. Essentially, this

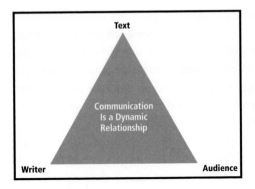

Figure 2   The rhetorical situation is the relationship between writer, text, and audience.

means knowing what strategies will work to convince your audience to accept your message. As shown in Figure 2, this involves assessing and attending to the **rhetorical situation**—that is, to the relationship between writer, text, and audience. Think of the politician who might argue the same political platform but in strikingly different ways depending on what part of his constituency he's addressing; of the various ways mothers, students, or police officers might convey the same antidrug message to a group of middle school students; of how clothing retailers adapt their marketing message to suit the media in which they're advertising—magazines, radio, or television. In each case the *argument* has been determined by the unique relationship between the writer, the audience, and the text.

In constructing your own arguments every day, you undoubtedly also, consciously or not, evaluate your rhetorical situations. When you want to persuade your coach to let practice out early, you probably make your case face to face, rather than through a formal letter. When you ask for an extension on a paper, you most likely do so in a well-crafted email rather than a hasty after-class appeal. When you apply for a job or internship, you send a formal résumé and cover letter to indicate the seriousness of your interest. Here again we see that the success of your argument depends at least in part on your choice of text (verbal plea, written email, cover letter) in relation to the audience (coach, professor, potential employer) that you're addressing. All these examples are rhetorical acts in the form of oral and written arguments.

STUDENT WRITING

Read Esmeralda Fuentes's short narrative about the visual rhetoric she observes during the course of one day.

www.ablongman.com/envision/201

Understanding Visual Rhetoric

Yet persuasion happens through visual means as well: how you stand and make eye contact, how you format your professional documents, even how you capitalize or spell words in an email. Moreover, when you insert an image in an essay, create a poster to advertise a club sport, or draw a cartoon spoofing university policy, you are moving into the realm of **visual persuasion**—"writing" with images. From photographs to Websites, political cartoons to advertisements, these visual texts use rhetorical means to persuade an audience. Although some images may be more aesthetic than argumentative, many convey either inherent or explicit persuasive messages. Think about brochures, movie trailers, flyers, commercial Websites, and even comics; these are all created as arguments to convince audiences.

Since such strategies of persuasion occur through images—either alone or combined with words—rather than merely through words, they are called **visual rhetoric**. A documentary is produced and edited specifically to suggest a particular point of view; the illustration in a children's book provides a way to read a story; the sequential cartoons of a comic strip offer powerful commentary on American society. In each example, the writer chooses the best visual representation for the message of the text. The study of visual rhetoric provides you with the means to understand how and why such choices are made, and what the significance of these decisions is in the larger culture in which we live.

ANALYZING TEXTS RHETORICALLY

Think of your favorite comic strips or political cartoons. Although they may seem purely aesthetic, merely informative about current events, or just plain funny, they do serve as an important mode of communicating ideas. For example, the comic antics of Dilbert or of Pig and Rat from *Pearls Before Swine* may not appear to carry any strong arguments about our society, human nature, or social relations. However, if you look closely at the details—the choice of words, the composition of the image, the particular colors, layout, character placement, and design—then you can gain a deeper understanding of the cartoon's message. This is what we mean by analyzing texts rhetorically.

Consider the following argument, made by cultural critic Scott McCloud as part of his book, *Understanding Comics:*

> When pictures are more abstracted from "reality," they require greater levels of perception, more like words. When words are bolder, more direct, they require lower levels of perception and are received faster, more like pictures.

What's significant about this quote is not only *what* McCloud says about the relationship between words and images but also *how* he says it. In effect, we can look to this brief passage as an example of a persuasive use of rhetoric, in which McCloud makes very deliberate choices to strengthen his point. Notice how he uses comparison-contrast (pictures versus words), qualified language ("reality"), and parallel structure (both sentences move from "When" to a final phrase beginning with "more like") to persuade his audience of the way pictures and words can operate in similar ways. Such attention to detail is the first step in rhetorical analysis—looking at the way the writer chooses the most effective means of persuasion to make a point.

To fully appreciate McCloud's rhetorical decisions, however, we need to consider the passage in its original context. As you can see in Figure 3, McCloud amplifies his argument by creating what we call a **hybrid text**—a strategic combination of words and images.

This complex diagram relies on the visual-verbal relationship itself to map out the complicated nature of how we understand both written text and pictures. The repetition and echoes that we found in the quoted passage are graphically represented in Figure 3; in fact, translated into comic book form, the division between word and image breaks down. It becomes a visual continuum that strongly suggests McCloud's vision of the interrelationship between these rhetorical elements. The power of this argument comes from McCloud's strategic assessment of the rhetorical situation: he, the **author,** recognizes that his **audience** (people interested in visual media) would find a **text** that relies on both visual and verbal elements to be highly persuasive.

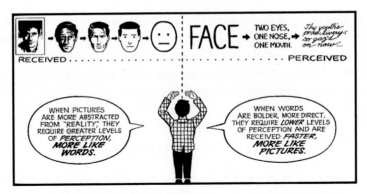

Figure 3   Scott McCloud writes in the medium of cartoons to explain comics.
Source: Courtesy of Scott McCloud.

McCloud's example is also instructive for demonstrating the way word and image can collaborate in modern arguments. Today more than ever, rhetoric operates not just through word choice, but also through choice of multimedia elements—images in a TV commercial, sounds accompanying a radio program, the font and color of a Website or flyer, even the layout strategies of this book. So we need to develop skills of analysis for all rhetorical texts. We need to envision argument as writing across diverse media and in turn develop **multimedia literacy,** or a careful way of reading, analyzing, and understanding media (visual, verbal, and other rhetorical texts).

Analyzing a Comic Strip

Comic strips are a productive starting point for examining how an understanding of the rhetorical situation and compositional strategies work together to produce powerful texts. We can begin with the cartoon in Figure 4, looking closely at its detail and composition. Focusing first on the central, circular frame in the middle of the strip, we can see even within this single frame the power of rhetoric at work. When you look at the circular panel, what do you see?

You may see a split screen with two boys and two alien creatures; if you are more familiar with comic strips, you may identify the boy as Calvin from the cartoon *Calvin and Hobbes.* What is the *rhetorical function* of this image? The cartoon provides a dramatic enactment of a moment of crisis in this boy's life. The left side portrays the "real" Calvin, cast in green liquid, an expression of alarm on his face. The white air bubbles surrounding him suggest his panic and amplify the impression of fear. In contrast, the right side of the cartoon features a different Calvin, his head opened up to reveal a mechanical brain, his eyes wide and staring like a boy possessed. It seems a standard body-snatcher science fiction scenario, complete with a pair of aliens preparing to refasten Calvin's spiky blonde hair on top of this new brain. As an individual image, this panel taps into a message of fear and childhood imagining, with the aliens readying Robot Calvin to take over the functions of the real Calvin's life.

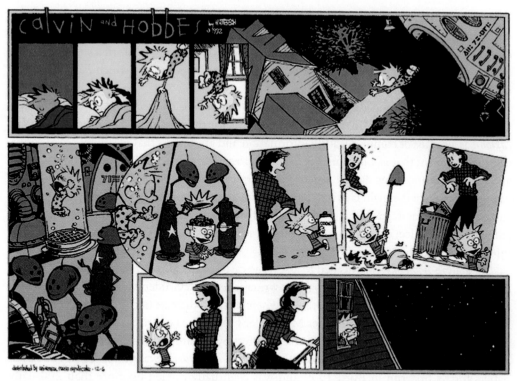

Figure 4   This *Calvin and Hobbes* cartoon conveys meaning through its colorful combination of sequential images.

Let's think about how the meaning of a cartoon changes when it is integrated into a full strip. When we view still frames in succession, we find that meaning becomes more complex in a wonderful array of possible interpretations. When read in conjunction with images of a stolen cookie jar, broken lamp, and discarded math book, Calvin's crisis takes on a slightly different meaning. As we arrive at the frame of Calvin gesticulating to his mother, her eyes narrowed with skepticism, we realize that the cartoon itself represents a moment of storytelling; the strip in effect juxtaposes Calvin's version of reality with his mother's. The final frame reveals the end of the tale, with Calvin banished to his room, staring out at the stars. These new elements add levels of meaning to the comic, as we are invited to ponder versions of reality, the power of childhood imagination, and the force of visual detail.

Watterson is hardly alone in the strategy of using his comic strip as a means of producing an argument or cultural critique. For instance, Aaron McGruder's *Boondocks* and Gary Trudeau's *Doonesbury* offer sharper, more critical messages about society through a combination of words and images.

 **STUDENT WRITING**

Read Jack Chung's interpretation of a *Calvin and Hobbes* cartoon strip.

www.ablongman.com/envision/202

In the *Boondocks* comic strip shown in Figure 5, McGruder argues for the power of political cartoons as a form of social commentary by having his protagonist, Huey, draw his own cartoon to comment on electoral politics. The irony in his line "Well, that's the key—not beating the reader over the head with your point" reveals the very way in which *Boondocks* does, in fact, make its point explicit for readers of the strip.

Significantly, McGruder subtitled his 2000 collection *The Boondocks: Because I Know You Don't Read the Newspapers*. In choosing these words for the title of his book, he presents his *cartoon* as a means of communicating information and arguments that we might see as equivalent to the news; that is, his comics persuade us to see current events, political controversies, and key issues concerning race in America in a certain light. This is shown in the second frame of Figure 5, where the main character, Huey, turns to cartooning itself as a way to craft a persuasive political message. He makes a rhetorical statement with his visual image and accompanying word choice; the drawing here is much more than merely an aesthetic, humorous, or informative text. It is a powerful rhetorical act.

To analyze *Boondocks*, we needed to assess the cartoon's *rhetorical situation* in drawing conclusions; we had to understand the way the writer (Aaron McGruder) took the audience (contemporary Americans) into consideration when creating the text (a comic strip, combining images and words). We can interpret McGruder's cartoon as offering a striking example of a rhetorical situation: although the Universal Press Syndicate had anticipated that this edgy strip would appear in between 30 and 50 newspapers, *Boondocks* was published in 160 newspapers for its first run in April 1999 and was eventually carried by more than 200 daily papers, and by 2005 it had been converted into an animated television series. McGruder's effective use of visual and verbal rhetoric to engage the topic of American race relations made his strip the most successful debut comic in the Universal Press Syndicate's history.

To apply this understanding of the rhetorical situation yourself, complete the following "Creative Practice." What is your analysis of these texts?

Figure 5   Cartoonist Aaron McGruder emphasizes the power of visual rhetoric in this comic strip.
Source: THE BOONDOCKS © 2002 Aaron McGruder. Dist. by UNIVERSAL PRESS SYNDICATE.

CREATIVE PRACTICE

Look at the *Penny Arcade* comic in Figure 6. Jot down your analysis of the elements of the cartoon: color, composition, characters, and action. Pay attention to facial expression, the use of symbols, and the changes between the panels. Then ask yourself: What persuasive statement does the cartoon convey? What is its argument? What is the message for readers?

Figure 6   *The Hipness Threshold* cartoon depicts the adventures of Gabe and Tycho as they accompany their friend Charles into an Apple Computer store, while in a blog entry, the cartoonist Jerry Holkins addresses Apple culture more broadly. *Source:* Penny Arcade, Inc. www.penny-arcade.com

Having done so, now read the following excerpt from one of the cartoonists' blog posts that accompanied the online publication of this comic. In it, Jerry Holkins makes a very similar argument—but in words. In what ways does this different rhetorical situation (blog versus Web comic) influence the way he makes his argument?

The way Apple projects its brand, however, has nothing to do with the underlying technology. It could not be more divorced from it. So if they want to create largely empty stores staffed exclusively by young hardbodies in ill-fitting t-shirts, it's open season. It's possible that each manifestation of this chain does not resemble the others, that each one is not populated with the scrubbed, tousled young things of the sort one sees in serious teen dramas. You'll forgive me if I don't believe that. I'd say it's far more likely that there is a single Apple Store, connected by a series of geographically distinct portals.

I don't put this out there to imply that the places I have to go to get technology or software are somehow superior, because they aren't. They're horrid. But at least I never feel underdressed.

As these examples demonstrate, we can gather a tremendous amount of information from a seemingly simple comic strip. Indeed, different readers will make different interpretations. This is what we mean by **visual arguments:** each viewer makes a separate interpretation of the image.

As we learn to develop our *visual literacy*, we can make more and better-informed interpretations of such intriguing visual texts. And, as we will soon see, these skills of visual analysis will help you approach other kinds of texts rhetorically: political speeches, scholarly articles, letters to the editor about timely issues, even instant messaging and—as we just learned—blog posts.

STRATEGIES FOR ANALYZING PERSUASIVE TEXTS

We've learned that rhetoric works as a means of persuading an audience to embrace the argument of the author. This is also true for the arguments *you make* about a text. In other words, rhetoric also applies to the texts you craft to persuade someone to accept your interpretation of a specific cultural or political artifact.

Why is it important for you to hone your skills in analyzing texts? Well, as we've seen, a single text visual can yield multiple interpretations. Your task is to argue convincingly—and persuade your audience—to see the text the way you see it. Your challenge as a student of writing and rhetoric is not only to identify the argument contained by a text but also to craft your own interpretation of that text. This involves a careful assessment of the ways in which the elements of the rhetorical situation work together to produce meaning in a text. In many cases your analysis will also address the interplay of words and images. Your analysis can take many forms: a written essay, an oral report, a visual argument, or a combination of these. Practice in analyzing the arguments of others is one of the best ways to develop your own persuasive skills.

Analyzing Editorial Cartoons

We can look at political cartoons—or **editorial cartoons** as they are also called—for another set of visual arguments to help us further develop effective strategies for analysis and interpretation. Editorial cartoons offer a rich resource for this sort of work since, as culture critic Matthew Diamond asserts, they "provide alternative perspectives at a glance because they are visual and vivid and often seem to communicate a clear or obvious message" (270). From the densely symbolic eighteenth-century plates of William Hogarth, to the biting social satire of *Punch*'s illustrators, to the edgy work of political cartoonists such as Ann Telnaes and Mike Luckovich in this century, the editorial cartoon has emerged as a succinct, powerful tool for writers to contribute to public dialogue on contemporary issues.

In the drawing by Daryl Cagle, for instance (see Figure 7), the particular face is recognizable to most twenty-first-century readers: the impish smile, the circular, black-frame glasses, and the prep-school tie identify this figure almost immediately as the young actor who plays Harry Potter in the film series.

Figure 7   This cartoon by Daryl Cagle uses a striking symbol to make its argument. *Source:* Daryl Cagle, Cagle Cartoons, Inc.

However, through one strategic substitution, Cagle transforms this image from illustration into commentary; he replaces the famous lightning bolt scar on Potter's forehead with a dollar sign. Cagle's Potter has been branded not by his encounter with a nearly omnipotent wizard but by his face-off with American capitalism. In this way, Cagle uses visual elements in his editorial cartoon to comment on the way this children's book hero has become a lucrative pop culture franchise.

Figure 8 Mike Luckovich's "Statue of Liberty" circulated widely in newspapers and on the Internet after September 11, 2001. *Source:* By permission of Mike Luckovich and Creators Syndicate, Inc.

For a more politically charged example, let's look at a powerful cartoon created by Pulitzer Prize-winning artist Mike Luckovich, depicting the Statue of Liberty crying in the aftermath of the attacks on the World Trade Center on September 11, 2001. As you examine Figure 8, ask yourself: What is the persuasive message of this political cartoon? Write down your interpretation, and be sure to consider the elements of the rhetorical situation as well as specific details that you observe.

Perhaps, in your attempts to write a rhetorical analysis of this cartoon's meaning, you commented on the statue's childlike features, suggestive of innocence or vulnerability. You might have remarked on the nose and hair as seeming particularly Caucasian and asked: What message does this send about who is American? You might also have integrated the history associated with this statue into your interpretation. Is Luckovich offering an argument about how America's role as a haven for the oppressed and as a steward of peace and goodwill was attacked on September 11?

Some students reading this cartoon have argued that it casts an ironic eye on the history of America; they read the Statue of Liberty as crying about the abuses of civil rights in the wake of the attacks. Others claim that the composition of the cartoon—the visual details of the crying eye and childish face—suggests that this country is more vulnerable than previously thought. As you consider the rhetorical situation for the cartoon (the way in which it was written in the wake of the attacks), reflect on how different audiences might respond to its power.

Practicing Rhetorical Analysis

Before choosing your own text for rhetorical analysis, let's look closely at the strategies you can use to analyze a text and arrive at your own interpretation.

In Figure 9, for instance, you will find a hybrid argument on the national debate over the Pledge of Allegiance. To get started composing an interpretation of this text, first notice which specific verbal and visual elements stand out as you look at the cartoon.

The drawing itself suggests a generic classroom in America: several elementary school students, diverse in terms of gender and race, face the flag in the standard, patriotic pose, their

Figure 9   Gary Markstein conveys the controversy
over the constitutionality of including the
phrase "under God" in the Pledge of
Allegiance. *Source:* Gary Markstein and
Copley News Service

teacher looking on. The flag, as you might expect, is center stage—but it is significantly limp and uninspiring. This strategic rendering of the flag becomes complicated by the words that accompany the image: "one nation, under nothing in particular." Not only has "God" been removed from the pledge, but with the clever substitution of "under nothing in particular," cartoonist Gary Markstein seems to speaks to the fear of raising a generation of Americans—and a future America—with no faith. His drawing of the disgusted teacher appears to embody the argument of the cartoon. Her mental thought, "God help us," voices an older generation's frustration and worry in the face of these young nihilists. In this way, you might argue, the cartoonist has taken the controversy over the use of "God" in the Pledge of Allegiance to an extreme; he has strategically used both word and image to create a powerful argument about this issue, as powerful as any written article found in a *Wall Street Journal* op-ed piece.

Like Markstein's editorial cartoon, the following excerpt from an editorial by Samuel P. Huntington comments on the debate over the Pledge of Allegiance. This debate was ignited by Michael Newdow, who filed a lawsuit against his daughter's school district, arguing that the words "under God" in the Pledge amounted to an unconstitutional endorsement of religion. A federal court ruled in favor of Newdow, but the Supreme Court reversed that decision in June 2004. No final decision has been made on the issue of whether or not the words "under God" violate the Constitution's provisions against the endorsement of religion by the government. As you read the excerpt, consider how Huntington's argument compares to Markstein's cartoon. Are they both making the same argument in different ways? Or is there a difference in what each text argues?

"Under God"

Michael Newdow is right. Atheists are outsiders in America.

Samuel P. Huntington

The battle over the Pledge of Allegiance has stimulated vigorous controversy on an issue central to America's identity. Opponents of "under God" (which was added to the pledge in 1954) argue that the United States is a secular country, that the First Amendment prohibits rhetorical or material state support for religion, and that people should be able to pledge allegiance to their country without implicitly also affirming a belief in God. Supporters point out that the phrase is perfectly consonant with the views of the framers of the Constitution, that Lincoln had used these words in the Gettysburg Address, and that the Supreme Court—which on Monday sidestepped a challenge to the Pledge of Allegiance—has long held that no one could be compelled to say the pledge.

The atheist who brought the court challenge, Michael Newdow, asked this question: "Why should I be made to feel like an outsider?" Earlier, the Court of Appeals in San Francisco had agreed that the words "under God" sent "a message to unbelievers that they are outsiders, not full members of the political community."

Although the Supreme Court did not address the question directly, Mr. Newdow got it right: Atheists are "outsiders" in the American community. Americans are one of the most religious people in the world, particularly compared with the peoples of other highly industrialized democracies. But they nonetheless tolerate and respect the rights of atheists and nonbelievers. Unbelievers do not have to recite the pledge, or engage in any religiously tainted practice of which they disapprove. They also, however, do not have the right to impose their atheism on all those Americans whose beliefs now and historically have defined America as a religious nation.

In composing your analysis of this text, you would need to follow a familiar process: First, look carefully at all the elements in the text. You might create a list of your observations or use the prewriting checklist at the end of this chapter to help you read the text more closely. Then, speculate about the meaning of each element. How does it contribute to the whole? Finally, complete the rhetorical triangle (see Figure 2) for the text, assessing who the author is, who the intended audience is, and what the argument of the text is, based on your observations of the details.

CREATIVE PRACTICE

Using the political cartoon shown in Figure 10, create your own hybrid text. First, jot down your observations about the cartoon; think about its rhetorical situation (its audience, author, and message) and determine a context (when and where you think it appeared). Next, develop an interpretation of the cartoon's meaning. Finally, fill in the blank tablet to clarify that argument for future readers. When you are done, move into a small group and share your work—both your written analysis and your hybrid text. Discuss what you have learned in producing oral, written, and cartoon texts, and how each text conveys your argument.

Figure 10 In this modified version of John Deering's cartoon, the words on the tablet have been removed, opening up many possibilities for alternative meanings. *Source:* By permission of John Deering and Creators Syndicate, Inc.

STUDENT WRITING

See Jeff Enquist's analysis of a cartoonist's commentary on the media representation of Catholic priests as part of a larger social issue dealing with the place of religion in American culture.

www.ablongman.com/envision/203

As you completed your work for the "Creative Practice," you probably found that your additions to the blank tablet altered the cartoon's meaning in fundamental ways. Perhaps you inserted words that referred to religion, September 11, the war with Iraq, or the 2006 Danish cartoon controversy—in this way, you practiced the art of rhetoric that, through the combination of word and image, contributed a very specific political message or strong social commentary. Or perhaps you drew something in the tablet instead, using *visual persuasion* as your means of practicing rhetoric.

When we gave this exercise to our students, some offered the words "We support the USA" or "Women for equal rights" while others suggested filling in the blank with a visual text—a photo of Hillary Clinton or a drawing of a Muslim woman lifting her burka to expose her heels. In the actual published version from the 2001 *Arkansas Democrat Gazette,* cartoonist John Deering made the tablet present the ironic words "To the Taliban: Give us Osama Bin Laden or we'll send your women to college." Thus, Deering used the ongoing search for Osama Bin Laden as a springboard for lampooning cultural differences in gender roles; his words suggest international and cultural differences among countries. His cartoon practiced visual and verbal means of persuasion, both of which are important to consider when we are analyzing and writing about a text.

COLLABORATIVE CHALLENGE

To begin writing about cartoons as powerful rhetorical acts, get into groups of three and turn to the Internet, a vast resource for finding visual rhetoric, to locate political cartoons that address the same issue from diverse national perspectives. Go to the Chapter 1 resource page of the *Envision* Website, and select two or three cartoons from Daryl Cagle's Professional Cartoonist Index. Compare how different countries craft persuasive visual arguments about the same issue with remarkably divergent messages. Working collaboratively, write an analysis of each cartoon, and prepare to share your interpretations with the rest of the class. Be sure to describe elements of the visual text in detail and discuss how each contributes to the rhetorical force of the image.

www.ablongman.com/envision/204

What we can learn from this practice with rhetoric is that the relationship between interpretation and argument is a complex one. Although the author might intend to produce a certain argument, at times the audience may offer a slightly different interpretation. Our task as readers and writers is both to study a text carefully and to learn how to persuade others to see the text as we see it.

One powerful example of how texts can be read in multiple ways occurred in 2002 when Pulitzer Prize-winning cartoonist Doug Marlette created a political cartoon following the 9/11 attacks (see Figure 11). The title of the cartoon, "What Would Mohammed Drive?" makes a clear link between the Muslim religion and terrorism, as depicted by the nuclear warhead in the Ryder truck.

The cartoon caused a firestorm of protest from the Muslim community in America, including death threats on the cartoonist. Marlette responded by asserting that "the objective of political cartooning 'is not to soothe and tend sensitive psyches, but to jab and poke in an attempt to get at deeper truths, popular or otherwise'" (quoted in Moore). Marlette's own words reveal that cartoons are not merely humorous texts but rather, as we have seen, they are rhetorical—they intend to persuade.

Figure 11 Doug Marlette received death threats after publishing this cartoon. *Source:* Courtesy of Doug Marlette

Look again at the cartoon and ask yourself *how* it attempts to jab or poke. What elements of composition, framing, shading, and layout suggest to you the target of Marlette's jab? How does the title set up or shape possible readings of the cartoon? How might this cartoon be read differently by an American audience, an Arab audience, and an Arab-American audience? How might it be interpreted in the United States or in the Middle East as conveying a different persuasive message?

Some might argue that the cartoon takes the announced threat of terrorists potentially using trucks to carry out nuclear attacks and reproduces it without irony. Another reader analyzing the cartoon could say that it mocks the government issuing the warning about post-September 11 terrorists. A third reader could point to the caricature of the driver and state that the cartoon makes fun of people of Arab descent. These varied ways of reading and responding to the text depend on both *audience* and *context*, bringing to light the importance of the rhetorical situation. They also reveal the importance of learning effective means of persuading others to see the text through a certain interpretative lens or way of reading the cartoon.

Let's turn now to Doug Marlette's writing to see how he used the art of rhetoric to persuade his many readers to see the cartoon from his perspective. Marlette's article stands as another persuasive text for us to analyze. As you read this article, originally published in the *Columbia Journalism Review*, use some of the same strategies of analysis that we've used on comics and cartoons throughout the chapter. Ask yourself: Who is his audience? How does he position himself as author? What is his argument? What evidence does he use to support that argument? Which parts are the most persuasive? Which are the least persuasive? What visual images does he convey with words? Are you persuaded by his argument?

I WAS A TOOL OF SATAN

Doug Marlette

Last year, I drew a cartoon that showed a man in Middle Eastern apparel at the wheel of a Ryder truck hauling a nuclear warhead. The caption read, "What Would Mohammed Drive?" Besides referring to the vehicle that Timothy McVeigh rode into

Marlette uses a provocative title to capture his readers' attention.

Marlette begins his article by establishing the context behind it. Notice how he implicitly defends the cartoon by describing how it was intended not just to poke fun at Mohammed but at Christian evangelicals as well. The play on words at the end of this paragraph gives the readers their first taste of the humorous, slightly irreverent tone and the close attention to style that characterize this piece.

In the second paragraph, Marlette uses specific examples of the threats he received to construct a rather unfavorable image of the people offended by his cartoon.

He recounts his response to the protests and comes to one of the most important points of his essay: that he is an equal opportunity offender, having penned cartoons that had enraged many different groups. By moving the question away from an issue of Islam to a larger issue of tolerance, Marlette sets up the issues of censorship and freedom of speech that are the real subjects of this essay.

Oklahoma City, the drawing was a takeoff on the "What Would Jesus Drive?" campaign created by Christian evangelicals to challenge the morality of owning gas-guzzling SUVs. The cartoon's main target, of course, was the faith-based politics of a different denomination. Predictably, the Shiite hit the fan.

Can you say "fatwa"? My newspaper, *The Tallahassee Democrat*, and I received more than 20,000 e-mails demanding an apology for misrepresenting the peace-loving religion of the Prophet Mohammed—or else. Some spelled out the "else": death, mutilation, Internet spam. . . . "What you did, Mr. Dog, will cost you your life. Soon you will join the dogs . . . hahaha in hell." "Just wait . . . we will see you in hell with all jews. . . ." The onslaught was orchestrated by an organization called the Council on American-Islamic Relations. CAIR bills itself as an "advocacy group." I was to discover that among the followers of Islam it advocated for were the men convicted of the 1993 bombing of the World Trade Center. At any rate, its campaign against me included flash-floods of e-mail intended to shut down servers at my newspaper and my syndicate, as well as viruses aimed at my home computer. The controversy became a subject of newspaper editorials, columns, Web logs, talk radio, and CNN. I was condemned on the front page of the Saudi publication *Arab News* by the secretary general of the Muslim World League.

My answer to the criticism was published in the *Democrat* (and reprinted around the country) under the headline *With All Due Respect, an Apology Is Not in Order*. I almost felt that I could have written the response in my sleep. In my thirty-year career, I have regularly drawn cartoons that offended religious fundamentalists and true believers of every stripe, a fact that I tend to list in the "Accomplishments" column of my résumé. I have outraged Christians by skewering Jerry Falwell, Catholics by needling the pope, and Jews by criticizing Israel. Those who rise up against the expression of ideas are strikingly similar. No one is less tolerant than those demanding tolerance. Despite differences of culture and creed, they all seem to share the notion that there is only one way of looking at things, their way. What I have learned from years of this is one of the great lessons of all the world's religions: we are all one in our humanness.

In my response, I reminded readers that my "What Would Mohammed Drive?" drawing was an assault not upon Islam but on the distortion of the Muslim religion by murderous fanatics—the followers of Mohammed who flew those planes into our buildings, to be sure, but also the Taliban killers of noncompliant women and destroyers of great art, the true believers who decapitated an American reporter, the young Palestinian suicide bombers taking out patrons of pizza parlors in the name of the Prophet Mohammed.

Then I gave my Journalism 101 lecture on the First Amendment, explaining that in this country we do not apologize for our opinions. Free speech is the linchpin of our republic. All other freedoms flow from it. After all, we don't need a First Amendment to allow us to run boring, inoffensive cartoons. We need constitutional protection for our right to express unpopular views. If we can't discuss the great issues of the day on the pages of our newspapers fearlessly, and without apology, where can we discuss them? In the streets with guns? In cafes with strapped-on bombs?

Although my initial reaction to the "Mohammed" hostilities was that I had been there before, gradually I began to feel that there was something new, something darker afoot. The repressive impulses of that old-time religion were now being fed by the subtler inhibitions of mammon and the marketplace. Ignorance and bigotry were reinventing themselves in the post-Christian age by dressing up as "sensitivity" and masquerading as a public virtue that may be as destructive to our rights as religious zealotry. We seem to be entering a Techno Dark Age, in which the machines that were designed to serve the free flow of information have fallen into the hands of an anti-intellectual mobocracy.

Twenty-five years ago, I began inciting the wrath of the faithful by caricaturing the grotesque disparity between Jim and Tammy Faye Bakker's televangelism scam and the Christian piety they used to justify it. I was then working at *The Charlotte Observer,* in the hometown of the Bakkers' PTL Club, which instigated a full-bore attack on me. The issues I was cartooning were substantial enough that I won the Pulitzer Prize for my PTL work. But looking back on that fundamentalist religious campaign, even though my hate mail included some death threats, I am struck by the relative innocence of the times and how ominous the world has since become—how high the stakes, even for purveyors of incendiary doodles.

One of the first cartoons I ever drew on PTL was in 1978, when Jim Bakker's financial mismanagement forced him to lay off a significant portion of his staff. The drawing showed the TV preacher sitting at the center of Leonardo Da Vinci's *Last Supper* informing his disciples, "I'm going to have to let some of you go!" Bakker's aides told reporters that he was so upset by the drawing that he fell to his knees in his office, weeping into the gold shag carpet. Once he staggered to his feet, he and Tammy Faye went on the

Notice the way that Marlette also condemns the "murderous fanatics" he describes based on an ongoing pattern of behavior—a rhetorical decision that makes his critique seem less reactionary and more thoughtful.

In this paragraph, he evokes the First Amendment and ends with an implicit comparison between America, with its civil liberties, and more militaristic and war-torn countries. Notice the power of the rhetorical questions that he uses at the end of the paragraph, asking readers to consider the alternatives to American freedom of speech.

At this point, he returns to describing his career as an equal opportunity offender, shifting the focus off Islam and instead discussing his troubles with evangelical Christians. By mentioning the death threats he received for his cartoons about the PTL Club (a televangelist show hosted by Jim and Tammy Bakker in the 1980s], he draws an implicit comparison here between Christian fundamentalists and what he calls Islamic "fanatics."

Although he doesn't reproduce his 1978 cartoon here, he offers a clear description to his readers.

This exchange brings humor back into the piece and demonstrates Marlette's seemingly flippant response to his critics.

Again, Marlette takes time to implicitly defend himself against claims of targeting Islam by describing how he has offended other religious groups as well.

Here Marlette cleverly plays on the idea of cartooning by pausing to assert that the reaction of his critics is "cartoonish" and exaggerated.

air and, displaying my cartoons, encouraged viewers to phone in complaints to the *Observer* and cancel their subscriptions.

Jim Bakker finally resigned in disgrace from his PTL ministry, and I drew a cartoon of the televangelist who replaced him, Jerry Falwell, as a serpent slithering into PTL paradise: "Jim and Tammy were expelled from paradise and left me in charge."

One of the many angry readers who called me at the newspaper said, "You're a tool of Satan."

"Excuse me?"

"You're a tool of Satan for that cartoon you drew."

"That's impossible," I said. "I couldn't be a tool of Satan. *The Charlotte Observer*'s personnel department tests for that sort of thing."

Confused silence on the other end.

"They try to screen for tools of Satan," I explained. "Knight Ridder human resources has a strict policy against hiring tools of Satan."

Click.

Until "What Would Mohammed Drive?" most of the flak I caught was from the other side of the Middle East conflict. Jewish groups complained that my cartoons critical of Israel's invasion of Lebanon were anti-Semitic because I had drawn Prime Minister Menachem Begin with a big nose. My editors took the strategic position that I drew everyone's nose big. At one point, editorial pages were spread out on the floor for editors to measure with a ruler the noses of various Jewish and non-Jewish figures in my cartoons.

After I moved to the Northeast, it was Catholics I offended. At *New York Newsday,* I drew a close-up of the pope wearing a button that read " No Women Priests." There was an arrow pointing to his forehead and the inscription from Matthew 16:18: "Upon This Rock I Will Build My Church." The *Newsday* switchboard lit up like a Vegas wedding chapel. *Newsday* ran an apology for the cartoon, a first in my career, and offered me a chance to respond in a column. The result—though the paper published it in full—got me put on probation for a year by the publisher. That experience inspired the opening scene of my first novel, *The Bridge.*

* * *

But how do you cartoon a cartoon? It's a problem of redundancy in this hyperbolic age to caricature an already extravagantly distorted culture. When writers try to censor other writers, we're in Toontown. We are in deep trouble when victimhood becomes a sacrament, personal injury a point of pride, when irreverence is seen as a hate crime, when the true values of art and religion are distorted and debased by fanatics and zealots, whether in the name of the God of Abraham, Isaac, and Jacob, the Prophet Mohammed, or a literary Cult of Narcissus.

It was the cynically outrageous charge of homophobia against my book that brought me around to the similarities between the true believers I was used to dealing with and the post-modern secular humanist Church Ladies wagging their fingers at me. The threads that connect the CAIR and the literary fat-was, besides technological sabotage, are entreaties to "sensitivity," appeals to institutional guilt, and faith in a corporate culture of controversy avoidance. Niceness is the new face of censorship in this country.

The censors no longer come to us in jackboots with torches and baying dogs in the middle of the night. They arrive now in broad daylight with marketing surveys and focus-group findings. They come as teams, not armies, trained in effectiveness, certified in sensitivity, and wielding degrees from the Columbia journalism school. They're known not for their bravery but for their efficiency. They show gallantry only when they genuflect to apologize. The most disturbing thing about the "Mohammed" experience was that a laptop Luftwaffe was able to blitz editors into not running the cartoon in my own newspaper. "WWMD" ran briefly on the Tallahassee Democrat Web site, but once an outcry was raised, the editors pulled it and banned it from the newspaper altogether.

The cyberprotest by CAIR showed a sophisticated understanding of what motivates newsroom managers these days—bottom-line concerns, a wish for the machinery to run smoothly, and the human-resources mandate not to offend. Many of my e-mail detractors appeared to be well-educated, recent emigres. Even if their English sometimes faltered, they were fluent in the language of victimhood. Presumably, victimization was one of their motives for leaving their native countries, yet the subtext of many of their letters was that this country should be more like the ones they emigrated from. They had the American know-how without the know-why. In the name of tolerance, in the name of their peaceful God, they threatened violence against someone they accused of falsely accusing them of violence.

With the rise of the bottom-line culture and the corporatization of news gathering, tolerance itself has become commodified and denuded of its original purpose. Consequently, the best part

---

Marlette now comes to one of the focal points of his discussion: the way censorship is enforced not by angry critics but by a culture of "niceness" that is afraid to offend.

The reference to the Columbia journalism school would have extra force considering that this piece was originally published in the *Columbia Journalism Review*. Here, also, he clearly articulates the central point of his extended Mohammed story: that the most "disturbing thing" was that critics were able to influence his editors into refusing to run the cartoon.

Having begun his argument applauding American principles—namely, freedom of speech—he now demonstrates the way that corporate structure and an ideology of tolerance (both hallmarks of American culture) are actually operating in conflict with First Amendment rights.

of the American character—our generous spirit, our sense of fair play—has been turned against us.

Tolerance has become a tool of coercion, of institutional inhibition, of bureaucratic self-preservation. We all should take pride in how this country for the most part curbed the instinct to lash out at Arab-Americans in the wake of 9/11. One of the great strengths of this nation is our sensitivity to the tyranny of the majority, our sense of justice for all. But the First Amendment, the miracle of our system, is not just a passive shield of protection. In order to maintain our true, nationally defining diversity, it obligates journalists to be bold, writers to be full-throated and uninhibited, and those blunt instruments of the free press, cartoonists like me, not to self-censor. We must use it or lose it.

Political cartoonists daily push the limits of free speech. They were once the embodiment of journalism's independent voice. Today they are as endangered a species as bald eagles. The professional troublemaker has become a luxury that offends the bottom-line sensibilities of corporate journalism. Twenty years ago, there were two hundred of us working on daily newspapers. Now there are only ninety. Herblock is dead. Jeff MacNelly is dead. And most of the rest of us might as well be. Just as resume hounds have replaced newshounds in today's newsrooms, ambition has replaced talent at the drawing boards. Passion has yielded to careerism, Thomas Nast to Eddie Haskell. With the retirement of Paul Conrad at the *Los Angeles Times*, a rolling blackout from California has engulfed the country, dimming the pilot lights on many American editorial pages. Most editorial cartoons now look as bland as B-roll and as impenetrable as a 1040 form.

We know what happens to the bald eagle when it's not allowed to reproduce and its habitat is contaminated. As the species is thinned, the eco-balance is imperiled.

Why should we care about the obsolescence of the editorial cartoonist?

Because cartoons can't say "on the other hand," because they strain reason and logic, because they are hard to defend and thus are the acid test of the First Amendment, and that is why they must be preserved.

What would Marlette drive? Forget SUVs and armored cars. It would be an all-terrain vehicle you don't need a license for. Not a foreign import, but American-made. It would be built with the same grit and gumption my grandmother showed when she faced down government soldiers in the struggle for economic justice,

---

He ends this paragraph by clarifying his interpretation of the First Amendment, specifically with relation to journalism. He then uses a cliché to emphasize his point.

Notice the analogy he makes between political cartoonists and bald eagles. It operates on two levels, on the one hand emphasizing that they are endangered and on the other hand suggesting that cartoonists represent America's freedoms.

His references on this page to important political cartoonists (Herbert Block, Jeff MacNelly, Paul Conrad) underscore his message about the decline of political cartooning as a genre.

In the next paragraph he returns to his metaphor of the bald eagle, developing it into a richer analogy.

As he moves toward his conclusion, Marlette draws his essay together by echoing and slightly revising the title of the cartoon that started the controversy and demonstrating the way that images carry symbolic weight.

and the courage my father displayed as a twenty-year-old when he waded ashore in the predawn darkness of Salerno and Anzio. It would be fueled by the freedom spirit that both grows out of our Constitution and is protected by it—fiercer than any fatwa, tougher than all the tanks in the army, and more powerful than any bunker-buster.

> Marlette solidifies his connection to great contributors to American culture by referring to great American writers and trailblazers, from novelist John Steinbeck (the Joads are the family from *The Grapes of Wrath*) to cultural icon Ken Kesey and astronaut Neil Armstrong.

If I drew you a picture it might look like the broken-down jalopy driven by the Joads from Oklahoma to California. Or like the Cadillac that Jack Kerouac took on the road in his search for nirvana. Or the pickup Woody Guthrie hitched a ride in on that ribbon of highway, bound for glory. Or the International Harvester Day-Glo school bus driven cross-country by Ken Kesey and his Merry Pranksters. Or the Trailways and Greyhound buses the Freedom Riders boarded to face the deadly backroads of Mississippi and Alabama. Or the moon-buggy Neil Armstrong commanded on that first miraculous trip to the final frontier.

What would Marlette drive? The self-evident, unalienable American model of democracy that we as a young nation discovered and road-tested for the entire world: the freedom to be ourselves, to speak the truth as we see it, and to drive it home.

> In his final paragraph, Marlette repeats his new catch phrase and uses it to provide a final comment on his vision of America and its inherent freedoms.

In his written argument, Marlette describes the observations he has made about the public's response to his cartoons. This process parallels the work you have done in walking across campus and observing rhetoric or in listing your observations of the visual detail found in the *Calvin and Hobbes* cartoon. Notice how specific Marlette is in describing the reactions to his cartoons and how concretely he conjures up American identity through the imagery of the bald eagle and the driven vehicle. These are *rhetorical moves,* strategic choices he has made as a writer in deciding how best to persuade his readers (especially those outraged by the cartoons) to see his drawing from a different point of view. Just as Markstein picked the most appropriate words and images for inside his Pledge of Allegiance cartoon, Marlette picked the most appropriate words and metaphors to use in his article.

WRITING A RHETORICAL ANALYSIS

As you turn now to write a longer, more sustained rhetorical analysis of a text, you'll be putting into practice all the skills you've learned so far in this chapter. You'll need to write down your observations of the text; spend time discussing them in detail, as we have done with the many examples we've worked on so far; and use these observations as evidence to make an argument that will persuade others to see the text the way you see it.

It's crucial to remember that when you write a rhetorical analysis, you perform a rhetorical act of persuasion yourself. Accordingly, you need to include the key elements of analytical

AT A GLANCE *Selecting a Visual Rhetoric Image*

When choosing a visual text for analysis, ask yourself the following questions:

- Does the image attempt to persuade the audience?
- Are there sufficient elements in the image to analyze?
- What do you know about the author or the intended audience?
- What's your own interpretation of this image?

writing that we've learned so far: (1) have a point of interpretation to share with your readers, (2) take time to walk readers through concrete details to prove your point, and (3) lead your readers through the essay in an engaging and convincing way. But of all these, the most important is your argument, your "take" or interpretation of the text—your **thesis.**

Developing a Thesis Statement

Perhaps the single most important part of your writing will be your **thesis statement,** the concise statement of your interpretation of your chosen text. To understand thesis statements, let's work through an example. Imagine, for instance, that you want to write an argument about the editorial cartoons in Figures 12 and 13. Both cartoons comment on recent debates about immigration policy. How might you develop a thesis statement that persuasively conveys your interpretation of how these cartoons contribute to the debate surrounding the status of undocumented immigrants?

Start by jotting down what you see; make close observations about these cartoons. Then use questions to bring your argument into focus and to make a specific claim about the images. The end product will be a *working thesis.* The process of developing your thesis might look like this:

Figure 12   Cartoon by Daryl Cagle about the immigration debate.
Source: Daryl Cagle, Cagle Cartoons, Inc.

1. **Write down your observations.** *Close observations:* Both pictures focus, literally or symbolically, on the border between the United States and Mexico and on the way that we set up fences (or vault doors) to keep illegal immigrants out. Both also show holes in those barriers: one focuses on people running through a hole in the fence; the other shows a small door in the vault that looks as if it's been propped open from the inside. The words are interesting, too. In the Cagle cartoon, the big sign says

Figure 13 This cartoon by Michael Ramirez uses a powerful visual image of the United States. *Source:* Michael Ramirez and Copley News Service

"Keep out," while the smaller signs are designed to draw people in. In the Ramirez cartoon, the small sign says "Cheap labor welcome," contradicting the message of the large, high-security door that blocks access to the United States.

2. **Work with your observations to construct a preliminary thesis statement.**
   First statement: Both cartoons focus on the contradiction in American border policy.
3. **Refine your argument by asking questions that make your statement less general.**
   Ask yourself: How? What contradictions? To what effect? How do I know this?
4. **Revise your preliminary thesis statement to be more specific; perhaps include specific evidence that drives your claim.**
   Revised statement: The cartoons in Figures 12 and 13 focus on the contradictions in American border policy by showing that on the one hand, the American government wants to keep illegal immigrants out, but on the other hand, economic forces encourage them to enter the United States illegally.
5. **Further polish your thesis by refining your language and asking questions about the implications of your working thesis statement.**
   Ask yourself: What do you find interesting about this observation? How does it tap into larger social or cultural issues?
6. **Write your working thesis to include a sense of the implications of your claim. Sometimes we call this the "So What?" of your claim.**
   Working thesis: The political cartoons in Figures 12 and 13 offer a pointed commentary on the recent immigration debate, suggesting ways the official government stance against illegal immigration is undermined by economic forces that tolerate, if not welcome, the entry of undocumented workers into the United States.

Figure 14   Mike Thompson's cartoon uses visual and verbal arguments to make a powerful statement about rising gas prices. *Source:* Mike Thompson and Copley News Service.

This activity should show you that a strong, argumentative thesis does more than state a topic: it makes a claim about that topic that you will develop in the rest of your paper. Let's look at one more example to further consider ways to produce sharp, clear, and persuasive thesis statements. The examples that follow are a series of thesis statements about Mike Thompson's cartoon in Figure 14, published in 2006 in reaction to rising gas prices.

Thesis #1: Mike Thompson's cartoon is very powerful.

Assessment: This thesis relies too heavily on subjective opinion; the author offers no criteria for evaluating the cartoon or a context for understanding the statement.

Thesis #2: Mike Thompson's drawing shows his opinion about SUVs.

Assessment: This thesis statement rests too much on a broad generalization rather than specific analysis.

Thesis #3: In response to rising gas prices, Mike Thompson draws a powerful editorial cartoon about the relationship between driving SUVs and consuming fossil fuels.

Assessment: This thesis statement merely states a fact and makes a broad claim rather than offering a focused interpretation of the cartoon. It needs to explain how the cartoon was powerful.

Thesis #4: In his 2006 editorial cartoon "Aptly Named," Mike Thompson persuasively plays with the term *fossil fuel* to suggest that SUVs and the "wanton consumption" of gasoline represent an outdated approach to transportation that needs to recognize its own imminent extinction.

Assessment: Of the four examples, this thesis provides the most provocative and specific articulation of the author's interpretation of the significance of Thompson's cartoon.

AT A GLANCE *Testing Your Thesis*

Do you have a specific and interesting angle on your topic?

- Does it offer a statement of significance about your topic?
- Is the thesis sharp enough (not too obvious)?
- Could someone argue against it (or is it just an observation)?
- Is it not too dense (trying to compact the entire paper) or too simplistic (not developing your point thoroughly)?

A strong argument, driven by a strong thesis statement, is at the heart of any successful essay. Let's look at how one student, Jason Benhaim, combines effective strategies of analysis with a carefully crafted thesis statement to compose his own rhetorical analysis of a recent editorial cartoon.

TAPPING INTO THE AMERICAN PSYCHE

Using Bird Flu to Critique the American Government

What comes to mind when you hear the phrase "Hurricane Katrina"? Does it conjure up pitiful images of human suffering or evoke a sense of anger at the American government's failure to respond? What about the phrases "war in Iraq" or "obesity epidemic"? "Enron scandal"? "Global warming"? "Monica Lewinsky"? Indeed, the media has ground these key phrases so deeply into the American psyche that their mere mention triggers a particular emotional response in even the most socially unaware audience. The fact that all audiences automatically associate these key phrases with certain images, ideas, and feelings makes their invocation a powerful tool for all varieties of social commentators, especially political cartoonists. Certainly, political cartoonists employ several readily apparent methods of condensing as much meaning as possible into a single frame, including the use of symbols, such as having an eagle represent an entire country, or simple artistic decisions, such as portraying Uncle Sam as aging and frail instead of youthful and muscular. However, the cartoonist's ability to take advantage of the associations the public already has concerning certain current events is often overlooked. A recent cartoon by Eric Devericks provides a powerful example of the way in which cartoonists can combine manipulation of classic symbols with allusion to

Notice the way Jason begins his essay with a series of evocative questions that directly engage readers.

In his first paragraph, he carefully sets up the context for his argument—that cartoonists tend to work with symbols or issues that automatically provoke a ready-made response in their audience.

By the end of the paragraph, Jason has moved from the context to his thesis statement, which refers to the specific cartoon he will be discussing.

The placement of the cartoon here is quite strategic: by including it in his first paragraph, he presents it as visual evidence to readers, making a much more powerful argument than if he had simply appended it to the end of his paper.

Jason spends his first main body paragraph describing the cartoon, drawing readers' attention to key details. Notice how, as the paragraph progresses, Jason moves from description to analysis.

Jason argues persuasively by using concrete details from his careful analysis of the cartoon.

Jason includes a strong transition here to move readers' attention from the Uncle Sam figure to that of the bird perched on the end of his rifle.

Notice the way Jason revises his own initial description of Uncle Sam to sharpen his argument about how the inclusion of the bird influences the way we read the cartoon as a whole.

a current event, in this case the imminent bird flu epidemic, in order to construct a visual-verbal argument speaking to issues that extend beyond the current event in question.

The central image of the Devericks cartoon is a crotchety old Uncle Sam staring intently through a

Source: Eric Devericks/The Seattle Times

pair of binoculars, his rifle at the ready. Because he faces to the right, the direction in which Americans read, Uncle Sam appears forward-looking and vigilant. However, the details of Uncle Sam's figure hint at his shortcomings. Though armed, Uncle Sam's frail and thin limbs betray his weakness. In the context of the cartoon, his white hair only serves to emphasize his old age, and even his characteristic bowtie contributes to his appearing old-fashioned. His antique rifle, so outdated to be equipped with a bayonet, most directly conveys a sense of his being behind the times. The scowl on Uncle Sam's face indicates a certain stubbornness, as though he is obstinately clinging to obsolete means of combating dangerous adversaries.

Uncle Sam's presentation alone constitutes an argument regarding the American government's outdated militaristic obsession and could potentially stand alone as a complete political cartoon. However, when coupled with the image of the sickly bird labeled with the cartoon's only words, "bird flu," the danger for America in focusing solely on military endeavors becomes immediately apparent. The bird's mere presence indicates that the specter of disease is wholly capable of bypassing America's military defense. Indeed, the bird's highly significant position atop the rifle further suggests that America's military might is not only ineffective against disease but actually supports its presence—without the rifle, the disease-carrier would have no place to perch! In light of the bird's position atop his weapon, Uncle Sam's binoculars become useless and even detrimental. His focus on enemy attackers blinds him to the possibility of other dangers. The presence of this sickly bird, representative of an impending costly and potentially life-threatening epidemic, wholly undermines Uncle Sam's vigilant appearance. Despite its simplicity and scarcity of words, the Devericks cartoon makes a clear statement: the American government's focus on its military endeavors results in a dangerous ignorance regarding other critical issues.

Though bird flu provides an excellent example of an issue potentially ignored by the American government in favor of war, the bird perched on the end of Uncle Sam's rifle could easily be replaced by a symbol of a different issue facing America. For example, Devericks could just as easily have argued that America's militaristic attitude detracts from its focus on a crumbling educational system or its president's plummeting polls. The bird's tired and sickly appearance indicates that it bypassed Uncle Sam's defenses without much effort, suggesting that America's military defenses are equally susceptible to infiltration by other nonmilitary dangers.

Merely noting America's recent infatuation with war efforts constitutes a mildly effective statement, but using bird flu as a tangible example of why such an attitude is detrimental to the health of the United States brings the message home. Portraying the American eagle as weakened and sickly might make for a startling image, but captioning such an image with a modern phrase forces people to consider bird flu in a different light. Allusion to bird flu adds extra punch to this political cartoon. Even if its audience knows nothing about the details of bird flu, Devericks can at least count on their associating the phrase with a sense of helplessness, panic, or fear. Certainly the mere thought of an epidemic is frightening, but for Devericks bird flu merely shines light on what ought to be the American public's main fear—will their government be able to handle it?

> In his penultimate paragraph, Jason strengthens his argument by speculating about alternative ways the cartoon might have been drawn. The summation sentence at the end of this paragraph is a key moment when Jason firmly articulates his interpretation of the cartoon.
>
> Notice the way Jason carefully offers a summary of his argument here without sounding repetitive. He ends his essay with a provocative question that points readers back to his interpretation of this cartoon: that it is ultimately less a commentary on bird flu than a critique of the government.

 ## AT A GLANCE *Visual Rhetoric Analysis Essays*

- Do you have a sharp point or thesis to make about the visual text?
- Have you selected key visual details to discuss in support of your main point?
- Do you lead readers through your analysis of the text by discussing important details in sequence? These include:
    - Visual composition, layout, and imagery
    - Verbal elements in the text
    - Color, shading, and arrangement of items
    - Caption or title of the image
- Do you have an effective title, main point, introduction, body, and conclusion?
- Have you included the image in the essay?

TURNING TO TEXTS OF YOUR CHOICE

As you turn now to selecting your own texts for rhetorical analysis, consider the ways the lessons you've learned in this chapter can help you approach the task. Keep in mind the need to begin with observations—whether it is of rhetorical texts all around your campus or the most provocative texts in the newspapers or online. As you select a text for analysis, think back to the cartoons or comics you found most striking in this chapter—perhaps the steroids cartoon, the *Boondocks* strip, or the Pledge of Allegiance cartoon. Each of these texts conveys a powerful message through words and images, verbal and visual rhetoric. Spend some time working on your thesis before composing the entire draft. Make sure your angle is sharp and your interpretation is complex. Consider working through a counterargument as well.

When you choose your own text for rhetorical analysis, make sure you pick one that offers a persuasive point. Also, in your own writing, avoid simply describing the elements you see in the work that you're analyzing. Instead, zoom in on specific details and comment on their meaning. Make a persuasive argument by using *specific* evidence to support your analysis of how the text succeeds at convincing an audience to see an issue in a particular way. This is key to crafting a persuasive and effective rhetorical analysis.

✔ PREWRITING CHECKLIST

Comics and Cartoons

- ❑ **Topic:** What key issue is the comic or cartoon addressing?
- ❑ **Story:** On the most basic level, what is happening in the cartoon?
- ❑ **Audience:** In what country and in what historical moment was the cartoon produced? In what type of text did it first appear? A journal? A newspaper? Online? Was this text conservative? liberal? radical? feminist? How does it speak to this audience?
- ❑ **Author:** What do you know about the artist? What kinds of cartoons does he or she regularly produce? Where does he or she live and publish? What kinds of other writing does this person do?
- ❑ **Argument:** What is the cartoon's message about the issue? Is there irony involved (does the cartoon advocate one point of view, but the cartoonist wants you to take the opposite view)?
- ❑ **Composition:** Is this political cartoon a single frame or a series of sequential frames? If the latter, how does the argument evolve over the series?
- ❑ **Word and image:** Does the cartoon rely exclusively on the visual? Or are word and image both used? What is the relationship between the two? Is one given priority over the other? How does this influence the cartoon's overall persuasiveness?
- ❑ **Imagery:** What choices of imagery and content does the artist make? Are the drawings realistic? Do they rely on caricatures? Does the artist include allusions or references to past or present events or ideas?
- ❑ **Tone:** Is the cartoon primarily comic or serious in tone? How does this choice of tone create a powerful rhetorical impact on readers?

❏ **Character and setting:** What components are featured by the cartoon? A person? An object? A scene? Think about how character and setting are portrayed. What are the ethnicity, age, socioeconomic class, and gender of the characters? Do they represent actual people? Are they fictional creations? How are these choices rhetorical strategies designed to tailor the cartoon and its argument to its intended audience?

❏ **Cultural resonance:** Does the cartoon implicitly or explicitly refer to any actual people, events, or pop culture icons? What sort of symbolism is used in the cartoon? Would the symbols speak to a broad or narrow audience? How does the cultural resonance function as a rhetorical strategy in making the argument?

WRITING PROJECTS

1. **Personal Narrative:** Complete the "Creative Practice" on page 10. Recall Alex's observations of rhetoric on her way to class; conduct a similar study of the rhetoric in your world. Write your reflections into a *personal narrative essay.* Discuss which types of visual, verbal, bodily, or architectural rhetoric were most evident, which were most subtle, and which you found the most persuasive.

2. **Rhetorical Analysis:** Choose a political cartoon on a current issue and write a *rhetorical analysis.* You might find an appropriate cartoon in a recent issue of *Newsweek*, in a collection such as Charles Brooks's *Best Editorial Cartoons of the Year*, or online through the *Envision* Website resource page for Chapter 1 (www.ablongman.com/ envision/200). Use the prewriting checklist to help you write a rhetorical analysis of the cartoon. If you choose to analyze more than one cartoon on the same issue, introduce all your texts in the opening paragraph, and spend some time analyzing each one in detail. Make sure that your argument raises a larger point about rhetorical attributes of all the texts you are comparing.

3. **Comparative Rhetorical Analysis of Text and Image:** After you've begun project 2, search through recent newspapers, newsmagazines, or a news database like LexisNexis to find an article that addresses the same issue. Write a *comparative analysis* of the text and the political cartoon. What is each one's argument, and what rhetorical strategies does each one use to effectively make that argument? You may want to use the prewriting checklist in looking at the political cartoon. If you want to take a historical approach to this assignment, choose both a political cartoon and an article that span across the historical spectrum but focus on one issue, such as racial profiling, immigrant workers, or what's "hip" in the entertainment industry. You might consult articles and cartoons from *The Onion's* "Our Dumb Century" or from online archives available through the *Envision* Website. For whatever texts you choose, write a *comparative historical analysis essay* in which you analyze how the cartoon and article use rhetoric to address a pressing issue of the time. Be sure to include specific details about each text, shape your observations into a thesis using the process on page 74, and don't forget a title.

Visit **www.ablongman.com/envision** for expanded assignment guidelines and student projects.

from *Envision*

What convinced you to buy that new pair of cross-trainers, to try that new sports drink, to purchase that new cell phone calling plan, or even to decide which college to attend? Chances are some sort of text combining words and images—whether it was a printed advertisement, television or radio commercial, billboard, or brochure—influenced your decision. Consider the street scene in Figure 15. What strategies of persuasion does the striking iPod banner ad use? Notice the simple design, the contrast between the bright background color and the dark silhouette, and the strategic use of white that draws your eye from the iPod in the figure's hand to the logo and slogan at the top of the image. How does this ad appeal to you? Does it appeal to your own enthusiasm for music that allows you to identify with the dancer? Or does it draw you in logically, asking you to identify yourself with one type of iPod because of its technical features?

Think now about other advertisements you have seen. How does the look of an ad make you pause and pay attention? Does a magazine ad show someone famous, a good-looking model, or characters you can identify with emotionally? Does a television spot tell a compelling story? Does a brochure offer startling statistics or evidence? Perhaps it was not one but a combination of factors that you found persuasive. Often we are moved to action through persuasive effects that are so subtle we may not recognize them at first; we call these effects **rhetorical strategies**—techniques used to move and convince an audience.

Ads offer us a productive means of analyzing rhetorical strategies because they represent arguments in compact forms. An ad has little room to spare; persuasion must be locked into a single frame or into a brief 30-second spot. Advertisements represent one of the most ubiquitous forms of persuasion. The average adult encounters 3000 of these compact, powerful arguments—that is, advertisements—every day (Twitchell, *Adcult* 2). Consider all the places ads appear nowadays: not just in magazines or on the television or radio but also on billboards and computer screens; on the sides of buses, trains, and buildings; in sports stadiums and movie theaters; and even spray-painted on sidewalks.

Figure 15   This eye-catching iPod ad from Stockholm, Sweden, draws the audience immediately into its argument.
Source: © Alyssa J. O'Brien, 2006

You probably can think of other places you've seen advertisements lately, places that may have surprised you: in a restroom, on the back of a soda can, on your roommate's T-shirt. As citizens of what cultural critic James Twitchell calls "Adcult USA," we are constantly exposed to texts that appeal to us on many levels. In this chapter, you'll gain a working vocabulary and concrete strategies of rhetorical persuasion that you can use when you turn to craft your own persuasive texts. The work you do here not only will make you a savvy reader of advertisements but also will equip you with skills you can use to become a sharper, more strategic writer of your own arguments.

CHAPTER PREVIEW QUESTIONS

- What specific strategies of argumentation work as persuasion?
- What role do the rhetorical appeals of logos, pathos, and ethos play in persuasion?
- What is the effect of exaggeration in these appeals?
- How does an awareness of context work to create a persuasive argument?
- How can you incorporate strategies of persuasion in your own writing?

ANALYZING ADS AS ARGUMENTS

By analyzing advertisements, we can detect the rhetorical choices writers and artists select to make their points and convince their audiences. In this way we realize that advertisers are rhetoricians, careful to attend to the *rhetorical situation*. We can find in advertisements specific strategies of argumentation that you can use to make your case in your own writing:

- Advertisers might use **narration** to sell their product—using their ad to tell a story.
- They might employ **comparison-contrast** to encourage the consumer to buy their product rather than their competitor's.
- They might rely upon **example** or **illustration** to show how their product can be used or how it can impact a person's life.
- They might use **cause and effect** to demonstrate the benefits of using their product.
- They might utilize **definition** to clarify their product's purpose or function.
- They might create an **analogy** to help make a difficult selling point or product—like fragrance—more accessible to their audience.
- They might structure their ad around **process** to demonstrate the way a product can be used.
- They might focus solely on **description** to show you the specifications of a desktop system or a new SUV.
- They might use **classification and division** to help the reader conceptualize how the product fits into a larger scheme.

These strategies are equally effective in both visual and written texts. Moreover, they can be used effectively to structure both a small unit (part of an ad or, in a more academic text, a paragraph or section of an essay) and a larger one (the entire ad or, in an academic paper, the argument as a whole).

Even a single commercial can be structured around multiple strategies. The famous "This Is Your Brain on Drugs" commercial from the late 1980s used *analogy* (a comparison to something else—in this case comparing using drugs and frying an egg) and *process* (reliance on a sequence of events—here, how taking drugs affects the user's brain) to warn its audience away from drug use. In this 30-second spot, the spokesperson holds up an egg, saying, "This is your brain." In the next shot, the camera focuses on an ordinary frying pan as he states, "This is drugs." We as the audience begin to slowly add up parts A and B, almost anticipating his next move. As the ad moves to the visual crescendo, we hear the words, "This is your brain on drugs" and the image of the egg sizzling in the frying pan fills the screen. The final words seem almost anticlimactic after this powerful image: "Any questions?"

These strategies function just as persuasively in print ads as well. For example, look at the advertisement for Rusk hair spray in Figure 16, an ad designed to draw the viewer's eye through the visual argument. What the reader notices first are the striking pictures of the golden-haired model, somewhat flat hair on one side and voluminous curls on the other, exemplifying the powerful *comparison-contrast* strategy that is echoed in many levels of the ad. The entire ad is bisected to reflect this structure, opposing "problem" to "solution" and literally dividing the main caption—"Go from ordinary . . . to Extraordinary"—in half. What bridges the divide, both literally and figuratively, is the strategically positioned can of hairspray, tilted slighted toward the right to reinforce emphasis on the *example/illustration* of a satisfied Rusk-user. By centralizing the red-capped canister in this way, the ad therefore also establishes a persuasive *cause and effect* argument, implicitly suggesting that using this hairspray allowed this girl to overcome the perceived challenges of limp hair.

Within written texts, the use of such strategies provides a similar foundation for a persuasive argument. As you read the following online article from Slate.com, look carefully to see which strategies author Seth Stevenson utilizes to make his argument about recent iPod commercials.

Figure 16   This problem-solution ad for Rusk hairspray uses several strategies of argumentation.

YOU AND YOUR SHADOW

*The iPod ads are mesmerizing. But does
your iPod think it's better than you?*

Seth Stevenson

The Spot: Silhouetted shadow-people dance in a strenuous manner. Behind them is a wall of solid color that flashes in neon shades
of orange, pink, blue, and green. In each shadow-person's hand is
an Apple iPod.

I myself own an iPod, but rarely dance around with it. In part
because the earbuds would fall out (Does this happen to you? I
think I may have narrow auditory canals) and in part because I'm
just not all that prone to solitary rump-shaking. It's a failing on
my part. Maybe if I were a silhouette I might dance more.

All that said, these are very catchy ads. I don't get sick of watching them. And yet I also sort of resent them, as I'll later explain.

First, let's talk about what the ads get right. For one, the songs
(from groups like Jet and Black Eyed Peas) are extremely well-chosen.
Just indie enough so that not everybody knows them; just mainstream enough so that almost everybody likes them. But as good
as the music is, the visual concept is even better. It's incredibly
simple: never more than three distinct colors on the screen at any
one time, and black and white are two of them. What makes it so
bold are those vast swaths of neon monochrome.

This simplicity highlights the dance moves, but also—and more
importantly—it highlights the iPod. The key to it all is the silhouettes. What a brilliant way to showcase a product. Almost everything that might distract us—not just background scenery, but
even the actors' faces and clothes—has been eliminated. All we're
left to focus on is that iconic gizmo. What's more, the dark black
silhouettes of the dancers perfectly offset the iPod's gleaming white
cord, earbuds, and body.

This all sounds great, so far. So what's not to like?

For the longest time, I couldn't put my finger on it. And then
I realized where I'd seen this trick before. It's the mid-1990s campaign for DeBeers diamonds—the one where the people are shadows, but the jewelry is real. In them, a shadow-man would slip a
diamond ring over a shadow-finger, or clasp a pendant necklace
around a ghostly throat. These ads used to be on television all the
time. You may recall the stirring string music of their soundtrack,
or the still-running tagline: "A Diamond Is Forever."

As part of his online series "Ad Reportcard," Stevenson uses a format not usually associated with academic writing—notice here he sets up the commercial under discussion in a separate section before even starting his essay.

Stevenson's chatty voice is very appropriate for his online audience

Notice the way Stevenson defers his thesis, although he gives us a sense of his approach toward the ads (resentment).

In this section, Stevenson relies on **description** to set up the foundation for his discussion of the ads; yet, notice that he is somewhat selective, emphasizing the elements that are most important for his analysis—namely, the way the use of silhouettes emphasizes the product.

The rhetorical question here points to the turn in his piece from description to analysis, the point where the reader will come closer to understanding his resentment.

At this point in the article, Stevenson moves to **description** and **example** to set up the powerful **comparison-contrast** strategy that he develops further in the next paragraphs.

By **comparing** the iPod commercials to the DeBeers campaign, Stevenson can clearly articulate his ambivalent feelings about Apple's ads. In his semihumorous interjection, Stevenson returns to the **contrast** between himself and the Apple silhouettes with which he started the article.

Like the iPod ads, these DeBeers ads used shadow-people to perfect effect. The product—in this case, diamonds—sparkles and shines on a dusky background. But what bothered me about the spots was the underlying message. They seem to say that we are all just transient shadows, not long for this world—it's our diamonds that are forever. In the end, that necklace is no overpriced bauble. It's a ticket to immortality!

My distaste for these ads stems in part from the fact that, with both the iPod and the diamonds, the marketing gives me a sneaking sense that the product thinks it's better than me. More attractive, far more timeless, and frankly more interesting, too. I feel I'm being told that, without this particular merchandise, I will have no tangible presence in the world. And that hurts. I'm a person, dammit, not a featureless shadow-being! If you prick me, do I not write resentful columns?

Notice how he builds on his **comparison** by opening his concluding paragraph with an **analogy**, using a simile ("like diamond jewelry") that reminds the reader of the connection he has established between the two campaigns.

Like diamond jewelry, the iPod is designed and marketed to draw attention to itself, and I think (I realize I'm in a minority here) I prefer my consumer goods to know their place. If I did it over, I might opt for an equally functional but slightly more anonymous MP3 player. One that deflects attention instead of attracting it. Because I'm the one with the eternal soul here—it's my stuff that's just transient junk.

Grade: B–. Perfectly executed. Mildly insulting message.

COLLABORATIVE CHALLENGE

Visit an online repository of commercials, such as those linked through the *Envision* Website. With a partner, browse through several commercials, selecting two or three in particular that you find persuasive. Discuss what strategies of argumentation you see at work in these visual rhetoric texts. Try to find an example of each approach listed earlier in the chapter. Write a short paragraph analyzing one of the commercials; compare your interpretation with a partner. Then share your work with the rest of the class.

www.ablongman.com/envision/205

UNDERSTANDING THE RHETORICAL APPEALS

The rhetorical strategies we've examined so far can be filtered through the lens of classical modes of persuasion dating back to 500 BCE. The formal terms are *logos, pathos,* and *ethos.*

Each type of rhetorical appeal represents a mode of persuasion that can be used by itself or in combination. As you might imagine, a text may employ a combined mode of persuasion, such as "passionate logic"—a rational argument written with highly charged prose, "goodwilled pathos"—an emotional statement that relies on the character of the speaker to be believed, or "logical ethos"—a strong line of reasoning employed by a speaker to build authority. Moreover, a text may use rhetorical appeals in a combination that produces an *overarching effect,* such as irony or humor. You might think of humor as one of the most effective forms of persuasion. Jokes and other forms of humor are basically appeals to pathos because they put the audience in the right emotional state to be receptive to an argument, but they can also involve reasoning or the use of the writer's authority to sway an audience.

Since they appear so frequently in combination, you might find that conceptualizing logos, pathos, and ethos through a visual representation helps you to understand how they relate to one another (see Figure 17).

As you read this chapter, consider how each text relies upon various rhetorical appeals to construct its message.

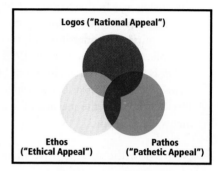

Figure 17   Rhetorical appeals are intersecting strategies of persuasion.

 AT A GLANCE *Rhetorical Appeals*

- *Logos* entails rational argument: appeals to reason and an attempt to persuade the audience through clear reasoning and philosophy. Statistics, facts, definitions, and formal proofs, as well as interpretations such as syllogisms or deductively reasoned arguments, are all examples of means of persuasion we call "the logical appeal."
- *Pathos,* or "the pathetic appeal," generally refers to an appeal to the emotions: the speaker attempts to put the audience into a particular emotional state so that the audience will be receptive to and ultimately convinced by the speaker's message. Inflammatory language, sad stories, appeals to nationalist sentiments, and jokes are all examples of pathos.
- *Ethos* is an appeal to authority or character; according to Aristotle, *ethos* means the character or goodwill of the speaker. Today we also consider the speaker's reliance on authority, credibility, or benevolence when discussing strategies of ethos. Although we call this third mode of persuasion the "ethical appeal," it does not strictly mean the use of ethics or ethical reasoning. Keep in mind that ethos is the deliberate use of the *speaker's character* as a mode of persuasion.

Appeals to Reason

Logos entails strategies of logical argument. As a writer, you use logos when you construct an essay around facts and reason; in general, an argument based on logos will favor the use of logic, statistical evidence, quotations from authorities, and proven facts. In the opening pages of this chapter, for instance, we used logos—quotations and statistics about advertising—to persuade you about the omnipresence of advertising in today's culture. Scholars often rely on logos in this way to make persuasive academic arguments. Consider, for instance, the way Laurence Bowen and Jill Schmid use *logos* as a strategy of persuasion in this passage from "Minority Presence and Portrayal in Mainstream Magazine Advertising: An Update":

> Some might argue that the small number of minorities featured in mainstream magazine advertising may be due to a very deliberate media strategy that successfully targets minorities in specialized and minority media. However, each of the magazines analyzed does have a minority readership and, in some cases, that readership is quite substantial. For example, according to *Simmons 1993 Study of Media and Markets,* the Hispanic readership of *Life* is 9.9%, yet the inclusion of Hispanics in *Life's* advertisements was only .8%. *Cosmopolitan* has a 11.3% Black readership, yet only 4.3% of the advertisements included Blacks; 13.3% of the magazines' readership is Hispanic and only .5% of the advertisements use Hispanics.

Notice how the authors drive their point home through reference to their research with mainstream magazines as well as to statistical data that they have both uncovered and analyzed. The inclusion of this concrete information and examples makes their argument much more convincing than had they provided a more general rebuttal to the statement that begins their paragraph. In this way, appeals to logic can take on many forms, including interpretations of "hard evidence," such as found in syllogisms (formal, structured arguments), reasoned arguments, closing statements in law, inferences in the form of statistical models, and appeals to "common sense" or cultural assumptions.

In advertising, the mode of persuasion we call logos often operates through the written text; significantly, the Greek word *logos* can be translated as "word," indicating the way in which we, culturally, often look to words as repositories of fact and reason. Let's see how the Chevron ad featured in Figure 18 presents a reasoned argument.

The type of logos-based reasoning found in the Chevron ad appears in many ads that you may also be familiar with: think, for instance, of a computer ad that juxtaposes a striking photo of a laptop with a chart detailing its processor type, memory capacity, screen size, and graphics features; a car ad that offsets a glossy showroom photo with safety ratings and positive reviews from *Car & Driver* and *Motor Trend;* or a commercial for a bank that features a smiling agent listing the reasons to open a checking account at that branch. In each case, the advertisement drives its point through facts, evidence, and reason.

In fact, some might argue that logos as an appeal underlies almost all advertising, specifically because most advertising uses an implicit *causal argument:* if you buy this product, then you or your life will be like the one featured in the ad. Sometimes the associations are explicit: if you use Pantene shampoo, then your hair will be shinier; if you buy Tide detergent, then your clothes will be cleaner; if you buy a Volvo sedan, then your family will be safer driving on the road. Sometimes the *cause-and-effect* argument is more subtle: buying Sure deodorant

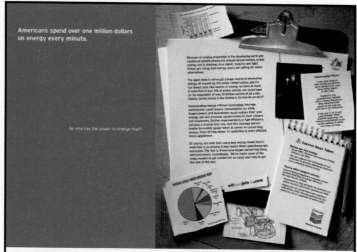

On the left side, the written text, set in relief against a vivid green background, sets up the problem using a striking statistic and poses the key question ("so who has the power to change that?") that governs the rest of the ad.

The right side provides the answer to the question, using a variety of research-based evidence including a memo, a fact sheet, a pie chart, a schematic, and a bar chart. Note that even the very abundance of materials is persuasive, suggesting that the ad's argument is based in fact rather than simply option.

Figure 18   The Chevron ad relies on a logical argument to persuade the reader.

will make you more confident; drinking Coke will make you happier; wearing Nikes will make you perform better on the court. In each case, logos, or the use of logical reasoning, is the tool of persuasion responsible for the ad's argumentative force.

The ad for Crest Whitening Strips in Figure 19 offers us a useful example of how logos can operate in more subtle ways in an ad—through visual as well as verbal argumentation. When we first look at the ad, our eyes are drawn immediately to the model's white smile, positioned near the center of the two-page spread. Our gaze next moves up to her eyes and then down again to the two juxtaposed close-up shots of her teeth.

These two close-ups carry the force of the argument. They are before-and-after stills, demonstrating, in brilliant color, the whitening power of Crest. The contrast between the two images makes a deliberate logos appeal by constructing a *cause-and-effect* argument. The captions for these two close-ups confirm the message imparted by the images and solidify the visual promise of the ad. The final small box insert is our last visual stop; it shows the product and suggests the solution to the logical equation at work in this ad. The fact that the ad's words, "Your new

STUDENT WRITING

Fred Chang analyzes Apple Computer's reliance on logos in its advertising battle with Intel.

www.ablongman.com/envision/206

Figure 19   In this Crest Whitening Strips advertisement, inset images offer visual evidence for the
              ad's argument.

smile," appear beneath the photo of the product—as the conclusion of the logical argument—
reinforces the persuasive message that Crest indeed will give its users such white teeth. To put
the logic plainly: if people brush with this product, then they too will achieve this result. In
this way, the ad relies on logos to attract and convince its audience.

Logical Fallacies

When crafting your own written analysis of advertisements, be careful not to rely on mistaken
or misleading uses of logos, commonly called **logical fallacies.** The causal strategy underlying most advertising can be seen as an example of faulty logic, for surely it is fraudulent to suggest that wearing a certain brand of clothing will make you popular or that drinking a certain
beer will make you attractive to the opposite sex. In classical rhetoric, this fallacy of causality
is called a ***post hoc ergo propter hoc* fallacy**—namely, the idea that because something happened first (showering with an aloe-enhanced body gel), it is the direct cause of something that
happened afterward (getting great grades on your midterms). A similar effect can be produced
by the ***cum hoc ergo propter hoc* fallacy**, often called a *correlation-causation* fallacy. According to this model, because two unrelated events happen at the same time (are correlated), they
are interpreted as cause and effect. For instance, the following is an example of a *cum hoc* fallacy: (1) a teenager plays his varsity basketball game wearing his new Air Jordans; (2) the
teenager makes many key rebounds and jump shots while playing the game; (3) the Air Jordans caused his success in the game. You can probably think of many commercials that rely
on these two particular logical fallacies.

AT A GLANCE *Logical Fallacies*

- ***The post hoc fallacy:*** confusing cause and effect
- ***The cum hoc fallacy:*** interpreting correlation as causation
- ***The hasty generalization:*** drawing a conclusion too quickly without providing enough supporting evidence
- ***The either-or argument:*** reducing an argument to a choice between two diametrically opposed choices, ignoring other possible scenarios
- ***Stacking the evidence:*** offering evidence for only one side of the issue
- ***Begging the question:*** using an argument as evidence for itself
- ***The red herring:*** distracting the audience rather than focusing on the argument itself

However, in those same commercials, we see more and more cases of advertisers guarding themselves against claims of false causality. For instance, consider the typical weight-loss advertisement. "I lost 31 pounds in 3 months using this nutritional plan!" one happy dieter exclaims on camera. The camera shows an old video clip of the subject at her previous weight, and then it moves to the newly trimmed-down version, usually with a trendy hairstyle and tight-fitting clothes—a clear before-and-after strategy. However, more and more often, you now find these images captioned with one telling phrase: "These results not typical." This disclaimer points to advertisers' recognition that they, like other rhetoricians, need to be careful in their use of logos as an argumentative appeal.

Appeals to Emotion

Roughly defined as "suffering" or "feeling" in its original Greek, the term *pathos* actually means to put the audience in a particular mood or frame of mind. Modern derivations of the word *pathos* include *pathology* and *pathetic,* and indeed we speak of pathos as "the pathetic appeal." But pathos is more a technique than a state: writers use it as a tool of persuasion to establish an intimate connection with the audience by soliciting powerful emotions. For instance, consider the way the following paragraphs foster an emotional reaction from the reader:

> Dorsey Hoskins' father Bryan felt a tingling in his arm. The diagnosis—an inoperable brain tumor. Six months later, he died at the age of 33, leaving his wife to raise Dorsey and sister Hattie.
>
> Fortunately, Bryan bought life insurance when he married, and again when his daughters were born. Thanks to Bryan's foresight, Dorsey, Hattie, and their mom are taken care of.
>
> Are you prepared should the very worst happen?

This passage relies on a pathos appeal on many levels. Clearly, the very premise of the piece—moving from tragedy, to a sense of tempered relief, to personal identification—is designed to evoke a sympathetic response. Looking more closely, however, suggests that even the more subtle stylistic choices also contribute to the emotional appeal. Notice, for example, the power of word choice: the author initially introduces Bryan as "Dorsey Hoskins' father," establishing him from the first in terms of his daughter and, ultimately, her loss; the author withholds Bryan's age for three sentences, at which point he can disclose it to accentuate the tragedy of his early death; finally, after the powerful, opening anecdote, the author uses the second person to draw the audience itself into the piece through the pointed rhetorical question.

It shouldn't be a surprise to discover that this passage is in fact taken from an advertisement for life insurance or that the pathos of the text is echoed by the emotional charge of a close-up photograph of 5-year-old Dorsey, which serves as the background for the advertisement. We encounter ads that rely on pathos all the time, and indeed, the visual composition of an ad often taps our emotions in ways we barely recognize.

Let's look closely at another advertisement that relies on creating an emotional connection with the audience to sell its product. In the spring of 2006 Volkswagen launched a new marketing campaign aimed at pitching safety rather than sportiness; the "Safe Happens" commercials revolve around an unexpected moment of collision and its surprisingly reassuring aftermath (Figure 20). In this particular commercial, the viewer finds herself transported into the interior of an automobile. At this point, there is no clue as to the car's make or model; the camera shots are all of the car's occupants, a group of friends in their late twenties or early thirties. The camera focuses on each face in turn, identifying them as the points of identification and creating a bond between the characters and the viewer. We encounter them in the middle of a friendly, light-hearted conversation, the women gently teasing the men about crying at the end of the movie they have just watched. The exchange is informal and comfortable, the mood light.

Figure 20   The final frame from a Volkswagen commercial reinforces the
             audience's identification with the occupants of the damaged vehicle
             and extends the pathos appeal of the ad's narrative.

In a second, everything changes. Replicating in real-time the experience of a car accident, the commercial cuts the characters off midsentence with a screech of brakes, blinding headlights, and the sound of a collision. The viewer, an invisible passenger in the car, feels the same surprise and horror as the main characters. The camera focus abruptly changes

 **STUDENT WRITING**

Cyrus Chee's rhetorical analysis reads the appeals to pathos in two poster ads for contemporary films about the Holocaust.

www.ablongman.com/envision/207

and moves us outside the vehicle; we become bystanders, watching a nondescript SUV plow into the white sedan that we identify as *our* car, the power of the collision captured with harsh accuracy. As the screen goes black, suddenly silence prevails, except for the uneven clatter of a rolling hubcap.

After a couple of seconds, the image reappears, and we see our former companions, unharmed, standing outside the battered vehicle. This first moment of product identification is captioned by an unusual voice-over; the camera zooms in on one of the female passengers, who looks with disbelief at the wreck and whispers, "Holy . . . ." The implied expletive is silenced by a quick cut to a more traditional car-commercial shot: the Jetta, in a spotless white showroom, slowly revolving on a turntable. Even here, beyond the end of the commercial's central narrative, the pathos appeal is reinforced. The rotating car is clearly not a showroom model; the dented driver's side door identifies it once again as *our* car, the one that kept the main characters safe. The written caption reinforces this association, proclaiming "Safe Happens" (playing with the female character's final words) and then announcing that Jetta has received the government's highest safety rating. This moment of logos appeal becomes doubly persuasive because of the viewer's emotional engagement with the commercial: we feel that we ourselves have survived the crash and we look to the Jetta as the reason.

Pathos does not only operate through triggering the highs and lows of emotion in its audience; sometimes the appeals, though still speaking to the visceral more than the rational, are more subtle. Patriotism, indignation, excitement—all these effects can be linked to the pathos appeal. Consider the Porsche commercial showing a sleek red car speeding along a windy mountain road, the Ford Escape TV spot featuring the rugged SUV plowing through a muddy off-road trail, or the Cooper Mini ad using uniqueness as a selling point for the little car. Each of these ads uses pathos to produce a specific feeling in viewers: I want to drive fast, wind in my hair; I want to get off the beaten path, forge a new frontier; I want to stand out in a crowd, make a statement.

You are probably even more familiar with another type of pathos appeal—the appeal to sexuality. Clearly, "sex sells." Look at Victoria's Secret models posed in near nudity or recent Abercrombie and Fitch catalogs featuring models more likely to show off their toned abs than a pair of jeans, and you can see how in many cases advertisers tend to appeal more to nonrational impulses than to our powers of logical reasoning. Perfume and cologne advertisers in particular often use the rhetoric of sexuality to sell their fragrances, whether it be Calvin Klein's Obsession or Armani's Acqua Di Gio. Such ads work cleverly to sell perfume, not on the merits of the scent or on its chemical composition but through the visual rhetoric of sexuality and our emotional responses to it.

COLLABORATIVE CHALLENGE

Find five advertisements from recent magazines—for instance, *Cosmo*, *Vogue*, *Seventeen*, *GQ*, *Details*, *Esquire*—that use sexuality to sell their products. In your group compare the use of pathos in these ads. When is this appeal an effective marketing strategy? When does it seem ineffectual or inappropriate?

PART GOOD. PART BAD.
THAT'S MAN'S ESSENCE.
NEW AXE ESSENCE

Figure 21   This Axe cologne ad relies on humor to market its scent.

One final—and perhaps most pervasive—pathos appeal deserves mention at the close of this section. Looking at Figure 21, we can see yet another typical use of pathos to drive an argument.

It is humor that underlies the visual argument of this ad; by depicting a monk wearing sunglasses and enjoying a game of golf at a new resort, this advertisement from Beijing, China, provides a particularly amusing rendering of how consumer goods and services can transform life. If you think about it, as a culture we tend to be quite persuaded by humor; against our more rational impulses, the ads that make us laugh are usually the ones we remember. To prove this point, you need only think back to last year's Superbowl ads: Which ads do you remember? Which ads did you talk over with your friends during and after the game? Probably most of those memorable commercials relied on humor—or "humos" as one of our students, David Baron, named it. The arguments made by these ads may not always be the most logically sound, but the way they foster a connection with the audience makes them persuasive nonetheless.

Exaggerated Uses of Pathos

Although these strategies of persuasion successfully move their audience, sometimes advertisers exaggerate the appeal to emotion for more dramatic effect.

Consider the case of exaggerated pathos found in the Listerine campaign from the early twentieth century. In the 1920s, Gerard Lambert introduced the term *halitosis* into the popular vocabulary as a marketing strategy; he used it to convince Americans that Listerine was their only alternative to public embarrassment from bad breath (Twitchell, *Adcult* 144). Regardless of the fact that Listerine's primary use at the time was as a hospital disinfectant, Lambert transformed American culture through his successful use of **false needs.**

AT A GLANCE *Exaggerated Uses of Pathos*

- *Over-sentimentalization:* distracting the audience from evidence or issues
- *The scare tactic:* capitalizing on the audience's fears to make a pitch
- *The false need:* amplifying a perceived need or creating a completely new one
- *The slippery slope fallacy:* suggesting that an event or action will send the audience spiraling down a "slippery slope" to a serious consequence

In Figure 22, we see an example from the 1950s of this famous ad campaign. The words of the headline, spoken by the two women in the upper-right corner ("He's Hanging Himself Right Now!"), are a bit cryptic so that the reader has to look to the image in the center of the ad to understand its message. The drawing of the man and woman dancing makes a direct correlation between personal hygiene and romantic relationships, creating a sense of *false need* in the consumer for the product. In this case, the woman's averted head suggests her rejection of the suitor. Moreover, as you can see, the ad also uses the **scare tactic;** the disapproval on the faces of the women at the side table arouses in viewers a fear of rejection. The way the dancing woman's body turns away from the man augments this pathos appeal. Having deciphered the meaning of the ad from the image, the words now seem to confirm the idea in the headline that the man stands little chance of a romantic encounter. Image and text collaborate here to produce a powerful emotional reaction in the audience. Moreover, the threat of impending loss signifies a successful use of the **slippery slope,** an argument asserting that one thing leads to a chain of events that results in an undesirable conclusion: in this case, bad breath leads to solitude and loneliness.

Many contemporary advertising campaigns also operate in a similar fashion, defining a problem and then offering up their product as a solution: think, for instance, of Clearasil's acne cream or Ban Invisible Solid deodorant. Take a moment now to think about times in your life when you may have been motivated to purchase a product through *false need:* have you ever bought a man's or

Figure 22   This Listerine ad uses appeals to pathos to persuade readers to use its product.

woman's razor? pump-up basketball shoes? an angled toothbrush? curl-enhancing mascara? a transparent band-aid? What other examples of false needs or exaggerated pathos can you recall?

CREATIVE PRACTICE

The written copy that follows is from the Listerine print ad featured in Figure 22. As we've seen, the more prominent visual and verbal elements rely primarily on pathos to drive their arguments. Read the copy from the ad over carefully and analyze the rhetorical strategies at work there. Does it also rely on pathos? At which parts? What other strategies or appeals do you see at work in the text? Why do you think the copywriter chose to employ those rhetorical strategies at those points in the argument?

"Mark my words," Edith went on, "by the time they've gone twice around the dance floor, he'll get the complete brush-off from her."

"But why?" Polly queried. "He's so attractive . . . seems so attentive . . ."

"Indeed he is. And he's been wangling this date for weeks. Poor guy . . . he's through before he even starts . . . and he'll never know why*."

This sort of thing can happen, and usually does, when people are careless about halitosis* (unpleasant breath).

How About You?

Are you guilty? The insidious thing about halitosis is that you, yourself, may not realize it is present. So at the very moment you want to be at your best, you may be at your worst . . . offending needlessly.

Sometimes, of course, halitosis comes from some systemic disorder. But usually—and fortunately—it is only a local condition that yields to the regular use of Listerine Antiseptic as a mouth wash and gargle.

Why Run Such a Risk?

Don't risk offending others. And don't trust to makeshifts. Put your faith in Listerine Antiseptic which millions have found to be an *extra-careful* precaution against halitosis. Really fastidious people look up to Listerine Antiseptic as a part of their passport to popularity. It's so easy, so delightful to use, so lasting in effect.

Sweetness for Hours

Listerine Antiseptic is the *extra-careful* precaution because it sweetens and freshens the breath, *not for seconds or minutes . . . but for hours, usually.* Your breath, indeed your entire mouth, feels wonderfully fresh and clean.

Never, never omit Listerine Antiseptic before any date where you want to be at your best. Better still, get in the habit of using it night and morning for that clean, fresh feeling.

Appeals to Character and Authority

The last of the three appeals that we'll look at in this chapter is *ethos*, "character." Perhaps you have used ethos in other disciplines to mean an argument based on ethical principles. But the *rhetorical* meaning of the term is slightly different: according to Aristotle, ethos works as a rhetorical strategy by establishing the goodwill or credibility of the writer or speaker. In fact, as a writer you use ethos every time you pick up a pen or proofread your essay—that is, you construct an argument in which your power to persuade depends on credibility, your word choice, your tone, your choice of examples, the quality of your research, your grammar and punctuation. All these factors contribute to your ethos as an author.

Let's look to one of the articles we've already encountered in this chapter to see the subtle ways in which an author can create ethos. Below are the opening lines of Seth Stevenson's "You and Your Shadow":

> I myself own an iPod, but rarely dance around with it. In part because the earbuds would fall out (Does this happen to you? I think I may have narrow auditory canals) and in part because I'm just not all that prone to solitary rump-shaking. It's a failing on my part. Maybe if I were a silhouette I might dance more.

Notice the way in which Stevenson immediately establishes why he feels authorized to talk about iPods: "I myself own an iPod." He is not an uninformed critic; from the first, he sets himself up as an iPod owner, someone familiar with the product—and by extension with the advertising. He also goes to lengths to establish a connection with his audience and gain their trust. By confessing that he rarely dances around with his iPod and then using this as an excuse to draw in his audience ("Does this happen to you?"), he more firmly ingratiates himself with his readers, many of whom have probably had the same experience. In this way, he deliberately constructs his ethos from the opening lines of his essay so that he can then launch into his analysis with the full confidence of his audience.

Clearly, ethos can be a very powerful tool for establishing trust and therefore facilitating the persuasiveness of an argument. Companies have long recognized the persuasive power of ethos. In fact, a brand logo is in essence ethos distilled into a single symbol: it transmits in a single icon the entire reputation of a company, organization, or brand identity. From the Nike swoosh to McDonald's golden arches, the NBC peacock, or the Apple computer apple, symbols serve to mark (or brand) products with ethos.

Yet the power of the brand logo as a seat of ethos relies on the company's overall reputation with the consumer—a reputation that the company carefully cultivates through advertising campaigns. Many companies, for instance, trade on ethos by using celebrity endorsements in their advertising campaigns. Although a rational appeal is at work behind some endorsements—having basketball superstar LeBron James sell basketball shoes, for instance, makes sense—many campaigns rely not only on the celebrity's suitability for selling a product but also on the person's star appeal, character, and goodwill. Consider the power of the famous "Got Milk?" campaign. Here's the argument: if this celebrity likes milk, shouldn't we? Indeed, when we see Kelly Clarkson—or others, such as Serena Williams, Nelly, Ben Roethlisberger, or Jackie Chan—sporting the famous milk moustache, we find the ad persuasive because these celebrities are vouching for the product. We look to their goodwill as public figures, to their character as famous people putting their reputation on the line.

While the impact of a famous spokesperson can be a powerful use of ethos, celebrity endorsement is only one way to create this sort of appeal. Sometimes the *lack* of fame can be a strategic tool of the trade. Consider the Apple "Switch" ad campaign that featured everyday people stepping into the role of spokesperson for the Apple computer system. These ads featured everymen or everywomen of various ages, nationalities, and professions speaking directly into the camera about their reasons for changing from PCs to Apple computers. The combination of an unknown spokesperson, a clear example, a simple white background, and a slightly choppy film style—designed to seem edited and somewhat amateur—brought an ethos to the campaign based not on star power but on no-nonsense use and everyday application. In assessing the rhetorical situation for creating its ads, Apple recognized an important fact: for a large part of its audience, ethos would derive not from the flash of a celebrity smile but from identification with real-life Apple users.

Sometimes an ad features a corporate ethos to establish the credibility of the company. Microsoft's "We See" campaign, for instance, sells not software but a company image. One representative ad from this campaign depicts young children at work in a classroom. What makes the ad visually interesting is that the image includes white shadowy sketches that transform the children into successful future versions of themselves. Complemented by the header, "We see new skills, tomorrow's inventions," and the closing tagline, "Your potential. Our passion," the ad becomes a window into the future, Microsoft's image of the new generation. The message of the ad relies heavily on ethos: Microsoft cares about America's youth and wants to help them realize their dreams.

Figure 23   This Longines ad from Beijing, China, uses corporate ethos to market its watch through the image of the man's character and the words "Elegance is an Attitude."

In contrast to the Microsoft ad that promotes its corporate ethos rather than a particular product, many ads sell products directly through appeals to character. In Figure 23, for example, a Longines watch ad makes its pitch through words and images: the line, "Elegance is an Attitude" suggests that both the company and the wearer of the company's product can share in elevated ethos. The visual image reinforces this idea through the representation of a well-dressed man standing confidently in a black jacket and pinstriped shirt. He looks directly out at the viewer, potentially catching the eye of possible viewers and literally standing in for corporate ethos.

COLLABORATIVE CHALLENGE

With a partner, look at the car advertisements in Figures 24 and 25. How does each use specific argumentative strategies and rhetorical appeals to make its argument? Choose one of the ads and brainstorm with your partner a way in which the company might market the same car through an ad that relies primarily on a different strategy or appeal. Sketch out your hypothetical ad—including both image and copy—and share it with the class, discussing how the shift in appeal affected your understanding of the rhetorical situation and the effectiveness of the ad.

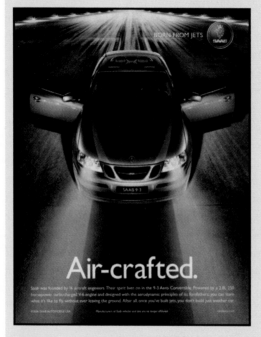

Figure 24   An advertisement for a Saab.

Figure 25   An advertisement for the Ford Escape hybrid.

Misuses of Ethos

One consequence of relying on ethos-driven arguments is that sometimes we come to trust symbols of ethos rather than looking to the character of the product itself. This tendency points us to the concept of **authority over evidence**—namely, the practice of overemphasizing authority or ethos rather than focusing on the merits of the evidence itself, a strategic exaggeration of ethos that helps entice audiences and sell products.

The most prominent examples of *authority over evidence* can be found in celebrity endorsements; in many commercials, the spokesperson sells the product not based on its merits but based on the argument, "Believe what I say because you know me, and would I steer you wrong?" However, the American public has become increasingly skeptical of such arguments. Living in a world where rumors of Pepsi-spokesperson Britney Spears's preference

AT A GLANCE: *Misuses of Ethos*

- *Authority over evidence:* placing more emphasis on ethos than on the actual validity of the evidence
- *Ad hominem:* criticizing an opponent's character (or ethos) rather than the argument itself

for Coke circulate on the Internet, Tiger Woods's $100 million deal with Nike makes front page news, and a star like former Sprite spokesperson Macaulay Culkin publicly announces, "I'm not crazy about the stuff [Sprite]. But money is money" (Twitchell, *Twenty* 214), the credibility of celebrity endorsements is often questionable.

Often, companies deliberately attempt to undermine the ethos of their competition as a way of promoting their own products. You probably have seen ads of this sort: Burger King arguing that their flame-broiled hamburgers are better than McDonald's fried hamburgers; Coke claiming its soda tastes better than Pepsi's; Visa asserting its card's versatility by reminding consumers how many companies "don't take American Express." The deliberate *comparison-contrast* builds up one company's ethos at another's expense. At times, however, this technique can be taken to an extreme, producing an ***ad hominem*** argument—that is, an argument that attempts to persuade by attacking an opponent's ethos or character. We see *ad hominem* at work most often in campaign advertisements, where candidates end up focusing less on the issues at hand than on their opponents' moral weaknesses, or in commercials where companies attack each other for the way they run their businesses rather than the quality of their products. In other words, this strategy attempts to persuade by reducing the credibility of opposing arguments.

Exaggerated Ethos Through Parody

Another strategy of persuasion is attacking ethos through **parody,** or the deliberate mocking of a text or convention. Parody has long been recognized as an effective rhetorical strategy for making a powerful argument. To see how this happens, let's turn to an ad designed by TheTruth.com, an innovative anti-tobacco organization (see Figure 26). Through the strategic use of setting, character, font, and layout, this ad deliberately evokes and then parodies traditional cigarette advertising to make its claim for the dangers of smoking.

Even if you are not familiar with the Masters Settlement Act, you probably have seen some of the Marlboro Country ads, often showing the lone cowboy or groups of cowboys riding across a beautiful, sunlit western American landscape. During the early part of its campaign, TheTruth.com recognized the

 STUDENT WRITING

Amanda Johnson, in her analysis of a Barbie parody ad, and Georgia Duan, in her reading of cigarette advertising, explore the construction of body image in the media and the use of parody in ads.

www.ablongman.com/envision/208

Figure 26   This TheTruth.com antismoking ad attacks ethos through parody.

impact of the long tradition of cigarette advertising on the public and decided to turn this tradition to its advantage. In the TheTruth.com parody version, however, the cowboy's companions do not ride proudly beside him. Instead, they are zipped up into body bags—an image that relies on exaggerated ethos and employs pathos to provoke a strong reaction in the audience. By producing an ad that builds on and yet revises the logic of Philip Morris's ad campaign, TheTruth.com could get past false images (the happy cowboy) to get at its idea of the "truth": that by smoking cigarettes "You Too Can Be an Independent, Rugged, Macho-Looking Dead Guy." The visual complexity of the image (and the combination of appeals) resonates powerfully by evoking the audience's familiarity with cigarette advertisements to pack some of its punch.

CONSIDERING CONTEXT

As you can tell from examining ads in this chapter, a successful argument must take into account not only the *rhetorical situation* but also the context, or the right time and place. That is why promotional trailers for the ABC series *Invasion*—featuring big-budget scenes of a Florida hurricane—could captivate audiences in the early summer of 2005 but horrify and outrage that same audience two months later in the wake of hurricanes Katrina and Rita. In ancient Greece rhetoricians called this aspect of the rhetorical situation **kairos**—namely, the contingencies of time and place for an argument.

In your own writing, you should consider *kairos* along with the other aspects of the rhetorical situation: audience, text, and writer. As a student of rhetoric, it is important to recognize the *kairos*—the opportune historical, ideological, or cultural moment—of a text when analyzing its rhetorical force. You undoubtedly already consider the context for persuasive communication in your everyday life. For instance, whether you are asking a friend to dinner or a professor for a recommendation, your assessment of the timeliness and the appropriate strategies for that time probably determines the shape your argument takes. You pick the right moment and place to make your case. In other words, the rhetorical situation involves interaction between audience, text, and writer *within* the context or *kairos*.

Consider, for instance, Coca-Cola's ad campaigns. Coke has exerted a powerful presence in the advertising industry for many years, in part because of its strategic advertising. During World War II, Coke ran a series of ads that built its beverage campaign around the contemporary nationalistic sentiment. What you find featured in these ads are servicemen, international landscapes, and inspiring slices of Americana—all designed to respond to that specific cultural moment.

Look at Figure 27, an advertisement for Coke from the 1940s. This picture uses pathos to appeal to the audience's sense of patriotism by featuring a row of seemingly carefree servicemen, leaning from the windows of a military bus, the refreshing Cokes in their hands producing smiles even far away from home. The picture draws in the audience by reassuring them on two fronts. On the one hand, it builds on the nationalistic pride in the young, handsome servicemen who so happily serve their country. On the other, it is designed to appease fears about the hostile climate abroad: as both the picture and the accompanying text assure us, Coca-Cola (and the servicemen) "goes along" and "gets a hearty welcome."

Figure 27   This Coca-Cola ad used *kairos* to create a powerful argument for its World War II audience.

The power of this message relates directly to its context. An ad such as this one, premised on patriotism and pride in military service, would be most persuasive during wartime when many more people tend to support the spirit of nationalism and therefore would be moved by the image of the young serviceman shipping off to war. It is through understanding the *kairos* of this advertisement that you can appreciate the strength of the ad's rhetorical appeal.

USING STRATEGIES OF PERSUASION

As you can tell from our work in this chapter, ads convey complex cultural meanings. Recognizing their persuasive presence everywhere, we realize the need to develop our ability to make better-informed interpretations of ads around us. You can pursue your study of ads by conducting your own careful rhetorical analyses of these visual-verbal texts. You'll find over and over again that ads are a microcosm of many of the techniques of persuasion. From billboards to pop-ups on the Internet, ads employ logos, pathos, and ethos to convey strong messages to specific audiences. We've learned how compact and sophisticated these texts are. Now it's time to apply those insights in your own writing.

As you begin to perform your individual analyses of advertisements, consider the way your own writing, like the ads we've discussed, can "sell" your argument to the reader. Consider the rhetorical situation and the specific *kairos* of your argument. What *strategies of argumentation* and *rhetorical appeals* would be most effective in reaching your target audience? Do you want to use narration, a humorous analogy, or a stirring example to forge a connection with your readers based on pathos? Or is your analysis better suited to logos, following a step-by-step process of reading an ad, drawing on empirical evidence, or looking at cause and effect? Perhaps you will decide to enrich your discussion through cultivating your ethos as a writer, establishing your own authority on a subject or citing reputable work done by other scholars. It is probable that in your essay you will use many strategies and a combination of appeals; as we saw in the advertisements presented earlier, from the Crest Whitening Strips ad to the Coca-Cola campaign, a successful argument uses various rhetorical strategies to persuade its audience.

While focusing on the individual strategies, don't forget to keep an eye on the composition of your argument as a whole. Just as an ad is designed with attention to layout and design, so you should look at the larger organization of your essay as key to the success of your argument. As you approach the organization of elements in your essay to maximize your persuasiveness, even a question like "Where should I insert my images?" has profound implications for your argument. Consider the difference between an essay in which the image is embedded in the text, next to the paragraph that analyzes it, and one with the image attached as an appendix. In your writing, use the persuasive power of visual rhetoric more effectively by allowing the reader to analyze the images alongside the written explanations. Use similar careful attention to organization, placement, and purpose as you begin your own analysis and craft your own rhetorical argument.

✓ PREWRITING CHECKLIST

Analyzing Advertisements

- ❑ **Content:** What exactly is the ad selling? an object? an idea? both?
- ❑ **Message:** How is the ad selling the product? What is the persuasive message that the ad is sending to the audience?
- ❑ **Character and setting:** What is featured by the ad? An object? a scene? a person? How are these elements portrayed? What are the ethnicity, age, socioeconomic class, and gender of any people in the advertisement? How do these choices relate to the ad's intended audience and reflect deliberate rhetorical choices?
- ❑ **Story:** On the most basic level, what is happening in the advertisement?
- ❑ **Theme:** What is the underlying message of the ad (beyond "buy our product")?
- ❑ **Medium:** What medium was the advertisement produced in? television? print? radio? How did this choice suit the rhetorical purpose of the ad and accommodate the needs of a particular audience?

❑ **Historical context:** In what country and at what historical moment was the advertisement produced? How do the demands of context shape the persuasive appeals at work in the ad? How does the ad reflect, comment on, challenge, or reinforce contemporary political, economic, or gender ideology? How does this commentary situate it in terms of a larger trend or argument?

❑ **Word and image:** What is the relationship between the word (written or spoken) and the imagery in the ad? Which is given priority? How does this relationship affect the persuasiveness of the advertisement?

❑ **Layout:** How are the elements of the ad arranged—on a page (for a print ad) or in sequence (for a television commercial)? What is the purpose behind this arrangement? How does the ad's organization lead the reader through—and facilitate—its argument?

❑ **Design:** What typeface is used? What size? What color? How do these decisions reflect attention to the ad's rhetorical situation? How do they function in relation to the ad's rhetorical appeals?

❑ **Voice:** What voice does the text use to reach its audience? Is the language technical, informal, personal, authoritative? Is the voice comic or serious?

❑ **Imagery:** What choices did the advertiser make in selecting imagery for this ad? If it is a static print ad, does the ad feature a line drawing or a photograph? Is the photograph black and white? a close-up? a panoramic shot? If the advertisement is drawn from television, what are the pace and sequence of the images? Where does the camera zoom in? What does it focus on? Does the ad feature a close-up or a long shot? Is the image centered? completely captured in the frame? Is it cut off? If so, how? Does it feature a head-on shot? a three-quarter shot? Whose point of view, if any, is the viewer supposed to assume?

❑ **Rhetorical appeals:** How does the advertiser use the images to work in conjunction with rhetorical appeals? For instance, does the image reinforce an appeal to reason? Is it designed to produce an emotional effect on the audience? Does the use of a certain style, such as black-and-white authority, contribute to the ethos of the ad?

❑ **Strategy of development:** What strategy of development does the ad rely on? narration? definition? comparison-contrast? example or illustration? classification and division? How do these strategies contribute to the ad's persuasive appeal?

❑ **Cultural resonance:** Does the ad use ethos—in the form of celebrities, famous events or places, or recognizable symbols—to increase its persuasiveness? If so, how does that establish audience or a particular relationship to a cultural moment?

WRITING PROJECTS

1. **Rhetorical Analysis:** Choose two or three ads for the same product and analyze the strategies of persuasion these ads use to reach specific audiences. To find your ads, you might visit an ad archive such as those linked through the Chapter 2 resources on the *Envision* Website, or look at old magazines in your school library. Alternatively, you can use current print or television advertisements as your sources and select ads that show-

case an exaggeration of rhetorical appeals, such as logical fallacies, exaggeration of pathos, misuse of ethos, parody, or self-referential ads. Use the prewriting checklist to help you analyze the appeals at work in the ads and to help you develop your argument about the persuasion in these texts. Be sure to address how *strategies of argumentation* operate and what the effects are on the audience as well as a description of context: where and when was the ad published and to whom? Refer back to the rhetorical triangle on page 54 to help you.

2. **Contextual Analysis:** Write a contextual analysis on the *kairos* of the Coca-Cola campaign. Examine, for instance, another Coke ad from the 1940s through the Adflip link on the *Envision* Website. Do some preliminary research and read about this era: explore the time, place, and culture in which the ad appeared. Ask yourself: How do the rhetorical choices of the ad you selected reflect an awareness of this context? How does the ad use the particular tools of logos, pathos, and ethos to comment upon or criticize this cultural moment?

3. **Historical Analysis:** Working in groups, look at several ads from different time periods produced by the same company. Some possible topics include ads for cigarettes, cars, hygiene products, and personal computers. Each member of your group should choose a single ad and prepare a rhetorical analysis of its persuasive appeals. Share your analyses and collaborate to explore how this company has modified its rhetorical approach over time. As you synthesize your argument, be sure to consider in each case how the different rhetorical situations inform the strategies used by the ads to reach their target audience. Collaborate to write a paper in which you chart the evolution of the company's persuasive strategies and how that evolution was informed by *kairos*.

4. **Cultural Analysis:** Write a paper in which you compare two ad campaigns and examine the ideology behind specific constructions of our culture. Does one campaign portray gender- or race-specific ideas? How do the tools of persuasion work to produce each message? What larger message is conveyed by the reliance on such cultural ideals or notions of identity? What representations of sexuality, gender roles, or class are presented by these ads? Write up your findings and then present them to the class, holding up examples of the ads to discuss in support of your analysis.

Visit **www.ablongman.com/envision** for expanded assignment guidelines and student projects.

A CLOSER LOOK AT THE THREE RHETORICAL APPEALS: INDIVIDUALLY AND IN TANDEM

Aristotle writes in the Book I of his treatise *On Rhetoric* that "Of the [means of persuasion] provided through speech there are three species: for some are in the character [*ethos*] of the speaker, and some in disposing the listener in some way [*pathos*], and some in the argument [*logos*] itself, by showing or seeming to show something" (I: 37). Understanding each of these means of persuasion is the first step that must be taken before one can perform or write a **rhetorical analysis**: an evaluation of a written or spoken text that identifies and critiques an author's use of the three rhetorical appeals. As you read on page 85, "Each type of rhetorical appeal represents a mode of persuasion that can be used by itself or in combination." Therefore, although this section will break down each rhetorical appeal individually, you should always keep in mind that one type of rhetorical appeal is often used in conjunction with another type of rhetorical appeal.

> For example, has a teacher ever told you that "if you fail to turn in a preliminary assignment that your grade on the final version will suffer?"

Two rhetorical appeals are hard at work in this example. The first of the two is logos. The audience is presented with a cause-effect scenario that takes the form of a correlative claim: if the student fails to hand in an initial exercise, he or she will see a significant reduction in his or her grade. The second rhetorical appeal that is in play is pathos, found in the words "your grade…will suffer." Here, the instructor is trying successfully to evoke fear.

ETHOS

The projected character or credibility that an author establishes inside or outside a text is called **ethos**. Rhetors (writers or speakers who consciously use rhetoric) establish their credibility in a number of ways: through their intelligence (does the rhetor come across as believable or scholarly?), through their good reasoning (does the rhetor's appeal seem reasonable or logical?), and through being fair-minded (is the rhetor treating the opposing argument or an opposing audience with respect?). If a rhetor is successful presenting himself or herself as sincere and/or thoughtful, that rhetor may be said to possess a strong ethos.

In contrast, ethos may be said to be weak if the rhetor comes across as biased or shallow in his or her treatment of the opposing side's arguments and evidence. In order to avoid such shortcomings, the rhetor must support his or her position with authoritative testimony, specific examples, and documented research.

Ethos may be established both inside and outside of the text, regardless of what type of text the text is: whether it is an advertisement, a letter to the editor, or a thesis-based argument.

Intrinsic ethos, or the credibility that a rhetor establishes inside a text, can be detected by looking for evidence that the rhetor comes across as knowledgeable or fair-minded. **Extrinsic ethos**, in contrast, refers to the respect that a rhetor possesses outside of the written or spoken words. Extrinsic ethos, therefore, involves the rhetor's reputation, the rhetor's standing in the academic or professional community (including his or her position or title as well as the identity and reputation of his or her place of work), and the rhetor's body of accomplishments or publications.

Here are some questions that you should consider when deciding how to establish your own ethos or how to judge another rhetor's ethos:

1. Have I used reasonable arguments? In making those arguments, have I considered the concerns of my audience or possible effects on them?
2. Have I avoided exaggerating my claims inappropriately?
3. Have I acknowledged other points of view? Have I done so with respect?
4. Have I established that I am credible on the issue?
5. Have I provided enough information for my audience to decide that what I am saying is credible?
6. Have I presented arguments in a manner that shows I respect my audience? Have I presented my arguments and evidence in a manner that shows I respect the arguments and the evidence of the opposing side?

PATHOS

Sharon Crowley and Debra Hawhee assess the issues that face the rhetor who is deciding whether or not to utilize pathos as follows:

> An audience may bring a certain emotional state of mind to a rhetorical situation, and if so, the rhetor needs to decide whether this state of mind is conducive to their acceptance of [his or her] proposition. If it is not, [he or she] needs to change their [state] of mind. (*Ancient Rhetorics for Contemporary Students*, 3rd edition 210).

Your goal, therefore, in terms of recognizing and evaluating an author's use of pathos is partially to recognize whether the author is successful in changing the audience's emotional state.

Keep in mind that direct appeals to the reader to feel an emotion (for example, "You should be crying now") are rarely effective. Instead, creating an emotion with words usually requires recreating the scene or event that would in "real" circumstances arouse the emotion.

But emotional appeals are only one type of appeal to pathos. Other equally important appeals to pathos involve creating a sense of identification between the rhetor and the audience based on shared values or shared identity. The second of these types of appeals may be as simple as the rhetor using the pronoun *we* or *our* to include his or her audience linguistically in his or her plight. Such an appeal may also be complex, based both upon the audience's emotions and on the audience's patriotism or shared love of one's country. Consider the following speech by Bill Pullman's character of the President in the movie *Independence Day* (1996):

Good morning. In less than an hour, aircraft from here will join others from around the world. And you will be launching the largest aerial battle in the history of mankind.

Mankind—that word should have new meaning for all of us today.

We can't be consumed by our petty differences anymore.

We will be united in our common interests.

Perhaps it [is] fate that today is the 4th of July, and you will once again be fighting for our freedom, not from tyranny, oppression, or persecution—but from annihilation.

We're fighting for our right to live, to exist.

And should we win the day, the 4th of July will no longer be known as an American holiday, but as the day when the world declared in one voice:

> *"We will not go quietly into the night!*
> *We will not vanish without a fight!*
> *We're going to live on!*
> *We're going to survive!"*

Today, we celebrate our Independence Day!

(Online Speech Bank, *American Rhetoric,* tr. Michael E. Eidenmuller)

Although fictional, President Whitmore's speech wonderfully illustrates how rich pathetic appeals can be and how well emotional appeals and appeals based on identification can work together. President Whitmore's speech also powerfully shows how pathos and the next appeal we will talk about, **logos**, can work together in the line "And should we win the day…" Here, structurally, what we have is a correlative claim: if we win, the 4th of July will be transformed; but the power of the claim also resides in the language and the appeals to both the audience's sense of identity and their emotions.

LOGOS

The appeal to logos involves what we often think of as *the argument itself*: the explicit reasons, the choices in terms of structure or language, the decisions as far as using a causal argument or a definition argument or an argument based upon analogy. A logical argument usually convinces its audience because of the perceived merit and reasonableness of the claims and proof offered in support of the overall thesis.

Sometimes logical agreements succeed because they call upon premises or objects of agreement that the arguer considers to be understood. Objects of agreement are basically either facts or values. For example, a person who writes an article advocating mandatory corporate day-care in a magazine such as *Parenting* might present certain "facts" (for example, most parents are frustrated with the current day-care system) and "values" (for example, children's well-being is more important than corporate profits) as objects of agreement. Of course the facts may not be the facts and readers may not agree with the values assumed, which is one reason why it is important to know your audience. Some premises will have to be supported further, but basically every argument has to begin from certain objects of agreement that it presents as shared between arguer and audience.

One way of thinking about the rhetorical appeal of logos is to think about it in terms of every conscious decision that a rhetor makes in terms of diction, structure, arrangement, evidence, and rhetorical strategy. The decision to include a statistic or a piece of testimony supporting one's claim is an example of logos, as is the claim itself. Other questions that you could consider in terms of identifying and then critiquing appeals to logos include the following:

1. Where has the rhetor chosen to put the thesis? Is the thesis stated or implied?
2. How has the rhetor organized his or her paragraphs? Do the paragraphs begin with claims that he or she then attempts to prove?
3. What types of claims or what strategies does the rhetor use to make his or her point?
4. What forms of evidence does the rhetor call upon?
5. How does the rhetor use punctuation, figures of speech, images, premises or other rhetorical maneuvers to assist his or her written or spoken text?

THE RHETORICAL APPEALS IN UNISON

Although the rhetorical appeals have very separate and specific functions, it is important to understand how they work together. A sound, persuasive argument will simultaneously establish a strong intrinsic ethos for the writer, appeal to the audience's emotions or sense of identity or shared values, and present cogent proofs in a logical and coherent manner. For example, in his "Letter from a Birmingham Jail," Martin Luther King, Jr. utilizes the three rhetorical appeals to support his assertion that African Americans can not continue to wait for civil rights. Below, we have briefly analyzed a passage from the "Letter" in order to demonstrate the ways in which the three rhetorical appeals work together in unison to achieve a specific purpose.

King argues that it is difficult for African Americans to wait for equality:

> When you suddenly find your tongue twisted and your speech stammering as you seek to explain to your six-year-old daughter why she can't go to the public amusement park that has just been advertised on television, and see tears welling up in her eyes when she is told that Funtown is closed to colored children. . . (78)

In this passage, King's reference to his daughter helps to build his intrinsic ethos because his audience, the white clergymen of Birmingham, will be disposed to see King as a compassionate and kindly man who is troubled because his daughter is being treated unfairly because of her race. King's ethos is bolstered because this example reveals that he is a loving father who also cares about justice in a broader sense.

This passage also demonstrates an effective use of pathos as King reaches out to his audience's sense of identity and emotions. To begin with, the clergymen he is addressing are most likely fathers themselves (and most of his overhearers would be parents as well). Hence the description of having to explain prejudice to a child will presumably prompt the audience and overhearers to imagine how they would feel having to explain to their own children that they would be denied some of the pleasures of childhood merely because of their skin color. Notice that King enhances the identification with his audience by using *you* rather than *I* to describe the parents' response. This emotional appeal predisposes the audience to agree with King.

Finally, this passage demonstrates an effective use of logos when, in using his daughter as an example, King provides a specific piece of evidence to support his thesis that segregation is wrong and harmful and should be stopped. Objects of agreement that children grow up quickly and children who are being harmed by injustice cannot wait for change support King's thesis. His daughter stands in for all of the African American children who are harmed in various ways by segregation.

It is important, also, to remember that examples of the rhetorical appeals that we locate can be strong or weak. If a rhetor offends his or her audience, those lines that are offensive are examples of weak ethos: where the rhetor harms his or her credibility. If a rhetor includes information that is faulty or outdated, that information constitutes a weak example of logos and it also has a direct and negative effect on the author's intrinsic ethos.

When you look for evidence of the rhetorical appeals, do not approach that task with the notion that only one rhetorical appeal is in play. Intentionally and unintentionally, the rhetorical appeals often exist in tandem to create a successful or unsuccessful text.

Americans seem to have a preference for logical arguments. We want scientific proof. Or so we say. If we think about it, we realize that we are often persuaded by things that are not and indeed cannot be proven scientifically. That's not a bad thing. It's a human thing. Humans aren't just logical, and our arguments needn't just be logical either. As we've already noted, for Aristotle, logos was just one of the three appeals used in persuasion, alongside ethos and pathos. Although Aristotle wrote a whole treatise on logic, he realized that not everything could be decided logically. Thus he was a proponent of rhetoric, and he realized that ethos and pathos often move audiences.

One place where we often see arguments that depend on pathos and ethos rather than logos to persuade us is in advertising. Much of advertising rests on what we would call faulty logic. Car ads, for example, basically tell us that the car is cool (or hot, depending on the slang we prefer), and that we should buy it, with the unstated point that the coolness of the car will transfer to us. If we tried to construct a logical argument from that, a car ad would look something like:

> **Premise of most car ads**: That car is hot
> **Unstated Minor Premise**: If I own that car, I'd be hot too.
> **Conclusion**: Buy that car!*

Does that work? Not logically, because the premise itself is unprovable: the "hotness" of the car is a matter of values rather than something logically provable. The "hotness" is a matter of the car's ethos or it might be considered an appeal to pathos, to our interests, but it certainly isn't logos. But while that might make the argument illogical, it makes it no less persuasive—just ask the auto industry!

Many such arguments rest on ideas that can't be determined logically. For instance, you can't logically prove who is the best person for president would be, because there's no objective way to prove "best" in this case.

That said, as intelligent consumers of the messages were hear, we should know when we are being told something that's illogical or a fallacy (they aren't the same thing, though they are often used synonymously). We should know what persuasion is based on so that we can make thoughtful and ethical considerations and decisions about the messages around us.

---

*The logical formula here is an enthymeme, or a syllogism with one part unstated. You'll read more about enthymemes and syllogisms on page 110.

JUST A MATTER OF OPINION?

Does that mean that ideas that aren't based on logical reasoning should just be cast aside as "just your opinion"? Many arguments are based on people's opinions, and opinions are very rhetorically based. Sometimes we cut off discussion saying, "Well, that's just your opinion." But that's not really saying much, and it shouldn't be the end of an earnest discussion on a worthwhile matter. People have a right to their opinions, certainly, but that doesn't preclude them changing their opinions. To terminate discussion saying "that's just his opinion" is a bit insulting; it's saying that the ideas expressed won't hold up to scrutiny, that the person hasn't really thought the matter through enough to be challenged. Certainly, there are times when it's appropriate to not pursue an argument based on someone's opinion. When your friend's dad says pineapple is the best thing on pizza but you think it's disgusting, there's little reason to argue; there's little at stake for you, or for the greater good, so let the man have his pizza the way he wants it, and be respectful of his taste! But when you think that you deserve another shift at work and your boss disagrees, you probably don't want to just say "it's just her opinion," and leave it at that. If you believe in something, you should be willing to respect someone else's ideas enough to scrutinize them—and hold yours up to scrutiny as well.

While we often decide that "it's just not worth arguing about, since it's his opinion," at other times we make an (often unstated) presumption that good, strong arguments are based on "facts" and poor or weak arguments are based on opinions. But if we understand more about ethos, pathos, and logos, we realize that often both opinions and facts are really based on values, on subjective beliefs rather than on philosophically logical proofs.

Where do our opinions come from? They come from our experiences, our values, the values of our community. The excerpt included here from the book *From Inquiry to Argument* explores the idea of understanding our values.

LOGICAL REASONING

We might draw a distinction between rhetorical reasoning and logical reasoning. Both should be ethical, both should be honest and fair, but both do not have to be beyond scientific proof. Misuses of pathos or ethos, as discussed earlier (pages 80–103), are equally problematic.

Syllogisms and Enthymemes

Before understanding faulty logic, you need to understand logic. Aristotle theorized about syllogisms, the basic formula for deductive reasoning, and enthymemes. A syllogism consists of a major premise, a minor premise and a conclusion.

The classical syllogism that you have probably all heard is this one:

Major Premise: All men are mortal
Minor Premise: Socrates is a man
Conclusion: Therefore, Socrates is mortal.

It is deductive reasoning, in that we deduce the conclusion from the premises. If the major premise and minor premise are both "true" (that is, logically provable), then the conclusion must be as well. In logic, something can be a formal fallacy if one of the premises is not true. For instance,

Major Premise: Some men are immortal
Minor Premise: Socrates is a man
Conclusion: Therefore, Socrates is immortal.

Because the major premise is not true, the conclusion can't be true, and that's a deductive fallacy.

You've also heard of inductive reasoning. That's when you argue from particulars to universals. Inductive reasoning is, in the technical realm of logic, not 100% provable, and thus, in a sense, inductive reasoning is always open to fallacy. But that doesn't mean that inductive arguments aren't viable arguments. It just means they don't rise to the level of logical proof. Here's an example of inductive reasoning:

Premise: Everyday in the past, the law of gravity has held
Conclusion: Therefore, the law of gravity will continue to hold today.

Technically speaking, the way that argument is structured, the logic is flawed—it's not enough to say (logically speaking) that just because something has happened every other day it will definitely happen today (think, for example, of this being a case of human behavior instead: because the baby has never walked before, she won't walk today. That doesn't make sense, because we know things can change). But just because something isn't provable in the strict logical sense doesn't mean it can't be a good argument, an ethical argument, a sensible argument.

Logical Fallacies

Earlier we briefly discussed logical fallacies (see pages 88–89). A logical fallacy is, simply, an error in reasoning. Faulty logic may come from an error in a syllogism or it may be an error in some other path to reasoning. We recognize the example about the baby above to be a fallacy. What's wrong with that argument? It assumes that things will always stay the way they are, it fails to consider cause appropriately. Those errors make it a fallacy.

How can we recognize fallacies beyond strict formal logical fallacies? We can group fallacies (those that fall beyond strict logical proof) into three categories: they may be fallacies in **relevance**, fallacies in **ambiguity**, or fallacies in **presumption**.

Fallacies of **relevance** rely on premises that aren't really relevant to the conclusion being made. These include *ad hominem* attacks, appeals to authority, appeals to consequence, or appeals to pity (see the list that follows this discussion for more on each of these fallacies). Remember, these might be very persuasive arguments, but that doesn't preclude them being fallacies.

Fallacies of **ambiguity**, which include the straw man fallacy and equivocation, twist language in some way so as to confuse or confound the listener.

Fallacies of **presumption**, as the name suggests, contain false premises. The most common of these are false dilemma, circular reasoning/begging the question, hasty generalization, slippery slope, *post hoc,* or any superstition or other cause/consequence that doesn't follow.

Some places to learn more about fallacies (and to see more examples)
http://www.fallacyfiles.org/

INQUIRING ABOUT FACTS AND INFORMATION

from *From Inquiry to Argument*

Read the following excerpt, then respond as indicated below:

> A friend working one summer near Polar Bear Pass on Bathurst Island [in the Arctic] once
> spotted a wolf running off with a duck in its mouth. He saw the wolf bury the duck, and
> when the wolf left he made for the cache. He couldn't find it. It was open, uncomplicated
> country. He retraced his steps, again took his bearings, and tried a second time. A third time.
> He never found it. The wolf, he thought, must have a keener or at least a different way of
> holding that space in its mind and remembering the approach. The land then appeared to
> him more complicated. . . .
>
>   One can only speculate about how animals organize land into meaningful expanses for
> themselves. The worlds they perceive, their Umwelten, are all different.* The discovery of
> an animal's Umwelt and its elucidation require great patience and experimental ingenuity,
> a free exchange of information among different observers, hours of direct observation, and
> a reluctance to summarize the animal. This, in my experience, is the Eskimo hunter's
> methodology. Under ideal circumstances it can also be the methodology of Western science.†

—Barry Lopez, "The Country of the Mind," *Arctic Dreams*

Writer's Journal

Write a few paragraphs in response to the Lopez passage. Are you reminded of any experiences of your own? Have you ever been struck by the complete otherness of someone else's
experience? Strive for an entry of about 150 words.

UNDERSTANDING FACTS AND INTERPRETATION

When we write to advocate for a position, just giving our opinion is not enough. Especially
in the civic and academic communities, people want to know why: why what we say is true
and why we believe as we do. In other words, we are expected to provide evidence for the

---

*The world we perceive around an animal is its environment: what it sees is its Umwelt, or self-world. A spe-
cific environment contains many Umwelten, no two of which are the same. The concept, developed by
Jakob von Uexkull in 1934, assumes that the structure of the organs of sense perception, the emphasis each
receives, the level of their sensitivity, and the ability of each to discriminate, are different in all animals.

†In practice, the two methodologies usually differ. The Eskimo's methods are less formal than those of the
scientist, but not necessarily less rigorous. By comparison, Western scientists often fall far short on hours of
observation; and they usually select only a few aspects of an animal's life to study closely. The Eskimo's ecological approach, however, his more broad-based consideration of an animal's interactions with many, some
seemingly insignificant, aspects of its environment, is increasingly becoming a Western approach.

ideas we write about. Facts—observations, descriptions, reports, and statistics that are accepted as true—and their interpretations and explanations make up the bulk of evidence. And most of the time our contact with these facts is very much secondhand: we deal in reports of facts, not personal knowledge, in much of our discourse. Much of our information comes to us via the media, and it is information that has been analyzed, shaped, and placed in context for our consumption. The process of acquiring information from media sources, be they books, television, or the Internet, is considered "secondary research." "Primary research" is investigation into events, opinions, or phenomena that produces new facts and new understandings.

Our civic and academic discourse communities have a particular way of processing information and constructing knowledge, but the passage from Barry Lopez shows that this way is not the only way. Our construction of knowledge emphasizes verifiable facts, and seeking facts constitutes much of the time spent in inquiry.

Facts, Just the Facts

In detective fiction, investigators claim to want "just the facts," but in real life determining what is a fact is not simple. At first, it may seem obvious what a fact is: a fact is a fact, the way "a rose is a rose." But, actually, facts are hard to define. David Crystal, the editor of a one-volume encyclopedia of information, *The Cambridge Factfinder*, notes that the definition of "fact" in the *Oxford English Dictionary* (OED) is one of the longest because so many complications come into play. As Crystal says, "There are facts about fictions . . . and fictions about facts. . . . There are situations where we cannot decide whether something is fiction or fact. . . . There are near-facts . . . , transient facts . . . , qualified facts . . . , arguable facts . . . , politically biased facts . . . , and contrived facts" (v).

Even some cut-and-dried facts turn out to have complications. In providing the flying times between major world cities, the *Factfinder* notes that "in order to travel between two points, it is [often] necessary to change aircraft. . . . Time between flights has not been included" (431). In other words, the flying times listed are ideal; if you are planning a trip, these facts may be misleading. In another case, the *Factfinder* lists the top twenty world languages, plus numbers of native speakers and total population numbers of countries where the languages are official. But a note explains that some languages are only one of several official ones, and therefore the official-language population figures are "over-estimations"—that is, they are not strictly true (448).

We want and expect our facts to be "truth[s] known by actual observation or authentic testimony," as the OED defines them (qtd. in Crystal: v). Nevertheless, facts sometimes collide with reality, as the examples above show. Crystal recommends that whoever uses facts should be informed about the complications. He writes, "A fact-book . . . must always remember to warn readers if 'there's something they should know' before swallowing a 'fact' whole" (v).

Establishing Facts as Factual

In the construction of facts from events, observations, and experiences, mere agreement is not enough to guarantee accuracy. All too often in human history, what people have agreed was factual was later shown to have been wildly untrue. You recognize the list: the world is flat; the sky is an inverted dome to which the stars are attached; the sun and moon revolve around the earth; diseases are caused by various body fluids being out of balance; leeches cure illness by sucking out excess blood; and many others. As time goes by, old "facts" are corrected and new facts are turned up—new planets and elemental particles discovered, medical techniques invented, and so on.

The last few years have seen numerous alterations or rejections of previously accepted facts. For example, the estimated age of the universe has been downsized from twenty billion to between fourteen and seven billion years, on the basis of sophisticated calculation methods. Two independent studies discovered the paradoxical "fact" that "the universe may be only about half as old as the oldest stars and galaxies it contains" (Hotz, "Universe").

Sometimes the commonplace "facts" of daily life turn out to be mere shadows. An article in the February 20, 1995, *Philadelphia Inquirer* reported that the concept of race has been found to be scientifically invalid. "Race is a social construct derived mainly from perceptions conditioned by events of recorded history, and it has no basic biological reality," according to C. Loring Brace, a biological anthropologist at the University of Michigan (Hotz, "Scientists").

Personal experience or witness makes strong claims to truth, but it is often not enough to ensure that a reported event is "true." Any number of factors can come into play to falsify or distort a person's observation or experience. Distractions, strong emotions, and physical positioning all can affect what a person reports as factual. You may have heard the story of the class interrupted by a gun-wielding thug, as the students later report; in actuality, the interruption was staged, and the intruder was holding a banana, yet the students perceived and reported a weapon was used because of their expectations.

"Fact insurance" comes in the form of the requirement that facts be verifiable. Observations and reports are needed from more than one person, from different and competing points of view, and over a period of time in order to ensure that something is a fact. Although many people over many decades have insisted they have seen the Loch Ness monster, the fact of its existence has not been verified from the competing vantage point of science: there are no unambiguous pictures or evidence of the feeding, breeding, nesting, or other activities of a huge creature in the lake.

The scientific method is an important way our culture ensures facts. Evidence derived from the scientific method has been tested by controlled observations or experiments. Such scientific method has proven the fact that water always boils at the same temperature, 212 degrees Fahrenheit or 100 degrees Centigrade, at the air pressure of earth at sea level.

The more variables affecting an event, the more difficult it is to establish the facts. In each academic discipline, the process developed to construct knowledge is often a variation of the scientific method.

The requirement that facts be verified means that we expect proof of what is factual in addition to expecting evidence in support of ideas. Lacking proof, we may agree that, in regard to certain facts, the "jury is out," that we do not know what the facts are. Or we may agree to accept certain facts as probable, although proof is inadequate.

In our discourse community, people expect others to be rational about their interpretations: thinkers should work from similar assumptions about how to construct and interpret facts. We expect, for example, that thinkers will assume that events have a cause or happen for a reason.

We expect them to avoid certain other assumptions—for example, that outer-space aliens intervene in human affairs. In the case of severe flooding in which no one died, for instance, to assume that spiritual beings exist and that the people in the flooded area were saved by angels who bore them away to higher ground would be to rest one's interpretation on assumptions that are not generally credited in our culture today. Beyond basing interpretations on accepted assumptions, reasoners and thinkers are expected to use logic, cause-and-effect reasoning, and common natural laws.

THE CONSTRUCTION OF KNOWLEDGE

Inference

According to the OED, facts should be kept separate from "what is merely inferred" and "conjecture[d]" and from "the conclusions which may be based upon [them]" (qtd. in Crystal: v). In real life and in discussions about issues, such a separation is not so easily achieved. Many things that people report as facts are actually a result of inference. People naturally "read into" and interpret what they have experienced, just as they use inference in the act of reading.

Here's an example. Imagine you happen to be walking along a street staring at your feet, deep in thought, when a car crash occurs immediately in front of you. You glance up immediately and survey the scene. You catch the signal light for the traffic on your street just as it changes to red. You thus infer that the car traveling in your direction had the green light as it crossed the intersection and that the car from the side street was running an orange or red light. You may then report to the police that the car on the side street was speeding and going through a red light when it hit the other car. But this is not actually a fact, however accurate it might be. It is an inference you have made.

When people infer, they create meaning out of facts. This may involve constructing a cause, attributing a reason, imaging an effect, or connecting seemingly opposed or contradictory facts to make them coherent. The scientific method makes constant use of inference; when an event occurs over and over in an experimental situation, the scientist infers that it will always occur under the same conditions. So water boils at the same temperature (at sea level) in both the lab and your kitchen. When we do the inferring, we feel pretty certain of our interpretation. But we are often in the position of accepting that what is reported is actually a fact. Unless we can question an eyewitness, observer, or researcher, we have to go on secondhand knowledge.

With all due respect to the excellence of the *Cambridge Factfinder,* many of the fact sets in it are not "pure." For example, the list "Evolution of Early Humans" must contain knowledge created by inferences. Until someone invents a time machine, we have no way of verifying anything about the development of early human life. However, by studying the evidence we have (skeletal remains, early tools, primitive paintings, fossils and bones of early animals and plants, and so forth), numerous trained experts over many decades have inferred much about what these early people looked like, their time periods and range, and so on. In accepting this information as factual, we are accepting knowledge constructed by authorities we trust. New discoveries and new methods of analysis will constantly change the "facts" about human evolution.

Judgments

Facts and inferences based on them are further interpreted when writers apply values and make judgments and also present information in the context of their conclusions. Then, when we receive information, we interpret it for ourselves; we make additional inferences, view them through the perspective of our values, and draw additional conclusions from them.

Articles that we read in the newspaper or information that we hear about is often a mixture of fact, inference, and judgment. We hope, as we read reports of facts, that the writers have the pertinent experience, knowledge, rationality, and goodwill to infer causes, results, and relationships that are in line with reality.

When reading or using sources it's important to recognize and differentiate what is factual and what is interpretation, what is evidence that can be trusted, and what is judgment.

To summarize:

Fact: verifiable event, occurrence
Inference: knowledge created by putting facts together
Judgment: a conclusion about facts and inferences created by applying values

Characteristics of Evidence

In order for evidence to be accepted as weighty, it must possess the following characteristics: it must be representative, relevant, sufficient, specific, and reliable.

Representative

Evidence should be typical and not exceptional. Relying on unusual examples or nonrepresentative situations can cause you to defend a weak or shaky conclusion. To maintain, for example, that severe childhood illnesses have the positive effect that their sufferers overachieve in athletics because ice skater Scott Hamilton suffered from a nutrition absorption deficiency syndrome as a child yet went on to win Olympic gold is to rely on an exceptional example. It would be more reasonable, in this case, to modify the claim and cite examples of more typical youths with childhood illnesses who grew up to lead healthy and normal lives.

Relevant

Evidence should truly support the point that is being made. A student who is discussing police brutality in a nearby city should provide facts and figures about instances of unwarranted force used during arrests. To describe the officers' tough-looking leather jackets, heavy clubs, and dangling handcuffs and assert that they strut around like thugs is to stray from the subject. The police force's uniforms and equipment have nothing to do with their treatment of suspects. The appearance and equipment are relevant only if, for example, you can cite a study that showed aggressively garbed and equipped police to be more abusive than police with sedate uniforms and hidden paraphernalia.

Sufficient

There should be several strong pieces of evidence, not just one. The more evidence, the better. If there is only one fact or example that supports a point, there is always the possibility that it is an exception. In addition to quantity, a sufficient amount of evidence usually includes a variety of types of evidence: some examples, reasoning, details, and so on. For example, to support the position that liberal arts degrees can lead to good jobs after graduation, you might include examples of friends' job-hunting success, comments from corporate personnel directors found in a newspaper report, and statistics from your college's placement office about last year's graduates. These provide a breadth of support from a variety of different angles for your point of view.

Specific

Evidence should "name names" and cite numbers whenever possible. Evidence needs to be concrete in order to be convincing. Stating that murders have declined in the United States recently is general and vague. But citing the latest statistics that show that homicide in New York City was down in 1996 compared with the previous year provides specific and convincing support.

Reliable

The quality of evidence should be high. Facts and information should be accurate, recent, and complete; reasoning should be logical. Authorities should be well credentialed in the appropriate field. If the support is the result of research, the sources should be acknowledged and should be acceptable to the audience.

INQUIRING INTO VALUES

Reactions and Opinions

from From Inquiry to Argument

Read the following selections carefully, then respond as indicated below:

> Freedom is perhaps the most resonant, deeply held American value. In some ways, it defines the good in both personal and political life. Yet freedom turns out to mean being left alone by others, not having other people's values, ideas, or styles of life forced upon one, being free of arbitrary authority in work, family and political life. . . . And if the entire social world is made up of individuals, each endowed with the right to be free of others' demands, it becomes hard to forge bonds of attachment to, or cooperation with, other people, since such bonds would imply obligations that necessarily impinge on one's freedom.

> —Robert N. Bellah, Richard Madsen, William M. Sullivan,
> Ann Swidler, and Stephen M. Tipton, *Habits of the Heart:*
> *Individualism and Commitment in American Life*

> Never was the human mind master of so many facts and sure of so few principles.

> —George Santayana, "Later Speculations,"
> *Character and Opinion in the United States*

Writer's Journal

Choose one of the passages above and respond by explaining what the passage means to you. Strive for an entry of 150 words.

Most of us honestly admit that our response to things we read is a mix of emotional reactions, value judgments, and thoughts. We may be able to still our emotions long enough to examine and comprehend content, for example, when writing a summary, but our overall reaction to something we read will result from our feelings as much as from our thoughts.

Our emotional reaction may be caused by any number of features of a text, but the power of that reaction lies deep in our own personality, background, and culture. Both our rationality and our emotional makeup are the result of membership in a discourse community. We have been taught how to reason along certain lines. We have absorbed a way of looking at the world, and often we have been charged with automatic reactions to certain ideas and issues.

The academic community values reasoned judgment and evidenced opinions, as well as thematic, unified discourse. Other discourse communities, some within our own society, may have other values they hold higher than that of reasoning: the wisdom of an elder or religious leader, for example, or the teachings embodied in a religious document or the procedures and life choices handed down by tradition. In this book, the highest valuation is placed on reasoned analysis.

Values also come into play, however—values about which reasonable people will differ. This difference in values derives from the discourse communities in which each person has been raised and has been residing in as well as from the individual's reasoning about what it is good to believe.

So, beyond reasoning, we can work to comprehend the underlying values that cause us to react emotionally and to think along different lines from others. Only through such self-understanding can we grasp the differences in opinion that separate us from others. And, through examining the components of our own reactions, we can determine whether there are hidden contradictions in our values and whether we fully stand by these values.

WHAT ARE VALUES AND HOW DO THEY INFLUENCE OUR OPINIONS?

Values are beliefs about what is important in life, in our lives in particular but also in the lives of people as a community. Values endorse certain kinds of behavior. We are likely to share many broad values with those in our local, regional, and national community, and even internationally with all people around the world. The rights to survival and freedom are supported by most people and nations, at least in theory. These are values that are close to being universally sanctioned. Many such values have come to be formalized as principles, rules, or laws that provide guidance in many circumstances. In our culture, the Ten Commandments, the Declaration of Independence, the Bill of Rights, the Golden Rule, the judgments of the Supreme Court and appellate courts, and folk wisdom ("the apple doesn't fall far from the tree"; "no guts, no glory") are some of the sources for the principles we turn to for guidance in making judgments.

Although sometimes we deliberately inject our values into an argument or consciously refer to them as we read, our values often come into play as assumptions—that is, as ideas we believe and consciously or unconsciously apply as we respond to a text. If the text confirms our values, we are likely to approve it and enjoy reading it. A person who believes strongly in order may read an essay supporting the enlargement of the police force with approval. If a text affronts our values, however, we may feel rage or disgust. For example, someone who strongly values artistic creativity may be angered by an article advocating the elimination of federal funding for the arts.

Many texts fall between entrancing us and outraging us. Perhaps the value they engage is one we hold but not strongly, so our response is lukewarm. If we only mildly value exploration, an article arguing increased support for NASA might make little impression on us. When some of our values are supported while others are not, we may have a mixed reaction to what we read. Someone who disdains taxation and values the enterprising spirit may feel mixed about an article advocating the funding of small business start-ups through increased taxation.

In any single case, whether our response to a text is reasonable or not can be determined only through a careful examination of our own values. When we think an argument is extremely persuasive, we should try to determine where it meshes with values we already hold. Then we should go on to examine the argument itself to determine whether it is solid. For example, someone may initially find persuasive an article in support of laws permitting concealed weapons. On recognizing that the article plays into two of her highest values, individualism and personal freedom, she can realize that her acceptance of the argument is due not to its strength but to her personal value system. She needs to read the argument analytically to define whether it truly is logical and well supported.

THE HIERARCHY OF VALUES

Some values cover most everything we do in our lives; they are "global," or overarching. Other values are more local, or situational, and pertain only to one aspect of our lives. A mother may value consistency and fairness in parenting, and these values may come into play constantly in her daily life. Her childless sister may hold similar values but may enact them only when she babysits her nieces and nephews. Often, the weight you place on a particular value results from the situation you're in. You may barely realize how much you value privacy until you are stuffed in a dorm room for three. Your long-awaited first professional job may reveal to you just how much you value a flexible daily schedule and going outside four walls for some part of every day.

Although we hold some values unconditionally—that is, regardless of the situation—many other of our values are conditionally important. Simply, we all rank some values higher than others. For most people, survival is a higher value than pleasure, for example. For many parents, their children's survival is a higher value than their own survival. Most people in our culture would agree that honesty is a clear and obvious value that should always apply, but in some situations honesty would be outranked by survival. For example, few would consider it wrong to lie to a person holding a knife to your throat if the lie would defuse the threat to your safety. A text may appeal to some of your values and not others, or it may appeal to values you rank less highly than others; in each of these cases, your response may be mixed.

One way of categorizing values is to break them down into global, or overarching, values and situational values. Examples of overarching values are survival, truthfulness, integrity. Examples of places where situational values come into play are the workplace, college, social life, home, and place of worship.

Values Conflict

As you and your class constructed a lengthy list of values, you may have noticed that some of them contradict others. A valuation of tradition, for example, would be undermined by valuing the new or novelty. It is probably fair to say that, for many values you might hold, an equal and opposite value is held by somebody else. As Robert Bellah and his coauthors emphasize in their book *Habits of the Heart,* American life has a values conflict at its core: the values of cooperation and service, crucial to a functioning community, conflict with the dearly held values of individualism and freedom (23–25).

Conflicts about values occur in all of us. For example, the value of self-preservation may conflict with the value of adventure when a person decides to take up a dangerous sport. Or perhaps, in such a case, the value of self-preservation is outweighed because there are several opposing values—adventure, the value of having a daring reputation, and the value of excitement brought by indulging in risky behavior.

An amusing example of a personal value conflict occurred at a community protest of a nightclub featuring topless dancing. An observer noticed that one protester left the others to venture inside. The bar visitor later admitted he couldn't resist seeing what such a place was like. At first, taking action against what he considered to be obscene dancing in his town, the man ended up valuing curiosity more than solidarity with the protest. (He said he still opposed the topless dancing however.)

Psychological studies indicate that a typical inner value conflict of adolescence tends to be resolved differently depending on the person's sex. In a far-ranging landmark study of women's and men's attitudes about morality, Carol Gilligan identified two approaches to values: "The morality of rights is predicated on equality and centered on the understanding of fairness, while the ethic of responsibility relies on the concept of equity, the recognition of differences in need. While the ethic of rights [involves] . . . balancing the claims of other and self, the ethic of responsibility rests on . . . compassion and care" (164–65). Gilligan's study showed that in the transition to adulthood, men and women experience the same dilemma over whether "integrity" or "care" is the higher value. The upbringing (or, as we might say, the discourse communities) of the two sexes is significantly different however, so that for most men and women "this dilemma generates the recognition of opposite truths. Men's upbringing emphasizes separation and independence, resulting in an 'ethic of rights,' while the emphasis on relationships and attachment in women's upbringing supports their adoption of an 'ethic of care'" (164).

When you examine your values, you will probably discover that your situational values are different from those on your list of overarching values. You may also find that your situational values conflict somewhat. For example, you may decide that at work, being polite, reserved, and professional are significant for you. However, your behavior at a friend's party might be governed by different values: letting loose, being spontaneous, acting "natural." Or after looking over your various situational lists, you may decide that "fitting in with others" and "conforming to a situation" are two overarching values for you that you apply, with different effects, in your workplace and in your social life.

Values Change

The way a person ranks values may shift over time, along with the person's changing experiences, life situation, and psychological needs. Maturity and parenthood may cause someone to downgrade the value of competitiveness and upgrade good sportsmanship and teamwork, for example. William Perry, who researched the cognitive development of adolescents, discovered that maturity is characterized by the realization that "there is a diversity of opinion about what is good and what is right. . . . Truth is no longer conceived as absolute and singular but multiple and infinite" (qtd. in Belenky et al.: 62–63). Younger children tend to believe that values are rock solid. But adults may see values as relative to a situation because the "meaning of an event depends on the context in which that event occurs and on the framework that the knower uses to understand that event" (10).

Values Serve Needs

You've probably noticed that people believe what they want to believe or what helps them get through their lives with the least distress or most enjoyment. In other words, sometimes values serve our needs, and this makes them convenient to hold whether or not they are defensible in a rational manner. It is often most difficult to be objective about the values that "keep us going" in our daily lives.

Psychologist Abraham Maslow identified a hierarchy of needs, organized from most to least crucial. As a person's lower-level needs are satisfied, he or she moves on to address higher-level needs. In other words, those who can't pay the rent are not usually too consumed with actualizing their sculpting talents. Maslow wrote that, beyond the basic physical needs for water, food, shelter, and the like, people's needs are "for safety, belongingness and identification, for close love relationships, and for respect and prestige" (21). The highest need is for "self-actualization," the ability to put all one's talents to use. You may find this structured way of examining needs helpful as you sort out the sources of your own values.

Students may be focused on self-esteem or self-actualization needs because their other needs are being met or their expectations (as for material comforts) are temporarily reduced or suspended. Some are preoccupied with their future needs for food and shelter, and sometimes students find themselves in dire straits, having to forage for food in friends' refrigerators or borrow couches and floors for sleeping because of changes in a marginal economic situation.

Sometimes what we may claim to be values verge closely on being rationalizations. These ideas serve as crutches to keep us going or as licenses that allow us to behave in a way not supportable by reason. If you are not familiar with the term *rationalization*, look it up, and also ask friends what they think it means. Don't confuse a "rationalization" with a "reason." While reasons are supposed to be clearly thought out and logical, rationalizations are merely wishful explanations. You can consider a rationalization an excuse for a reason—that is, a "decoy" meant to distract its owner from acknowledging the actual impulses that lie deeper down.

People sometimes spout values instead of admitting to failure or fear or to deny they care about an unpleasant consequence. This common habit of avoidance among humans appears to be the cause of many sayings:

"Practical knowledge is what counts."
"Smart as a whip but doesn't know to come in out of the rain."
"Don't be a stool pigeon."
"I'd rather be poor but happy."
"Everybody's doing it."
"I'm only a little bit bad."

You may recognize that many of these sayings are clichés—that is, stale phrases, timeworn, unimaginative, and easy to come by. They represent one of the worst aspects of a discourse community: the possibility that the language of the community will supply the thinking for the individuals within it. Some individuals prefer to think in formulas and to operate on impulse rather than on reason. They ache to follow the crowd (satisfying their need for belonging) rather than think things through for themselves. As the above list reveals, there is a cliché for every occasion, a formula to justify any and all beliefs and actions.

Almost any value can get out of hand and become a crutch supporting irrational needs or a license to perform antisocial or questionable behavior. For example, loyalty to and love of one's group can, if extreme, lead to provincialism, ethnocentrism, prejudice, stereotyping, superstition, overreliance on traditional practices, and resistance to change. A tragic example of extremism in loyalty was the mass suicide of the thirty-nine members of the Heaven's Gate cult during the visit of the Hale-Bopp comet in spring 1997 (Bruni 1).

VALUE ACTIVATORS

Our emotional reaction to a piece of writing may be prompted by any number of features of the text: the topic, the way the topic is treated, or the language effects created by the writer. Certain topics themselves affect all of us emotionally to a certain extent—child abuse, abortion, crime, international crises involving slaughter, bombings, starvation, and so on. Other times our personal histories sensitize us to particular issues. A person with a close gay friend may have a heightened awareness of discrimination against homosexuals.

A highly emotional response may also be sparked by the way a topic is treated. A satiric treatment of a person or institution that we respect may "get our goat." A blameful discussion of the poverty that can befall single mothers, for example, may enrage someone who has researched divorce and single motherhood or whose sister is an unmarried mother. A negative or mocking appraisal of our favorite candidate's honesty may set us off long before we reach the middle of the article.

Writers who wish to play on readers' feelings can manipulate language to create effects. They use imagery, emotionally tinged words, repeated phrases, or language patterns that create drama and heighten feelings. In such texts, rhetoric is consciously employed to promote a claim. To be sure, all writers make use of rhetoric. How much a reader is affected depends on the extent to which the reader meshes with the writer's intended audience and how extreme the rhetoric is. When the language of a text is designed to provoke heavily emotional reactions, we speak of the text as *biased* or *slanted*. Such slanting usually goes beyond the style of language used; it often involves omitting evidence and information that might moderate or contradict the point of view taken in the text. Some writers deliberately adopt extreme styles in order to irritate mainstream readers. Being a gadfly or iconoclast is a time-honored role in Western culture: such writers take an adversarial or exaggerated stance just to touch off debate and inspire the flow of ideas.

ASSUMPTIONS AND VALUES IN REASONING: TOULMIN LOGIC

It's hard to get away from values and assumptions about them. Typically, values lie underneath arguments as unspoken assumptions. Although no one would maintain that you shouldn't argue with reference to values, it's a good idea to know what your assumptions are and also to take the assumptions of your intended audience into account.

British logician Stephen Toulmin showed how values (as well as beliefs) serve as assumptions that connect a claim to the evidence or data offered for it. Toulmin's term for such an assumption is warrant. A warrant is an assumption, often hidden, that "licenses" or permits us to use the facts of the situation as support for the claim. The assumption asserts a value or belief. For example, if you observe that your neighbor drives a British Sterling, you might reason that she is materialistic. Diagramed according to Toulmin logic, this bit of reasoning looks like this:

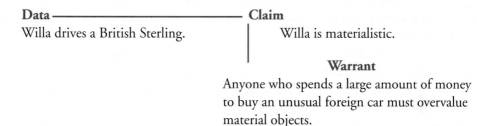

Data ——————————————————— **Claim**
Willa drives a British Sterling.   Willa is materialistic.

                                         Warrant
Anyone who spends a large amount of money to buy an unusual foreign car must overvalue material objects.

Here, the claim about Willa is based on your observation of the car she drives. But the idea that makes the claim possible is an assumption, a value judgment, that owning an expensive and unusual foreign car makes the owner materialistic. Without that assumption (or some other), Willa's car is just a car, and you can learn nothing about her from it.

For this bit of reasoning to work, both the audience and the arguer must agree on the truth of the assumption or warrant and its applicability to the claim. In presenting an argument, the writer must identify common ground shared with the audience. This common ground provides the assumptions or warrants that form the hinge of the argument. Most of the time, people within a discourse community hold similar values and make similar assumptions, but, within a large discourse community, there is lots of room for variety. Among college students, values are quite diverse, depending on background and length of exposure to the college environment. Students sometimes discover that beliefs shared by friends at home are not shared by those in their dormitory. A new college student might, for example, assume that using borrowed or faked identification to get into bars is a brazen violation of drinking laws, an outrageous, shabby, and even dangerous behavior. To her shock, she may learn that her dorm mates consider this action no big deal.

Widespread beliefs held by a cohesive community or group constitute what the social sciences call *mores*. Such values are not as formal or as consciously held as morals, but they nevertheless strongly govern the behavior of the group. The unspoken mores of a community work to produce *norms*, "a standard, model, or pattern [of behavior] regarded as typical" ("Norm"). Rules of politeness are norms. In the United States, for example, it used to be a norm for men to take off their hats when entering a building because of the belief that a man's wearing a hat inside was rude (women's hats, being decorative, were permitted indoors). This norm has disappeared among younger Americans, to the extent that many are surprised to learn it ever existed. Another norm that has changed is how people behave when they are victorious. Today, it is common for winners, from Olympic champions to schoolyard victors, to celebrate themselves by punching one or both fists in the air; in the past, such boastful, "I'm great" gestures were considered poor sportsmanship, especially when made by amateurs. Norms are more than just etiquette however. They cover all our interactions: how we behave in elevators, at parties, and in the cafeteria.

When your assumptions are not acceptable to your audience, you must provide backing for them. Toulmin makes the point that all warrants have backing—that is, material that supports the warrant, but the backing is not always out in the open. When your assumptions are not congruent with those of the audience, you need to be explicit about your backing. Otherwise, your claim is likely to be rejected. In the example above, the backing might include such statements as "a Sterling costs $45,000"; "only one in a thousand Americans owns a Sterling"; "it requires a large amount of money and effort to acquire an unusual foreign car"; "people who make such efforts are materialistic."

Toulmin acknowledged that even with backing, a claim is still only likely rather than definitely true, and so he added another element to the mix, the qualifier. The qualifier is a word, like "probably," that softens the claim. The reservation is a statement that, if true, invalidates the claim. In this example, a reservation might be "Willa's rich aunt asked her to use the car while she spends the year abroad." Or "Willa's company assists junior executives in the purchase of a high-status car." If the reservation is true, then the claim is false.

Diagramed completely according to Toulmin's structure, this argument looks as follows:

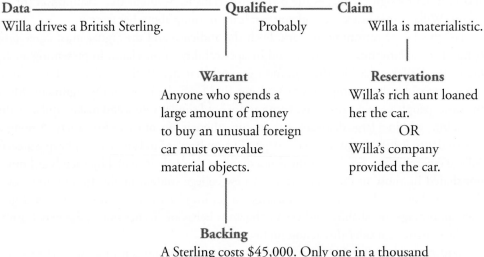

Data ———————————————— **Qualifier** ———— **Claim**
Willa drives a British Sterling.   Probably   Willa is materialistic.

Warrant   **Reservations**
Anyone who spends a   Willa's rich aunt loaned
large amount of money   her the car.
to buy an unusual foreign   OR
car must overvalue   Willa's company
material objects.   provided the car.

Backing
A Sterling costs $45,000. Only one in a thousand
Americans owns a Sterling. It requires a large amount
of money and effort to acquire an unusual foreign car.
People who make such efforts are materialistic.

Exploring Assumptions

Examine the reasoning expressed in the statements below. For each, try to determine the assumptions that allow the stated conclusion to be drawn. Then, decide whether you feel that assumption warrants the conclusion. Finally, diagram the statements according to Toulmin format.

1. I see that girl walking three dogs in the park every day. She must really love dogs.
2. The president held three press conferences this summer. I guess his popularity is increasing.

3. More and more people seem to be fishing from Cauman Bridge every time 1 pass it. It must be a good fishing spot.
4. The Food and Drug Administration forced a recall of twenty-five million pounds of beef. The FDA is sure doing a good job of watching out for the health of Americans.
5. Seven men were arrested on charges of conspiring to kill an organized crime kingpin so they could take over his illegal drug business. It's a crime that our government is letting these mob activities go on, only stepping in when murder is threatened.

One of the best ways to engage a text rhetorically is to look at how an author utilizes the rhetorical appeals to persuade his or her audience. This may be done either by looking at a single persuasive text or by looking at two persuasive texts that tackle the same topic. To demonstrate how a rhetorical analysis might be written, we have chosen to discuss two arguments on the topic of gay straight alliance clubs from the April 14, 2000 issue of *CQ Researcher*.

AT ISSUE:

Should high schools permit "gay-straight alliance" clubs?

YES:

Jim Anderson
Communications director, Gay, Lesbian and Straight Education Network

WRITTEN FOR *THE CQ RESEARCHER*

Considerable media attention has been paid over the past few months, to gay-straight alliance (GSA) controversies in Utah, Louisiana and Orange County, Calif. In each instance, school boards either considered or took action to prevent students from exercising their federally protected right under the Equal Access Act.

While these battles and controversies have been intriguing, it is, perhaps, more interesting to consider the stories that have not made the news.

Little attention has been paid to the approximately 700 gay-straight alliances that are currently meeting in high schools from coast-to-coast. These school communities accepted or embraced the students and their efforts, and not as a result of judicial mandate. Instead, they recognized their professional, if not moral, responsibility to do so.

Should other high schools permit the creation of gay-straight alliances? To answer the question, we need to define gay-straight alliances and to discuss why students are forming them in such numbers. A gay-straight alliance is formed by lesbian, gay, bisexual and transgender (LGBT) students and their straight classmates. These students join together to support one another and to address concerns about the misinformation and ignorance that too often result in anti-gay harassment or violence at school.

Their concerns are well-founded. Studies by the federal Centers for Disease Control and Prevention (CDC) show that lesbian, gay and bisexual students are more than four times as likely as their heterosexual classmates to be threatened with or injured by a weapon while at school.

The Gay, Lesbian and Straight Education Network found similarly disturbing trends. In a recent national survey, we found that 61 percent of LGBT students experience verbal harassment, 27 percent physical harassment and 14 percent outright physical assault while at school.

This harassment and isolation may negatively affect students' self-esteem and school performance. Such experiences may explain why national mainstream organizations such as the American Counseling Association and the National Association of Social Workers have recently endorsed gay-straight alliances.

Every student is entitled to a supportive, safe and affirming learning environment. With this goal in mind, we urge schools not only to permit gay-straight alliances but also to encourage and foster their existence.

NO:

Peter LaBarbera
Senior analyst, Family Research Council

WRITTEN FOR *THE CQ RESEARCHER*

School districts should not allow the formation of gay-straight alliances on their campuses. These groups, where they already exist, have become de facto homosexuality booster clubs—causing unnecessary divisions and distractions and subjecting the entire student body to one-sided propaganda. Moreover, they are part of a movement that promotes radical identities and dangerous sexual practices to vulnerable, confused teens.

The gay-straight alliances are part of an ingenious strategy by pro-homosexuality and trans-sexuality groups like the Gay, Lesbian and Straight Education Network (GLSEN) to inject their unhealthy sexual and gender ideologies into the classroom. Students rally around the "rights" of gay, bi or even trans (transgender) classmates who, it is true, are ostracized and sometimes mistreated by their peers.

But while GLSEN and other groups have artfully "spun" the issue of youth homosexuality into one of "discrimination," it is really about behavior and parents' rights to guide their children's moral decisions.

In Massachusetts, taxpayers subsidize the formation of gay-straight alliances—there are now 185—through state grants for GSA projects.

Across the country, educators are wasting valuable school time by allowing GSAs to promote extreme notions to the entire student body. Students rarely get to hear the other side of the debate, and they fear expressing their opposition to homosexuality because of the schools' politically correct embrace of homosexuality.

The National Education Association, the American Civil Liberties Union, GLSEN and their allies promote GSAs in the name of school "safety." But schools shouldn't promote homosexual identities to troubled kids when studies show that homosexual males have drastically shorter life spans. This is due to the risky sexual behavior that flourishes in the promiscuous "gay" world. At a March conference sponsored by GLSEN's Boston affiliate, speakers from the state's Education Department approvingly discussed "queer sex" acts to an audience made up mostly of students ages 14–21.

Parents must resist an agenda that uses schools' authority to confirm impressionable youth in harmful lifestyles. As one former homosexual has noted, "From every medical and health aspect—up to and including the probability of becoming infected with AIDS—it is tragic, even criminal, to lead a child into homosexuality because he or she showed some degree of confusion in adolescence."

RHETORICAL ANALYSIS—UNDERSTANDING THE APPEALS

Quick, which of the two arguments is more convincing? Jim Anderson's in favor of high schools permitting gay straight alliance clubs or Peter LaBarbera's opposing high schools' decisions to allow gay straight alliance clubs? The answer you arrive at by performing a rhetorical analysis could be that either author's argument is stronger for its intended audience. Your goal in the rhetorical analysis is to assess each author's effectiveness in using the three rhetorical appeals and to conclude that one author's argument is more effective overall for its intended audience because of the way that author uses one, two, or all three rhetorical appeals.

Before we proceed, we must identify each author's intended audience. Although both writers, Jim Anderson and Peter LaBarbera, composed their arguments for the *CQ Researcher*, and their audiences share certain traits, it is also clear from reading the two arguments that the authors have two very different audiences in mind. What traits do the two authors' audiences share? We can determine these by looking at the authors' joint publication choice: the *CQ Researcher*. *CQ Researcher* is published weekly in print, and offered forty-four times a year online to libraries, universities, and researchers who subscribe, and it attempts to give in depth coverage to a single topic each issue. In addition to each edition featuring a bibliography, each edition features a pair of opposing arguments from politicians, academics, or people connected by their vocations to the issue. Both Anderson's and LaBarbera's audiences, therefore, are interested in topics of debate, either because they are politically minded or because they are pursuing research on a particular topic: in this case, gay-straight alliance clubs. Anderson's and LaBarbera's audiences are also similar in that they would be made up of adults voting-age and older and would include all races and both genders. There is, however, an important characteristic that differentiates the two authors' intended audiences: degree of partisanship. Whereas Jim Anderson, who supports gay-straight alliance clubs in high schools, attempts to convince those who are neutral and perhaps slightly opposed to his position as well as supporters, Peter LaBarbera is addressing exclusively those who support his position. LaBarbera's choice is problematic, given the fact that the readers of the *CQ Researcher* cover every pole of the liberal to conservative spectrum. He will have to be careful to avoid offending those who disagree with his position. Now we are ready for the next stage of the rhetorical analysis: an evaluation of each author's use of the rhetorical appeals.

Let's begin by comparing the two authors' extrinsic ethos. Extrinsic ethos refers to the credibility that an author possesses outside of the argumentative text itself. Jim Anderson is the Communications Director of the Gay, Lesbian and Straight Education Network. Based upon his position and his organizational affiliation, what level of credibility should we attach to Anderson outside of the argument? The nature of his position and his role as director of communications leads us to conclude both that he is trained and well educated and that he is frequently called upon to communicate with the press and the public. This suggests strong extrinsic ethos. His organizational affiliation, in contrast, points to exactly what position he will be taking: supporting gay-straight alliance clubs. Although this does not necessarily translate as weak extrinsic ethos, it does mean that Anderson will have to work to convince a neutral or opposing audience that he is not biased. Peter LaBarbera is the Senior Analyst for the Family Research Council, a conservative think tank. Even if you did not know that the Family Research Council is a conservative think tank, the phrase "family research" should clue you in to what stand LaBarbera will be taking on the question of whether high schools should permit gay-straight alliance clubs. Similarly to Anderson, LaBarbera will have to work to convince a neutral or opposing audience that he is not biased in terms of character. LaBarbera's title and position indicates that he is an expert in tabulating, compiling, and assessing data. In this regard, LaBarbera's extrinsic ethos is strong.

In order to grasp Jim Anderson's intrinsic ethos, we need to ask a series of questions. Is he fair-minded? Does he cite knowledgeable authorities and provide outside evidence to back his claims? Does he treat the opposing side with respect? Anderson succeeds in all three of these endeavors, and avoids alienating an opposing audience, because he is careful to build his credibility slowly, over the course of his entire argument. He uses the first three paragraphs to set up the question that he asks in the opening sentence of the fourth paragraph: "Should other high schools permit the creation of gay straight alliances?" (321) By asking this question overtly, he is suggesting to an opposing audience that support for gay straight alliance clubs is not a foregone conclusion and that it is a stance that must be carefully considered before being defended. He proceeds to justify a need for a definition of gay-straight alliance clubs and offers a warrant for why those clubs have become necessary (victimization of gay students). He then calls upon the statistical findings of two national organizations, one of which is his own: the federal Centers for Disease Control and Prevention and the Gay, Lesbian and Straight Education Network. Finally, after invoking the support of the American Counseling Association and the National Association of Social Workers, he makes an ethical plea: "Every student is entitled to a supportive, safe, and affirming learning environment" (321). Once he has presented a full defense of gay straight alliance clubs, he is comfortable stating the position that he would like his audience to take: "not only to permit gay straight alliances but also to encourage and foster their existence" (321).

Peter LaBarbera's intrinsic ethos, in contrast, is poor, not because of the position he is taking but because of the way he addresses the opposing side. His overriding disrespect for the proponents of gay straight alliance clubs can be seen in two different ways: through his use of language and characterization, and through his use of quotation marks. Consider the diction or word choice that LaBarbera incorporates in the opening sentence of the second paragraph: "The gay-straight alliances are part of an ingenious strategy by pro-homosexuality and transsexuality groups like the Gay, Lesbian and Straight Education Network (GLSEN) to inject their unhealthy sexual and gender ideologies into the classroom" (321). In choosing words like "ingenious" to describe the opponents' method, "inject" to describe how organizations supporting gay rights get their information into the classrooms, and "unhealthy" to describe the "ideologies" that organizations like GLSEN promote, LaBarbera risks alienating both readers who have not yet made up their mind about gay straight alliance clubs and supporters of gay civil rights. LaBarbera's use of quotation marks presents an even greater chance that he will lose the support of an opposing or neutral audience. Consider the first instance where LaBarbera uses quotation marks. LaBarbera writes:

> Students rally around the "rights" of gay, bi, or even trans (transgender) classmates, who,
> it is true, are ostracized and sometimes mistreated by their peers. (321)

Any credibility that LaBarbera might gain by the concession that he makes at the end of the sentence (that gays are "sometimes mistreated") is undermined by his decision to put quotation marks around the word *rights*. The reader may wonder, "Does LaBarbera believe that gays, bisexuals, and transsexuals do not deserve rights?" On multiple occasions later in LaBarbera's argument, he uses quotation marks in a manner that calls into question whether he respects his opposing audience. For example, he writes that "GLSEN and other groups have artfully `spun' the issue of youth homosexuality into one of `discrimination'" (321). Does he not believe that what gays face is discrimination? Each instance where LaBarbera comes across as unnecessarily antagonistic may solidify a neutral or opposing reader's opinion that LaBarbera disrespects the opposing side. The end result is that LaBarbera may lose credibility in all but the staunchest supporter's mind.

Ethos is not the only measure of whether a piece of persuasive writing is weak or strong. In fact, you read earlier in this chapter that "many rhetoricians . . . have considered pathos the strongest of the appeals." Whereas in terms of ethos, Anderson's argument is stronger, in terms of pathos, LaBarbera's argument is stronger. LaBarbera excels in making the audience fear for the morality of students. One way in which he does this is by identifying gay straight alliance clubs as a threat. LaBarbera concludes his opening paragraph by suggesting that "[gay straight alliance clubs] are part of a movement that promotes radical identities and dangerous sexual practices to vulnerable, confused teens" (321). Even if we disagree with LaBarbera's stance, we must recognize the emotional impact of his word choices: "a movement," "radical identities," "dangerous sexual practices," and "vulnerable, confused teens." Each phrase asks LaBarbera's audience to feel the same concern that he feels regarding the implementation of gay straight alliance clubs. Jim Anderson, on the other hand, does not take full advantage of the fact that he is making an argument that is based upon empathizing (and sympathizing) with the plight of gay and bisexual students, who are "more than four times as likely as their heterosexual classmates to be threatened with or injured by a weapon while at school" (321). Although Anderson provides a statistic, he could have also made the statistic personal by identifying one such victim of anti-gay or anti-bisexual harassment by name if that person was willing.

In terms of logos, Anderson and LaBarbera adopt completely different strategies; and it is up to you to make the case that one of the strategies is more successful. Anderson begins by giving a context for an argument on the topic of gay straight alliance clubs. He then proceeds to offer a definition of gay straight alliances that suggests the twofold purpose of such organizations is to open up communication between homosexuals and heterosexuals and to help spread awareness of the obstacles that many gay students face. He waits until the final sentence of his argument to state the position that he would like his audience to take (in support of gay straight alliances), but not until he makes an assertion that few teachers and parents would disagree with: "Every student is entitled to a supportive, safe, and affirming learning environment" (321). LaBarbera, in contrast, opens with the thesis or position that he wants his audience to support: "School districts should not allow the formation of gay straight alliances on their campuses" (321). He proceeds to attach as much negativity and long-term risk as he can to the effect of high schools allowing gay straight alliance clubs to form.

Ultimately, if you conclude in your rhetorical analysis that Jim Anderson's argument supporting gay straight alliance clubs is stronger, you are most likely building your case on Anderson's effective use of ethos, whereas if you conclude that LaBarbera's argument opposing gay straight alliance clubs is more persuasive you are building your case both on LaBarbera's substantial use of pathos and on the fact that his intended audience supports his position.

RHETORICAL ANALYSIS AND STASIS THEORY— DETERMINING WHAT'S AT ISSUE IN A TEXT

You already know something about **stasis theory**, about the categories of questions for thinking about what is at issue in a topic. When you do rhetorical analysis, particularly of a persuasive text, it's important to know what arguments are being made, and one way to recognize the arguments is to think of what kinds of issues are being discussed.

Determining "what's at issue" in a debate is crucial to understanding the topic, proceeding with research, and finding a solution. But arguers rarely stop to identify the kind of issue they are debating. Imagine two educators disagreeing over whether a national school exit test should come at the end of the eighth or twelfth grades. They will probably not stop to tell their audience, "The issue we are debating here concerns what course of action to take." Yet the reader analyzing their arguments needs to have a general system for describing what kind of issue is being addressed.

The first four stases are "hierarchical", meaning they build on each other and there must be agreement in an earlier stasis before there can be agreement in a later one. So, for example, before two historians can agree about the **causes** of terrorism, they must agree not only that terrorism exists (a matter of **conjecture**) but also on how to **define** it. Similarly, before two policy analysts can agree on a proposal of how to deal with terrorism, they must agree that it exists (**fact**), on how exactly it should be **defined**, on what **causes** and **effects** it has, and on its **value**. Then they can debate a plan of **action**. The stasis of **jurisdiction** stands outside this hierarchy but it can relate to any of the other questions. Thus before the policy that the analysts working for the executive branch agree upon can be implemented, it must be agreed that it is the executive branch that has a right to make such decisions.

FIRST STASIS: CONJECTURE (OR FACT AND DEFINITION)

The questions in this stasis concern the existence, nature, and attributes of subjects. Arguments about whether something existed or exists, happened or is happening belong in this stasis. Some disagreements concern how or whether a potential "fact" can be verified, and some disagreements go deeper and question whether the status of "fact" is even possible in some cases.

Identifying facts can depend on prior definitions. We saw this with the recent recategorization of Pluto. Because there was disagreement on what constituted a planet, there was disagreement about which bodies in space should be categorized as planets. Once the definition was changed, the categorization was changed.

There are other instances when arguers agree on some set of "facts" but disagree on how they should be labeled or characterized. For example, we may agree that a friend of ours has taken a car, but disagree on whether to call that fact "borrowing" or "stealing."

SECOND STASIS: CAUSE

If we agree that something exists or happened, we may next naturally question what brought it about. Causes are usually matters of probable argument rather than factual demonstration when people are involved, since it is usually impossible to recreate human events in order to test a causal hypothesis, while controlling all the potentially influential variables.

Predictions—forecasts of what will happen—are essentially questions about cause since our speculations about what might happen depend on what causes we think could bring about a certain effect, whether we think those causes are likely to occur, and whether we agree upon what kinds of effects a certain event might cause.

THIRD STASIS: VALUE (OR QUALITY OR EVALUATION)

Many perspectives can gather around questions of quality and value. What quality does the thing have? Is it good or bad of its kind, beautiful or ugly, moral or immoral, or at any of the fine gradations between these extremes? These disagreements can also concern what kind of evaluation to make in the first place. Should a person, a politician for example, be judged only in one area of performance, or for character overall? Should a work of art be evaluated morally, or only aesthetically?

Often participants in a discussion about values find they actually share the same values but disagree over how to weight or order them according to importance in a given case. They must use some key value to help them create a hierarchy of other values from most to least important.

FOURTH STASIS: ACTION

If we agree that a situation exists and we evaluate it negatively, we next naturally ask what, if anything, can be done about it. (In fact, one argumentative strategy pushes to action as the issue under debate, as though agreement existed on the preceding issues. Rebuttal then requires moving the issue back down the stases.)

There can be many different arguments over what the best possible course of action might be. Thus arguments in this stasis frequently concern feasibility and trade-offs. We can often agree on what should be done ideally, but not on what is actually possible given the available resources. We can also debate who has the authority or responsibility to take action; in fact, some arguments for courses of action spend much of their time trying to "create" an audience that will act.

We can also agree that a situation exists and evaluate it positively, concurring that we'd like to see the situation maintained (although others might argue against us). Maintaining the *status quo* and arguing that we *should* maintain it also belong within the action stasis.

QUESTIONS OF JURISDICTION

During an argument in any of the preceding stases, but particularly in questions of evaluation and action, someone may challenge someone else's right to conduct or even to participate in the discussion. Does a particular group have the right to make decisions about the issue? Is one group interfering in another's domain? How do we determine the appropriate forum in which to conduct the argument?

Jurisdictional arguments can be raised in many kinds of controversies. Is it America's right to evaluate China's human rights policies? Do certain powers belong to Congress, to the States, or to the people? Who has the right to decide what a person can do with his or her body? Because such questions do not directly tackle the arguments advanced within the four stases outlined above, they form a separate stasis. Jurisdiction, however, does not follow the first four stases in sequential order. Instead, it is a kind of underlying stasis which attempts to shift the conversation to a different forum or to redistribute the authority for making decisions about the subject. It is ultimately a question of who can debate and who can decide.

THE RHETORIC OF "SETTING AN ISSUE"

Classifying an issue according to its stasis is a useful stage in the arts of inquiry, discussion, and argument. Arguers making or responding to a case can try to set or change the issue to their advantage.

The order of the stases (from fact and definition to cause, to value, to action) is an important feature of the system since it reveals the consequences of setting an issue in a certain stasis. Setting an issue in the third or fourth stasis, for example, frequently assumes agreement in the first or second; in some situations that agreement may be unwarranted. An arguer may propose action for a situation that the audience has yet to identify as a problem. The audience is pressured to see the situation as a problem, however, simply because a solution has been proposed. Similarly, in some situations and with some audiences, arguing in the first or second stasis will immediately create agreement in the third or fourth. For example, a case for the disappearance of a certain species of fish (first stasis) will function with some very receptive audiences as a call to action (fourth stasis). So setting the issue in a particular stasis can be a powerful rhetorical strategy.

Let's look at the pair of articles from *CQ Researcher*. The way they are presented underscores the point here about stasis theory: the whole section is titled "AT ISSUE". What is "at issue" in the overriding question "Should high schools permit 'gay-straight' alliance clubs?" In which stasis is that question? That's pretty simple—should it be done is a question of **action**. But are the articles only discussing action? Let's consider them with more depth.

Jim Anderson's "yes" argument begins with points that related to the fact/definition stasis: he points out that there has been "considerable media attention" to this subject, and that school boards have considered or taken action. He doesn't dispute anything there, he just says what has happened. He makes a point that is in the stasis of fact/definition, but it's not a controversial point, as far as he is concerned.

He then goes on to say that what is more interesting is what hasn't made the news (paragraph two), and that's the "approximately 700 gay-straight alliance" clubs that are already meeting. Again, he's making a point about the existence of these clubs, but that's not what's controversial. He notes that "These school communities accepted or embraced the students and their efforts, and not as a result of judicial mandate. Instead, they recognized their professional, if not moral, responsibility to do so." In terms of the stases, he's suggesting *why* schools formed these clubs (that's a point about cause/effect), and saying that the cause was professional and/or moral duty. That last part sounds a lot like value, and it's a good example of how cause/effect and value are very intertwined. He's stating the idea that forming these clubs was morally right. Certainly someone could interject their own perspective here and say no, they are not, but Anderson is not arguing this point—he makes this move and believes his audience agrees, because he doesn't argue this point.

Then, in paragraph four, he raises the question of whether there should be more of these clubs in other high schools. We can see there that he has moved to action after making some presumptions about existence, cause and value. But then he makes an interesting move. From that question about action—"Should other high schools permit the creation of gay-straight alliances"— he jumps back to the definition stasis and the causal stasis, saying that "To answer the question, we need to define gay-straight alliances and to discuss why students are forming them in such numbers.' What's the rhetorical effect of the way he is arranging these arguments so far?

Anderson offers a definition of these alliances in the rest of paragraph four. Is the definition particularly controversial? Would we say he is making an argument with this definition? Why or why not? Is his definition of the alliances purely definitional, or does he pull in elements of cause/effect and value as well? How does he do this? Why might he be doing it?

In the next three paragraphs, Anderson builds his argument with arguments from various authorities, using statistics to make his case. All of these are examples of arguments that state the existence of threats and harassment, which point out arguments in cause/effect stasis: the statistics prove that these threats exist, and these threats have an effect ("This harassment and isolation may negatively affect students' self-esteem and school performance"). He also makes subtle value arguments here—the affects are negative, the trends are disturbing.

Anderson ends the argument with a clear statement of action, dependent on a sentence that has to do with fact/definition, cause, and value: "Every student is entitled [the idea that students are entitled to something harkens back to the idea that our rights exist] to a supportive, safe and affirming learning environment" [the implication is that such an environment will have an effect on students; furthermore, the implication is that it will be a positive affect]. Based on arguments of fact/definition, cause/effect and value, Anderson makes his argument: yes, these clubs should exist.

If we think about it, it makes sense that any argument about an action should be made on points about cause/effect and value—we generally decide that we want to do things because we believe they will have positive effects. We have coffee in the morning because we believe it will have an effect (it will caffeinate us) and that effect will be good (it will make us alert). Anderson has used the hierarchy of the stases—whether consciously or not—to establish this argument about an action he favors. The extent to which he goes into each point has to do with the constraints of his rhetorical situation: his audience, the genre, the source, the limitations of space.

EXERCISE

Look at Peter LaBarbera's "no" argument about gay-straight alliance clubs. Does he, like Anderson, make arguments in other stases to construct his point that the clubs should not be permitted in high schools? How can you compare their arguments using the way each constructs points in the various stases? Does LaBarbera use one stasis more than others to make his point?

The final type of text that we are going to have you look at with regards to rhetorical analysis is a speech pulled from literature. For this particular case, we have selected a speech from George Orwell's novella *Animal Farm*. Below, we have given a context for the speech.

Night fell on the Manor Farm and all the animals in the barn gathered just after Mr. Jones, the farm's drunken owner, had gone to bed. Old Major, the wisest and most respected animal on the farm, had had a dream the night before that he wanted to share with the other animals. Old Major "was so highly regarded on the farm that everyone was ready to lose an hour's sleep in order to hear what he had to say." All the animals settled in to listen to him speak.

The speech begins:

"Comrades, you have heard already about the strange dream that I had last night. But I will come to the dream later. I have something else to say first. I do not think, comrades, that I shall be with you for many months longer, and before I die, I feel it my duty to pass on to you such wisdom as I have acquired. I have had a long life, I have had much time for thought as I lay alone in my stall, and I think I may say that I understand the nature of life on this earth as well as any animal now living. It is about this that I wish to speak to you.

"Now, comrades, what is the nature of this life of ours? Let us face it: our lives are miserable, laborious, and short. We are born, we are given just so much food as will keep the breath in our bodies, and those of us who are capable of it are forced to work to the last atom of our strength; and the very instant that our usefulness has come to an end we are slaughtered with hideous cruelty. No animal in England knows the meaning of happiness or leisure after he is a year old. No animal in England is free. The life of an animal is misery and slavery: that is the plain truth.

"But is this simply part of the order of nature? Is it because this land of ours is so poor that it cannot afford a decent life to those who dwell upon it? No, comrades, a thousand times no! The soil of England is fertile, its climate is good, it is capable of affording food in abundance to an enormously greater number of animals than now inhabit it. This single farm of ours would support a dozen horses, twenty cows, hundreds of sheep-and all of them living in a comfort and a dignity that are now almost beyond our imagining. Why then do we continue in this miserable condition? Because nearly the whole of the produce of our labour is stolen from us by human beings. There, comrades, is the answer to all our problems. It is summed up in a single word-Man. Man is the only real enemy we have. Remove Man from the scene, and the root cause of hunger and overwork is abolished for ever.

"Man is the only creature that consumes without producing. He does not give milk, he does not lay eggs, he is too weak to pull the plough, he cannot run fast enough to catch rabbits. Yet he is lord of all the animals. He sets them to work, he gives back to them the bare minimum that will prevent them from starving, and the rest he keeps for himself. Our labour tills the soil, our dung fertilises it, and yet there is not one of us that owns more than his bare skin. You cows that I see before me, how many thousands of gallons of milk have you given during this last year? And what has happened to that milk which should have been breeding up sturdy calves? Every drop of it has gone down the throats of our enemies. And you hens, how many eggs have you laid in this last year, and how many of those eggs ever hatched into chickens? The rest have all gone to market to bring in money for Jones and his men. And you, Clover, where are those four foals you bore, who should have been the support and pleasure of your old age? Each was sold at a year old-you will never see one of them again. In return for your four confinements and all your labour in the fields, what have you ever had except your bare rations and a stall?

"And even the miserable lives we lead are not allowed to reach their natural span. For myself I do not grumble, for I am one of the lucky ones. I am twelve years old and have had over four hundred children. Such is the natural life of a pig. But no animal escapes the cruel knife in the end. You young porkers who are sitting in front of me, every one of you will scream your lives out at the block within a year. To that horror we all must come-cows, pigs, hens, sheep, everyone. Even the horses and the dogs have no better fate. You, Boxer, the very day that those great muscles of yours lose their power, Jones will sell you to the knacker, who will cut your throat and boil you down for the foxhounds. As for the dogs, when they grow old and toothless, Jones ties a brick round their necks and drowns them in the nearest pond.

"Is it not crystal clear, then, comrades, that all the evils of this life of ours spring from the tyranny of human beings? Only get rid of Man, and the produce of our labour would be our own. almost overnight we could become rich and free. What then must we do? Why, work night and day, body and soul, for the overthrow of the human race! That is my message to you, comrades: Rebellion! I do not know when that Rebellion will come, it might be in a week or in a hundred years, but I know, as surely as I see this straw beneath my feet, that sooner or later justice will be done. Fix your eyes on that, comrades, throughout the short remainder of your lives! And above all, pass on this message of mine to those who come after you, so that future generations shall carry on the struggle until it is victorious.

"And remember, comrades, your resolution must never falter. No argument must lead you astray. Never listen when they tell you that Man and the animals have a common interest, that the prosperity of the one is the prosperity of the others. It is all lies. Man serves the interests of no creature except himself. And among us animals let there be perfect unity, perfect comradeship in the struggle. All men are enemies. All animals are comrades."

At this moment there was a tremendous uproar. While Major was speaking four large rats had crept out of their holes and were sitting on their hindquarters, listening to him. The dogs had suddenly caught sight of them, and it was only by a swift dash for their holes that the rats saved their lives. Major raised his trotter for silence.

"Comrades," he said, "here is a point that must be settled. The wild creatures, such as rats and rabbits-are they our friends or our enemies? Let us put it to the vote. I propose this question to the meeting: Are rats comrades?"

The vote was taken at once, and it was agreed by an overwhelming majority that rats were comrades. There were only four dissentients, the three dogs and the cat, who was afterwards discovered to have voted on both sides. Major continued:

"I have little more to say. I merely repeat, remember always your duty of enmity towards Man and all his ways. Whatever goes upon two legs is an enemy. Whatever goes upon four legs, or has wings, is a friend. And remember also that in fighting against Man, we must not come to resemble him. Even when you have conquered him, do not adopt his vices. No animal must ever live in a house, or sleep in a bed, or wear clothes, or drink alcohol, or smoke tobacco, or touch money, or engage in trade. All the habits of Man are evil. And, above all, no animal must ever tyrannise over his own kind. Weak or strong, clever or simple, we are all brothers. No animal must ever kill any other animal. All animals are equal.

"And now, comrades, I will tell you about my dream of last night. I cannot describe that dream to you. It was a dream of the earth as it will be when Man has vanished. But it reminded me of something that I had long forgotten. Many years ago, when I was a little pig, my mother and the other sows used to sing an old song of which they knew only the tune and the first three words. I had known that tune in my infancy, but it had long since passed out of my mind. Last night, however, it came back to me in my dream. And what is more, the words of the song also came back-words, I am certain, which were sung by the animals of long ago and have been lost to memory for generations. I will sing you that song now, comrades. I am old and my voice is hoarse, but when I have taught you the tune, you can sing it better for yourselves. It is called Beasts of England."

Rhetorical Appeals

Look back at the first paragraph. What do you see happening there? How are both intrinsic and extrinsic ethos operating? What about pathos and logos? Are they doing anything in the first paragraph?

Sticking with the first paragraph, what is Old Major's conception of his audience? Does he unify, create, or speak to a specific audience? How? What language choices has he made that reflect his idea of his audience?

Now, looking at the first three paragraphs, identify specific rhetorical choices that Old Major has made in order to convince his audience.

Do the three rhetorical appeals interact in the first three paragraphs? If so, how?

Considering the entire speech, trace the uses of intrinsic ethos, extrinsic ethos, logos, and pathos. How does each operate throughout the entire speech? How and when do they interact? What effects do they have?

Is any one rhetorical appeal most responsible for the success of the speech? Why or why not?

Stasis Theory

Look at the second paragraph of the speech. In which stasis is Old Major's argument in that paragraph? Why?

Consider the following quote of Old Major: "Why then do we continue in our miserable condition? Because nearly the whole of the produce of our labour is stolen from us by human beings." In which stasis is this argument?

"Remove Man from the scene, and the root cause of hunger and overwork is abolished forever," says Old Major. In which stasis is this argument?

Let's say the core of Old Major's argument is this: *Animals are slaves because of man.* Look at his speech and find how he uses each stasis to support this claim.

Stasis 1:

Stasis 2:

Stasis 3:

Stasis 4:

What do you think are the effects of the ways that Old Major uses the stases? What impact will his use of the stases have on his audience? Why?

III

INQUIRY AND EVIDENCE

ARGUMENT OF INQUIRY—
WHAT IS IT? WHAT'S THE POINT?

Too often, we think of arguments as being about proving someone right or wrong. But an argument of inquiry doesn't aim to prove right or wrong.

What is the point of an argument of inquiry? If your intent isn't to convince someone of something, or persuade readers to act in some way, what is the point of argument? An argument of inquiry seeks to examine our opinions, why we hold them, and whether we want to continue to hold them. You may be tempted to think of argument of inquiry as primarily an argument with yourself, since it's your inquiry that is most significant. And that's a good way to think of the argument. But you don't have to be the sole audience of an argument of inquiry. In argument of inquiry, you might be helping your audience to increase their knowledge, resolve some doubt, consider new interpretations about information, or examine contradictions.

What are you inquiring about? An argument of inquiry is not always about deciding on "facts" or something that can be determined empirically or logically. Unless you are beginning a project with significant empirical evidence, most arguments of inquiry are looking into the truths, values or opinions we hold. In argument of inquiry, we may be seeking, defending, or interrogating a position. Why does some idea shape our experiences? How might we judge our experiences and their relationship to other experiences and other situations?

We might think of argument of inquiry as a dialogue. This dialogue may be with ourselves or with others who are concerned about the issue. Those concerned about the issue are not limited to *our* readers, but may also include those whom *we* are reading. In other words, we can think of an argument of inquiry as the beginning of a conversation with texts that influence us, with things we are reading, hearing, or seeing.

The point of argument of inquiry is to lead us and our readers to the "right" questions, questions that are useful to ask, that will deepen our understanding of a situation. Perhaps they complicate our understanding or critique it. They shouldn't be easy questions, but should be compelling. Through argument of inquiry and the questions we ask, we should test out our opinions and convictions.

Writing argument of inquiry can be quite a challenge, in part because of the importance of thinking about your audience as inquiring with you. But, as is always the case in thinking about readers as you write, you need to think about providing detail for your readers so that they can really join in the inquiry. Without enough detail, your audience won't be able to follow along the lines of inquiry you are considering.

Storytelling may be the most familiar and fundamental of all discourse genres. All of us, no matter our background, can think of stories that we have heard or read. If you were asked to describe examples of stories, you might think of those in movies, television shows, or works of fiction; the familiarity of such examples might lead us to conclude that the purpose of most storytelling is entertainment or diversion. You might also think of stories you have heard from parents or grandparents about when they were young, things they have done in the past, places they have been; these stories tell us about our family history and where we come from.

But thinking of those same examples, have those stories *only* been entertaining or informative? Can stories also be arguments? Can they offer ideas that persuade us to believe in or value something, or even make us decide to take a course of action? Think of what is implied in the phrase "the moral of the story." The idea that stories have a moral is probably most familiar to us through fables or fairy tales. For example, consider the old fable from Aesop, about the tortoise and the hare, in which the hare, so confident that he can beat the tortoise in a race, diverts his attention from the race and dawdles, while the tortoise slowly but steadily carries on to the goal and wins the race because of his persistence. When we hear the story, we realize that it is not just a silly story about animals; it becomes an observation about how and why people act the way they do. We see it as making an argument about human behavior. Thinking of stories as arguments, then, requires us to think about this everyday genre in a different way. While we may think of stories as primarily telling details of *what* happened as opposed to *why* something happened or why the occurrence has significance, the most interesting stories tell not only what but also prompt us to think about how, why, and why it matters.

We might be accustomed to thinking of stories and argumentative papers as being distinct genres. But both can argue, and both have much in common. Stories—particularly stories that narrate events from a first-person point-of-view—make observations about what happens and speculate about why things happen, just as arguments posit observations and hypotheses about those observations. Indeed, among the selections in the **Readings** (Section VIII) at the end of this volume, you'll see that the researched, academic arguments use stories in various ways. In particular, narrative is used to help establish a sense of inquiry; that is, telling a story is often a good way to demonstrate your inquiry and to engage your reader in sharing that sense of inquiry with you.

The "Overview and Appreciation" of the "Knowing Our History" report, for instance, begins by telling a story about how the report came into being. Prof. Ira Berlin tells of the inquiry that established the exigence for the course and its subsequent report, and relates the details of that inquiry as a story. He begins with the phrase "It was no secret," a phrase that suggests what will be revealed and has a narrative tone to it:

It was no secret that slavery had some relationship to the founding of the Maryland Agricultural College, predecessor of the University of Maryland, as the university celebrated its 150th anniversary in 2006. Charles Benedict Calvert, the prime mover in the college's creation, was a slaveholding planter, as were many of the members of the state legislature that authorized the college's establishment and the trustees who governed the new institution. Some of the first faculty members held slaves, and many of the students came from slaveholding families. It could be no other way in Maryland, as slavery touched every aspect of life. Slaveholders, who controlled much of the state's wealth, transformed that wealth into political power, which, in turn, allowed them to shape the state's culture. (ii)

In this opening paragraph, Berlin reports the broad relationship between the University and slavery, but does so with select, telling details. Also in this opening paragraph, he shows keen awareness of his audience: members of the current University specifically, but also others who may be affected by "the state's culture"—that is, Marylanders past and present.

In the next paragraph, Berlin continues to speak to and shape a sense of the various parts of his audience. Who might care about this issue? Can we tell by what stories are told or the way the story of the project is shaped? Look at Berlin's second paragraph:

Nonetheless, many students, faculty and friends of the university in 2006 were appalled to learn of its roots in the odious institution of chattel bondage. Some believed that information had been withheld from them in an effort to whitewash the university's past. Others shared the embarrassment of Americans who had but recently discovered that the entire lower end of Manhattan was underlaid by a slave cemetery, or that President George Washington housed his slaves on the site of the Liberty Bell in Philadelphia, or that the national Capitol in Washington was constructed in part by slaves. Still others saw no special revelation in the "discovery" of the university's slave past, but wanted a full accounting. Did slaves clear the land, build the buildings and feed the students at the newly established Maryland Agricultural College?

Broadly speaking, we can see that Berlin thought his audience to be people with some connection to the University. We can also see that he addresses their connection and interest in the issue, regardless of how they believe we in the 21st century should feel about 150 year old actions; that is, he addresses people's interest rather than their views on how we should respond to the past. Berlin's artful prose can draw in not only various positions on the issue but also various elements of the story of slavery in America.

Berlin uses narrative elements throughout this brief overview. He notes that students in History 429 had to, in a sense, figure out the "story" of slavery and its many characters in order to come to some kind of conclusion about their research: "Piecing together those lives requires not only a close reading of the sources but also an imaginative reconstruction of a world that is no more. History 429 thought its way back to mid-19th century Maryland" (ii). His overview also uses narrative to offer a summary of the report itself. He tells about the complex lives of founders Calvert and Hallowell and offers us a brief version of their stories. Berlin has called us into the inquiry as members of the University and uses stories—of the state, of the course, of the founders—to whet our appetite to read more.

Prof. Eric Uslaner also begins his article, "Trust, Civic Engagement, and the Internet," with two narrative anecdotes. Without any formal introduction, these first two paragraphs plunge the reader into the controversy about the "good" and the "bad" internet that Uslaner explores in his research. Consider how you as a reader react to these two anecdotes. Chances are, they feel very familiar; you have heard stories like them about the internet, and so it is easy for you as a reader to be drawn into Uslaner's inquiry. "Yes," you might think, "there are times when the internet is a great place and times when it is a dangerous place." Uslaner's anecdotes are not long; they offer only minimal detail rather than extensive description. Consider whether you would be more persuaded by more detail, or whether this minimal detail is persuasive precisely because it offers enough for us, as readers, to fill our own experiences of the internet into Uslaner's broad framework. It might be the case that the minimal detail here actually allows for more reader identification; we see just enough to recognize the situations he introduces and then we fill in our own experiences, perhaps engaging *more* in his inquiry.

What else can we say about Uslaner's audience here? These opening anecdotes are broadly familiar enough for nearly any contemporary American reader to recognize, but is his audience nearly any contemporary American reader? After the first two paragraphs, he asks the question "Which is the real Internet, the good Net or the bad Net?" (224). This is not a rhetorical question; Uslaner invites us into his inquiry very directly. From here, he recognizes the two sides of this question and those who stand on both sides, those he later in the paragraph refers to as the "[s]upporters of the good Net approach" and "adherents to the bad Net theory." Between these two sides, however, he also refers to "we" in his reference to Putnam's ideas about decreasing membership in groups. Uslaner will continue to refer to "we" Americans and will also address "you" in his narrative scenarios repeatedly, as when he writes "When you enter an Internet chat room, you can hide your identity" (225). Again and again throughout the article, Uslaner draws his readers into his inquiry and his ideas in this way, asking us to consider our experiences of the Net. But does this mean that every "you" is Uslaner's primary audience? Not exactly. He writes to an academic audience, even if his tone is somewhat less formal than we might expect from a political studies journal. But don't mistake the readability of Uslaner's prose with the sophistication of his audience; he expects his audience to be familiar with his references, to understand his use of data, to follow the complexity of his arguments. Using narratives helps him take a complicated issue and address it in a meaningful way. You can use that approach with any kind of argument, to any kind of audience.

Uslaner's use of narrative shows us another strategy often employed by academic writers. He recycles one of his opening anecdotes in another article that we have included here, "Trust Online, Trust Offline." In that article, written for a different audience, he uses the anecdote about Alex Salcedo and his family not in the beginning but in the body of his argument. Uslaner uses another narrative earlier in this short argument. After an opening paragraph that introduces the issue and its exigence—again with a clear question articulating his inquiry— in the second paragraph, Uslaner employs a narrative about himself discussing his work as a way to contextualize his research. He mentions a lunch with a colleague at which they discussed Uslaner's work. Later in the article, he brings up the discussion with the colleague again:

My colleague asked: You say trust is not based upon experience, but what about the Internet? All sorts of danger lurks there; just to get online one must establish a firewall, because people are constantly trying to hack into your system. He runs a virus checker constantly and at least once a week uses a spyware search utility to see which companies are trying to track his every move. His email has a spam filter to isolate the dozens of daily invitations to pornographic Web sites and other attempts to sell him stuff he doesn't want. Then there is the teenager haven of instant messaging, which, we now learn, is a major source of identity theft online. So how can we expect people to suffer through all of this insecurity and still believe that most people can be trusted? My colleague thinks the Internet is a source of trust and mistrust. But the Internet really depends upon trust rather than creates trust. (28)

Uslaner uses his colleague as a character to serve as a kind of "everyone," a stand-in for the reader here who no doubt is asking the same kinds of questions. We identify with the character of the friend, and so in putting that character into the story, Uslaner has accomplished many things rhetorically: not only has he called up the situation at issue, but he actively engages us in its exigence and his inquiry, all while developing an *ethos* of friendly credibility.

But narratives are not always intended for audiences who have experiences similar to those of the narrator. Sometimes, narratives are used to tell a story that is very different from the reader's experience; indeed, in a situation in which readers may not directly identify with the experiences of the teller, narrative is a good genre to employ because we *are* all familiar with the idea of a story and characters, and so we take in a story more readily than we might take in information otherwise. Such is the case with Martin Luther King, Jr.'s "Letter from a Birmingham Jail." Here, Rev. King addresses the clergymen who have written the public statement calling for an end to the demonstrations in Birmingham. In their statement, we can see the way the clergymen, from a range of denominations and faiths, draw on a common bond of religious beliefs and a shared need for a solution to the racial issues of the area. King uses a similar tactic here, drawing on stories about those such as "Apostle Paul [who] left his little village of Tarsus and carried the gospel" across his world as analogies of the current situation in Birmingham. Soon after, King uses the same technique we saw in Berlin's "Overview and Appreciation" of recounting the story of how the problem he addresses arose. Following on one of King's famous lines, "Injustice anywhere is a threat to justice everywhere," and on his statement of the four basic steps of any nonviolent campaign, King narrates the series of events that led to his coming to Birmingham. The characters in his story are both specifically named— Rev. Shuttlesworth, Mr. Connor—and unnamed; the greatest of the unnamed here are the "we" King refers to repeatedly. This "we," unlike the "we" of Uslaner's tales of the Internet, does *not* refer to the direct addresses, the ""Fellow Clergymen" of King's salutation. Who are the "we" of King's story? Though never explicitly named, we recognize that the "we" are those who fought injustice with King, specifically the Alabama Christian Movement for Human Rights. But the actual "we" would have included many people who were not explicitly members of that organization and, more importantly, the "we" calls in all of King's readers. Using "we" is a clear rhetorical tactic here because readers insert themselves into a "we." In a sense, King here is building his audience with that pronoun.

Because King's primary undertaking here is to refute the appeal of the clergymen's statement, it makes sense that he begins with some kind of common ground, with the familiar references to Christian stories and his own recounting of the events leading up to the situation.
King's direct audience likely does know the story of how the demonstrations came to occur,
though they may not "know" the story from King's perspective, as King is telling it. But later
in the "Letter," after he has refuted some of their claims, he uses other narratives to appeal to
his audience, to draw in their emotions. Interestingly, although King's audience has not experienced these stories, he uses "you" as the pronoun to address them:

> I guess it is easy for those who have never felt the stinging darts of segregation to say wait.
> But when you have seen vicious mobs lynch your mothers and fathers at will and drown
> your sisters and brothers at whim; when you have seen hate filled policemen curse, kick,
> brutalize, and even kill your black brothers and sisters with impunity; when you see the
> vast majority of your twenty million Negro brothers smothering in an air-tight cage of
> poverty in the midst of an affluent society; when you suddenly find your tongue twisted
> and your speech stammering as you seek to explain to your six-year-old daughter why she
> can't go to the public amusement park that has just been advertised on television, and see
> the tears welling up in her little eyes when she is told that Funtown is closed to colored
> children, and see the depressing clouds of inferiority begin to form in her little mental sky,
> and see her begin to distort her little personality by unconsciously developing a bitterness
> toward white people; when you have to concoct an answer for a five-year-old son asking
> in agonizing pathos: "Daddy, why do white people treat colored people so mean?"; when
> you take a cross country drive and find it necessary to sleep night after night in the uncom-
> fortable corners of your automobile because no motel will accept you; when you are humil-
> iated day in and day out by nagging signs reading "white" and "colored"; when your first
> name becomes "nigger" and your middle name becomes "boy" (however old you are) and
> your last name becomes "John," and when your wife and mother are never given the
> respected title "Mrs."' When you are harried by day and haunted by night by the fact that
> you are a Negro, living constantly at tip-toe stance never quite knowing what to expect
> next, and plagued with inner fears and outer resentments; when you are forever fighting
> a degenerating sense of "nobodiness"; —then you will understand why we find it difficult
> to wait.

King's very point in this long sentence filled with small narratives is that his direct readers
don't know these stories, and so he tells them, using "you" as a pronoun, to insert his audience
into these unfamiliar situations to make them feel the experience as best as he is able.

Berlin, Uslaner and King give us different examples of narratives and different ways to
address those narratives to audiences, but these are only three out of many possible examples;
in the end, you must decide for your own essay who your audience is, how you will begin, how
you will address your audience, and how you will depict your experiences. But regardless of
whom your narrative is for and how it will be structured, think carefully about the relationship between the experiences that you describe and the argument of inquiry for which those
experiences serve as evidence. In particular, be sure that you describe your experiences in

enough detail that readers can be persuaded to accept your experiences as credible. As we saw in the above examples, that does *not* necessarily mean making your narrative long, but, rather, means that you **show** your readers what happened rather than just **telling** them, that you engage them in your story by using details that make it easy for them to imagine what it was like to have the experience. Finally, think about how you can signal the relationship between the experience and the inquiry. How will you show the transition from your narration of what happened to you as an individual to your inquiry about how your observations relate to larger concerns? Is it simply about changing from declarative sentences to questions? Can you also show the shift in pronoun use (from focusing on "I," "me," and "my," to emphasizing "we," "our," and "us"), as Berlin, Uslaner and King do? Combining a number of rhetorical strategies to draw in your audience will probably work best.

ACTIONS

from *Style: Lessons in Clarity and Grace*

Suit the action to the word, the word to the action.

—William Shakespeare, HAMLET, **3**.2

I am unlikely to trust a sentence that comes easily.

—William Gass

UNDERSTANDING THE PRINCIPLES OF CLARITY

Making Judgments

We have words enough to praise writing we like: *clear, direct, concise,* and more than enough to abuse writing we don't: *unclear, indirect, abstract, dense, complex.* We can use those words to distinguish these two sentences:

> 1a. The cause of our schools' failure at teaching basic skills is not understanding the influence of cultural background on learning.

> 1b. Our schools have failed to teach basic skills because they do not understand how cultural background influences the way a child learns.

Most of us would call (1a) too complex, (1b) clearer, more direct. But those words don't refer to anything *in* those sentences; they describe how those sentences make us *feel.* When we say that (1a) is *unclear,* we mean that *we* have a hard time understanding it; we say it's *dense* when *we* struggle to read it.

The problem is to understand what is *in* those two sentences that makes us feel as we do. Only then can we rise above our too-good understanding of our own writing to know when our readers will think it needs revising. To do that, you have to know what counts as a well-told story. (To profit from this lesson and the next three, you must be able to identify VERBS, SIMPLE SUBJECTS, and WHOLE SUBJECTS. See the Glossary.)

Telling Stories About Characters and Their Actions

This story has a problem:

> 2a. Once upon a time, as a walk through the woods was taking place on the part of Little Red Riding Hood, the Wolf's jump out from behind a tree occurred, causing her fright.

We prefer something closer to this:

✓ 2b. Once upon a time, Little Red Riding Hood was walking through the woods, when the Wolf jumped out from behind a tree and frightened her.

Most readers think (2b) tells its story more clearly than (2a), because it follows two principles:

- Its main characters are subjects of verbs.
- Those verbs express specific actions.

Those two principles seem simple, but they need some explanation.

Principle of Clarity 1: Make main characters subjects.   Look at the subjects in (2a). The simple subjects (boldfaced) are *not* the main characters (italicized):

2a. Once upon a time, as a **walk** through the woods was taking place on the part of *Little Red Riding Hood, the Wolf's* **jump** out from behind a tree occurred, causing *her* fright.

The subjects in that sentence do not name its characters; they name actions expressed in the abstract NOUNS *walk* and *jump:*

SUBJECT	VERB
a **walk** through the woods	was taking place
the *Wolf's* **jump** out from behind a tree	occurred

The whole subject of *occurred* does have a character *in* it: the ***Wolf's** jump,* but *the Wolf* is only attached to the simple subject *jump;* it is not *the* subject.

Contrast those abstract subjects with the concrete subjects (italicized and boldfaced) in (2b):

2b. Once upon a time, ***Little Red Riding Hood*** was walking through the woods, when ***the Wolf*** jumped out from behind a tree and frightened *her.*

The subjects and the main characters are now the same words:

SUBJECT/CHARACTER	VERB
Little Red Riding Hood	was walking
the Wolf	jumped

Principle of Clarity 2: Make important actions verbs.   Now look at how the actions and verbs differ in (2a): its actions are not expressed in verbs but in abstract nouns (actions are bold-faced; verbs are capitalized):

2a. Once upon a time, as a **walk** through the woods WAS TAKING place on the part of Little Red Riding Hood, the Wolf's **jump** out from behind a tree OCCURRED, causing her **fright**.

Note how vague the verbs are: *was taking, occurred*. In (2b), the clearer sentence, the verbs name specific actions:

✓ 2b. Once upon a time, Little Red Riding Hood WAS WALKING through the woods, when the Wolf JUMPED out from behind a tree and FRIGHTENED her.

> ***Here's the point:*** In (2a), the sentence that seems wordy and indirect, the two main characters, Little Red Riding Hood and the Wolf, are not subjects, and their actions— *walk, jump,* and *fright*—are *not* verbs. In (2b) the more direct sentence, those two main characters are subjects and their main actions are verbs. That's why we prefer (2b).

Fairy Tales and Writing for Grown-ups

Writing in college or on the job may seem distant from fairy tales, but it's not, because most sentences tell stories. Compare these two:

3a. The Federalists' argument in regard to the destabilization of government by popular democracy was based on their belief in the tendency of factions to further their self-interest at the expense of the common good.

✓ 3b. The Federalists argued that popular democracy destabilized government, because they believed that factions tended to further their self-interest at the expense of the common good.

We can analyze those two sentences as we did the ones about Little Red Riding Hood and the Wolf.

Sentence (3a) feels dense for two reasons. First, its characters are not subjects. Its simple subject is *argument*, but the characters are *Federalists, popular democracy, government,* and *factions* (characters are italicized; the simple subject is boldfaced):

3a. *The Federalists'* **argument** in regard to the destabilization of *government* by *popular democracy* was based on *their* belief in the tendency of *factions* to further *their* self-interest at the expense of the common good.

Second, most of the actions (boldfaced) are not verbs (capitalized), but rather abstract nouns (also boldfaced):

3a. The Federalists' **argument** in regard to the **destabilization** of government by popular democracy WAS BASED on their **belief** in the **tendency** of factions to FURTHER their self-interest at the expense of the common good.

Notice the long whole subject of (3a) and how little meaning is expressed by its main verb *was based:*

WHOLE SUBJECT	VERB
The Federalists' argument in regard to the destabilization of government by popular democracy	was based

Readers think (3b) is clearer for two reasons: first, the actions (boldfaced) are verbs (capitalized):

3b. The Federalists ARGUED that popular democracy DESTABILIZED government, because they BELIEVED that factions TENDED TO FURTHER their self-interest at the expense of the common good.

Second, its characters (italicized) *are* subjects (boldfaced):

3b. The *Federalists* argued that *popular democracy* destabilized government, because *they* believed that *factions* tended to further *their* self-interest at the expense of the common good.

Note that all those subjects are short and specific:

WHOLE SUBJECT/CHARACTER	VERB/ACTION
the Federalists	argued
popular democracy	destabilized
they	believed
factions	tended to further

In the rest of this lesson, we look at actions and verbs; in the next, at characters and subjects.

VERBS AND ACTIONS

Our principle is this:

A sentence seems clear when its important actions are in verbs.

Look at how sentences (4a) and (4b) express their actions. In (4a), actions (boldfaced) are not verbs (capitalized); they are nouns:

4a. Our **lack** of data PREVENTED **evaluation** of UN **actions** in **targeting** funds to areas most in **need** of **assistance**.

In (4b), on the other hand, the actions are almost all verbs:

✓ 4b. Because we LACKED data, we could not EVALUATE whether the UN HAD TARGETED funds to areas that most NEEDED ASSISTANCE.

Readers will think your writing is dense if you use lots of abstract nouns, especially those derived from verbs and ADJECTIVES, nouns ending in *-tion, -ment, -ence,* and so on, *especially when you make those abstract nouns the subjects of verbs.*

A noun derived from a verb or adjective has a technical name: *nominalization.* The word illustrates its meaning: When we nominalize *nominalize,* we create the nominalization *nominalization.* Here are a few examples:

VERB	→	NOMINALIZATION	ADJECTIVE	→	NOMINALIZATION
discover	→	discovery	careless	→	carelessness
resist	→	resistance	different	→	difference
react	→	reaction	proficient	→	proficiency

We can also nominalize a verb by adding *-ing* (making it a GERUND):

She flies → her flying   We sang → our singing

Some nominalizations and verbs are identical:

hope → hope   result → result   repair → repair

We **REQUEST** that you **REVIEW** the data.

Our **request** IS that you DO a **review** of the data.

(Some actions also hide out in adjectives: *It is applicable* → *it applies* Some others: *indicative, dubious, argumentative, deserving.*)

No element of style more characterizes turgid writing, writing that feels abstract, indirect, and difficult, than lots of nominalizations, especially as the subjects of verbs.

Here's the point: In grade school, we learned that subjects are characters (or "doers") and that verbs are actions. That's often true:

subject	verb	object
We	discussed	the problem.
doer	action	

But it is not true for this almost synonymous sentence:

subject	verb			
The problem	was	the topic	of our	discussion.
			doer	action

We can move characters and actions around in a sentence, and subjects and verbs don't have to name any particular kind of thing at all. But when in most of your sentences you match characters to subjects and actions with verbs, readers are likely to think your prose is clear, direct, and readable.

Analyze the subject/character and verb/action in these sentences:

There is opposition among many voters to nuclear power plants based on a belief of their threat to human health.

Many voters oppose nuclear power plants because they believe that such plants threaten human health.

If you aren't sure whether you can distinguish verbs, adjectives, and nominalizations, turn these verbs and adjectives into nominalizations, and the nominalizations into adjectives and verbs. Remember that some verbs and nominalizations have the same form:

Poverty predictably **causes** social problems.

Poverty is a predictable **cause** of social problems.

analysis	believe	attempt	conclusion	evaluate
suggest	approach	comparison	define	discuss
expression	failure	intelligent	thorough	appearance
decrease	improve	increase	accuracy	careful
emphasize	explanation	description	clear	examine

Create sentences using verbs and adjectives from Exercise 2. Then rewrite them using the corresponding nominalizations (keep the meaning the same). For example, using *suggest, discuss,* and *careful,* write:

I SUGGEST that we DISCUSS the issue CAREFULLY.

Then rewrite that sentence into its nominalized form:

My **suggestion** is that our **discussion** of the issue be done with **care**.

Only when you see how a clear sentence can be made unclear will you understand why it seemed clear in the first place.

DIAGNOSIS AND REVISION

You can use the principles of verbs as actions and subjects as characters to explain why your readers judge your prose as they do. But more important, you can also use them to identify sentences that your readers would want you to revise, and then revise them. Revision is a three-step process: diagnose, analyze, rewrite.

1. **Diagnose**

   a. Ignoring short (four- or five-word) introductory phrases, underline the first seven or eight words in each sentence.

      <u>The outsourcing of high-tech work to Asia by</u> corporations means the loss of jobs for many American workers.

   b. Then look for two things:
      • You underline abstract nouns as simple subjects (boldfaced).

         The ***outsourcing*** <u>of high-tech work to Asia by</u> corporations means the loss of jobs for many American workers.

      • You read seven, eight, or more words before getting to a verb.

         <u>The outsourcing of high-tech work to Asia by</u> corporations (10 words) **means** the loss of jobs for many American workers.

2. **Analyze**

   a. Decide who your main characters are, particularly flesh-and-blood (more about this in the next lesson).

      The outsourcing of high-tech work to Asia by **corporations** means the loss of jobs for **many American workers.**

   b. Then look for the actions that those characters perform, especially actions in nominalizations, those abstract nouns derived from verbs.

      The **outsourcing** of high-tech work to Asia by corporations means the **loss** of jobs for many American workers.

3. **Rewrite**

   a. If the actions are nominalizations, make them verbs.

      outsourcing → outsource   loss → lose

   b. Make the characters the subjects of those verbs.

      corporations outsource   American workers lose

   c. Rewrite the sentence with SUBORDINATING CONJUNCTIONS like *because, if, when, although, why, how, whether,* or *that.*

      ✓ Many middle-class American workers are losing their jobs, **because** corporations are outsourcing their high-tech work to Asia.

Some Common Patterns

You can quickly spot and revise five common patterns of nominalizations.

1. The nominalization is the subject of an empty verb such as *be, seems, has,* etc.:

> The **intention** of the committee IS to audit the records.

  a. Change the nominalization to a verb:

> intention → intend

  b. Find a character that would be the subject of that verb:

> The intention of **the committee** is to audit the records.

  c. Make that character the subject of the new verb:

> ✓ *The committee* **INTENDS** to audit the records.

2. The nominalization follows an empty verb:

> The *agency* CONDUCTED an **investigation** into the matter.

  a. Change the nominalization to a verb:

> investigation → investigate

  b. Replace the empty verb with the new verb:

> conducted → investigated

> ✓ The *agency* **INVESTIGATED** the matter.

3. One nominalization is the subject of an empty verb and a second nominalization follows an empty verb:

> Our **loss** in sales WAS a result of their **expansion** of outlets.

  a. Revise the nominalizations into verbs:

> loss → lose   expansion → expand

  b. Identify the characters that would be the subjects of those verbs:

> **Our** loss in sales was a result of **their** expansion of outlets.

  c. Make those characters subjects of those verbs:

> we lose   they expand

  d. Link the new CLAUSES with a logical connection:
- To express simple cause: *because, since, when*
- To express conditional cause: *if, provided that, so long as*
- To contradict expected causes: *though, although, unless*

Our **loss** in sales	→	*We* **LOST** sales
was the result of	→	**because**
their **expansion** of outlets	→	*they* **EXPANDED** outlets

4. **A nominalization follows *there is* or *there are:***

> There IS no **need** for *our* further **study** of this problem.

   a. Change the nominalization to a verb:

> need → need study → study

   b. Identify the character that should be the subject of the verb:

> There is no need for **our** further study of this problem.

   c. Make that character the subject of the verb:

> no need → we need not   our study → we study

> ✓ *We* **NEED** not **STUDY** this problem further.

5. **Two or three nominalizations in a row are joined by prepositions:**

> We did a **review** of the **evolution** of the brain.

   a. Turn the first nominalization into a verb:

> review → review

   b. Either leave the second nominalization as it is or turn it into a verb in a clause beginning with *how* or *why:*

> evolution of the brain → how the brain evolved

> ✓ First, *we* **REVIEWED** the **evolution** of the *brain.*

> ✓ First, *we* **REVIEWED** how *the brain* **EVOLVED**.

 QUICK TIP

> When you start to revise a complicated sentence, it will probably fit one of these three patterns: *X because Y*, *If X, then Y*, *Although X, Y*. Think of the meaning of the sentence, then try out these patterns.

Some Happy Consequences

When you consistently rely on verbs to express key actions, your readers benefit in many ways:

1. Your sentences are more concrete, because they will have concrete subjects and verbs. Compare:

> There was an affirmative **decision** for **expansion.**

> ✓ *The Director* **DECIDED** to **EXPAND** the program.

2. Your sentences are more concise. When you use nominalizations, you have to add articles like *a* and *the* and prepositions such as *of, by,* and *in.* You don't need them when you use verbs and conjunctions (italicized):

> A **revision** *of* the program WILL RESULT *in* **increases** *in* our **efficiency** *in the* **servicing** *of* clients.

> ✓ *If* we **revise** the program, we **can serve** clients more **efficiently.**

3. **The logic of your sentences is clearer.** When you nominalize verbs, you have to link actions with fuzzy prepositions and phrases such as *of, by,* and *on the part of.* But when you use verbs, you link clauses with precise subordinating conjunctions such as *because, although,* and *if:*

> Our more effective presentation of our study resulted in our success, despite an earlier start by others.
>
> ✓ **Although** others started earlier, we succeeded **because** we presented our study more effectively.

4. **Your sentence tells a more coherent story.** This next sequence of actions distorts their chronology. (The numbers refer to the real sequence of events.)

> Decisions[4] in regard to administration[5] of medication despite inability[2] of an irrational patient appearing[1] in a Trauma Center to provide legal consent[3] rest with the attending physician alone.

When we revise those actions into verbs and reorder them, we get a more coherent narrative:

> ✓ When a patient appears[1] in a Trauma Center and behaves[2] so irrationally that he cannot legally consent[3] to treatment, only the attending physician can decide[4] whether to medicate[5] him.

A COMMON PROBLEM SOLVED

You've probably had this experience: you think you've written something good, but your reader thinks otherwise. You wonder whether that person is just being difficult, but you bite your tongue and try to fix what should be clear to anyone who can read Dr. Seuss. When that happens to me (regularly, I might add), I almost always realize—eventually—that my readers are right, that they see where my writing needs work better than I do.

Why are we so often right about the writing of others and so often wrong about our own? It is because we all read into our own writing what we want readers to get out of it. That explains why two readers can disagree about the clarity of the same piece of writing: a reader who knows its content better is likely to think the passage is more clearly written than is a reader who knows less about it. Both are right. Degrees of clarity are in the eye of more or less informed beholders.

That is why we need to look at our own writing in a way that is almost mechanical, that sidesteps our too-good understanding of it. The quickest way is to underline the first seven or eight words of every sentence. If you don't see in those words a character as a subject and a verb as a specific action, you have a candidate for revision.

 QUICK TIP

When you start revising a longer piece of work, look first at those passages that were hard to write because you didn't fully understand your ideas. We all tend to write badly when we're unsure about what we want to say or how to say it.

One sentence in each of these pairs is clear, expressing characters as subjects and actions as verbs; the other is indirect, with actions in nominalizations and characters often not in subjects. First, identify which is which. Then circle nominalizations and highlight verbs. If you are good at grammar, underline subjects. Then put a "c" over characters that seem to perform actions.

1a. Some people argue that atmospheric carbon dioxide does not elevate global temperature.

1b. There has been speculation by educators about the role of the family in improving educational achievement.

2a. Smoking during pregnancy may cause fetal injury.

2b. When we write concisely, readers understand easily.

3a. Researchers have identified the AIDS virus but failed to develop a vaccine to immunize those at risk.

3b. Attempts by economists at defining full employment have been met with failure.

4a. Complaints by editorial writers about voter apathy rarely offer suggestions about dispelling it.

4b. Although critics claim that children who watch a lot of television tend to become less able readers, no one has demonstrated that to be true.

5a. The loss of market share to Japan by domestic automakers resulted in the disappearance of hundreds of thousands of jobs.

5b. When educators discover how to use computer-assisted instruction, our schools will teach complex subjects more effectively.

6a. We need to know which parts of our national forests are being logged most extensively so that we can save virgin stands at greatest risk.

6b. There is a need for an analysis of library use to provide a reliable base for the projection of needed resources.

7a. Many professional athletes fail to realize that they are unprepared for life after stardom because their teams protect them from the problems that the rest of us adjust to every day.

7b. Colleges now have an understanding that yearly tuition increases are now impossible because of strong parental resistance to the soaring cost of higher education.

Now revise the nominalized sentences in Exercise 4 into sentences with verbs. Use its paired verbal version as a model. For example, if the verbal sentence begins with *when,* begin your revision with *when:*

Sentence to revise:	**2a.** Smoking during pregnancy may lead to fetal injury.
Model:	**2b.** When we WRITE concisely, readers UNDERSTAND more easily.
Your revision:	**2a.** When pregnant women SMOKE . . .

EXERCISE 6

Revise these next sentences so that the nominalizations are verbs and characters are their subjects. In (1) through (5), characters are italicized and nominalizations are boldfaced.

1. *Lincoln's* **hope** was for the **preservation** of the Union without war, but the *South's* **attack** on Fort Sumter made war an **inevitability.**
2. **Attempts** were made on the part of the *president's aides* to assert *his* **immunity** from a *congressional* subpoena.
3. There were **predictions** by *business executives* that the *economy* would experience a quick **revival.**
4. *Your* **analysis** of my report omits any data in **support** of *your* **criticism** of my **findings.**
5. The *health care industry's* **inability** to exert cost **controls** could lead to the *public's* **decision** that *congressional* action is needed.

In sentences 6 through 10, the agents are italicized; find the actions and revise.

6. A *papal* appeal was made to the world's rich *nations* for assistance to those facing the threat of *African* starvation.
7. Attempts at explaining increases in *voter* participation in this year's elections were made by *several candidates.*
8. The agreement by the *class* on the reading list was based on the assumption that there would be tests on only certain selections.
9. There was no independent *business-sector* study of the cause of the sudden increase in the trade surplus.
10. An understanding as to the need for controls over drinking on campus was recognized by *fraternities.*

In 11 through 15, only the nominalizations are boldfaced; find or invent the characters and revise.

11. There is **uncertainty** at the CIA about North Korean **intentions** as to **cessation** of missile **testing**.
12. Physical **conditioning** of the team is the **responsibility** of the coaching staff.
13. **Contradictions** among the data require an **explanation.**
14. The Dean's **rejection** of our proposal was a **disappointment** but not a **surprise** because our **expectation** was that a **decision** had been made.
15. Their **performance** of the play was marked by **enthusiasm** but lacked intelligent **staging.**

EXERCISE 7

Revise these sentences. At the end of each is a hint. For example:

> Congress's **reduction** of the deficit resulted in the **decline** of interest rates. [because]
> ✓ Interest rates DECLINED because Congress REDUCED the deficit.

1. The use of models in teaching prose style does not result in improvements of clarity and directness in student writing. [Although we use . . .]
2. Precision in plotting the location of building foundations enhances the possibility of its accurate reconstruction. [When we precisely plot . . .]
3. Any departures by the members from established procedures may cause termination of membership by the Board. [If members . . .]
4. A student's lack of socialization into a field may lead to writing problems because of his insufficient understanding about arguments by professionals in that field. [When . . ., . . ., because . . .]
5. The successful implementation of a new curriculum depends on the cooperation of faculty with students in setting achievable goals within a reasonable time. [To implement . . ., . . .]

TWO QUALIFICATIONS

Useful Nominalizations

I have so relentlessly urged you to turn nominalizations into verbs that you might think you should never use one. But in fact, you can't write well without them. The trick is to know which to keep and which to revise. Keep these:

1. **A nominalization as a short subject refers to a previous sentence:**

    ✓ **These arguments** all depend on a single unproven claim.

    ✓ **This decision** can lead to positive outcomes.

    Those nominalizations link one sentence to another in a cohesive flow.

2. **A short nominalization replaces an awkward** *The fact that:*

    The fact that she ACKNOWLEDGED the problem impressed me.

    ✓ Her **acknowledgment** of the problem impressed me.

    But then, why not this:

    ✓ *She* IMPRESSED me when *she* ACKNOWLEDGED the problem.

3. **A nominalization names what would be the OBJECT of the verb:**

    I accepted *what she* REQUESTED [that is, *She requested* **something**].

    ✓ I accepted her **request.**

This kind of nominalization feels more concrete than an abstract one. However, contrast *request* above with this next sentence, where *request* is more of an action:

> Her **request** for **assistance** CAME after the deadline.

✓ She REQUESTED **assistance** after the deadline.

4. **A nominalization refers to a concept so familiar to your readers that to them, it is a virtual character (more about this in the next lesson):**

✓ Few problems have so divided us as **abortion** on **demand.**

✓ The Equal Rights **Amendment** was an issue in past **elections.**

✓ **Taxation** without **representation** did not spark the American **Revolution.**

Those nominalizations name familiar concepts: *abortion* on *demand, amendment, election, taxation, representation, revolution.* You must develop an eye for nominalizations expressing a common idea and those that you can revise into a verb:

> There is a **demand** for a **repeal** of the **inheritance** tax.

✓ We DEMAND that Congress REPEAL the **inheritance** tax.

Clarity, Not Simplemindedness

Your readers want you to write clearly, but not in Dick-and-Jane sentences. This was written by a student aspiring to academic sophistication:

> After Czar Alexander II's emancipation of Russian serfs in 1861, many freed peasants chose to live on communes for purposes of cooperation in agricultural production as well as for social stability. Despite some communes attempts at economic and social equalization through the strategy of imposing low economic status on the peasants, which resulted in their reduction to near poverty, a centuries-long history of social distinctions even among serfs prevented social equalization.

In his struggle to write clearly, he revised that paragraph into something that sounds as if it were written by a 12-year-old:

> In 1861, Czar Alexander II emancipated the Russian serfs. Many of them chose to live on agricultural communes. There they thought they could cooperate with one another in agricultural production. They could also create a stable social structure. The leaders of some of these communes tried to equalize the peasants economically and socially. As one strategy, they tried to impose on all a low economic status. That reduced them to near poverty. However, the communes failed to equalize them socially. This happened because even serfs had made social distinctions among themselves for centuries.

Some argue that all sentences should be short, no more than 20 or so words. But most mature ideas are too complicated to express in Dick-and-Jane sentences. When that student applied those principles to his primer-style sentences, he revised again:

After Russian serfs were emancipated by Czar Alexander II in 1861, many chose to live on agricultural communes, hoping they could cooperate in working the land and establish a stable social structure. At first, some who led the communes tried to equalize the new peasants socially and economically by imposing on everyone a low economic status, a strategy that reduced them to near poverty. But the communes failed to equalize them socially because the serfs had for centuries observed their own social distinctions.

Those sentences are long but clear, because the writer consistently aligned major characters with subjects and actions with verbs.

SUMMING UP

We can represent these principles graphically. As we read, we mentally integrate two levels of sentence structure. One is a relatively fixed grammatical sequence of subject and verb (the empty box is for everything that follows the verb):

Fixed	Subject	Verb	————

The other level of sentence structure is based on its characters and their actions. They have no fixed order, but readers prefer them matched to subjects and verbs. We can graphically combine those principles:

Fixed	Subject	Verb	————
Variable	Character	Action	————

Keep in mind that readers want to see characters not just *in* a subject, as in these two:

The ***president's* veto of the bill** infuriated Congress.

The **veto of the bill by *the president*** infuriated Congress.

Instead, they want to see the character *as* the subject, like this:

✓ When ***the president***$_{subject}$ VETOED$_{verb}$ the bill, ***he***$_{subject}$ INFURIATED$_{verb}$ Congress.

When you frustrate those expectations, you make readers work harder than they should have to. So keep these principles in mind as you revise:

1. Express actions in verbs:

The **intention** of the committee is improvement of morale.

✓ The committee **INTENDS** to improve morale.

2. Make the subjects of those verbs the characters associated with those actions.

> A decision by **the dean** in regard to the funding of the program by **the department** is necessary for adequate **staff** preparation.

> ✓ **The staff** CAN PREPARE adequately, only after **the dean** DECIDES whether **the department** WILL FUND the program.

3. Don't revise these nominalizations:

   a. They refer to a previous sentence:

   > ✓ **These arguments** all depend on a single unproven claim.

   b. They replace an awkward *The fact that*:

   > **The fact that she strenuously objected** impressed me.

   > ✓ **Her strenuous objections** impressed me.

   c. They name what would be the object of a verb:

   > I do not know **what she INTENDS**.

   > ✓ I do not know **her intentions**.

   d. They name a concept so familiar to your readers that it is a virtual character:

   > ✓ Few problems have so divided us as **abortion** on **demand**.

   > ✓ The Equal Rights **Amendment** was an issue in past **elections**.

CHARACTERS

from *Style: Lessons in Clarity and Grace*

Whatever is translatable in other and simpler words of the same language, without loss of sense or dignity, is bad.

—Samuel Taylor Coleridge

When character is lost, all is lost.

—Anonymous

UNDERSTANDING THE IMPORTANCE OF CHARACTERS

Readers think sentences are clear and direct when they see key ACTIONS in their VERBS. Compare (1a) with (1b):

1a. The CIA feared the president would recommend to Congress that it reduce its budget.

1b. The CIA had fears that the president would send a recommendation to Congress that it make a reduction in its budget.

Sentence (1a) is a third shorter than (1b), but some readers don't think it's much clearer. But now compare (1b) and (1c):

1b. The CIA had fears that the president would send a recommendation to Congress that it make a reduction in its budget.

1c. The fear of the CIA was that a recommendation from the president to Congress would be for a reduction in its budget.

Every reader thinks that (1c) is less clear than either (1a) or (1b).

The reason is this: In both (1a) and (1b), important characters are short, specific SUBJECTS of verbs (characters are italicized, subjects boldfaced, verbs capitalized):

1a. ***The CIA*** FEARED ***the president*** WOULD RECOMMEND to Congress that ***it*** REDUCE its budget.

1b. ***The CIA*** HAD fears that ***the president*** WOULD SEND a recommendation to Congress that ***it*** MAKE a reduction in its budget.

But the two subjects in (1c) are not concrete characters, but abstractions (boldfaced).

> 1c. The **fear** of the *CIA* was that a **recommendation** from the *president* to *Congress* WOULD BE for a **reduction** in its budget.

The different verbs in (1a) and (1b) make some difference, but the abstract subjects in (1c) make a bigger one.

> ***Here's the point:*** Readers want actions in verbs, but even more they want characters as their subjects. We give readers a problem when for no good reason we do not name characters in subjects, or worse, delete them entirely, like this:
>
> > 1d. There was fear that there would be a recommendation for a budget reduction.
>
> Who fears? Who recommends? Who reduces? It is important to express actions in verbs, but the *first* principle of a clear style is this: Make the subjects of most of your verbs short, specific, and concrete—the main characters in your story.

DIAGNOSIS AND REVISION

Finding and Relocating Characters

To get characters into subjects, you have to know three things:

1. when you haven't done that
2. if you haven't, where you should look for characters
3. what you should do when you find them (or don't)

For example, this sentence feels indirect and impersonal.

> Governmental intervention in fast-changing technologies has led to the distortion of market evolution and interference in new product development.

We can diagnose that sentence:

1. **Skim the first seven or eight words:**

   > Governmental intervention in fast-changing technologies has led <u>to the distortion of market evolution and interference in new product development.</u>

   In those first words, readers want to see characters as the subjects of verbs. But in that example, they don't.

2. **Find the main characters.** They may be POSSESSIVE PRONOUNS attached to NOMINALIZATIONS, OBJECTS of PREPOSITIONS (particularly *by* and *of*), or only implied. In

that sentence, one main character is in the ADJECTIVE *governmental;* the other, *market,* is in the object of a preposition: *of market evolution.*

3. **Skim the passage for actions involving those characters, particularly actions buried in nominalizations.** Ask *Who is doing what?*

governmental **intervention**	→	*government* **intervenes**
distortion	→	*[government]* **distorts**
market **evolution**	→	*markets* **evolve**
interference	→	*[government]* **interferes**
development	→	*[market]* **develops**

To revise, reassemble those new subjects and verbs into a sentence, using CONJUNCTIONS such as *if, although, because, when, how,* and *why:*

✓ **When** a *government* **INTERVENES** in fast-changing technologies, *it* **DISTORTS** how *markets* **EVOLVE** or **INTERFERES** with their ability to **DEVELOP** new products.

Be aware that just as actions can be in adjectives (*reliable* → *rely*), so can characters:

Medieval *theological* debates often addressed issues considered trivial by modern *philosophical* thought.

When you find a character implied in an adjective, revise in the same way:

✓ *Medieval theologians* often debated issues that *modern philosophers* consider trivial.

> ***Here's the point:*** The first step in diagnosing your style is to look at your subjects. If you do not see your main characters there expressed in a few short, concrete words, you have to look for them. They can be in objects of prepositions, in possessive pronouns, or in adjectives. Once you find them, look for actions they are involved in. Then make those characters the subjects of verbs naming those actions.

Reconstructing Absent Characters

Readers have the biggest problem with sentences devoid of *all* characters:

A decision was made in favor of doing a study of the disagreements.

That sentence could mean either of these, and more:

We decided that I should study why they disagreed.

I decided that you should study why he disagreed.

The writer may know who is doing what, but readers might not and so usually need help. Sometimes we omit characters to make a general statement.

Research strategies that look for more than one variable are of more use in understanding factors in psychiatric disorder than strategies based on the assumption that the presence of psychopathology is dependent on a single gene or on strategies in which only one biological variable is studied.

But when we try to revise that into something clearer, we have to invent characters, then decide what to call them. Do we use *one* or *we,* or name a generic "doer"?

✓ If *one/we/researchers* are to understand what causes psychiatric disorder, *one/we/they* should use research strategies that look for more than one variable rather than assume that a single gene is responsible for psychopathology or adopt a strategy in which *one/we/they* study only one biological variable.

To most of us, *one* feels stiff, but *we* may be ambiguous because it can refer just to the writer, or to the writer and others but not the reader, or to the reader and writer but not others, or to everyone.

But if you avoid both nominalizations and vague pronouns, you can slide into PASSIVE verbs (I'll discuss them in a moment):

To understand what makes patients vulnerable to psychiatric disorders, strategies that look for more than one variable **SHOULD BE USED** rather than strategies in which it **IS ASSUMED** that a gene causes psychopathology or only one biological variable **IS STUDIED**.

In some cases, characters are so remote that you have to start over:

There are good reasons that account for the lack of evidence.

✓ I can explain why I have found no evidence.

 QUICK TIP

When you are explaining a complicated issue to someone involved in it, imagine sitting across the table from that person, saying *you* as often as you can:

Taxable intangible property includes financial notes and municipal bonds. A one-time tax of 2% on its value applies to this property.

✓ **You** have to pay tax on **your** intangible property, including **your** financial notes and municipal bonds. On this property, **you** pay a one-time tax of 2%.

If *you* seems not appropriate, change it to a character that is:

Taxpayers have to pay tax on their intangible property, including their financial notes and municipal bonds. **They** pay . . .

Abstractions as Characters

So far, I've discussed characters as if they had to be flesh-and-blood people. But you can tell stories whose main characters are abstractions, including nominalizations, so long as you make them the subjects of a series of sentences that tell a story. Here's a story about a character called *freedom of speech,* two nominalizations.

✓ No right is more basic to a free society than **freedom of speech. Free speech** served the left in the 1960s when it protested the Vietnam War, and **it** is now used by the right when it claims that speech includes contributions to political organizations. **The doctrine of free speech** has been embraced by all sides to protect themselves against those who would silence unpopular views. As a legal concept, **it** arose . . .

The phrase *freedom of speech* (or its equivalents *free speech* and *it*) is a virtual character because we are so familiar with it and because it is the subject of a series of sentences and is involved in actions such as *served, is used, has been embraced,* and *arose.*

But when you do use abstractions as characters, you can create a problem. A story about an abstraction as familiar as *free speech* is clear enough, but if you surround a less familiar abstract character with a lot of other abstractions, readers may feel that your writing is dense and complex.

For example, few of us are familiar with *prospective* and *immediate intention,* so most of us are likely to struggle with a story about them, especially when those terms are surrounded by other abstractions (actions are boldfaced; human characters are italicized):

The **argument** is this. The cognitive component of **intention** exhibits a high degree of **complexity. Intention** is temporally divisible into two: prospective **intention** and immediate **intention**. The cognitive function of prospective **intention** is the **representation** of a *subject*'s similar past **actions,** *his* current situation, and *his* course of future **actions**. That is, the cognitive component of prospective **intention** is a **plan**. The cognitive function of immediate **intention** is the **monitoring** and **guidance** of ongoing bodily **movement**.

—Myles Brand, *Intending and Acting*

We can make that passage clearer if we tell it from the point of view of flesh-and-blood characters (they are italicized; "denominalized" verbs are boldfaced and capitalized):

✓ *I* ARGUE this about intention. It has a complex cognitive component of two temporal kinds: prospective and immediate. *We* use prospective intention to REPRESENT how *we* have ACTED in our past and present and how *we* will ACT in the future. That is, *we* use the cognitive component of prospective intention to help *us* PLAN. *We* use immediate intention to MONITOR and GUIDE *our* bodies as *we* MOVE them.

But have I made this passage say something that the writer didn't mean? Some argue that any change in form changes meaning. In this case, the writer might offer an opinion, but only his readers could decide whether the two passages have different meanings, because at the end of the day, a passage means only what a careful and competent reader thinks it does.

Here's the point: Most readers want the subjects of verbs to name the main characters in a story and those main characters to be flesh-and-blood. But often, you must write about abstractions. When you do, turn them into virtual characters by making them the subjects of verbs that tell a story. If readers are familiar with your abstractions, no problem. But when they are not, avoid using lots of other abstract nominalizations around them. When you revise an abstract passage, you may have a problem if the hidden characters are "people in general." You can try we or a general term for whoever is doing the action, such as researchers, social critics, one, and so on. But the fact is, unlike many other languages, English has no good solution for naming a generic "doer."

EXERCISE 8

Before you revise these next sentences, diagnose them. Look at the first six or seven words (ignore short introductory phrases). Then revise so that each has a specific character as subject of a specific verb. To revise, you may have to invent characters. Use *we, I,* or any other word that seems appropriate.

1. In recent years, the appearance of new interpretations about the meaning of the discovery of America has led to a reassessment of Columbus's place in Western history.
2. Decisions about forcibly administering medication in an emergency room setting despite the inability of an irrational patient to provide legal consent is usually an on-scene medical decision.
3. Tracing transitions in a well-written article provides help in efforts at improving coherence in writing.
4. Resistance has been growing against building mental health facilities in residential areas because of a belief that the few examples of improper management are typical.
5. With the decline in network television viewing in favor of cable and rental DVDs, awareness is growing at the networks of a need to revise programming.

CHARACTERS AND PASSIVE VERBS

More than any other advice, you probably remember *Write in the active voice, not in the passive.* That's not bad advice, but it has exceptions.

When you write in the active voice, you typically put

- the agent or source of an action in the subject
- the goal or receiver of an action in a DIRECT OBJECT:

	subject	verb	object
Active:	I	lost	the money
	character/agent	action	goal

The passive differs in three ways:

1. The subject names the goal of the action.
2. A form of *be* precedes a verb in its PAST PARTICIPLE form.
3. The agent or source of the action is in a *by*-phrase or dropped entirely:

	subject	be + verb	prepositional phrase
Passive:	The money	was lost	[by me].
	goal	action	character/agent

The terms *active* and *passive,* however, are ambiguous, because they can refer not only to those two grammatical constructions but to how a sentence makes you *feel.* We call a sentence *passive* if it feels flat, regardless of whether its verb is actually in the passive voice. For example, compare these two sentences.

We can manage the problem if we control costs.

Problem management requires cost control.

Grammatically, both sentences are in the active voice, but the second *feels* passive, for three reasons:

- Neither of its actions—*management* and *control*—are verbs; both are abstract nominalizations.
- The subject is *problem management,* an abstraction.
- The sentence lacks flesh-and-blood characters entirely.

To understand why we respond to those two sentences as we do, we have to distinguish the literal meanings of *active* and *passive* from their figurative, impressionistic meanings. In what follows, I discuss grammatical passives.

Choosing between Active and Passive

Some critics of style tell us to avoid the passive everywhere because it adds a couple of words and often deletes the agent, the "doer" of the action. But in fact, the passive is often the better choice. To choose between active and passive, you have to answer three questions:

1. **Must your readers know who is responsible for the action?** Often, we don't say who does an action, because we don't know or readers won't care. For example, we naturally choose the passive in these sentences:

    ✓ The president WAS RUMORED to have considered resigning.

    ✓ Those who ARE FOUND guilty can BE FINED.

    ✓ Valuable records should always BE KEPT in a safe.

If we do not know who spread rumors, we cannot say, and no one doubts who finds people guilty or fines them or who should keep records safe. So those passives are the right choice.

Sometimes, of course, writers use the passive when they don't want readers to know who did an action, especially when the doer is the writer: For example,

> Because the test was not done, the flaw was uncorrected.

2. **Would the active or passive verb help your readers move more smoothly from one sentence to the next?** We depend on the beginning of a sentence to give us a context of what we know before we follow the sentence to read what's new. A sentence confuses us when it opens with information that is new and unexpected. For example, in this next short passage, the subject of the second sentence gives us new and complex information (boldfaced), before we read more familiar information that we recall from the previous sentence (italicized):

> We must decide whether to improve education in the sciences alone or to raise the level of education across the whole curriculum. **The weight given to industrial competitiveness as opposed to the value we attach to the liberal arts** new information WILL DETERMINE active verb *our decision.* familiar information

In the second sentence, the verb *determine* is in the active voice, ***will determine*** *our decision*. But we could read the sentence more easily if it were passive, because the passive would put the short, familiar information (*our decision*) first and the new and complex information last, the order we all prefer:

> ✓ We must decide whether to improve education in the sciences alone or raise the level of education across the whole curriculum. *Our decision* familiar information WILL BE DETERMINED passive verb **by the weight we give to industrial competeness as opposed to the value we attach to the liberal arts.** new information

I discuss where to put old and new information in a sentence in the next lesson.

3. **Would the active or passive give readers a more consistent and appropriate point of view?** The writer of this next passage reports the end of World War II in Europe from the point of view of the Allies. To do so, she uses active verbs to make the Allies a consistent sequence of subjects:

> ✓ By early 1945, *the Allies* HAD essentially DEFEATED active Germany; all that remained was a bloody climax. *American, French, British, and Russian forces* HAD BREACHED active its borders and WERE BOMBING active it around the clock. But *they* HAD not yet so DEVASTATED active Germany as to destroy its ability to resist.

But had she wanted to explain history from the point of view of Germany, she would have used passive verbs to make Germany the subject/character:

> ✓ By early 1945, *Germany* HAD essentially BEEN DEFEATED; passive all that remained was a bloody climax. *Its borders* HAD BEEN BREACHED, passive and *it* WAS BEING BOMBED passive around the clock. *It* HAD not BEEN SO DEVASTATED, passive however, that *it* could not RESIST.

Some writers switch from one character to another for no apparent reason. Avoid this:

> By early 1945, *the Allies* had essentially defeated Germany. *Its borders* had been breached, and *they* were bombing it around the clock. *Germany* was not so devastated, however, that *the Allies* would meet with no resistance. Though *Germany's population* was demoralized, *the Allies* still attacked German cities from the air.

Pick a point of view and stick to it.

Here's the point: Many writers use the passive verb too often, but it has important uses. Use it in these contexts:

- You don't know who did an action, readers don't care, or you don't want them to know.
- You want to shift a long and complex bundle of information to the end of its sentence, especially when it also lets you move to its beginning a chunk of information that is shorter, more familiar, and therefore easier to understand.
- You want to focus your readers' attention on one or another character.

EXERCISE 9

In the following, change all active verbs into passives, and all passives into actives. Which sentences improve? Which do not? (In the first two, active verbs that could be passive are italicized; verbs already passive are boldfaced.)

1. Independence is **gained** by those on welfare when skills are **learned** that the marketplace *values*.
2. Different planes of the painting are **noticed**, because their colors **are set** against a background of shades of gray that are **laid** on in layers that cannot be **seen** unless the surface is **examined** closely.
3. In this article, it is argued that the Vietnam War was fought to extend influence in Southeast Asia and was not ended until it was made clear that the United States could not defeat North Vietnam unless atomic weapons were used.
4. Science education will not be improved in this nation to a level sufficient to ensure that American industry will be supplied with skilled workers and researchers until more money is provided to primary and secondary schools.
5. The first part of Bierce's "An Occurrence at Owl Creek Bridge" is presented in a dispassionate way. In the first paragraph, two sentinels are described in detail, but the line, "It did not appear to be the duty of these two men to know what was occurring at the center of the bridge" takes emotion away from them. In paragraph 2, a description is given of the surroundings and spectators, but no feeling is betrayed because the language used is neutral and unemotional. This entire section is presented as devoid of emotion even though it is filled with details.

The "Objective" Passive vs. *I* / *We*

Some scholarly writers claim that they should not use a first-person subject, because they need to create an objective point of view, something like this:

> Based on the writers' verbal intelligence, prior knowledge, and essay scores, their essays **were analyzed** for structure and evaluated for richness of concepts. The subjects **were** then **divided** into a high- or low-ability group. Half of each group **was** randomly **assigned** to a treatment group or to a placebo group.

Contrary to that claim, academic and scientific writers use the active voice and the first-person *I* and *we* regularly. These next passages come from articles in respected journals:

✓ This paper is concerned with two problems. How can **we** best handle in a transformational grammar certain restrictions that . . ., To illustrate, **we** may cite . . ., **we** shall show . . .

✓ Since the pituitary-adrenal axis is activated during the acute phase response, **we** have investigated the potential role . . . Specifically, **we** have studied the effects of interleukin-l . . .

Here are the first few words from several consecutive sentences from *Science,* a journal of great prestige:

✓ **We** examine . . ., **We** compare . . ., **We** have used . . ., Each has been weighted . . ., **We** merely take . . ., They are subject . . ., **We** use . . ., Efron and Morris describe . . ., **We** observed . . ., **We** might find . . .

> —John P. Gilbert, Bucknam McPeck, and Frederick Mosteller,
> "Statistics and Ethics in Surgery and Anesthesia," *Science*

It is not true that academic writers always avoid the first person *I* or *we*.

Passives, Characters, and Metadiscourse

When academic writers do use the first person, however, they use it in certain ways. Look at the verbs in the passages above. There are two kinds:

• One kind refers to research activities: *study, investigate, examine, observe, use*. Those verbs are usually in the passive voice: *The subjects were observed* . . .
• The other kind of verb refers not to the subject matter or the research, but to the writer's own writing and thinking: *cite, show, inquire*. These verbs are often active and in the first person: *We will show* . . . They are examples of what is called METADISCOURSE. Metadiscourse is the language you use when you refer not to the substance of your ideas, but to yourself, your reader, or your writing:
    —your thinking and act of writing: *We/I will explain, show, argue, claim, deny, suggest, contrast, add, expand, summarize* . . .

—your readers' actions: *consider now, as you recall, look at the next example . . .*

—the logic and form of what you have written: *first, second; to begin; therefore, however, consequently . . .*

Metadiscourse appears most often in introductions, where writers announce their intentions: *I claim that . . ., I will show . . ., We begin by . . .*, and again at the end, when they summarize: *I have argued . . ., I have shown . . .*

On the other hand, scholarly writers use the first person less often to describe specific actions they performed as *part* of their research. We rarely find passages like this:

> To determine if monokines elicited an adrenal steroidogenic response, **I** ADDED preparations of . . .

The writer of the original sentence used a passive verb, *were added,* to name an action that anyone can perform, not just the writer:

> To determine if monokines elicited a response, **preparations** . . . WERE ADDED.

A passive sentence like that, however, can create a problem: its writer dangled a modifier. You dangle a modifier when an introductory phrase has an *implied* subject that differs from the *explicit* subject in the following or preceding CLAUSE. In that example, the implied subject of the INFINITIVE VERB *determine* is *I* or *we: I determine* or *we determine.*

> [So that **I** could] determine if monokines elicited a response, preparations WERE ADDED.

But that implied subject, *I,* differs from the *explicit* subject of the clause it introduces—**preparations** *were added.* When the two differ, the modifier dangles. Writers of scientific prose use this pattern so often, though, that it has become standard usage in their community.

We might note that this impersonal "scientific" style is a modern development. In his "New Theory of Light and Colors" (1672), Sir Isaac Newton wrote this charming first-person account of an experiment:

> I procured a triangular glass prism, to try therewith the celebrated phenomena of colors. And for that purpose, having darkened my laboratory, and made a small hole in my window shade, to let in a convenient quantity of the sun's light, I placed my prism at the entrance, that the light might be thereby refracted to the opposite wall. It was at first a very pleasing diversion to view the vivid and intense colors produced thereby.

 QUICK TIP

Some teachers prohibit the use of *I* everywhere in the writing of their students not because it is wrong, but because inexperienced writers begin too many sentences with *I think . . .,* *I believe . . .*, and so on. Others forbid *I* because they want to discourage students from writing a narrative account of their thinking: *First I read . . ., Then I considered . . .* On those two occasions, follow their advice.

Here's the point: Some writers and editors avoid the first person by using the passive everywhere, but deleting an I or we doesn't make a researcher's thinking more objective. We know that behind those impersonal sentences are still flesh-and-blood people doing, thinking, and writing. In fact, the first-person I and we are common in scholarly prose when used with verbs that name actions unique to the writer.

EXERCISE 10

The verbs in 1 through 4 below are passive, but two could be active because they are metadiscourse verbs that would take first-person subjects. Revise the passive verbs that should be changed into active verbs. Then go through each sentence again and revise nominalizations into verbs where appropriate.

1. It is believed that a lack of understanding about the risks of alcohol is a cause of student bingeing.
2. The model has been subjected to extensive statistical analysis.
3. Success in exporting more crude oil for hard currency is suggested here as the cause of the improvement of the Russian economy.
4. The creation of a database is being considered, but no estimate has been made in regard to the potential of its usefulness.

The verbs in 5 through 8 are active, but some of them should be passive because they are not metadiscourse verbs. Revise in other ways that seem appropriate.

5. I argue that the indigenous peoples engaged in overcultivation of the land leading to its exhaustion as a food-producing area.
6. Our intention in this book is to help readers achieve an understanding not only of the differences in grammar between Arabic and English but also the differences in world-view as reflected by Arabic vocabulary.
7. To make an evaluation of changes in the flow rate, I made a comparison of the current rate with the original rate on the basis of figures I had compiled with figures that Jordan had collected.
8. We performed the tissue rejection study on the basis of methods developed with our discovery of increases in dermal sloughing as a result of cellular regeneration.

EXERCISE 11

In these sentences, change passive verbs into actives only where you think it will improve the sentence. If necessary, invent a rhetorical situation to account for your choice of active or passive. (Different answers are correct for this one.)

1. Your figures were analyzed to determine their accuracy. Results will be announced when it is thought appropriate.
2. Home mortgage loans now are made for thirty years. With the price of housing at inflated levels, those loans cannot be paid off in a shorter time.
3. The author's impassioned narrative style is abandoned and a cautious treatment of theories of conspiracy is presented. But when the narrative line is picked up again, he invests his prose with the same vigor and force.
4. Many arguments were advanced against Darwinian evolution in the nineteenth century because basic assumptions about our place in the world were challenged by it. No longer were humans defined as privileged creatures but rather as a product of natural forces.
5. For many years, federal regulations concerning wiretapping have been enforced. Only recently have looser restrictions been imposed on the circumstances that warrant it.

In these sentences, change passives to actives where appropriate and change nominalizations into verbs. Invent characters where necessary.

6. It is my belief that the social significance of smoking receives its clearest explication through an analysis of peer interaction among adolescents. In particular, studies should be made of the manner in which interactive behavior is conditioned by social class.
7. These directives are written in a style of maximum simplicity as a result of an attempt at more effective communication with employees with limited reading skills.
8. The ability of the human brain to arrive at solutions to human problems has been undervalued because studies have not been done that would be considered to have scientific reliability.

EXERCISE 12

The excerpt below is from an actual letter from the chancellor of a state university to parents of students. Except for the second word, *you,* why is the first part so impersonal? Why is the last part more personal? Change the first part so that you name in subjects whoever performs an action. Then change the second part to eliminate all characters. How do the two parts now differ? Have you improved the letter? This exercise raises the question of deliberate misdirection.

> As you probably have heard, the U of X campus has been the scene of a number of incidents of racial and sexual harassment over the last several weeks. The fact that similar incidents have occurred on campuses around the country does not make them any less offensive when they take place here. Of the ten to twelve incidents that have been reported since early October, most have involved graffiti or spoken insults. In only two cases was any physical contact made, and in neither case was anyone injured.
>
> U of X is committed to providing its students with an environment where they can live, work, and study without fear of being taunted or harassed because of their race, gender, religion, or ethnicity. I have made it clear that bigotry and intolerance will not be permitted and that U of X's commitment to diversity is unequivocal. We are also taking steps to improve security in campus housing. We at U of X are proud of this university's tradition of diversity . . .

NOUN + NOUN + NOUN

One more stylistic choice does not directly involve characters and actions, but we discuss it here because it can distort the match that readers expect between the form of an idea and the grammar of its expression. It is the long COMPOUND NOUN phrase:

> Early *childhood thought disorder misdiagnosis* often results from unfamiliarity with recent *research literature* describing such conditions. This paper is a review of seven recent studies in which are findings of particular relevance to *pre-adolescent hyperactivity diagnosis* and to *treatment modalities* involving *medication maintenance level evaluation procedures.*

Some grammarians claim we should never modify one noun with another, but that would rule out common phrases such as *stone wall, student center, space shuttle,* and many other useful terms.

But strings of nouns feel lumpy, so avoid them, especially ones you invent. When you find a compound noun of your own invention, revise, especially when it includes nominalizations. Reverse the order of words and find prepositions to connect them:

1	2	3	4	5
early	childhood	thought	disorder	misdiagnosis
misdiagnose	disordered	thought	in early	childhood
5	4	3	1	2

Re-assembled, it looks like this:

> Physicians misdiagnose[5] disordered[4] thought[3] in young[1] children[2] because they are unfamiliar with recent literature on the subject.

Revise the compound noun phrases in 1 through 4.

1. The plant safety standards committee discussed recent air quality regulation announcements.
2. Diabetic patient blood pressure reduction may be brought about by renal depressor application.
3. The goal of this article is to describe text comprehension processes and recall protocol production.
4. On the basis of these principles, we may now attempt to formulate narrative information extraction rules.

In these, unpack compound nouns and revise nominalizations.

5. This paper is an investigation into information processing behavior involved in computer human cognition simulation.

6. Enforcement of guidelines for new automobile tire durability must be a Federal Trade Commission responsibility.

7. The Social Security program is a monthly income floor guarantee based on a lifelong contribution schedule.

8. Based on training needs assessment reviews and on office site visits, there was the identification of concepts and issues that can be used in our creation of an initial staff questionnaire instrument.

A LAST POINT: THE PROFESSIONAL VOICE

Every group expects its members to show that they accept its values by adopting its distinctive voice. The apprentice banker must learn not only to think and look like one, but to speak and write like one, as well. Too often, though, aspiring professionals think they join the club only when they write in the club's most complex technical language. It is an exclusionary style that erodes the trust a civil society depends on, especially in a world where information and expertise are now the means to power and control.

It is true that some research can never be made clear to merely intelligent lay readers—but less often than many researchers think. Here is an excerpt from Talcott Parsons, a social scientist who was as influential in shaping his field as he was notorious for the opacity of his prose.

> Apart from theoretical conceptualization there would appear to be no method of selecting among the indefinite number of varying kinds of factual observation which can be made about a concrete phenomenon or field so that the various descriptive statements about it articulate into a coherent whole, which constitutes an "adequate," a "determinate" description. Adequacy in description is secured insofar as determinate and verifiable answers can be given to all the scientifically important questions involved. What questions are important is largely determined by the logical structure of the generalized conceptual scheme which, implicitly or explicitly, is employed.

We can make that clearer to moderately well-educated readers:

> When scientists lack a theory, they have no way to select from everything they could say about a subject only that which they can fit into a coherent whole that would be "adequate" or "determinate." Scientists describe something "adequately" only when they can verify answers to questions they think are important, and they decide what questions are important based on their implicit or explicit theories.

And we could make even it more concise:

> Whatever you describe, you need a theory to fit its parts into a whole. You need a theory to decide even what questions to ask and to verify their answers.

My versions lose the nuances of Parsons's style, but his excruciating density numbs all but his most masochistically dedicated readers. Most readers would accept the tradeoff.

Here's the point: Whether you are a reader or a writer, you must understand three things about a style that seems complex:

- It may be necessarily complex to express complex ideas precisely.
- It may needlessly complicate simple ideas.
- It may needlessly complicate complex ideas.

Einstein said that everything should be made as simple as possible, but no simpler. Neither should anything be made more complex than necessary. As a writer, your must recognize when you have committed that gratuitous complexity and, if you can, to revise it. When you do, you follow the Writer's Golden Rule: Write to others as you would have others write to you.

SUMMING UP

1. Readers judge prose to be clear when subjects of sentences name characters and verbs name actions.

Fixed	Subject	Verb	—————
Variable	Character	Action	—————

2. If you tell a story in which you make abstract nominalizations its main characters and subjects, use as few other nominalizations as you can:

    A nominalization is a **replacement** of a verb by a noun, often resulting in **displacement** of characters from subjects by nouns.

    ✓ When *a nominalization* REPLACES a verb with a noun, *it* often DISPLACES characters from subjects.

3. Use a passive if the agent of an action is self-evident:

    The voters REELECTED the president with 54 percent of the vote.

    ✓ *The president* WAS REELECTED with 54 percent of the vote.

4. Use a passive if it lets you replace a long subject with a short one:

    Research demonstrating the soundness of our reasoning and the need for action SUPPORTED *this decision.*

    ✓ *This decision* WAS SUPPORTED BY research demonstrating the soundness of our reasoning and the need for action.

5. Use a passive if it gives your readers a coherent sequence of subjects:

   ✓ By early 1945, *the Axis nations* had **BEEN** essentially **DEFEATED;** all that remained was a bloody climax. *The German borders* had **BEEN BREACHED,** and both *Germany and Japan* were being bombed around the clock. *Neither country,* though, had **BEEN** so **DEVASTATED** that *it* could not **RESIST.**

6. Use an active verb if it is a metadiscourse verb:

   The terms of the analysis must **BE DEFINED.**

   ✓ We must **DEFINE** the terms of the analysis.

7. When possible, rewrite long compound noun phrases:

   We discussed the **board**[1] **candidate**[2] **review**[3] **meeting**[4] **schedule**[5].

   ✓ We discussed the **schedule**[5] of **meetings**[4] to **review**[3] **candidates**[2] for the **board**[1].

Nene D Fofana
June 14, 2005
English101 paper2

I have had my love for traveling since I was a little girl as my parents used to say and this is still true. I like traveling to new places, meeting new people and discovering new culture. My love for living aboard led me to France, Morocco, Senegal, and Mali and now to the US. Each place where I have been teaches me something different. I learned Arabic in Morocco, more about Islam in Senegal, collected information about my ancestor in Mali and I am still learning English in the US. However, during all those encounter and meeting with people a lot of them made me the notice that I have a strong accent as all the Ivorian people. These remarks at first hurt my feelings, and made me give rude answers to my interlocutors. How can I, a proud descendant of 'la langue de Moliere' (French) speaker be insulted like this! I wondered. Once in vacation in Paris with my cousin and friends, I met one of my family relative who used to live abroad for more than ten years. While talking to him, he also made me the remark that I have a strong accent and time going on I realized that the more people I met, the more I realized that people were perhaps right and I start wondering about this word: Accent.

What is an accent and how can we define a person with an accent? In the definition given by the ESL Oxford dictionary, it is a particular way of pronouncing words that is connected with the country or with a social group. Basing myself on this definition, I can therefore assume that everybody got an accent.

Is it good or bad to have an accent? Where I came from, we consider ourselves as one of the best French speaking country after our dear mother 'La France'. It is with condescendence that we look at people speaking French with an accent. In Cote d'Ivoire, having an accent is synonym of bad education and consequently, of a low social position. Ivorian parents, in their desire to have well-educated children speaking French perfectly invest huge amount of money in schools and in special teachers known as "accent erasers". These 'accent erasers' are in general native French speakers, they are hired in their native country and send in the country where they give luxurious classes of French that is supposed to give a real French accent to the child.

Are we, people from Cote d'ivoire alone in our fight against accent? Surely, no, a few years ago, I read an article about Korea. This article by Kathy Marks (1) was about Korean parents who made lot of sacrifice to pay colossal amount of money for their children to learn perfect English, as it is the case of my dear Ivorian parents. However, they are somewhat different because the article stated that Korean parents in addition to English classes also paid for lingual surgery to make disappear their children accent. As Kathy Marks explains in her article published in the independent of january03, 2004: "the mastery of the English language is so highly prized that ambitious parents force their children to have a painful tongue surgery in order to give them pronunciation." The operation as describe by Kathy marks, involved sniping the thin tissue under the tongue to make it longer and supposedly nimbler. The procedure involves chopping half an inch of the frenulum is carried out on children under five.

This example of the surgery may be an extreme case, but it reflects the common thinking of thousand of millions of people for whom speaking English or French fluently without accent is a sign of social success. From Korea to Cote d'ivoire or anywhere else in the world, speaking French or English fluently is mandatory for economic reasons. In the third world country or the developing ones, the economic challenge is so high that parents think acting for the best of their child by using these torturous procedures. It is for them a way of giving a chance to the child in a society in which good schools and jobs are based on people's capacity to speak this languages. For other people, when facing native English or French speakers, the better thing to do is to try their best to hide or make disappear this accent. They take speech classes as the classes offered by Duke University in North Carolina : '(2) foreign accent surgery class.' The program targets foreign accent modification focusing on articulation and intonation and it is coordinate by a licensed speech-language pathologist. The prices ranged from 500 us dollars to 2000us.

As you can see, some people consider having an accent as pathology and other as a deterrent to their success in life. Instead of rejecting their accent, non-native speaker should carry their accent with pride and work in order to make other people accept it. I think that accent should be considered as the sign of the cultural identity that we all carry. Coming from diverse places and with different cultural background, we all express an accent while talking a language different from our native language one. In my perspective, accent as the recognition sign of an individual should be accepted and acknowledge as an individual primary characteristic. I can reflect this idea from the point made by Laureen tarabokia during the 4th annual composition and cultural studies conferences for students' writers at Georges Washington University in April 2005(3). She wrote that speaking to a person with a different accent is creating a culture at that specific moment. 'It's an intense interaction, a communication between two beings that strays from the truth that are held so strong in everyone of us, is where you find culture.' Accent is the reflect of each person native language when speaking a different language. If language is the basis of a group of people identity, then accent is the link that permits to refer to this group in a different environment, in a different country. Moreover, in our contemporary world focus on the globalization, the conservation of different ethnicity or accent is mandatory. In the perspective of considering the world as a planetary village, we should all keep in mind that this difference that brings us together. As Laurence tarabokia says again: "If there were complete unity and homogeneity, there would be no way to discover what we can learn from each other." The cultural difference is a unique and necessary link that has to be cultivated and keep alive in order to preserve the diversity of the world. Our planet inhabitants speak more than 6000 languages according to Michael E Krauss, director of the university of Alaska language center in Fairbanks. The existence of an accent in this perspective is the proof of the singularity and specificity of each language and thus the expression of a specific culture.

Sources

(2) Duke university web site

   Dukehealth1.org/surgery/speech_program-asp.

(1) Korean linguistic surgery by Kathy Marks

   www.thunderbay.indymedia.org/news/2004/01/10969.php

(3) Essay by Laureen Tarabokia

   www.gwu.edu/english/ccsc/2001-pages/laureen tarabokia.html.

IV

STASIS THEORY

STASIS THEORY—IDENTIFYING THE ISSUES
AND JOINING THE DEBATE

As you move into researching your topic and writing your final two papers, you are joining a debate. Without a sense of what is at issue in a disagreement, it can be difficult to decide where to begin one's own argument or to determine what even counts as arguable within a particular discourse. In his book *Political Communication*, Dan Hahn suggests that one reason there is apathy in American politics is because it is hard to find one's way into a debate:

> Anybody who has ever arrived late to a cocktail party knows how difficult it is to catch up. Every conversation you try to join is confusing. You don't know what has already been said, so you don't know what you should say. Sometimes you plunge in, only to have somebody say, "Yes, that was what Bill was saying a few minutes ago." After a few such embarrassing incidents, you learn either to keep your mouth shut or to change the subject as soon as you enter the group.
>
> Unfortunately, those are also the two options most people take when becoming aware of politics. Nobody bothers to explain what the societal conversation has already covered (although history courses try to do so). Nobody brings you "up to snuff" on the nature of the controversies, what the various sides are, and why people on those sides take the positions they do. All too many people conclude that politics is too complicated and give up.[1]

Perhaps you have felt this way when reading about a topic. Stasis theory offers a system for finding your way in, for getting "up to snuff" on a debate. The stases are like sorting bins for issues and questions. No matter what the subject, the issues can be put into one or more of the five categories described below. (Note that, collectively, the categories are called **stases**; each individual category is called a **stasis**.) If you keep these categories in mind while you read about a subject, you will find it easier to identify the separate issues in the discourse about it. Later, as you begin to fashion your own arguments, knowing where people tend to agree and disagree will assist you in knowing how to start and how to rebut counterarguments that assume agreement where it does not, in fact, exist.

As you prepare your stasis grid, you can use stasis theory to both anticipate debates and to recognize them when you see them.

THE STASES IN A DEBATE

We often wonder how the stases will help us as writers once we have figured out what to write about. Since we know the stases work as sorting bins to classify different types of arguments, and we know how to decide which stasis applies to our opposing arguments, we can use this

---

[1] Hahn, Dan F. *Political Communication: Rhetoric, Government, and Citizens.* 2nd ed. State College, PA: Strata Publishing, Inc.: 2003.

to devise a thesis that confronts our opposition in the right mode. But do the stases have any use to us as writers after we've formulated our thesis? The answer is an emphatic "yes!"

To understand how they are useful, we must first understand how the stases function differently in a large, multi-faceted debate as opposed to their use in our own individual arguments. In a large debate, we can trace the stases through the issues by posing them as a series of questions:

- Does X exist? How do we define X?
- What causes X? What are the consequences of X?
- Is X therefore a good thing or bad thing? Are the benefits of X worth the costs?
- What should we do about X? Should we implement X?
- Who decides any of these questions about X?

In doing this, we can map the arc of the debate, identify the points at which opposing sides are in disagreement, and decide where we, as participants, should intervene in the debate. For example, we may map the debate over same-sex marriage:

- How do we define marriage?
- What are the consequences of applying or ignoring that definition?
- Are the benefits of these consequences worth the costs?
- Should we legalize same-sex marriage?
- Who should make this decision—states, the federal government, a popular vote?

THE STASES IN YOUR ARGUMENT

When you as a writer sit down to say your piece about this issue, you may realize a couple of things. First, you may notice that the two major parties in the debate don't agree in any of the stases, so even though the debate is bogged down in definitional issues, the public discourse is centered on action. Second, you may notice that in order to establish your action claims, you must first establish your value claims, which in turn rely on the answer to the cause and consequence questions, which themselves require a definition to work from. Each question depends on the answer reached in the previous stasis.

Suddenly, you have to tackle five major questions instead of one, but fortunately, they're already organized into a logical sequence for you. Thus, in constructing your own argument, you can use the procedure of moving through the stases as an organizational technique. Depending on your position, then, a basic outline might look like one of these:

Definition: Marriage, a love bond between two consenting adults, is a fundamental right.
Consequence: By denying same-sex partners marriage, we are consequently withholding their human rights.
Evaluation: These human rights are more important than archaic traditions based on procreation.
Action (thesis):   We should legalize same-sex marriage.

-or-

Definition: Marriage is a procreative bond and a privilege.

Consequence: By extending these rights to same-sex couples, we de-emphasize the role of parenting and break down the family structure.

Evaluation: Upholding traditional family structures is more important than granting special rights to couples whose bond is not for the purpose of procreation.

Action (thesis):   We should reserve marriage for heterosexual couples.

Notice that taking this debate through the stases in both your own position and the opposing position or positions is also useful for invention. Here, for example, someone supporting same-sex marriage would notice that by starting with marriage as primarily procreative in purpose, the opposing side potentially paints itself into a corner, unless it is willing to stipulate that infertile heterosexuals cannot properly marry. Since few opponents of same-sex marriage are willing to go that far, the supporter now has a useful point of refutation. Someone opposing same-sex marriage, on the other hand, would notice that the definition they start with may lead them to a position they do not in fact hold, and therefore will want to modify their definition.

You will surely find that your argument is more complex than this: perhaps your definitional argument will require a few paragraphs, and your evaluation argument may require a few more. You may want to add a jurisdiction component to your action argument, or propose a compromise that bridges more than one position. Still, by following the shape of the larger debate using the stases, you will find that the logic of your argument follows more smoothly, and, if well managed, more convincingly.

When you read through your research, you may notice that individual authors often work through these stases, even though an author's thesis will focus on one stasis. As you read the articles you have found for your stasis grid, try to locate each article's thesis, identify its stasis, and then work backwards. Ask yourself whether the author builds an argument by using the conclusions drawn in the previous stasis. By analyzing how other authors work through the stases, you may well find yourself devising a claim structure for your own argument.

The following arguments can be placed into one key stasis, but if you see other possible issues, feel free to identify and classify them. Try to phrase each dispute as a "whether" question (e.g., "The question is whether the embargo should be lifted"; "the question is whether the defendant can get a fair trial in the state where the crime occurred").

1. Your friend's car rolled backwards into your car and dented it. You want her to pay to have it fixed, but she doesn't want to. She argues that she shouldn't pay because it wasn't her fault since you parked too close behind her.

   The question is whether . . .

   Stasis:

2. You have a disagreement with your professor about the penalty you received for not turning in an important assignment. She thinks you should not pass the course; you think you should be allowed to turn it in late and merely be marked down.

   The question is whether . . .

   Stasis:

3. You and your father argue about your favorite new CD. He says the lyrics are obscene. You respond that they are not obscene, because the language simply expresses the language of the street.

   The question is whether . . .

   Stasis:

4. You and your father continue to argue. He insists that the band is lousy and uses volume to make up for its lousy music. You try to convince him that the band is very talented.

   The question is whether . . .

   Stasis:

5. You accuse someone of stealing a $10 bill you left sitting on the table. The person you accuse denies it and suggests it wasn't stolen at all but that you still have the money and were just trying to make him look bad.

   The question is whether . . .

   Stasis:

6. You argue with your sister about whether or not the extremely cold weather is evidence of the "greenhouse effect." She doesn't believe in the theory at all, and you try to convince her, using the strange weather as evidence, that it does exist.

   The question is whether . . .

   Stasis:

7. Although your best friend loves *Jane Eyre*, you hate it. You argue over whether it is a good book.

   The question is whether . . .

   Stasis:

8. The reason you hate *Jane Eyre* so much is that you think it is actually a long lyric poem and you despise poetry. Your friend thinks this is ludicrous and argues that the book is clearly a novel in form.

   The question is whether . . .

   Stasis:

9. A police officer pulls you over for running a red light. You insist that the light was yellow when you crossed the intersection, but he gives you a ticket anyhow, saying that the light was clearly red.

   The question is whether . . .

   Stasis:

10. Desperate to escape the ticket, you tell the officer that even if the light was red, running it wasn't your fault, since you were afraid that stopping would cause a dangerous accident with the truck that was bearing down on you from behind. The officer replies that the truck was nowhere near you and hands you a $100 ticket.

    The question is whether . . .

    Stasis:

11. You and a friend are driving frantically around campus looking for a parking space. Your friend sees a 30-minute meter and tries to convince you that you should park there and risk the ticket instead of being late to class. You insist that you should continue to look.

    The question is whether . . .

    Stasis:

12. As you continue driving around, your friend asks, "What's the big deal over $25? We have a midterm!" You reply, "We'll only be five minutes late. That's not worth $25."

    The question is whether . . .

    Stasis:

V

CONSIDERING ANOTHER SIDE

MAINTAINING A POSITIVE STANCE WHEN CONSIDERING ANOTHER SIDE

You may have heard it said that "those who do not understand their opponents' arguments do not truly understand their own." This maxim applies with special force to academic writing. To present an academic argument in a responsible manner, then, one must first understand opposing perspectives before articulating one's own position. The "Considering Another Side" paper gives you a chance to explore the point of view of someone who is making an argument that is opposed (in some way) to the argument that you plan to make in the final paper, so that you will understand this opposing argument and will know how to respond to it effectively.

But arguing a position that you do not necessarily agree with can be a challenging task. We tend to want to view positions we disagree with as merely the opposites of our own positions, a viewpoint that makes it easy to see our opponents in a negative light. Thus, those who are in favor of abortion rights tend to see those who disagree with them as merely being *against* abortion rights, and they wonder how any sane person could possibly be against a woman's right to choose what to do with her body. Similarly, pro-life individuals view those who disagree with them as being merely opposed to the right to life, and they find it difficult to see how anyone could oppose a fetus's right to live. Viewing the opposing side in a negative light like this makes it easy to reduce the opposing side to a caricature of itself. When we conclude that only "our" viewpoint is right and that anybody who disagrees must be crazy, we stop making any attempt to understand the other side's point of view, and the debate can easily deteriorate into a polarizing, two-sided shouting match.

In sharp contrast to those types of arguments, one of the most important principles of making an academic argument is to recognize that just because two people disagree about an issue doesn't mean that one of them is rational and the other is just stupid or crazy. Most people have at least some good reasons to believe what they do. That doesn't mean that most people are always right; rather, it simply means that we should start with the assumption that everyone is being reasonable in their own way. In the end, we may be able to prove that our opponents are being unreasonable, but by beginning with the assumption that our opponents are reasonable people (rather than idiots who don't know what they're talking about), we establish ourselves as respectful arguers who care about finding the real truth rather than simply proving our opponents wrong. If we assume that opponents are being as logical as they can be, then we may even be able to pinpoint exactly where the opposing side's logic breaks down, and we can learn how to refute that faulty logic in our own argument.

This, then, is the trick to writing the "Considering Another Side" paper: You must be able to understand the logic of someone who would argue a thesis that is different from the one that you plan to argue in the final paper, so that when you write the final paper, you can understand their perspective and respond to their argument in a way that still supports your own final thesis. But it's all too easy to write this paper simply as a negative response to the thesis you will argue in the final paper. As we saw above, in the abortion debate, pro-choice activists want to see their opponents as anti-choice, and pro-life activists want to see opponents as anti-life. But each side presents itself as being "pro-"something (*pro*-choice or *pro*-life). In order to really understand a position on its own terms, then, you need to understand what people who hold that position are for, not just what they're against. What do they support? What do they value? What are they in favor of?

The easiest way to accomplish this in the "Considering Another Side" paper is to make yourself argue a **positive** or **affirmative** thesis. Make sure that you argue **for** something, not just **against** something. One of the potential problems with this approach, though, is that if your argument is *too* positive, readers may have trouble seeing your argument as an argument. So you must be able to make a positive argument while still acknowledging that disagreement is possible.

How do you do this? Here are some possible suggestions:

- State your thesis positively. That is, eliminate any uses of the word "not," and restate the thesis if necessary.
- Pick an audience that will agree with some important premises of your argument, so you can minimize explanation of those premises and spend most of your energy on the points that need more support. (You may even be able to use some of your sources to help guide you to a possible audience. Look at the sources that argue the position of the "Considering Another Side" paper, especially ones that focus on the positive side of the argument rather than just trying to tear down the other side—what audiences are they written to? Do they take certain premises for granted as assumptions that don't need much support? Do they present certain facts, definitions, or values as objects of agreement?) **Carefully explain what these premises are in your audience analysis!**
- Acknowledge the existence of debate/disagreement/other points of view in your introduction. (The template on page 24 of *They Say/I Say* can be especially helpful here.)
- Focus on using sources that **agree** with the thesis you are arguing in the "Considering Another Side" paper, so that you can concentrate your analysis on explaining why those sources are right.
- As much as possible, focus on **positive** evidence for the "Considering Another Side" thesis—in other words, what evidence is there that the CAS thesis is right. (Ideally, you shouldn't have to spend very much time refuting other evidence suggesting the CAS thesis is wrong, unless the sources you're using spend lots of time doing this.) It's okay to acknowledge that others can disagree with how the evidence is interpreted, and you can explain why that interpretation is incorrect, but focus on the evidence that you think supports your thesis; do not spend extensive time trying to refute opposing evidence unless there is no way to avoid doing so. You will have plenty of opportunity to refute opposing points of view in your final paper.

The more strategies like these that you can use to keep your argument positive or affirmative, the more likely it is that you will be able to understand the position of the "Considering Another Side" paper as it really is, instead of just presenting it as the opposite of what you actually believe. Although this seems much harder at first than simply making an opposing side seem ridiculous and illogical, it will allow you to argue your position in the final paper already having taken the opposition's logic into account. In the end, if you can demonstrate that you understand both an opposing side's logic and the limitations of that logic, the argument of your final paper will be much more convincing to an academic audience.

Many of the passages below (but not all!) contain logical fallacies. Identify the fallacious arguments, name the kind of logical error being made, and suggest how to correct it. If the passage is logically sound, explain why.

1. Chloroflurocarbons, found in many everyday items such as Styrofoam packaging, may significantly alter our future daily activities as their environmental effects become pronounced. All skin exposure to the sun must be drastically limited, and people will have to cut down on their outdoor exercise.

2. The panda may become extinct because its future is in jeopardy.

3. Abortion violates a baby's freedom of choice when the baby's life is cut short based on the dictatorial whims of its mother.

4. Lakisha, our best swimmer, eats oatmeal for breakfast every morning. Therefore, the whole team should start having oatmeal for breakfast so we can win more meets.

5. Mike was yelling racial slurs in the cafeteria. Such slurs are offensive to people and should be punished.

6. We had to go to war in Vietnam. If Vietnam had fallen to communism, all of Southeast Asia would have fallen to communism soon after.

7. We need to institute national testing at the high-school level. Without such tests, we doom our children to low expectations and low achievement.

8. If you do not help end these crimes, you may be the next victim.

9. We can't trust his opinions about this child care bill. After all, he divorced his wife and gave up custody of his own children.

10. My opponent has a soft attitude toward criminals. This soft attitude poses a danger to the community. Therefore, you shouldn't vote for my opponent.

11. Don't trust what your advisors tell you; my sister had to do a whole extra semester of classes because her advisor gave her bad advice.

from *BioCycle*

*This well-documented message—proven in many states—may hold the
key to reinvigorating public commitment to materials recovery and reuse.*

Matt Ewadinger and Scott Mouw

A recent survey in North Carolina shows the powerful impact of recycling as an economic development tool. It reflects similar results of data compiled by state offices, the U.S. EPA and the Institute for Local Self-Reliance. These reports all show how recycling means good business that goes far beyond the resources and energy conservation benefits long recognized.

The North Carolina Division of Pollution Prevention and Environmental Assistance conducted a survey to examine recycling's impact on jobs and the North Carolina economy. This survey follows up a similar effort conducted in 1994 and documents the growth of the recycling industry over the past decade. Some of the findings include:

- Recycling employs approximately 14,000 people across the state.
- In 1994, recycling employed 8,700 people, rising 60 percent in ten years to reach its current level.
- Recycling jobs as a percentage of the state's total employment has increased 40 percent in ten years, from 0.25 percent of the total labor force in 1994 to 0.35 percent in 2004.
- Fifty-four percent of the businesses surveyed forecast creating more recycling-related jobs in the next two years.
- Recycling employs more people than the biotech and agricultural livestock industries in North Carolina.
- The number of companies listed in the state's recycling markets directory has increased from 306 in 1994 to 532 in 2004, a 74 percent increase.

The recycling industry can be expected to continue its growth in North Carolina, with expansion of existing firms and the advent of new companies resulting in a rising level of employment in this sector. The two chief obstacles to growth are access to materials that are currently being thrown away and sent to landfills and, as is the case with many small- to medium-sized businesses, access to capital.

ACCESS TO KARMA OR CAPITAL?

In an ideal world, we would measure a recycling company's success based on its positive environmental impact. In a market-based economy, however, success is measured by a company's ability to start-up, grow and remain financially solvent. To help these companies be successful, the N.C. Recycling Business Assistance Center (RBAC) collaborated with Self-Help, the state's community development bank, to create the N.C. Recycling Business Loan Fund. The loan fund nurtures fledgling businesses until they become bankable and graduate to full-service private sector financing. Since the inception of the loan fund in 1999, despite a somewhat sluggish economy, Self-Help has made $1,175,300 in loans and leveraged an additional $1,617,810 from other financial sources resulting in a total of $2,793,110 lent to North Carolina-based recycling companies. Forty-three jobs have been created, 18 jobs have been retained that might otherwise have been lost and 18,782 tons per year of capacity have been developed.

The rationale for establishing a dedicated Recycling Business Loan Fund is that banks can be reluctant to fund start-ups or companies in untested sectors. While venture capital is designed to take on higher levels of risk, those firms often want only very large deals and those with some form of management participation. The loan fund is designed to fill the gap between bank loans and venture capital.

What types of loans are available? The loans are structured as market-rate debt, and can be used for working capital, inventory, equipment and real estate purchases. The staff at Self-Help is well skilled at tapping existing Small Business Administration funding pools and guarantee programs to help with the approval of riskier loans. Self-Help often uses SBA 504 and 7(A) guarantees in its underwriting.

For more information about the N.C. Recycling Business Loan Fund, contact Fred Broadwell. Environmental Finance Coordinator at (919) 956-4490, or e-mail him at fred@self-help.org, or visit the Self-Help website at www.self-help.org.

> Jobs connected to resource recovery businesses have increased 40 percent in the last ten years in North Carolina.

THE HUMAN FACE OF THE RECYCLING INDUSTRY

North Carolina's RBAC has developed "Recycling Means Business! The Impact of Recycling on North Carolina's Economy." Unlike other recycling employment and business studies concentrating on economic statistics, this document provides a snapshot of the many faces of North Carolina's recycling industry. The 42 companies featured are just a few of the 540 state based recycling operations listed in the N.C. Recycling Markets Directory. (See "New North Carolina Law Bans Pallet Disposal" sidebar on page 200 for a description of some of these companies.) The operations range from Fortune 500 manufacturers to single proprietor, family-owned businesses, handling hundreds of different types of materials and products. Some of these companies now occupy old textile factories and other industrial plants abandoned by some of the state's more traditional industries. A copy of Recycling Means Business! can be found at http://www.p2pays.org/ref/34/33912.pdf.

NORTH CAROLINA IS NOT UNIQUE

Every state could probably provide similar recycling success stories like those highlighted here. An amazing array of companies across the country help turn discarded materials into everyday products while creating jobs for our citizens and investment in our economy at the same time.

NEW NORTH CAROLINA LAW BANS PALLET DISPOSAL

The North Carolina General Assembly passed House Bill 1465, which bans the disposal of wooden pallets, as well as motor vehicle oil filters, rigid plastic containers that have a neck smaller than the body of the container and oyster shells. Wooden pallets may still be accepted for disposal at facilities permitted to accept only construction and demolition debris. HB 1465 was signed into law and becomes effective on October 1, 2009.

Pallets represent approximately four percent of all disposed waste in North Carolina, notes Scott Mouw of the state's Department of Environment and Natural Resources, coauthor of the accompanying article. A disposal ban would divert as much as 200,000 tons per year from disposal. "We were able to 'sell' the idea of the ban in part because of the extensive infrastructure that is already in place for recycling many of these materials, and the opportunities to grow that infrastructure," he explains. Talking points prepared in support of the ban cite a recent North Carolina study that identified over 100 pallet recycling companies covering all areas of the state, employing an average of 33 people per business. Eighty-five percent of these recyclers could sell more pallets if they had them, and could handle another 192,000 tons beyond current consumption. There also are over 160 facilities in North Carolina permitted to burn wood as fuel, with other large wood fuel users accessible in nearby states. Five large commercial composting operations and some smaller ones need more wood feedstock, including pallet wood. In addition, there are wood mulch operations. Value-added wood product manufacturers operating in the central and western regions of the state want more pallet wood as well.

To help companies like these thrive, states can help create and maintain a business climate that supports the success of recycling companies. Local communities and states can help with policies, programs and incentives that drive materials out of the waste stream and into the hands of recyclers. Some recyclers struggle to compete against relatively low tipping fees for materials. Access to capital, discussed previously, needs to improve. Maintaining a strong network of technical, economic development and business planning assistance can give companies a strong foundation for expansion and improvement. A need to raise public awareness of the recycling economy exists. Waste generators, decision-makers and the public should know about the economic development, as well as the environmental, benefits the recycling industry offers.

Recycling's environmental promise is matched by its ability to grow jobs and businesses and strengthen the overall economy. This message, now well documented, may hold the key to reinvigorating public commitment to recycling and to capturing the large amount of materials that are now mistakenly discarded as "waste."

Matt Ewadinger is manager of the North Carolina Recycling Business Assistance Center, a cooperative effort of the N.C. Department of Environment and Natural Resources and the N.C. Department of Commerce, Scott Mauw is Chief of the Community and Business Assistance Section of the N.C. Department of Environment and Natural Resources.

IN DEFENSE OF RECYCLING

from Social Research

By Allen Hershkowitz

Recycling may be the most wasteful activity in modern America: a waste of time and money, a waste of human and natural resources.... [T] here's no reason to make recycling a legal or moral imperative.

John Tierney (1996b, pp. 24, 26)

[T] he need to rethink our throwaway mentality has become obvious.... I have come to believe that the waste crisis—like the environmental crisis as a whole—serves as a kind of mirror in which we are able to see ourselves more clearly if we are willing to question more deeply who we are and who we want to be, both as individuals and as a civilization. Indeed, in some ways the waste crisis serves as perhaps the best vehicle for asking some hard questions about ourselves.... If we have come to see the things we use as disposable, have we similarly transformed the way we think about our fellow human beings?

Al Gore (1992, p. 167)

INTRODUCTION

The following article addresses the claims of a small but vocal chorus of antienvironmental interests that has tried to cast doubt on the value of recycling, perhaps the most widely practiced and most basic of all environmental policies. Over the years, similar attacks have been launched against reports that confirmed industry's damage to the earth's biodiversity, as well as those revealing the threats posed by lead poisoning, ozone depletion, and greenhouse warming. Given the overwhelming support shown toward recycling policies over the past decade, it is understandable that until recently the conservative- and corporate-inspired backlash against recycling was hidden from most Americans, played out instead by lobbyists working obscure but important legislative committees and regulatory agencies. However, as the infrastructure for recycling has expanded over the past fifteen years, and as demands by citizens and state and local officials that consumer-products companies accommodate higher levels of recycling have intensified, backlash attacks against recycling have become more public. In general, recycling is opposed by (1) conservative theorists and (2) executives and trade group lobbyists working for extractive industries, such as mining and timber, as well as those representing a few, large manufacturers of grocery products and plastics.

Revisionist critiques of recycling have been slow to emerge publicly because the documented economic and ecosystem benefits that recycling programs provide are substantial, and because recycling is no longer a marginal enterprise supported by a few active members of local environmental clubs. As the Environmental Protection Agency (EPA) reported in September 1996.

There are 7,500 recycling programs [in the United States] compared to 1,000 in 1988, and the number continues to grow. Now about 120 million people, or 48 percent of the population, have access to curbside collection programs. Further, over 3,000 yard waste composting facilities complement the collection programs (Shapiro, 1996).

In fact, recycling is today a global phenomenon, a big business with diverse supporters, providing important benefits to millions of people worldwide. It is precisely the challenge to this widely shared experience that makes attacks on recycling so reckless.

Although popular concern about unchecked consumption and dangerous and wasteful disposal practices has helped recycling to flourish in the United States since the early 1980s, it is still far from being solidly established national industrial policy. Of the twenty most industrially advanced democracies in the world, the United States ranks fifteenth in paper recycling and nineteenth (behind Mexico) in glass recycling.[1] According to the Congressional Research Service, "Other countries use less packaging than the United States, recycle more of it, and are considering [recycling] policy measures stronger than measures generally being considered in America" (McCarthy, 1991, p. 2). This, despite the fact that on a per capita basis, as well as in absolute amounts, the United States is far and away the largest generator of wastes of any nation on earth. The United States also maintains the highest per capita use of water and the highest per capita use of energy; in addition, it contributes the highest global percentage of air pollution from both stationary and mobile sources (Organization for Economic Cooperation and Development, 1996, pp. 75, 254–57).

Recycling can help lessen some of these environmental burdens and the economic costs they engender. Both "upstream" (in the manufacturing process) and "downstream" (in the waste disposal process), recycling provides meaningful benefits. As this report will make clear, few public policies provide as many advantages as does recycling:

1. Recycling conserves natural resources, such as timber, water, and mineral ores, from domestic and imported sources.
2. Recycling prevents pollution caused by manufacturing from virgin resources.
3. Recycling saves energy.
4. Recycling reduces the need for landfilling and incineration and helps avoid pollution produced by these technologies.
5. Recycling helps protect and expand manufacturing jobs in America.
6. Recycling engenders a sense of community involvement and responsibility.

The environmental and economic benefits of recycling have been broadly analyzed.[2] Few analysts dispute that recycling can help reduce global and local environmental burdens as well as the costs of administering, collecting, processing, and transporting garbage to landfills and incinerators. It is the only solid waste management strategy that offers the potential to generate revenue in the otherwise losing proposition that government faces regarding the collection and disposal of municipal waste. Of course, as a raw-material commodities business, recycling markets can't guarantee profits. No market does. Still, recycling industries now encompass billions of dollars in competitive investments and infrastructure worldwide. Yet whatever the financial risks of recycling, these in no way negate its environmental benefits. Though recycling draws its direction primarily from science and empirical economics, it is grounded as well in a philosophical belief that people throughout the world are interdependent, however isolated they may feel. Teaching children the value of recycling, as tens of thousands of parents and schools do each year, is not, as has been alleged, a merely sentimental gesture; rather, it helps cultivate an important awareness of one's relationship to others and responsibilities to them. Recycling confirms that people can do what is efficient and still do what is right, though it may mean minor adjustments in the way they collect and throw out garbage or choose to shop for everyday needs.

Recently, attacks on the philosophical premise and environmental value of recycling have gained visibility, challenging Americans to rethink their commitment to this highly popular environmental policy. These attacks have emerged from antigovernment and conservative organizations such as the Reason Foundation, the Cato Institute, the Competitive Enterprise Institute, and the National Center for Policy Analysis. These groups, which advocate the elimination of many, if not most environmental and public health regulations, have a severe view of local recycling ordinances, characterizing them as "the equivalent of Soviet planning" (Schaumburg and Doyle, 1994, p. 20) or "East European five-year plans" that burden Americans with "forced labor" and childhood "indoctrination" (Tierney, 1996b, pp. 24, 26). Such characterizations reveal the power that metaphors can hold over reality for ideologues, even at the expense of diminishing the evils of totalitarianism. They dismiss Americans' vigorous support of recycling—for two decades, public opinion polls have routinely concluded that more than seven out of ten Americans view recycling as an important solution to some of the planet's environmental problems (see, for examples, National Solid Waste Management Association, 1988; "Shades of Green," 1991, p. 1; and "Waste of a Sort," 1995, p. A1)—as being a consequence of "bizarre . . . misconceptions and mistaken assumptions that snowballed into a "national myth" ("Waste of a Sort," p. A1).

Certainly the most prominent, if not controversial, attack on the nation's growing commitment to recycling was published as a lengthy cover story, "Recycling Is Garbage," in the New York Times Magazine on June 30, 1996. In it, John Tierney, a staff writer for the magazine, argued that most recycling efforts are economically unsound and of questionable environmental value. Billions of dollars in profitable and ecologically productive investments in recycling have conserved millions of tons of resources, reduced pollution, saved energy, and produced tens of thousands of jobs. Yet Tierney described recycling as perhaps "the most wasteful activity in modern America." How could this be? Tierney's article was a challenge to all Americans committed to environmental protection. In fact, in the past thirty years, hundreds of volumes of text and data have documented the value and logic of recycling to industry and government alike. But "Recycling Is Garbage," which was replete with half-truths, stretched far to excerpt out-of-context or incomplete "facts" here and there from previously published reports issued by the Reason Foundation, a West Coast antigovernment group, as well as corporate public relations firms and consultants, and other interests ideologically or financially opposed to recycling. In so doing, Tierney constructed a manifesto against all the good documented benefits recycling provides. The article sought to turn recycling, and the values that underlie it, on its head. Although recycling efforts have proliferated in response to concerns about the global damage caused by wasteful consumption, "Recycling Is Garbage" referred to recycling as "the most primitive form of materialism: the worship of materials" (Tierney, 1996b, p. 53).

Had Tierney's tract been treated as just another antienvironmental voice among others, it would have gone largely unnoticed, as happened to the few similar attacks on recycling that came before it. But a cover story in the *New York Times Magazine* gets attention, and in this case it had important policy consequences. Excerpts of the article or echoes of its antirecycling theme were reprinted in more than two dozen major papers nationwide, and two days after the article's publication. New York City mayor Rudolph Giuliani denounced the city's recycling ordinance as "absurd" and "irresponsible," indicated his intention to ignore it, and supported his position by citing "an article in the *New York Times Magazine* . . . that called recycling a waste of time and money and suggested that the national drive to increase recycling was prompted by an irrational fear that available landfill space was rapidly disappearing"* Not surprisingly, conservative theorists and officials at virgin resources-based industries threatened by recycling would like other government officials to believe the public has indeed turned its back on recycling. As the executive director of the Vinyl Plastics Institute claimed, "the *New York Times* article was a picture in time accurately reflecting society" (*Plastic News*, 1996, p. 6).

I don't agree. This document is a response to the small but potentially influential group of antirecycling voices disrupting environmental progress. As the text that follows makes clear, and as many Americans seem to understand intuitively, antirecycling diatribes routinely distort the facts relating to recycling. Obviously, not all the materials found in the municipal waste stream can be recycled, nor can all consumer products be made from recycled materials. But the United States is certainly far from those practical limits. A much higher percentage of materials now discarded in the U.S. waste stream can be recycled, and the environment would certainly benefit if many of the products now made from virgin resources were manufactured from recycled resources instead. Virtually every issue put forth by those who take the antirecycling position has been subjected to thorough review and debate, producing volumes of research. Rarely do the facts support the antirecycling stance.

Those who argue that recycling has been oversold to the American public try to hit at the heart of recycling's environmental and economic value. Their arguments express four general concerns, none of which are accurate:

1. Recycling is itself a complex industrial process that consumes more resources than it saves, causes pollution, and doesn't really save trees, energy, or other natural resources.
2. Landfill space is available, convenient, and, unlike earlier dump sites, today's landfills pose no environmental problems.
3. Recycling is more expensive than landfilling.
4. Government mandates requiring recycling and subsidies offered in behalf of recycling are costly and distort free-market objectives and efficiencies.

This article refutes all of these arguments.

Undoubtedly, recycling will withstand this latest assault on common sense, good science, and sound economics. Like any good idea, especially one that threatens the world view of ideologues and entrenched profit-making interests or requires some adjustment in bureaucratic processes, recycling is an uphill battle. But it is one that mainstream America, whose commitment to environmental progress is well documented, is winning. Perhaps no other idea

---

New York Times, July 3, 1996, p. 1.

emerging out of the environmental movement has been so successful in garnering popular support and motivating the behavior of so many people throughout the world. This article is a brief attempt to confirm why this is so.

THE UPSTREAM BENEFITS: REDUCING POLLUTION AND THE USE OF VIRGIN RESOURCES

Manufacturing and Mining's Toxic Impacts

Using recycled materials helps avoid the air and water pollution typically caused by manufacturing plants that rely solely on unprocessed, virgin raw materials. Because using recycled materials reduces the need to extract, process, refine, and transport the timber, crude petroleum, ores, and so that are necessary for virgin-based paper, plastics, glass, and metals, recycling lessens the toxic air emissions, effluents, and solid wastes that these manufacturing processes create. It is virtually beyond dispute that manufacturing products from recyclables instead of from virgin raw materials—making, for instance, paper out of old newspapers instead of virgin timber—causes less pollution and imposes fewer burdens on the earth's natural habitat and biodiversity.

Antienvironmental theorists dismiss these benefits. The Cato Institute, a conservative research and advocacy group based in Washington, D.C, claims that state and local ordinances that promote recycling "neither conserve scarce resources nor help to protect the environment" (Schaumburg and Doyle, 1994, p. 1). According to the Reason Foundation, "Recycling itself can cause environmental harm. . . . As a result, the environmental costs of recycling may exceed any possible environmental benefits" (Scarlett, 1991, p. 1). Most recently, the benefits recycling provides in avoiding pollution caused at manufacturing plants were dismissed by John Tierney as follows: "[T]here are much more direct—and cheaper—ways to reduce pollution. Recycling is a waste of . . . natural resources . . . [and] a messy way to try to help the environment" (Tierney, 1996b, pp. 24, 44).

The Facts

In virtually all cases, recycling helps reduce or eliminate the pollution typically associated with the production and disposal of consumer products. As the following text makes clear, antirecycling interests who argue otherwise are either out of touch with or conveniently ignoring well known and widely documented environmental facts.

Paper Made from Timber

Think bundling your newspapers is "messy"? Not when compared with the process of making paper from virgin timber. While modern paper recycling mills produce no hazardous air or water pollution and no hazardous wastes (see, for example, Bronx Community Paper Company, 1994, 1996), the virgin pulp and paper industry is one of the world's largest generators of toxic air pollutants, surface water pollution, sludge, and solid wastes. A recent assessment of the virgin-timber based paper-making industry concluded that reducing hazardous discharges at paper mills worldwide to safe levels would cost $27 billion (International Institute for Environment and Development, 1996) . . .

THE DOWNSTREAM BENEFITS: DECREASING GARBAGE
AND THE NEED FOR LANDFILL SPACE

Landfills' Toxic Impacts

The most obvious and well-known advantage of recycling is that it leads to less garbage being buried in landfills, and environmental problems are the major reason more than ten thousand landfills have closed in the United States in the past fifteen years. Among the listed Superfund sites, the nation's most hazardous and contaminated locations, more than 20 percent (more than one of every five) are former municipal landfills (40 CFR 51, 52, and 60 Federal Register, 1996, p. 9909). The Reason Foundation dismisses contemporary concerns about the environmental impacts of landfills by claiming that "properly sited and operated, landfills pose little threat either to human health or to the environment" (Scarlett, 1991, p. 4). Predictably, John Tierney concurs. Here's how he put in "Recycling Is Garbage":

> [T]he simplest and cheapest option is usually to bury garbage in an environmentally safe landfill. . . .[T]here's little reason to worry about modern landfills, which by federal law must be lined with clay and plastic, equipped with drainage and gas-collection systems, covered daily with soil and monitored regularly for underground leaks (Tierney, 1996b, pp. 24, 28).

The Facts

Landfills are neither simple nor cheap, nor are they environmentally safe. Landfills generate hazardous and uncontrolled air emissions and also threaten surface and groundwater supplies. Landfills have contaminated aquifer drinking water supplies, wetlands, and streams throughout the United States—indeed, throughout the world—and the majority continue to do so. As detailed below, the list of toxic and hazardous chemicals emitted as gas or leaching as liquid from literally thousands of landfills defines a waste management option with wide-ranging pollution impacts. Among these documented pollutants are cyanide, dioxins, mercury, volatile organic compounds, methane and nonmethane organic compounds, greenhouse gases, hydrochloric acid, sulfuric acid, lead, and many others.

Conclusion

To be effective, recycling needs to draw upon corporate as well as governmental expenditures. It also requires a rethinking of long-held assumptions about our relationship to the earth's resources. Thus, it should come as no surprise that moving the manufacturing sector off its reliance on virgin resources and toward high-volume recycling is an uphill battle, despite the extraordinary support it enjoys throughout the industrialized world.

Nor should the fact be lost that recycling is a well-established, consensus-driven national policy goal. As Mike Shapiro at the EPA recently commented:

> We believe that recycling and composting, along with waste prevention, are vital components of the national approach to integrated solid waste management. More importantly, there's tremendous potential for growth in recycling and increased efficiencies as these municipal programs innovate and mature. Now is the time to invest our efforts in improving the cost-effectiveness of recycling so we can do it even better (Shapiro, 1996).

Meeting the needs of the present generation without compromising the ability of future generations to meet their own needs is the fundamental principle underlying the concept of sustainability. In both a material sense and in the way it fosters community participation and a concern for unseen people, faraway places, and future generations, few policies advance sustainability as much as recycling. The antirecycling message is being widely disseminated and, invariably, it is generating proenvironment responses from average citizens as well as representatives from all levels of government. Far from trashing recycling and impugning the motives its proponents, all sectors of the polity would do well, materially and spiritually, to embrace and help advance the sustainable, community-building, natural harmony it promotes.

Notes

1. OECD, 1995, p. 171. These rankings indicate recovery as a percentage of total discards for each commodity.
2. For some useful assessments see Denison and Ruston, eds., 1990; Denison, 1996; and Ackerman, 1997.

References

Bronx Community Paper Company, *Feasibility Study for the High-Grade Deinking Facility, New York, New York* (Birmingham, Ala.: Rust Engineering Company, September 4, 1994).

Bronx Community Paper Company, *Bronx Community Paper Company in the Harlem River Yard, Final Environmental Impact Statement* (April 25, 1996).

Gore, Al, Earth in the Balance (New York: Houghton Mifflin Company, 1992).

International Institute for Environment and Development, "Towards a Sustainable Paper Cycle," London (1996), cited in *Daily Environment Report* (August 5, 1996)..

McCarthy, J. E., *Recycling and Reducing Packaging Waste*: How The United States Compares to Other Countries (Washington, D.C.: Congressional Research Service, Library of Congress, 1991).

National Solid Waste Management Association, *Public Attitudes Towards Garbage Disposal* (Washington, D.C: NSWMA, 1988).

"Plastic Recycling Alliance to Close Doors," *Plastic News*, December 2, 1996.

"Plastics Recycling: Time for Last Rites?" *Plastics News*, September 30, 1996.

Schaumburg, Grant W. Jr., and Doyle, Katherine T., *Wasting Resources to Reduce Waste*: Recycling in New Jersey (Washington, D.C: Cato Institute, January 26, 1994), Policy Analysis No. 202.

Shapiro, Michael, "Sustainability and Recycling: A New Vision for the Future," paper presented at National Recycling Coalition Conference, Pittsburgh, Pennsylvania (September 19, 1996).

Standards of Performance for New Stationary Sources and Guidelines far Control of Existing Sources: Municipal Solid Waste Landfills, 40 CFR 51, 52, and 60 Federal Register 61:49 (March 12, 1996).

Solid Waste Disposal Criteria; Final Rule, 40 CFR Parts 257 and 258, Federal Register 56:196 (October 9, 1991).

"Testimony of the Natural Resources Defense Council before the U. S. Senate Subcommittee on Environmental Protection," Washington, D.C. (June 5, 1991).

Tierney, John, appearing on *New York Up-Close,* NY1 (June 28, 1996a).

Tierney, John, "Recycling Is Garbage," *New York Times Magazine*, June 30, 1996b.

"Union Carbide to Close HDPE Recycling Plant," in *Plastics News*, July 22, 1996.

THE ENVIRONMENTAL AND ECONOMIC FLAWS
OF RECYCLING PROGRAMS

Scott DeMuth
ENG101 sec0101

They can be seen everywhere. Bins and containers of all different shapes, sizes, and colors bearing the universal triangular recycling symbol are now on street corners, in office buildings, and in classrooms. They are so common, in fact, that I often find myself mistakenly placing garbage in recycling receptacles, and wondering what happened to the days when disposing of waste was a simple act that did not require reading the label on the container. Recycling has become an undeniable part of American culture. The images and testimonies of heroic citizens "doing their part" on television and various other forms of media have romanticized our view of recycling. Americans are recycling in such high volumes in part because they need to feel like they are personally making a difference. According to the United States Environmental Protection Agency, about 80 million tons of waste was recycled in 2005, accounting for 32 percent of all waste produced that year (www.epa.gov/epaoswer/non-hw/muncpl/reduce.htm). With such widespread participation in recycling programs, one would think that there existed conclusive evidence that recycling was the perfect alternative to conventional waste management techniques.

The truth is, however, that recycling is not as environmentally friendly or economically sensible as it is commonly believed, and in some cases it directly counteracts the goals of establishing recycling programs in the first place. Recycling may have some benefits, but the environmental and monetary costs involved necessitate a mandated reduction in recycled paper, plastic, and glass. Paper products should be deposited in landfills, and plastic and glass products should be reused for the same or similar purposes as they were originally produced. I argue that this is not insensitive, but exactly the opposite. As you will see, these actions are intended to serve the best interests of both society and the environment.

The Environmental Protection Agency cites as one of the benefits of recycling that it "allows more trees to remain standing" (www.epa.gov/msw/faq.htm). Many people buy into the "save the trees" mission, reasoning that recycling reduces the demand for wood pulp and increases the total stock of trees. Before I explain why the notion that recycling saves trees is faulty, I would like to make it clear that I do not disagree with the objective of saving trees itself, and I think it is very sensible for a number of reasons. First of all, trees maintain considerable amounts of aesthetic and recreational value, making them very desirable, especially to those who particularly enjoy being outdoors. Trees and forests also serve as invaluable habitats for countless species of wild animals and plants. Thirdly, and perhaps most importantly, trees serve a precious purpose in the sequestration of carbon dioxide, a gas that would cause serious global consequences if it were to be left unregulated. Although I agree that recycling will reduce the demand for wood pulp, taking this a few steps further will show that the reasoning that this increases the stock of trees is flawed. One of the fundamental laws of microeconomics states that supply will always meet demand. If the demand for wood pulp decreases, the quantity of wood pulp supplied will also decrease. The lumber plantations on which soft woods are raised and harvested will decrease the amount of new trees planted over the course of a few decades, until many are forced to shutdown. At this point the land on which the plantations were situated may be bought out by developers, who would clear the land and destroy any potential environmental value indefinitely. Indeed, recycling will reduce the demand for wood pulp, but the list of consequences continues from there. In the end, recycling paper actually results in a lower total stock of trees, defeating the original goal. The best response to this phenomenon is to levy a tax on the paper recycling industry in order to "reduce paper recycling and increase the number of trees" (Darby 1255).

As for plastic and glass recyclables, the issue is slightly different. In the words of an expert from The Environmental Defense Fund in the USA, "The diversity of plastic is really defeating its ability to be recycled" ("The Cost of Recycling"). The processes used to break down complex materials like glass and especially plastic are complicated, as well as costly. The end result is a material of much lower quality that "can only be used for low-grade products, like carpet fiber or supermarket carrier bags" ("The Cost of Recycling"). In addition, the energy required to transport and reduce these items to raw materials at least partly offsets the initial conservation from recycling. In light of these difficulties, it would make more sense to simply reuse products for the same purpose that they were originally intended, instead of putting forth the effort and the funds to break them down into raw materials to be manufactured again.

"We are running out of landfill space," argues Peter L. Grogan, President of the National Recycling Coalition, a strong recycling advocacy organization (Griffin). This is an interesting argument because so many recycling supporters stand by it, but it is nothing more than a misconception. Clark Wiseman, Professor of economics at Gonzaga University, explains that "at the current rate, all the nation's solid waste for the next 500 years" could fit into a landfill just 100 yards deep and 20 miles on each side (Griffin). Even the Environmental Protection Agency admits that "landfill space is plentiful on the national level" (www.epa.gov/msw/faq.htm). Equally deceptive and outdated are the claims that landfills are harmful because decomposing garbage releases methane, which seeps through the soil into the atmosphere, exacerbating the growing problem with global warming. It is true that when bacteria break down garbage in landfills, methane is produced, but in fact, this occurrence is usually advantageous. Most modern landfills are outfitted with equipment to recover the methane so that it can be burned to generate electricity ("Landfills: Is Wetter Better?" A320). In effect, the more garbage that is deposited in landfills, the more methane that is produced and recovered, and the more we can substitute away from harmful fossil fuel-burning electric power plants.

The thought of discontinuing recycling programs is very counterintuitive to the typical American conscience, because we are constantly bombarded by the ethical appeals of environmentalism. Americans need to feel like they are making a difference, and it is this "feel good factor" that is keeping recycling alive. However, we have to let the facts speak over our consciences and remind us that recycling is not as environmentally and economically beneficial as it is commonly believed. If our goal as a society is to serve the interests of the planet earth, then we should reduce recycling and invest in some more sensible waste management methods.

References

1. Baldwin, William. "Environmentalist, Spare That Tree." *Forbes.com*. 15 Aug. 2005 *Forbes Magazine*. 11 Apr. 2007 <http://www.forbes.com/opinions/freeforbes/2005/0815/0 12.html>

2. Black, Harvey. "Rethinking Recycling." *Environmental Health Perspectives*. 20 Nov. 1995. 11 Apr. 2007 <http://www.ehponline.org/docs/1995/103-11/focus2.html>

3. Cordato, Roy E. "Don't Recycle: Throw it Away!" *The Ludwig von Mises Institute*. Dec.1995. 11 Apr. 2007 <http://www.mises.org/freemarket_detail.asp?control=212>

4. Collins, Lyndhurst. "Recycling and the Environmental Debate: A Question of Social Conscience or Scientific Reason?" *Journal of Environmental Planning and Management* 39.3 (1996): 333–356. Informaworld. U of Maryland, McKeldin Lib. 15 Apr. 2007 <http://www.Informaworld.com/smpp/content ~content=a713676382>

5. Darby, Michael R. "Paper Recycling and the Stock of Trees." *The Journal of Political Economy* 81.5 (1973): 1253–1255. JSTOR. U. of Maryland, McKeldin Lib. 15 Apr. 2007 <http://www.jstor.org/ view/00223808/di950956/95p0062g/0?frame=frame&userID=8102c2be@umd.edu/01cce4405f00501 bd4015&dpi=3&config=jstor>

6. "End to Recycling Would Be a Step Backwards." *New Orleans City Business* 19.51 (1999): 18. *MasterFILE Premier*. EBSCOhost. U. of Maryland, McKeldin Lib. 15 Apr. 2007 <http://web.ebscohost. com/ehost/detail?vid=1&hid=8&sid=b41da2f3-2f58-4fbb-9ca8-02c627f2dbc3%40sessionmgr2>

7. Griffin, R. D. "Garbage crisis." (1992): 241–264. CQ Researcher Online. U. of Maryland, McKeldin Library. 19 Apr. 2007 <http://library.cqpress.com/cqresearcher/cqresrre19 92032006.>

8. "If There is Plenty of Landfill Space, Then Why Should I Recycle?" *Frequently Asked Questions about Recycling and Waste Management*. 23 Oct. 2006 *Environmental Protection Agency*. 19 Apr. 2007 <http://www.epa.gov/msw/faq.htm>

9. "Landfills: Is Wetter Better?" *Environmental Health Perspectives*. 106.7 (1998): A320–A321. 19 Apr. 2007 <http://www.pubmedcentral.nih.gov/pagerender.fcgi?artid=153312 4&pageindex=1>

10. MacGuire, Francis A.S. "Comments and Debates." *Journal of Environmental Planning and Management* 41.3 (1998): 403–410. Informaworld. U. of Maryland, McKeldin Lib. 15 Apr. 2007 <http://www.informaworld.com/smpp/content~content=a713676468>

11. "NRDC Report Trashes Recycling Critics." *Environmental Health Perspectives*. June 1997. 15 Apr. 2007 <http://www.ehponline.org/docs/1997/105-6/forum.html>

12. Read, Adam D., Paul Phillips, and Guy Robinson. "Landfill as a Future Waste Management Option in England: The View of Landfill Operators." *The Geographical Journal* 164.1 (1998): 55–66. JSTOR. U. of Maryland, McKeldin Lib. 15 Apr. 2007 <http://www.j stor.org/view/00167398/sp020013/ 02x0600b/0>

13. "Recycle." *Reduce, Reuse, and Recycle*. 8 Dec. 2006. *Environmental Protection Agency*. 19 Apr. 2007 <http://www.epa.gov/epaoswer/non-hw/muncpl/reduce.htm>

14. "The Cost of Recycling." *Geographical* 77.9 (2005): 36–37. *Academic Search Premier*. EBSCOhost. U. of Maryland, McKeldin Lib. 11 Apr. 2007 <http://web.ebscohost.com/ ehost/detail?vid=1&hid= 14&sid=8b156e0f-5959-48b5-9e93-9d2058904561%40session mgr2>

15. "What Effects Do Waste Prevention and Recycling Have on Global Warming?" *Frequently Asked Questions about Recycling and Waste Management*. 23 Oct. 2006 *Environmental Protection Agency*. 19 Apr. 2007 <http://www.epa.gov/msw/faq.htm>

VI

FINAL POSITION PAPER

PARTS OF A FULL ARGUMENT

So you have to write a ten-page research paper on a subject of your choosing and the question you might be asking is: how am I going to organize all of the research that I've done and the arguments that I intend to make into a cohesive document? One way to arrange the evidence and analysis that you've assembled is to use the same pattern of arrangement that classical rhetoricians used. Classical rhetors often used a regular pattern or outline to keep track of their arguments, especially because their speeches were often improvised or delivered from memory. Rhetors then adjusted and rearranged the pattern to suit the rhetorical situation. And while some classical rhetoricians disagreed on the names and numbers of the various parts of an argument, they all agreed a regular pattern helped audiences better understand and remember the arguments made. The arrangement of the six-part pattern (listed in the table below) has rhetorical purposes as well; each part builds on the others to increase the persuasiveness of an argument.

Parts		Ancient Terms	Purpose
1	Introduction	*exordium*	To establish exigence, to make the reader receptive to your arguments
2	Narration	*narratio*	To state your case, to give background information on your topic
3	Partition	*partitio*	To forecast your arguments, to provide your audience with an overview of your subject
4	Confirmation	*confirmatio*	To prove your claim/s to your readers, to provide evidence and analysis to support your arguments
5	Refutation	*refutatio*	To consider opposing arguments
6	Conclusion	*peroratio*	To summarize your claim/s, to enhance your ethos, to answer the question "so what?"

This six-part structure of a full argument is not necessarily a fixed one—that is, you can rearrange the parts to suit your argument, purpose, and audience. In some cases, your argument may not need an introduction, or you may decide that starting your paper with your refutation to answer your audience's objections is the best exigence for your argument. You may also want to shorten or lengthen your narration depending upon your audience's familiarity with the issue you are addressing. As you write an outline for your paper, you will probably not weight every part detailed below equally; almost certainly, you will reorder some of these parts to better suit your persuasive goals. Knowing the part of a full argument enables you to select and rearrange material systematically, the better to appeal to your intended audience.

INTRODUCTION

Most writers assume that an introduction must state an argument's purpose and "get the audience's attention," but introductions can do much more that this. You can use the introduction to

- establish exigence, convincing your readers of your subject's importance and of problems that need to be solved.
- begin to construct your ethos, building a relationship with your readers that helps them to identify with the persona you project.

Some arguments, however, may require no introduction because audiences may be familiar with the issue and might already agree with the claims made. Indeed, deciding what kind of introduction to write depends on the rhetorical situation. For this reason, classical rhetoricians suggested that students not write their introductions until after they had written the confirmation—believing that it was difficult for writers to know how to introduce an argument they had yet to make.

NARRATION

Before beginning to argue for a position, you may need to give your readers a background or history of the issue. The narration

- makes clear what happened or is happening that requires resolution or rethinking.
- introduces readers who know little about the topic to the information they need to follow the argument.
- reminds knowledgeable readers of the information they need to appreciate the issue.
- defines key terms your readers need to know to understand your paper.
- begins to shape how your want your audience to understand the context of the debate by telling the story of the debate as you want them to see it.

As you write this section, realize that you are not just providing all the information and detail you can; rather, you are selecting and phrasing the presentation of that information in a way that establishes exigence for and lays the foundation of your argument.

Some classical rhetoricians argued that the narration could be omitted if the audience was very familiar with the issue, but others disagreed, stating that the narration gave the issue prominence and to neglect it was to make the issue seem insignificant. Again, the decision as to what to include in your narration weighs heavily on the rhetorical situation.

PARTITION

Readers may find longer arguments (such as a research paper) difficult to follow, which is why rhetoricians often use a partition to act as a signpost showing the direction the arguments will follow. The partition is a brief section that

- narrows down the issue you will be supporting, giving you the opportunity to clarify which issues you will discuss, and, perhaps, which you will not.
- previews the coming parts of your argument without giving away the substance of your support.

This part serves as a necessary overview of the unfolding of the subject; think of it as a road map to the rest of your argument that your reader can study before proceeding on a journey through your claims and evidence, and perhaps even look back to as they continue through your argument.

CONFIRMATION

The confirmation is usually the longest part of an argument. It presents the best arguments for your case, and these arguments might consider issues of existence, definition, cause, effect, value, policy, and jurisdiction, depending on the rhetorical situation addressed. This part can contain

- positive arguments that support your position, relying on the common topics and lines of argument.
- evidence and analysis that support all of your arguments, including data and testimony from reliable authorities.

As you outline your argument, you will want to pay close attention to how you order your confirmation, thinking about which proofs are the strongest and which are the weakest. Knowing the weak points in your argument makes it easier to consider your audience's refutations, and often writers combine confirmation and refutation throughout the paper.

REFUTATION

The refutation considers arguments that might weaken your credibility or case. Although some students think that considering arguments against their case might lessen their argument's impact, composing a refutation has just the opposite effect for their writing. A well-written refutation contains

- arguments against positions opposed to yours.
- evidence that shows why your opponent's arguments are mistaken, misguided, too limited, or otherwise problematic.

The position of refutation in an argument is not fixed—it can appear at different points such as in the introduction, the narration, or the confirmation. Refutation can also be structured as a separate section before or after the confirmation, or it can be woven into the confirmation. For more information on refutation, see "Considering Refutation in Arrangement" on page 220.

CONCLUSION

Writing your conclusion should draw on your best skills because it can leave a lasting impression on your audience. A hastily written conclusion that simply enumerates major points made will not, in most cases, do justice to the significance of the issue you want to address. So while a conclusion should certainly summarize your major points and remind your reader of where they have been, it should also

- remind readers of the stake they have in the debate.
- use emotional appeals to highlight your major claims.
- leave your readers with a positive impression of your argument.

A good conclusion answers the "so what" question: so what has your audience gained by reading this, what might they do next with the perspective you have offered, what do they do next in thinking about this topic.

RESPONDING TO OPPOSING VIEWS:
REFUTING, CONCEDING, AND BRIDGING

You will hardly be surprised to hear that when arguing to a "hostile" audience a writer must respond to opposing views. After all, would the audience be hostile if it did not to some degree accept the arguments of the opposition? In fact, when addressing more neutral readers who might be undecided but who have heard opposing arguments, responding to opposing views is still important. The three strategies for responding to opposing views are **refuting**, **conceding** and **bridging**. Refuting is the most common and will often form a whole section of an argument (see "Parts of a Full Argument," p. 213–216). Conceding usually does not form whole sections of an argument. It usually occurs very quickly and may be used during both confirmation and refutation. Bridging usually occurs at a more global level, such as framing a more inclusive thesis statement.

REFUTING

Refutations are arguments that undo opposing views, responding to them and showing that your own arguments are more valid.

Why refute an argument?

- To make your own argument stronger
- To show that you have considered other possible conclusions in coming to your own conclusion
- To show that you are educated and knowledgeable on your topic and are aware of the opposition's arguments
- To more fully participate in the debate on the topic

What arguments should you refute? It depends on your audience.

- What arguments are they familiar with?
- What objections do you think they would raise?
- Are there popular arguments those opposing your thesis often take?

Refutation, however, should not be confused with "trashing." If you trash the opposition and/or its views, you not only damage your ethos (an injury to you), you fail to consider those views adequately and respectfully (an injury to your opponent); as a result, you fail to answer the questions those arguments raise for your audience (an injury to the community). Instead of trashing the opposition, ethical and authoritative rhetors offer thoughtful, supportable reasons why the opposition is wrong.

Strategies for Refuting

1. Show that their claims are applicable to one or part of the cases, but not to all.
2. Show that the thesis they assert is only applicable in rare cases.
3. Show that their thesis has overstated the case or exaggerated the issue.
4. Show that they have included irrelevant facts or details or irrelevant history.
5. Show that the causal connections they have made are unreasonable.
6. Show that their evidence or reasoning is not compelling.
7. Show that their definitions of key terms are invalid, out of context, or too broad.
8. Show that the evidence is used out of context.
9. Show that their position is outdated or irrelevant due to new facts.
10. Show that there are more choices than the ones they present.
10. Show that they have not presented statistics fairly or accurately.
12. Show that they beg the question (the evidence is the same as the thesis).
13. Show that their logic includes a logical fallacy.
14. Show that the unstated premise of their argument should not be accepted.

When refuting, pay careful attention to the logic behind the rhetor's statements. Is their unstated premise one that the audience would not accept? Have they elevated weaker values over stronger ones?

CONCEDING

Concessions are when you acknowledge the force of an opposing view. When you concede a point, you recognize its validity.

Why concede a point?

- To make you sound reasonable and fair-minded
- To show that you understand opposing arguments and are willing to consider them
- To diffuse your opponents' energy: you can take the wind out of their sails if you acknowledge the validity of some of their points

Some phrases indicating concession are: *granted*; *of course*; *X may be a good point, but . . .*; *I can understand X, yet . . .*; *Although X is true. . . .*

How do you decide when to concede? It can be tricky. Consider:

- the consequences of crediting the strongest opposing views without being able to attack them as well
- whether the concessions give the impression that you don't support your own position

If you find you are conceding most or all of the arguments to an opponent, rethink your position.

Once you offer a concession, follow up with an explanation of why your thesis is still correct and/or why the opposition's thesis is nevertheless wrong. Words that signal follow-up include: *nevertheless, still, however, but, yet, on the other hand, instead, conversely.*

Strategies for Conceding

1. Present the opposing view fairly and then move to your own position, marking it with words signaling a comeback (*Takaki argues that X. However, a strong case can be made against X.* or *Yet, a better case can be made for Y.*)
2. Show that you have thought about other positions (*I understand why some people are opposed to euthanasia. But I believe that . . . I've considered the moral arguments against euthanasia such as . . . But I've reached the conclusion that . . .*)
3. Acknowledge the validity of evidence or of a premise but refute it as not leading to the conclusion that has been drawn, or as not being correct or applicable in this case (*It is true that X . . . However, . . .*)
4. Acknowledge the prevalence of a belief and then question it (*Some people think that killing someone is morally worse than letting someone die. But is it?*)
5. Show that there are points of agreement, but then indicate where the parties diverge and why your position is the better one (*While we agree about X, we cannot accept Y.*)

BRIDGING OR INGESTING

Bridging is the technique of incorporating two conflicting positions into a single compatible one. Why attempt a bridging argument?

- To show that the positions are actually compatible in some important respects
- To seek a more moderate, middle position that acknowledges the partial validity of both of the extreme, opposed positions

Strategies for Bridging

1. Try to construct a higher value, a broader interest that both parties can identify with. Environmentalists and loggers, at odds over spotted owl habitat, nevertheless both value the forests of the Pacific Northwest. Similarly, if two groups disagree about what caused a major oil spill, you might point out their common desire to clean up the area and save wildlife.
2. Find points of commonality where people can reconcile their opposition, and remind them of the larger goals that unite them. Thus, if Catholics and Protestants are in opposition on some issue, you might appeal to their religious sensibility and bridge their differences by calling both groups "Christians." Using such a bridging term may allow opposing groups to work together despite some differing beliefs. In fact, this strategy is useful when two groups are at extreme odds or hold absolute beliefs and appear to be so far apart that no resolution can be achieved.
3. Invent a new term or concept, and in the process, creating a mediating position never before attempted. Faced with the extreme options of total government control of health-care delivery versus total reliance upon free-market competition, some policy analysts created a bridged position by taking features from both. They even named their approach with a term formed by taking a word from each of the opposed positions: *managed competition*.

Although "Parts of a Full Argument" seems to place confirmation (arguments supporting the thesis presented) before refutation (arguments that undo opposing views), the actual order of arguments depends on audience and purpose.

In some cases, you may need to refute opposing arguments with which your audience agrees before presenting positive arguments for your own position; in others, you may need to establish your own case before rebutting opposing arguments. Sometimes confirmation and refutation can be intertwined, addressing opposing points and presenting positive support issue by issue. For instance, an argument against distributing condoms in high schools could proceed in issue-oriented units, first presenting both refuting and confirming arguments regarding the moral implications of the policy, then refuting and confirming arguments regarding parental authority, and finally refuting and confirming arguments regarding health-related concerns.

There are some considerations, but no absolute rules, that can help with this decision:

- How recently has the audience heard opposing arguments? How entrenched is their opposition to your thesis?
- Do you need to clear some space before you start presenting your own views, or should you put forward your own position before you risk alienating them by disputing arguments with which they agree?
- Does an alternating approach allow you to answer objections as they arise or problematically prevent you from making your whole case at once?

The best approach is to outline the argument using several different arrangements and then to consider how each approach will affect your audience. How will the audience likely respond at each point in your argument? Once you have a draft or two, you might ask a reader or peer editor to briefly note what she is thinking while reading each paragraph of your paper:

- What questions arise as she reads?
- If you begin with refutation, does she want you to switch to offering positive arguments for your position?
- If you begin with confirmation, does she feel that you are skirting important opposing views?
- If you are alternating confirmation and refutation, does the back-and-forth arrangement make the argument difficult to follow or the position seem underdeveloped?

Combined, these steps will help you find an effective arrangement.

Regardless of whether you are writing an introduction, a paragraph in the body of an argument, or a conclusion, it is important that you establish a structure that will convey the overall goal or goals of that unit of thought. *The Academic Writer's Handbook* suggests two pieces of advice to follow: "giv[e] your paragraph a controlling idea and sticking to it" and "mov[e] from sentence to sentence with a plan" (Rosen 48, 49).

Because introductions and conclusions differ greatly from body paragraphs in terms of what the sections set out to accomplish in argumentative writing, this section will solely focus on body paragraphs.

Each body paragraph should focus on proving a single argumentative claim. To a certain extent, argumentative claims function as "paragraph-level theses" (Rosen 48). Only by proving all of the smaller paragraph-level theses can an author prove his or her overall thesis. There are several ways in which you can write the smaller paragraph level claims. The most straightforward of these is by composing a **premise based claim**. **Premises** often rely upon the word *since* or *because* to connect back to the larger thesis. For example, let's say you were asked to write a claim to support the overall thesis: *The death penalty in the U.S. should be abolished.* You might write as a connecting premise *since it is cruel and unusual punishment.* In such a paragraph, your primary smaller goal would be to prove that the death penalty constitutes "cruel and unusual punishment." An example of this type of argument paragraph proceeds below.

> The death penalty in the U.S. should be abolished since it amounts to cruel and unusual punishment. Such a conclusion can be justified not only from referring to the 1791 federal Bill of Rights, which outlaws "excessive bail...excessive fines [and] cruel and unusual punishments." Such a conclusion can also be supported by looking at the horrific particulars of the extended execution of Angel Diaz. Elizabeth Weil notes in an article from *The New York Times Magazine* that
>
> > because the execution team punctured the veins in Diaz's arm when putting in the intravenous catheters, forcing the drugs into the soft tissue instead, Diaz grimaced for as long as 26 minutes, suffering from 11-inch and 12-inch chemical burns on his left and right arms respectively, and took 34 minutes to die.
>
> Lethal injection was originally decided upon because it was considered a more humane form of capital punishment than sentencing someone to the electric chair or death by hanging. Looking at the Diaz example, it is clear that lethal injections can result in something no less barbarous or painful. For the sake of both the condemned and those forced to administer or witness such events, the death penalty should be abolished.

Notice how each sentence builds towards supporting the smaller argument that the death penalty constitutes a form of punishment that is both "cruel and unusual." Notice also how the last sentence of the argument claim paragraph ties the smaller claim to the overall thesis.

Premises are not the only method you might choose to construct your paragraph level claims. You might also choose one of the **special topics**, which are similar to the **common topics**, but are rarer and more specialized. The most straightforward of the special topics, and one of the most useful, is the **correlative claim**. A correlative claim is a cause and effect based claim that relies upon the following structure:

If x, then y

If we rewrote the premise-based death penalty argument as a correlative claim, it might look like this:

> *If the death penalty is eliminated, U.S. senators and citizens alike can once again argue with a straight face that the U.S. does not abide by cruel and unusual punishment.*

Clearly, the goal of the correlative claim above is different than the goal of the premise based claim but how so? If the writer uses the premise-based claim

> *The death penalty in the U.S. should be abolished since it is cruel and unusual punishment.*

the writer will have to prove that the death penalty constitutes "cruel and unusual punishment" and that, according to our laws, it is wrong. If the writer uses the correlative claim, the writer must prove instead that the U.S. is being hypocritical in allowing the death penalty to continue (given their outward objections to "cruel and unusual punishment") and that this hypocrisy would cease if the government outlawed the death penalty.

Although there are many other special topics, we especially recommend four to help with the composition of argumentative claims. These include *a fortiori* **claims**, **partitioning your subject to eliminate possibilities, arguing on the basis of consistency, and arguing on the basis of equivalency of results.** *A fortiori* **claims** argue on the basis of probability:

> If something occurs when it is not likely, it will certainly occur when it is likely; likewise, if something does not occur when it is likely, it will not occur when it is not likely.

Certain subjects will allow more easily for *a fortiori* claims than others. Take, for example, Title IX, the federal antidiscrimination statute that says that women athletes have to be given equal athletic opportunities and facilities to male athletes in direct proportion to the overall enrollment of men and women. Using an *a fortiori* strategy, we might write

> *If women athletes are the victims of gender discrimination with Title IX enforced, women athletes will be even more likely to be the victims of gender discrimination when Title IX is overturned.*

Partitioning your subject to eliminate possibilities provides another structure with which to write your argumentative claim. With this claim structure, your goal as a writer is to set certain conditions under which a certain position or stance should be taken and then prove that the position or stance should be taken or rejected.

For example, you could write:

The death penalty should be abolished if it constitutes "cruel and unusual punishment," if such a practice contradicts federal law, and if it has contributed to the United States losing the moral high ground on issues such as torture and detainee rights.

The last two formal special topics that you could use to structure your argumentative claims could be easily confused if you are not careful. **Arguments on the basis of consistency** involve cases in which you establish that something you are arguing for is consistent with something that is already in practice. **Arguments on the basis of equivalency of results** instead argue that what you are arguing for is no different from something that is already accepted.

VII

STYLE

Have you ever heard another student writer say, "Well, that teacher just didn't like my style, so I only got a C on the paper"? While some students might agree that their papers only succeed when the teacher "likes their style," classical rhetoricians and seasoned writers would heartily disagree with this claim. Why? Because rhetoricians and professional writers know that to communicate your ideas clearly you need to master many different styles so that you suit your style and your message to the needs of the rhetorical situation.

Different writing situations demand different styles. As Sharon Crowley notes in *Ancient Rhetorics for Contemporary Students*, "the community dictates the standards of rhetorical appropriateness . . . When ancient teachers of rhetoric counseled their students to use an appropriate style, they generally meant that a style should be suited to subject, occasion, and audience." For example, Michael Wilbon, a well-known *Washington Post* sports columnist, uses a more conversational style when he comments on LeBron James' NBA playing style, "He's not Jordan. He's more like Magic Johnson, and if not Magic then a super duper-size Scottie Pippen." Notice how Wilbon's use of short sentences, repetition, and colloquial terms such as "super-duper size" appeals to his audience of daily sport readers who are expecting an informal, entertaining sports analysis. However, readers of the *L.A. Time*s editorial assessing the aftermath of the Iraq war expect a serious subject to be treated in a more formal style. Christopher J. Fettweis, Assistant Professor of National Security Affairs at the U.S. Naval War College, writes of the war's potential aftermath, "Defeat in war damages societies quite out of proportion to what a rational calculation of cost would predict. The United States absorbed the loss in Vietnam quite easily on paper, for example, but the societal effects of defeat linger to this day. The Afghanistan debacle was an underrated contributor to Soviet malaise in the 1980s and a factor in *perestroika, glasnost* and eventually the dissolution of the Soviet Union. Defeats can have unintended, seemingly inexplicable consequences." Notice the marked difference in style—Fettweis uses words like *perestroika*, dissolution, inexplicable, and he rarely uses three-word sentences.

Indeed ancient rhetoricians taught their students that there were three levels of style: grand, middle, and plain. Grand style employed highly figurative language and elevated diction, while middle style used fewer figures and more commonplaces. Plain style meant writing in everyday language.

In English 101 gaining expertise in style means that you will learn the elements of good sentence composition, the principles of writing clearly, and figures of speech and thought. This section of the English 101 curriculum presents specific techniques and language skills that will help you get your message across as effectively as possible.

WHY DO I HAVE TO LEARN LANGUAGE SKILLS?
I ALREADY KNOW MY LANGUAGE.

Spoken/signed language and written language have significant differences, and most of these reside in the different circumstances in which they are used. When you speak or sign, you are usually interacting with someone in real time. Your interlocutor can reply, ask questions, and signal agreement or disagreement, confusion, surprise or boredom. If you see that a point hasn't gotten across, you can stop and rephrase—speaking and signing allow a special sort of self-editing. And you can use intonation, voice tone, speed of delivery, facial expressions and gestures to signal how you feel about something, to emphasize a point, and even to structure your talk. None of these tools is available in writing. When you write, you must anticipate how readers will react; you must figure out where the difficult points are and guide readers over them; and you have only one chance to be persuasive. When you talk to someone, that person may edge away when he's heard enough, but he's unlikely to try to sneak out of the room when you're in the middle of a sentence. Your reader has no such limitations. Unless that reader has some compelling reason to stick with you, your argument can easily lose its audience.

In speech or signing, then, we have a wealth of ways to create emphasis, to signal organization, and to keep interest. In writing, all this must be done with words on a page. Therefore, you must have a range of language tools available to help you move your reader through your text. Where you might signal the organization of a series of points by gesture, you will learn to use logical relations; where oral communication can indicate emphasis with loudness or stress, you will work on finding other ways to emphasize your points; where you might use your facial expressions to show your attitude towards what you are saying, you will work on using word choice and figurative language to give your reader the same information.

WHY DO WE HAVE TO PRACTICE ONE SKILL OVER AND OVER?

When you practice a language skill by playing around with a structure or a linguistic device, you won't produce a normal prose paragraph. But you will learn the skill well enough so that when you do need it, you will have it available. You should get used to playing with language, even though you may or may not use the results of any given exercise on the associated paper. An athletic analogy works well here: football players do weight training, but not because they labor under the delusion that they're going to carry a weight bench out onto the field and hold up the game while they demonstrate their abilities. Weight training is a way to develop the strength they need in order to be able to do their job well during the game. Similarly, by going through language exercises, you will be increasing your verbal agility. In some cases it may be every bit as boring as endless weight-training can be to the athletes, who, after all, stick with it because they're interested in what it enables them to do on the field or the court when it counts.

WHAT IS THE POINT OF LEARNING THE TERMINOLOGY—
"NOMINALIZATIONS," "ANTITHESIS," AND SO ON?

The language skills you are learning here are not entirely new to you. You've been using transition words most of your life, and you're familiar with examples of many of the figures of speech from advertising and casual conversation. However, there is a difference between knowing how to do something and knowing exactly what it is that you know. Being able to put a name to something can help you identify it when you see it again. Knowing the categories and how they are related will help you understand how best to make use of the techniques so that they work together smoothly to create effective prose.

Terminology is also valuable in diagnosing problems. Those of us with little knowledge of cars often go to our mechanics with no better description than that the car is making "a funny noise" or seems "a bit sluggish." It would be far more useful if we could describe the component that is malfunctioning or put a more precise description to the way the car is deviating from its normal operations. In any field in which it is important to be able to talk about how things work, practitioners find it useful to have clear and precise terminology both for organizing their own thinking and for communicating with others in the field.

As you work through the exercises in the language skills section, try to become more and more conscious of the details of how language is used—both how you use the skills you learn and how others outside the classroom provide examples of the skills you are practicing. You will find that a conscious awareness of language use will help your writing immeasurably.

WHAT IS RHETORICAL GRAMMAR?

from *Rhetorical Grammar*

To understand the subject matter of a book with the title *Rhetorical Grammar,* you'll obviously have to understand not only the meaning of both *rhetoric* and *grammar* but also their relationship to each other. *Grammar* is undoubtedly familiar to you. You've probably been hearing about, if not actually studying, grammar in your English classes since middle school. *Rhetoric,* on the other hand—and its adjective version, *rhetorical*—may not be familiar at all. So, to figure out what rhetorical grammar is all about, we'll begin with the familiar *grammar.*

If you're like many students, you may associate the idea of grammar with rules—various do's and don'ts that apply to sentence structure and punctuation. You may remember studying certain rules to help you correct or prevent errors in your writing. You may remember the grammar handbook as the repository of such rules.

But now consider another possibility: that YOU are the repository of the rules. You—not a book. Consider that there is stored within you, in your computer-like brain, a system of rules, a system that enables you to create the sentences of your native language. The fact that you have such an internalized system means that when you study grammar *you are studying what you already "know."*

Linguistic researchers now tell us that you began internalizing the rules of your language perhaps before you were born, when you began to differentiate the particular rhythms of the language you were hearing. In the first year of life you began to create the rules that would eventually produce sentences.

You were little more than a year old when you began to demonstrate your grammar ability by naming things around you; a few months later you were putting together two- and three-word strings, and before long your language took on the features of adult sentences. No one taught you. You didn't have language lessons. You learned all by yourself, from hearing the language spoken around you—and you did so unconsciously.

This process of language development is universal—that is, it occurs across cultures, and it occurs in every child with normal physical and mental development. No matter what your native language is, you have internalized its grammar system. By the time you were five or six years old, you were an expert at narrating events, at asking questions, at describing people and places, probably at arguing. The internalized system of rules that accounts for this language ability of yours is our definition of *grammar.*

When you study grammar in school, then, you are actually studying what you already "know." Note that the verb *know* needs those quotation marks because we're not using it in the usual sense. Your grammar knowledge is largely subconscious: You don't know consciously what you "know." When you study grammar you are learning *about* those grammar rules that you use subconsciously every time you speak—as well as every time you listen and make sense of what you hear.

But as you know, studying grammar also means learning other rules, the conventions of writing—rules that have nothing to do with the internalized rules that enable us to speak. When you write, you must pay attention to rules about paragraphing and sentence completeness and capital letters and quotation marks and apostrophes and commas and, perhaps the trickiest of all, spelling.

To be effective, however, writing also requires attention to rhetoric—and here is where the adjective *rhetorical* comes into the picture. *Rhetoric* means that your audience—the reader—and your purpose make a difference in the way you write on any given topic. To a great extent, that rhetorical situation—the audience, purpose, and topic—determines the grammatical choices you make, choices about sentence structure and vocabulary, even punctuation. Rhetorical grammar is about those choices.

This meaning of *rhetoric* is easy to illustrate: Imagine writing a letter to your best friend describing your first week at school this semester; contrast that with the letter on the same subject to your great-aunt Millie. Think of the differences there might be in those two letters, those two different rhetorical situations. One obvious difference, of course, is vocabulary; you wouldn't use the same words with two such different audiences. The grammatical structures are also going to be different, determined in part by the tone or level of formality. For example, you might use longer sentences in the more formal version, the letter to Aunt Millie:

> My roommate, Peter Piper, is a very nice fellow from New York City.

or

> My roommate, who grew up in New York City, is named Peter Piper.

In the letter to your buddy, you'd probably say,

> You'd like my roommate. He's a nice guy—from the Big Apple. And would you believe? His name is Peter Piper.

You would probably write this less formal version almost as easily as you speak; it sounds like something you'd say. The Aunt Millie letter, especially the sentence with the *who*-clause, would take a little more thought on your part. It doesn't sound as much like speech. In fact, a *who*-clause like that, set off by commas, is a modifier used almost exclusively in the written language.

Understanding rhetorical grammar, then, means understanding the grammatical choices available to you when you write and the rhetorical effects those choices will have on your reader. Aunt Millie will probably recognize—and approve of—your letter as evidence of a serious-minded, articulate student. She will feel assured that your twelve or more years of education have not been wasted. The good friend who gets your letter will hear your familiar voice and know that all is well.

You can think of the grammatical choices you have as tools in your writer's toolkit. You have a variety of tools for the differences in language that different rhetorical situations call for. To study grammar in this way—that is, to consider the conscious knowledge of sentence structure as your toolkit—is the essence of rhetorical grammar.

EXERCISE 1

from *Rhetorical Grammar*

Add punctuation to the following sentences—if they need it.

1. I took piano lessons for several years as a child but I never did like to practice.

2. I surprised both my mother and my former piano teacher by signing up for lessons in the Music Department here at school so now I practice every spare minute I can find.

3. My hands are small but I have exercised my fingers and now have managed to stretch an octave.

4. My fingers are terribly uncoordinated but every week the exercises and scales get easier to play.

5. I was really embarrassed the first few times I practiced on the old upright in our dorm lounge so I usually waited until the room was empty now I don't mind the weird looks I get from people.

6. Some of my friends clap their hands or tap their feet to help me keep time.

7. I have met three residents in the dorm who are really good pianists they've been very helpful to me and very supportive of my beginning efforts.

8. I often play my Glenn Gould records for inspiration and just plain enjoyment.

9. I'm so glad that Bach and Haydn composed music simple enough for beginners and that my teacher assigned it for me to play.

10. I'm looking forward to seeing the look on my mother's face when I go home at the end of the term and play some of my lessons from *The Little Bach Book* she will be amazed.

EXERCISE 2

Revise the following sentences, paying particular attention to the unparallel structures.

1. I can't decide which activity I prefer: to swim at the shore in July, when the sand is warm, or jogging along country roads in October, when the autumn leaves are at their colorful best.

2. The Baltimore Orioles' stadium at Camden Yards has all the virtues of the beloved ballparks of another era and is in the great tradition of classic baseball architecture.

3. I neither enjoy flying across the country nor particularly want to take the train.

4. The movie's starting time and whether we could afford the tickets were both more important to us than were the opinions of the reviewers.

5. Denny lost weight very slowly but said he didn't want to try the new diet drugs.

6. Bowling, like other sports, requires physical exertion and is the number one participation sport in the country.

7. I almost never watch television: There is either nothing on that appeals to me, or the picture disappears at a crucial moment.

8. Blue whales are the largest of all animals and up to 80 percent of them congregate seasonally in Antarctic waters.

EXERCISE 3

Revise the following passages to eliminate the vague pronouns. In some cases the most effective revision will be to turn *this* or *that* into a determiner. Another possibility is to combine the sentences.

1. The contractor for our house is obviously skeptical about solar energy. This doesn't surprise me.

2. The summer heat wave in the Midwest devastated a large portion of the nation's corn crop. That probably means higher meat prices for next year.

3. I know that I should give up junk food to get in shape for summer, but that is never easy to do.

4. We arrived at the airport two hours before our flight. I was glad to do it, realizing the importance of safety procedures.

5. If I would take time to study my computer manual, it would save me a lot of frustration.

6. Jeremy's father died when he was only six years old. That left the burden of raising him and his sister to his mother. Jeremy remembers that it wasn't easy for her.

7. My friend Abe nearly drowned several years ago when his boat capsized in Lake Erie. I assume that is the reason he became a confirmed landlubber and refuses to go fishing with me.

8. Last year my brother Chuck designed and built his own house—a beautiful rustic log cabin. It really amazed me, because when we were kids he did nothing but break things, especially my favorite toys. In fact, he was always in trouble because of that.

EXERCISE 4

It's important to recognize the passive voice when you see it—so that you'll know when you've used it and thus will use it deliberately and effectively. In the first section of this exercise, you'll transform active sentences into the passive voice; in the second part you'll do the opposite—change the passive into the active. And in the third part, the voice of the sentence is not identified: You'll have to figure it out.

A. Transform the following active sentences into the passive voice; remember that the direct object of the active functions as the subject in the passive.
   1. My roommate wrote the lead article in today's *Collegian.*
   2. Bach composed some of our most intricate fugues.
   3. My brother-in-law builds the most expensive houses in town.
   4. He built that expensive apartment complex on Water Street.
   5. The county commissioners try out a new tax-collection system every four years.
   6. Your positive attitude pleases me.
   7. Hurricane Katrina devastated the Gulf Coast in 2005.
   8. The number of flood victims overwhelmed the available facilities.

B. Transform the following passive sentences into the active voice; remember that the subject of the passive is the direct object in the active. (*Note:* If the agent is missing, you will have to supply one to act as the subject for the active.)
   1. The football team was led onto the field by the cheerleading squad.
   2. This year's cheerleading squad was chosen by a committee last spring.
   3. Bill's apartment was burglarized last weekend.
   4. A snowstorm is predicted for this weekend.
   5. The election of the student body officers will be held on Tuesday.
   6. Your car's oil should be changed on a regular basis.
   7. The suspect is being kept in solitary confinement.
   8. The kidnap victim has been found unharmed.

C. First decide if the following sentences are active or passive; then transform them.
   1. John Kennedy was elected president in 1960.
   2. Bill's grandmother nicknamed him Buzz when he was a baby.
   3. You should read the next six chapters before Monday.
   4. The cities in the Northeast have been affected by migration in recent years.
   5. Thousands of manufacturing jobs have been moved to Mexico.
   6. After the dot-com bubble burst, many employees of financial institutions were cheated out of their retirement savings.
   7. A number of executives from those companies have been sent to prison.

8. The streetlights on campus are finally being repaired.
9. Our company is trying out a new vacation schedule this year.
10. The plant will be closed for two weeks in July.

Revise the following passages by finding more precise alternatives to the italicized verbs. In some cases you will have to make changes other than just the verb substitution.

1. The small band of rebels *fought off* the army patrol for several hours, then *gave up* just before dawn. News reports about the event did not *give any specific details about* how many troops were involved.

2. The majority leader *has* a great deal of influence in the White House. He can easily *find a way around* the established procedures and go directly to the president, no matter what his party affiliation.

3. Several economists are saying that they *look forward to* an upturn in the stock market during the second half of the year. Others, however, maintain that interest rates must *stop their fluctuating* if the bull market is to prevail.

4. The night-shift workers took their complaints to the shop steward when the managers tried to *force* them into *giving up* their ten-cent wage differential.

5. The chairman of the Senate investigating committee *spoke against* the practice of accepting fees for outside speeches. He said that the new rules will *put a stop to* all such questionable fund raising. To some observers, such practices *are the same thing as* bribery. Several senators have promised to *come up with* a new compromise plan.

6. Dorm life changed drastically when colleges *did away with* their traditional "in loco parentis" role. In the old days, of course, there were always students who *paid no attention to* the rules. At some schools, where the administration would not *put up with* violations, students were routinely *kicked out*.

THE OVERUSE OF *BE*

Another major culprit contributing to flabbiness is the overuse of the linking-*be* (*am, is, are, was, were, have been, is being, might be,* and so on) as the main verb.[1] You'll recall from Chapter 1 that the *be* patterns commonly serve not only as topic sentences but as supporting

---

[1]This overuse of *be* refers only to its role as the main verb. *Be* also has a job to do as an auxiliary in the progressive tenses and in the passive voice.

sentences throughout the paragraph. You may be surprised, in checking a paragraph or two of your own prose, at how often you've used a form of *be* as the link between the known and the new information. An abundance of such examples—say, more than two or three in a paragraph—constitutes a clear "revise" message.

The following revised examples, sentences from this and earlier chapters, illustrate the substitution of more active, meaningful verbs:

Original:	The precise verb <u>isn't</u> always <u>available</u> when you need it.
Revision:	The precise verb *doesn't* always *come to mind* when you need it.
Original:	As a writer, you must <u>be aware of</u> your own inappropriate words.
Revision:	As a writer, you must *learn to spot* your own inappropriate words.
Original:	In fact, <u>we are not surprised to see</u> that nonpersonal voice in certain kinds of documents.
Revision:	In fact, *we've come to expect* that nonpersonal voice in certain kinds of documents.
Original:	Further, in writing <u>there are</u> certain modifiers, such as nonrestrictive clauses and phrases . . ., that we rarely use in speaking.
Revision:	Further, in writing *we use* certain modifiers. . . .

In this last example the culprit is an unnecessary *there are*. This use of *there are*, called a there transformation, along with the cleft transformation *it is*, both take *be*—and neither should be overused.

EXERCISE 6

Combine each of the following groups of sentences into a single sentence, using coordination and subordination. In some cases you may have to reword the sentence to make it sound natural. You can probably come up with more than one possibility for each.

1. The famous Gateway Arch is in St. Louis.
   Kansas City claims the title "Gateway to the West."

2. Our spring semester doesn't end until the second week of June.
   Many students have a hard time finding summer jobs.

3. Thomas Jefferson acquired the Ozark Mountains for the United States in 1803.
   That was the year of the Louisiana Purchase.
   We bought the Louisiana Territory from Napoleon.

4. Auto companies offered enticing cash rebates to buyers of new cars last January.
   Car sales increased dramatically.

5. The neighbors added a pit bull to their pet population, which now numbers three unfriendly four-legged creatures.
   We have decided to fence in our backyard.

6. The human circulatory system is a marvel of efficiency.
   It is still subject to a wide variety of degenerative diseases.

7. Carbohydrates—starches—are the body's prime source of energy.
   Fad diets that severely restrict the intake of starches are nearly always ineffective.
   Such diets can also be dangerous.

8. By 1890 the buffalo population of the West had been nearly wiped out.
   It now numbers about 60,000.
   About 400 ranchers in Colorado are raising buffalo for meat.

EXERCISE 7

Rewrite the following sentences to eliminate the dangling clauses and phrases. In some cases you may want to complete the clause; in others you may want to include its information in a different form.

1. Before mixing in the dry ingredients, the flour should be sifted.

2. Lightning flashed constantly on the horizon while driving across the desert toward Cheyenne.

3. There was no doubt the suspect was guilty after finding his fingerprints at the scene of the crime.

4. While waiting for the guests to arrive, there were a lot of last-minute details to take care of.

5. If handed in late, your grade on the term project will be lowered 10 percent.

6. After filling the garage with lawn furniture, there was no room left for the car.

7. While collecting money for the hurricane victims, the generosity of strangers simply amazed me.

8. The employees in our company who smoke now have to go outside of the building during their breaks if they want a cigarette, since putting the smoking ban into effect a month ago.

9. When revising and editing your papers, it is important to read the sentences aloud and listen to the stress pattern.

10. Your sentences will be greatly improved by eliminating dangling phrases and clauses.

Rewrite the following sentences to eliminate the dangling participles. In some cases you may want to expand the participles into full clauses.

1. Having endured rain all week, the miserable weather on Saturday didn't surprise us.

2. Hoping for the sixth win in a row, there was great excitement in the stands when the band finally played "The Star Spangled Banner."

3. Known for her conservative views on taxes and the role of government, we were not at all surprised when the Republican county commissioner announced her candidacy for the General Assembly.

4. Exhausted by the heat and humidity, it was wonderful to do nothing but lie in the shade and drink iced tea.

5. Having spent nearly all day in the kitchen, everyone agreed that my superb gourmet meal was worth the effort.

6. Feeling pressure from the environmentalists, the Clean Air Act was immediately put on the committee's agenda.

7. Obviously intimidated by a long history of defeats in Morgantown, there seems to be no way that our basketball team can beat the West Virginia Mountaineers on their home court.

8. Arriving unexpectedly on a weekend when I had two papers to finish and a big exam coming up, I didn't feel exactly overjoyed at seeing my parents.

Revise the following sentences to eliminate any instances of the broad-reference *which*.

1. My roommate told me she was planning to withdraw from school, which came as a complete surprise.

2. The first snowstorm of the season in Denver was both early and severe, which was not what the weather service had predicted.

3. The college library has finally converted the central card catalog to a computer system, which took over four years to complete.

4. The president had some harsh words for Congress in his recent press conference, which some observers considered quite inappropriate.

5. Wendell didn't want to stay for the second half of the game, which made Harriet rather unhappy.

6. We're having company for dinner three times this week, which probably means hot dogs for the rest of the month.

7. In his State of the Union message, the president characterized the last two years as a period of "unprecedented prosperity," which one economist immediately labeled "sheer hype and hyperbole."

8. The Brazilian government has grudgingly agreed to consider new policies regarding the rain forests, which should come as good news to everyone concerned about the environment.

EXERCISE 10

Problems of subject–verb agreement sometimes occur when modifiers follow the headword of the subject noun phrase:

- The <u>instructions</u> on the loan application <u>form was</u> very confusing.
- This <u>collection of poems</u> by several of my favorite romantic poets <u>were</u> published in 1910.

In these incorrect examples, the writer has forgotten that the headword determines the number of the noun phrase. To figure out the correct form of the verb, you can use the pronoun-substitution test:

The instructions [<u>they</u>] <u>were</u> very confusing.
This collection [<u>it</u>] <u>was</u> published in 1910.

Now test the following sentences to see if they are grammatical:

1. The statement on the income tax form about deductions for children and other dependents were simply not readable.

2. The type of career that many graduates are hoping to pursue pay high salaries and provide long vacations.

3. Apparently the use of robots in Japanese factories have been responsible for a great deal of worker dissatisfaction.

4. The problems associated with government deregulation have been responsible for the economic plight of several major airlines in recent years.

5. The government's deregulation policy regarding fares have also resulted in bargains for the consumer.

6. The inability to compete with those low airline fares are also responsible for the financial problems of the bus companies.

7. The impact of computers on our lives is comparable to the impact of the industrial revolution.

8. This new book of rules with its 100 ways to play solitaire really amaze me.

9. Carmen's collection of computer games and board games were really impressive.

10. The amount of money and time I spend on computer games is more than I can afford.

EXERCISE 11

Edit the following passages, paying particular attention to the nonstandard use of pronouns and to those with unclear referents.

1. I recall with great pleasure the good times that us children had at our annual family reunions when I was young. Our cousins and ourselves, along with some younger aunts and uncles, played volleyball and softball until dark. They were a lot of fun.

2. Aunt Yvonne and Uncle Bob always brought enough homemade ice cream for them and everyone else as well. There was great rivalry, I remember, between my brother and I over who could eat the most. Nearly everyone made a pig of himself.

3. It seemed to my cousin Terry and I that the grownups were different people at those family reunions. That may be true of family reunions everywhere.

4. Nowadays my father seems to forget about them good days and concentrates on the sad ones instead. He often tells my brother and myself about his boyhood during the Great Depression. He remembers the long years of unemployment for he and his whole family with very little pleasure. That doesn't really surprise me, because they were hard times.

EXERCISE 12

The following paragraphs are reproduced exactly as they were published—with one exception: *All internal punctuation has been removed; only the sentence-end marks have been retained.* Your job is to put the punctuation marks back into the sentences. (Don't forget hyphens and apostrophes!) As you know, punctuation rules are not carved in stone; consequently, in some places your version may differ from the original—and still be correct.

Management is still taught in most business schools as a bundle of techniques such as budgeting and personnel relations. To be sure management like any other work has its own tools and its own techniques. But just as the essence of medicine is not urinalysis important though that is the essence of management is not techniques and procedures. The essence of management is to make knowledge productive. Management in other words is a social function. And in its practice management is truly a liberal art.

The old communities family village parish and so on have all but disappeared in the knowledge society. Their place has largely been taken by the new unit of social integration the organization. Where community was fate organization is voluntary membership. Where community claimed the entire person organization is a means to a person's ends a tool. For 200 years a hot debate has been raging especially in the West are communities organic or are they simply extensions of the people of which they are made? Nobody would claim that the new organization is organic. It is clearly an artifact a creation of man a social technology.

—Peter F. Drucker (*The Atlantic Monthly*)

The charter school movement is not yet big. Just 11 states beginning with Minnesota in 1991 have passed laws permitting the creation of autonomous public schools like Northland a dozen more have similar laws in the works. Most states have restricted the number of these schools 100 in California 25 in Massachusetts in an attempt to appease teachers unions and other opponents. Nevertheless the charter movement is being heralded as the latest and best hope for a public education system that has failed to deliver for too many children and cannot compete internationally.

A handful of other places notably Baltimore Maryland and Hartford Connecticut are experimenting with a far more radical way to circumvent bureaucracy hiring a for profit company to run the schools.

—Claudia Wallis *(Time)*

EXERCISE 13

Please punctuate the following sentences using commas, semi-colons, and periods.

1. Joe was offered a new job yesterday that he really wanted in order to celebrate he hosted a party and invited everyone he knew.

2. Joe first chose the music he wanted to play at the party and then he downloaded some of those songs.

3. Cindy asked if she could bring Dave her friend from New York Heather and Jill.

4. When the party began no one wanted to dance instead they chatted with each other.

5. Once everyone became better acquainted people started to dance.

6. Joe told his neighbors about the party assuring them his friends would not create too much noise in fact he invited two of his neighbors to join the celebration.

7. The party continued on until 2 am with only a few people remaining longer to help Joe clean up.

8. Joe's friends congratulated him on his new job and said they wish they could stay later however most had to work the next day.

9. Joe thanked his friends for their help and their good wishes and after they left he went to bed.

EXERCISE 14

Please punctuate the following exercises correctly.

1. The Alistair Murphy who chairs the organization is the grandson of the one who founded it.

2. Alistair Murphy who chairs this organization and oversees the publication of its monthly magazine is one of the most sought-after speakers in the region.

3. Anyone who heard him speak could tell that he had done his research.

4. The chair hesitated to call on Roberta Graves who disagreed with the proposed budget.

5. The board decided to move headquarters out of the city where the rent is more expensive.

6. In one of the special issues Jane Yuen who has been around the longest wrote a provocative essay on forest resource management.

7. She argues that we need to punish all lumberjacks who clear cut forests irresponsibly.

8. The magazine which is highly acclaimed is approaching its fiftieth anniversary issue.

9. The issue that everyone is concerned about however is the one for which they have recruited a prominent yet controversial conservationist as guest editor.

10. The editorial board which likes to be prepared is bracing itself for the public response.

EXERCISE 15

The following citations are wrong. Without worrying about whether or not they are effective, *find and fix the mechanical mistakes.*

1. As one doctor argues, ". . . we are learning too much from this research to worry about ethical implications . . ." (Mansfield, 68).

2. Kenneth Burke asks "Do we simply use words, or do they not also use us?" (84).

3. According to Noam Chomsky, we need to "read what's presented to [us] with ordinary common sense, skeptical intelligence . . . the same way [we] would read Iraqi propaganda", (Chomsky, 38).

Rewrite with apostrophes

4. Two students, two books

5. Henry James, *The Beast in the Jungle*

6. One dog, one chew-toy

7. Fifty kittens, one litter box

8. France; immigration policy

9. Person; academic potential

Add *Its* or *It's*

10. _____ raining

11. _____ most salient feature

11. _____ not fair

13. _____ worth remembering

14. _____ digestive system

EXERCISE 16

Good academic writing is concise academic writing. Replace the phrasal verbs below with more effective verbs.

1. Come up with a more concise version of this sentence.

2. The punctuation convention calls for a comma.

3. All sentences are made up of one or more independent clauses.

4. We are in the process of coming up with sentences for you to correct.

5. Wordiness has an undesired effect of causing the reader to lose sight of what the true meaning of sentence is.

Some of the following sentences have pronoun problems. Find them and fix them.

1. When a student is in high school, they take the SATs.

2. At the University of Maryland, a student must pass certain "core classes." You must pass English 101, for example.

3. I used to love roller coasters as a kid. When one is on them, all the problems in the world are gone.

4. By hiring international laborers at slave wages, the employer is exploiting the economically weaker individual, manipulating a tilt in the global market to increase their profit margin.

5. I realized my first week in college that one cannot rely on another student for his/her his/her class notes.

6. A student's future should not depend on how much money their parents make.

FIGURES OF SPEECH: AN INTRODUCTION AND SAMPLING

Do you know what it's like to live with a messy roommate? Do you know what it's like to have to climb over a mountain of shirts and pants and mismatched shoes and three-week-old pizza boxes in order to reach your desk? I live in these conditions. My room is a pig sty. It's smelly. It's dirty. It's inhumane. I like to keep my side of the room neat, but neat does not exist in my roommate's world. There is dust on her dresser. There is dust on her desk. There is dust on her phone and on her bookshelf and on her computer. But does she care? No. The "clean me" I inscribed on the third row of her bookshelf is forming its own layer of dust. And the dirty socks kicked under her bed have lived there so long that her mattress is screaming for mercy. I sweep, she scatters. I stack, she stuffs. I pick up, she piles up. I try to influence her, but you know what they say—you can lead a horse to water. . . . I can't wait until this semester is over and I leave this room and this roommate behind in her own big cloud of dust.

What were you thinking as you read this paragraph? Did you become curious after the opening question? Did you feel you were in familiar territory with the expression "you can lead a horse to water . . ."? Did you share a sense of being overwhelmed when you read the lists of piled up clothes and garbage or the list of furniture and accessories collecting dust? Was the passage becoming overly dramatic with the sentences, "It's smelly. It's dirty. It's inhumane"? Did you sense that the socks were so bad that they could actually affect the mattress?

Perhaps you simply skimmed the paragraph; perhaps you noticed that the writing wasn't as dry as plain white toast. What spiced up this paragraph? At least twelve **figures of speech**. We use the phrase "figures of speech" casually to mean something like "it's just the way you say it." But **figures of speech** is a rhetorical term that refers to patterns in phrases that have a particular effect. Figures of speech, like other elements of rhetoric, are commonly used in written and spoken discourse. Start noticing them; bring good or bad or just plain interesting examples to class when you come across them. Some figures of speech are so effective that they become "sound bites," quotes that can be—and often are—repeated over and over again. Think about this for a minute. Like so many things you've learned this semester, figures naturally occur in our written and spoken discourse. But wouldn't it be strategic to craft figures of speech for your most important or effective arguments in your writing and speaking? You know—sentences or phrases that will stick out in people's minds and memories?

Look at the examples below. How would you describe the patterns that each uses?

Examples from the *New York Times*

(1) *The piano lesson to take before you buy a piano.*
        —Steinway Piano advertisement

(2) *You get on at 38th St. You get off in the 1600s.*
        —Historic Hudson Cruise advertisement

(3)   *Philadelphia is worried. New York is nervous. Boston is depressed.*
      —sports column on a baseball pennant race

(4)   *Lately I've begun to ask people I know whether they're in the market. Always their answer is yes; always they've gone the mutual fund route; always they have a worried look when they talk about it.*
      —Op-Ed article on the stock market

From History

(5)   *That's one small step for man, one giant leap for mankind.*
      —Neil Armstrong, landing on the moon, 1969

(6)   *The only thing we have to fear is fear itself.*
      —Franklin D. Roosevelt, encouraging Americans after the Great Depression, 1933

(7)   *The right is ours. Have it, we must. Use it, we will.*
      —Elizabeth Cady Stanton, calling for woman suffrage in the U.S., 1848

(8)   *Fellow-citizens! I will not enlarge further on your national inconsistencies. The existence of slavery in this country brands your republicanism as a sham, your humanity as a base pretense, and your Christianity as a lie. It destroys your moral power abroad; it corrupts your politicians at home.*
      —Frederick Douglass, protesting the American institution of slavery, 1852

(9)   *I came, I saw, I conquered.*
      —Julius Caesar, on crossing the Rubicon, 49 B.C.E.

From Literature

(10)   *You have seen how a man was made a slave; you shall see how a slave was made a man.*
      —Frederick Douglass, *Narrative of the Life of An American Slave*, 1845

(11)   *I am the poet of the woman the same as the man,*
And I say it is as great to be a woman as to be a man,
And I say there is nothing greater than the mother of men.
      —Walt Whitman, *Song of Myself,* 1855

(12)   *When angry, count four; when very angry, swear.*
      —Mark Twain, *Pudd'nhead Wilson,* 1894

(13)   *Keep, ancient lands, your storied pomp!" cries she*
With silent lips. "Give me your tired, your poor,
Your huddled masses yearning to breathe free,
The wretched refuse of your teeming shore.
      —Emma Lazarus, "The New Colossus," 1883

Categories of Figures

In the *Rhetorica ad Herennium,* a work of rhetorical theory from classical Rome, we find what we now often refer to generally as "figures of speech" divided into two categories, **figures of diction** and **figures of thought.** The author of the *Rhetorica ad Herennium* makes the distinction that "It is a figure of diction if the adornment is comprised in the fine polish of the language itself. A figure of thought derives a certain distinction from the idea, not from the words" (IV.xiii.18). Another way to distinguish the difference is between **schemes** and **tropes.** A **scheme** is considered a variation in the arrangement of words, while a **trope** is a variation of the way we expect a word or idea to be expressed.

There are many, many figures. In rhetorical theory, they are often known by their Latin or Greek names. We've included those here, but don't feel that you need to memorize them (though your family would certainly be impressed to hear such words rolling off your tongue when you go home at the end of the semester); it's more important to think about how you might use them in your writing and to recognize how they have rhetorical effect in the writing you read.

Schemes Involving Balance

Schemes involving balance by repeating structures, words, phrases, or clauses guide readers to see a balance or equivalence between items or ideas in the repeated structures.

Repeat the same structure in a series of words, phrases, or clauses (parallelism).

> *The agricultural age was based on plows and the animals that pulled them; the industrial age, on engines and the fuels that fed them. The information age will be based on computers and the networks that interconnect them.*

Repeat not only the same structure but also the same length (number of words or syllables) in parallel items (isocolon).

> *We have no salt, no meat, and no bread.*

Invert a phrase or sentence, creating its "mirror image" (antimetabole).

> *When the going gets tough, the tough get going.*

Create a mirror image of the structure without repeating the words (chiasmus).

> *Napoleon lost an army to a Russian winter, and the snows of Leningrad defeated Hitler.*

An **antitheses,** putting contrary, contradictory or correlative terms in parallel structures, is a particular kind of parallelism that frames a contrast between the balanced structures. You can create antithesis of words, phrases or clauses.

> *People believe many things that are false; they doubt many things that are true.*

> *To err is human; to forgive, divine.*

Schemes Involving Repetition

Like schemes of balance, schemes of repetition repeat structures or words, but these schemes work not by creating balance but by creating emphasis. Though we are often told not to be redundant or repetitive when we write, using repetition figuratively is not the same as being repetitive. These schemes help draw the reader's attention to the prose.

Repeat consonant sounds of adjacent words (alliteration).

> *He who laughs last laughs loudest.*

Repeat words at the beginning of a series of sentences, clauses, or phrases (anaphora).

> *Let us march to the realization of the American dream. Let us march on segregated housing. Let us march on segregated schools. Let us march on poverty* (Martin Luther King, Jr.).

Repeat words at the end of a series (epistrophe).

> *Your brother made the team, and your sister made the team. In fact, everyone in the family made the team.*

Repeat words beginning a phrase/clause in its ending (epanalepsis).

> *Boys will be boys.*

Repeat ending words from one sentence in the beginning of the next (anadiplosis).

> *To be a good writer, one must read. Read books, magazines, newspapers.*

Repeat the same word in different positions in a sentence (ploche).

> *People who need people are the luckiest people in the world.*

Repeat the same word root (polyptoton).

> *Love is an uncontrollable desire to be uncontrollably desired.*

Create a series in which each item grows stronger (climax).

> *I wondered, I worried, I panicked.*

Schemes Involving Omission

Schemes that involve omission leave out something readers expect to create rhythm or emphasis and to make the reader work along with the writer.

Omit conjunctions between items in a series (asyndeton).

> *Today I have to do my laundry, write a paper for English, call my mother, study for a physics test, go to practice, read a chapter in sociology, see my advisor, take a make-up quiz in calculus.*

Leave out words or phrases readers can supply mentally (ellipsis).

> *My parents gave me $100 for my birthday, my grandparents $50, and my aunt $30.*

A **climax** may also be seen as a scheme of omission when written without conjunctions.

> *He shoots, he scores, he wins the championship.*

Schemes of Interruption

Just as other schemes create balance or rhythm, schemes of interruption break the rhythm or pattern we expect. We use these schemes so regularly that we might think of them as grammatical rules more than figures of speech, but that demonstrates the way that figures are not so distinct from everyday speech.

Interrupting to add commentary (parentheses).

> *As you follow Route 66—now this is the important part—don't forget to turn left at the third light.*

Creating a two coordinating elements where the second explains or modifies the first (appositive).

> *George W. Bush, our current president, was previously governor of Texas.*

Tropes

Perhaps the most important and best known trope is **metaphor.** We often don't even realize how much of our language depends on metaphor, an implied comparison between two things that are not, on the surface, very similar, and **simile**, a direct comparison of two things that are not similar on the surface. Metaphors and similes help to shape the way we imagine an idea or concept.

> *You think you are king around here don't you?* (metaphor)
>
> *On life's journey, we expect to make many decisions about which way to turn.* (metaphor)
>
> *In the battle against cancer, surgeons may be considered the front line troops.* (metaphor)
>
> *You are acting just like an animal.* (simile)

In an **oxymoron,** we juxtapose two words with contrary meanings to draw attention to the contrast between them.

> *Celebrities lead public private lives.*
>
> *The late actor Erich von Stroheim became famous for playing roles best described as "the man we love to hate."*

In a **rhetorical question**, we presume the audience will find the answer for itself. This draws the audience into our thinking and helps our ideas resonate.

> *Why would the company suddenly decide to embark on a massive project to clean out its records?*

In **prosopopoeia,** we invent speakers and put words in their mouths that ask questions or express opinions and reactions. Such invention enlivens the points we are trying to make.

> *At this point in my argument someone might ask, "What's in it for you?"*

Prosopopoeia may also involve imagining famous people, dead or alive, speaking .

> *Lincoln would have said, "Pursuing this policy will lead to another civil war."*

In **personification**, we create roles and actions for, or put words in the mouths of, groups or animals or even of inanimate objects and abstractions. Again, as with prosopopoeia, our point becomes more lively and playful, and thus more memorable.

> *The betrayed Constitution asks, "Isn't the Bill of Rights enough?"*

In **irony**, words are meant to convey something different from their literal meaning. Irony is generally very dependant on its situation. Creating irony emphasizes a point we are trying to make without seeming to create such emphasis.

> *Oh, your mom is going to love to hear that you are quitting school to work as a horse trainer.*

> *The homeless survive in their cardboard palaces.*

In **overstatement**, or **hyperbole**, we exaggerate a point. This can often make the point clearer to the audience (though it may do so ironically).

> *I have had the worst day a human being could ever have.*

In **litotes**, we understate a point. As with overstatement, the point is emphasized or clarified for the reader.

> *One nuclear bomb can ruin your whole day.*

VIII

READINGS

African American Slavery and the University of Maryland
By the Students of History 429

AN OVERVIEW AND APPRECIATION

It was no secret that slavery had some relationship to the founding of the Maryland Agricultural College, predecessor of the University of Maryland, as the university celebrated its 150th anniversary in 2006. Charles Benedict Calvert, the prime mover in the college's creation, was a slaveholding planter, as were many of the members of the state legislature that authorized the college's establishment and the trustees who governed the new institution. Some of the first faculty members held slaves, and many of the students came from slaveholding families. It could be no other way in Maryland, as slavery touched every aspect of life. Slaveholders, who controlled much of the state's wealth, transformed that wealth into political power, which, in turn, allowed them to shape the state's culture.

Nonetheless, many students, faculty and friends of the university in 2006 were appalled to learn of its roots in the odious institution of chattel bondage. Some believed that information had been withheld from them in an effort to whitewash the university's past. Others shared the embarrassment of Americans who had but recently discovered that the entire lower end of Manhattan was underlaid by a slave cemetery, or that President George Washington housed his slaves on the site of the Liberty Bell in Philadelphia, or that the national Capitol in Washington was constructed in part by slaves. Still others saw no special revelation in the "discovery" of the university's slave past, but wanted a full accounting. Did slaves clear the land, build the buildings and feed the students at the newly established Maryland Agricultural College?

In the controversy over slavery stirred by the 150th anniversary celebration, the History Department saw a teachable moment. With the encouragement of university President C. D. Mote, Jr., Herbert Brewer, an advanced graduate student, and I organized History 429, "Knowing Our History: Slavery and the University of Maryland," an undergraduate course whose purpose was to explore, document and define the historic connections between African American slavery and the Maryland Agricultural College. Now, as the students' report goes to press, I am pleased to say that "Knowing Our History" was one of the most engaging and rewarding teaching experiences in my 30 years at the university.

The students of History 429 took their charge seriously and attacked the question of slavery's relationship to the university with energy, enthusiasm and intelligence. They quickly gained the assistance of many interested parties who shared their concerns and whom they thank in the report's acknowledgements. As they readily admit, their work was built on the work of others. Although the class took the long view of slavery's history—beginning in the 11th century Mediterranean and tracing the development of the slave-based plantation system across the Atlantic into the Caribbean, onto mainland North America, and finally to Prince George's County—I think it's safe to say most students were determined to find the smoking gun, the direct evidence that slaves cleared the land, constructed the buildings and worked in the dining halls.

But the smoking gun was not to be had, although the students searched with great diligence in archives, libraries and historical repositories on campus and off. In the process, however, they learned something far more important: that the past can also be reconstructed from a deep knowledge of the context of events and a full appreciation of the circumstances of the lives of men and women. Piecing together those lives requires not only a close reading of the sources but also an imaginative reconstruction of a world that is no more. History 429 thought its way back to mid-19th century Maryland.

Simply put, the Maryland Agricultural College was founded in response to a profound crisis in Maryland society, a crisis that was shaking Maryland's economy as its agricultural base faltered under the pressure of the greater productivity of western lands, changes in technology and the reorganization of labor. Not only were many Maryland farmers losing their place, but their sons and daughters also were leaving home, some for the West and some for cities like nearby Annapolis, Baltimore and Washington. The decline and depopulation created a deep sense of loss that was exacerbated by the larger national debate over slavery. That debate would soon explode in civil war.

Charles Calvert felt the crisis as a planter whose wealth rested on agriculture, and also as a politician appreciative of the challenges facing his class and his community. Fashioning himself an improving farmer, he spoke and wrote about ways to elevate Maryland agriculture through new techniques of farm management, the introduction of blooded stock and more productive crops and the creation of a cohort of educated farmers. He found a kindred spirit in Benjamin Hallowell, a self-taught scientist with long experience as an educator in Maryland and Virginia, whom Calvert and the board of trustees appointed the college's first president. But while Hallowell shared Calvert's interest in agricultural reform, his views on slavery differed radically. A member of the Society of Friends, Hallowell believed in his denomination's long-standing opposition to slavery. He and his family were deeply involved in the anti-slavery movement; his hometown of Sandy Spring was a station on the Underground Railroad and two distant cousins commanded black regiments—the famed Massachusetts 54th and 55th—during the Civil War. Hallowell accepted the college's presidency, but only upon condition that no slave labor would be used at the new campus.

Calvert and Hallowell sought to create an institution that, then as now, addressed the state's most pressing problems. Circumstances, however, confined what they could do and say. For one thing, though they both spoke frequently about the various measures of agricultural improvement, they dared not address the central element in the extant system of agriculture: slave labor. It was perhaps that which led Hallowell to resign within a month of his appointment, although the evidence points elsewhere. Slavery was the elephant in the room, which everyone recognized but no one could acknowledge.

But, as the students came to understand, the silence could not deny the undeniable. Political necessities may have forced both Calvert and Hallowell to avoid the direct discussion of slavery, but slavery's omnipresence—as a source of wealth, status and labor—made it clear that slaves were no silent partner in the establishment of the Maryland Agricultural College. The crisis created by their presence drove the decision to establish the college, and the wealth their labor produced made the college possible. In making the case for those connections, the students of History 429 make their greatest contribution toward an understanding of the university's relationship with slavery.

Representing the slaves' founding presence, the students discovered one Adam Francis Plummer, a favorite slave of Charles Calvert and also, through the convoluted ways in which whites and blacks mixed in a slave society, a Calvert kinsman as well. For the students, Plummer—who was literate, kept a journal, played a large role on the Calvert estate and himself had deep roots in Maryland society—became a person who could represent the mass of otherwise anonymous black men and women whose labor helped create the Maryland Agricultural College but whose voices remained mute in the historical record. Here, too, the students of History 429 expand the understanding of the university's beginnings.

In its origins, the students concluded, the Maryland Agricultural College—and, by descent, the University of Maryland—had three founders: a slaveholder, an abolitionist and the slaves themselves. Appreciating the connections that brought these three together is the work of this report, authored and edited by the students of History 429, who have come not only to know their history, but also to make it.

Ira Berlin
College Park, August 2009

HISTORY 429 STUDENT RESEARCHERS

Caroline Anderson is a junior double-majoring in government and politics and U.S. history. She is active on campus with the Student Government Association, University Student Judiciary and University Senate. She was a member of the Maryland Room research group and the steering committee for this report.

Tamara Arnold is a senior pursuing a double major in history and women's studies with a concentration in society and culture. She is vice president of Triota, the women's studies honors society at the University of Maryland. Her aspiration is to apply the skills she learned about society and culture to combat global issues such as poverty and education; in particular, her passion is social issues surrounding women and children. She was a member of the Riversdale research group and the public relations committee for this report.

Donald B. Caltrider Jr. is a junior double major in international business and history with a concentration in early modern Europe. Outside of school he is a private antiques dealer specializing in 19th-century photography, books and ephemera. At Maryland, Donny is a member of the Fencing Club and the Hinman CEOs program. He served as chair of the Maryland State Archives research group and was a member of the steering committee for this project.

Emma Coll is a senior majoring in history and American studies. She is the co-community service chair for the Mortar Board Senior Honors Society and was recently named a Philip Merrill Scholar. This year Emma will be completing departmental honors in American studies and will participate in the Chillum Internship Program, developing classes for elementary students. She hopes to pursue a graduate degree in educational policy. She was a member of the Maryland Room research group and the steering committee for this report.

Natalia Cuadra-Saez is a junior double-majoring in history and classics with a minor in religious studies. Her concentration in history is in African diaspora. She is a member of the Global Communities honors program and a member of the Primannum Honors Society. She was a member of the Maryland Room research group and the public relations committee for this report.

Jessica Dwyer-Moss is a senior double-majoring in government and politics and history. She is a member of the University Honors Program, Beyond the Classroom living and learning program and Pi Sigma Alpha political science honors society. President of the Maryland Shakespeare Players, she is very involved with the performing arts. She was a member of the Maryland Room research group and the writing committee for this report.

Christoff Funches is a senior anthropology major with a focus in archaeology. His academic interest is the history and archaeology of the African diaspora. He was a member of the Maryland State Archives research group and the writing committee for this report.

Mara James is a junior government and politics major and has a double minor in French and international development and conflict management. At Maryland, she was a member of College Park Scholars' Public Leadership program and the Beyond the Classroom program. She has been a trip leader for the alternative break program and helped organize the first alternative winter break trips. This summer, Mara traveled to Egypt and Israel to study religious conflicts. She was a member of the Maryland Room research group and the public relations committee for this report.

Rebekah Kass graduated in May with a bachelor's degree in history, with a concentration in Jewish history and an English minor. She wrote a senior thesis as part of the history honors program that focused on the decision to have an egalitarian bat mitzvah service within Conservative Judaism in America. Rebekah was president of the History Undergraduate Association as well as a member of Phi Alpha Theta history honors society and the Primannum Honor Society. She competed on the Maryland Academic Quiz Team and worked as a program assistant in the Department of Resident Life. Rebekah plans to pursue either a doctoral degree in history or a law degree after taking some time off. She was a member of the Maryland State Archives research group and served as the chair of the steering committee for this report.

Lauren Kaufman is a junior history major with an American history concentration. An active member of campus radio station WMUC-FM, Lauren is studying abroad in Copenhagen this semester. She was a member of the Maryland Room research group and the writing committee for this report.

Ross Krublit graduated in May with bachelor's degrees in history and geography and concentrations in American history and human geography. He was a College Park Scholar focusing on American cultures and a member of the Phi Alpha Theta history honors society. He has worked in the Undergraduate Technology Apprenticeship Program, assisting faculty in the College of Arts and Humanities with classroom technology. He planned to enroll in the World Union of Jewish Students' program on peace and social justice, a six-month internship in Jerusalem. He was a member of the Maryland State Archives research group and the public relations committee for this report.

Mike Kurkjian is a junior double-majoring in history and communication. He was a member of College Park Scholars' Media, Self and Society program, a member of the Maryland and Prince George's County historical societies research group and served as chair of the Public Relations Committee for this report.

Jasmine London is a senior English major with a concentration in African American literature and a minor in rhetoric. A native of Prince George's County and an African American, she is keenly interested in local connections to slavery. The experience has allowed her to know more about the county as well as enhance her awareness of slavery. She was a member of the Riversdale research group and the writing committee for this report.

Ana Rosas graduated in May with bachelor's degrees in history and Spanish language and literature, with a concentration in western European history. She participated in Harmony's Cross, a student a cappella group, and held board positions with the Latino Student Union and Latino Honors Caucus. She was inducted into the Maryland chapters of the history and Spanish honor societies, Pi Alpha Theta and Sigma Delta Pi. She is pursuing a master of science degree in information at the University of Michigan. She was a member of the Maryland State Archives research group and the writing committee for this report.

Jonathan Sachs is a senior majoring in government and politics. He completed College Park Scholars' Public Leadership program, is part of the government and politics honors program and is a Rawlings Undergraduate Leadership Scholar. He served as president of the student body, as president of the College Democrats and as a university senator. This year he is serving as student liaison to the city of College Park. He has also interned for two state delegates and U.S. House of Representatives Majority Leader Steny Hoyer and interned for the House Energy and Commerce Committee this summer. He was a member of the Riversdale research group and the public relations committee for this report.

Kevin Valdez graduated in May with a bachelor's degree in history and a concentration in U.S. history. He is attending Washington University's School of Law in St. Louis, Mo. He was a member of the Maryland and Prince George's County historical societies research group and the steering committee for this report.

Grace Waldron is a junior majoring in history and a lifelong resident of Silver Spring. She was a member of the Riversdale research group and served as chair of the writing committee for this report.

Shoshi Weiss is a senior majoring in history with a minor in linguistics. She completed College Park Scholars' American Cultures program and is a member of Hillel. She also works as a park ranger at the Frederick Douglass National Historic Site in Washington, D.C. She was a member of the Maryland and Prince George's County historical societies research group and the writing committee for this report.

INTRODUCING THE PROJECT

In 2006, the University of Maryland celebrated its 150th anniversary. This occasion naturally raised questions about the origins of the university. The Maryland Agricultural College, as the University of Maryland was then known, opened its doors to students shortly before the Civil War, and before Maryland abolished slavery in 1864. Its founder, Charles Benedict Calvert, was descended from a long line of slave-owning planters and owned 52 slaves in 1860, many of whom lived and worked on his Riversdale plantation, a portion of which forms a large section of the current campus.[1] While the founder's great wealth derived from slavery, the extent to which slavery was directly linked to the college remained unknown. Noted slavery historian and Distinguished University of Maryland Professor Ira Berlin explained, "If slaves didn't lay the bricks, they made the bricks. If they didn't make the bricks, they drove the wagon that brought the bricks. If they didn't drive the wagon, they built the wagon wheels."[2] What needed to be determined was the precise relationship between slavery and the college: whether slaves labored in the fields, prepared the students' meals or waited on the faculty, and how the college was connected to the institution of slavery once its first students arrived. The commemorative events and academic projects celebrating the university's historic anniversary mentioned slavery only in passing, and some students and community members protested what they saw as the university's avoidance of the issue. Andrew Vanacore, a reporter for the campus newspaper *The Diamondback,* wrote that "during the course of the year, as university officials celebrated the university's 150th anniversary by producing a documentary and accompanying book examining the university's history, no mention was made of slaves' roles in working the grounds that would become this university—only that Calvert owned slaves."[3]

In an effort to address community concerns and answer questions about the relationship between the university and slavery, university President C. D. Mote, Jr. authorized the creation of an undergraduate research team to investigate and report on the role slavery played in the school's development. Mote understood the university's quandary about slavery as a teachable moment. He charged Berlin and History Department lecturer Herbert Brewer with creating a two-semester undergraduate course, the first semester focusing on the broad history of slavery and the second semester on the research and production of a report—"Knowing Our History"—to be presented to the university community.

Berlin and Brewer held several informational meetings in the spring of 2008 to generate interest in the course and asked interested students to submit a detailed application. From approximately 60 applicants, Berlin and Brewer selected 25 students to participate in the course. The first semester, taught during the fall of 2008, focused on the history of slavery and the plantation system from a global perspective. Beginning with slave-driven sugar plantations in the Mediterranean region, the class studied the gradual movement of the plantation system across the Atlantic Ocean to South America, the Caribbean and mainland North America, as well as the simultaneous development of the transatlantic slave trade. The perspective narrowed as the semester progressed, examining slavery in the United States, then Maryland and finally Prince George's County. In the spring, equipped with essential background knowledge on slavery and the many forms it has taken throughout the world, the students focused on researching the precise relationship of slavery to the university's history and constructed this report.

The students formed four research teams in an effort to uncover as much information as possible about the relationship of the Maryland Agricultural College to slavery. Each team took responsibility for conducting research at one of several locations: the archives of the University of Maryland and of the state of Maryland; the Maryland and Prince George's County historical societies; and Riversdale, the estate of Charles Benedict Calvert. As research progressed, students found other historical repositories to investigate. The students in the class also formed three activity committees. A steering committee was responsible for coordinating the research for the entire project, a writing committee pieced together various drafts to give the report a single voice, and a public affairs committee organized media and public relations activities.

When the course and its ultimate goals were announced, reactions ranged from supportive to dismissive. "This is a major step for the university and the African-American community," read one response to *The Diamondback* article about the course. Others called the course "an incredible waste of precious dollars" and "a ridiculous project," and doubted whether the research would uncover any significant information, since the subject had been studied in the past. Some members of the community responded with concern: "All this does is create a racial divide among people where there doesn't need to be one," one person wrote. Another response directly posed the question at the core of the entire debate: "What [will] this report accomplish?"[4] The student researchers involved in the course had to confront this question themselves.

The class agreed that there were many compelling reasons to study the history of slavery at the University of Maryland. First, a full understanding of the past is a powerful tool. Slave masters sought to keep their slaves illiterate not only to limit their access to freedom, but also to prevent them from learning their own histories, from learning that there was no justification for their enslavement. Masters assumed that if slaves did not know and understand their history, they could not act upon it. The students in the class agreed that the same was true for themselves and all members of the university community; if they did not know their history, they could not act upon it.

Second, racial divides and tensions continue to beset American life. The recent election of President Barack Obama to the nation's highest office suggests to some that black people are now fully integrated into American society and that the nation has finally achieved racial equality. Despite Obama's victory, however, racism remains active, even on the university's campus. Just over a year ago, a noose was found hanging in a tree outside the Nyumburu Cultural Center, a campus venue where many black student activities occur.[5] Racism generally derives from ignorance, from assumptions and stereotypes that may or may not be accurate. Knowing our history and sharing it with others can help to combat racism by preventing ignorance and clarifying some of the myths and stereotypes surrounding American slavery and its long history.

Finally, the entire campus community has an interest in its origins. As individuals and as a nation, Americans are fascinated by their beginnings. But this curiosity, this desire for knowledge, often stops abruptly when faced with unpleasantness. The enslavement of Africans was one of the cruelest chapters in human history. The United States was built on this horrible and violent institution. If the university cannot come to terms with the truth of its origins in what many see as a new age of race relations, then it may never be able to face its past. By openly addressing the university's relationship to slavery and bringing it to public attention, the students of History 429 hope to understand the past they have inherited, even if they cannot fully make amends for it. This task, though difficult and contentious, is an important and necessary undertaking.

No discussion of race relations in the U.S. is complete without an acknowledgment of slavery and its impact on modern America. Although slavery was abolished nearly 150 years ago, its legacy remains. As Americans attempt to address issues of racial equality, interest in slavery has grown. The Maryland legislature and the Annapolis City Council recently issued apologies expressing their "regret for the role Maryland played in instituting and maintaining slavery."[6] Others, including the U.S. House of Representatives, have issued similar apologies.[7]

The University of Maryland is not the only educational institution to address these concerns. In the past decade, several other American universities have examined their relationships to the enslavement of African Americans. Faculty members and students at Brown and Yale universities have produced meticulously researched reports on their institutions' link to this dark aspect of American history. Archivists at the University of North Carolina constructed an online exhibit exploring the subject.[8] Recently, the College of William and Mary launched a five- to 10-year project to "explore the College's ownership of slaves and the complexities of race relations from the end of the Civil War to date."[9] Emory University is also conducting research, as well as planning an international symposium on slavery and universities tentatively scheduled for 2010.[10]

The University of Maryland approached the issue a bit differently. Mote charged undergraduate students with the task of investigating the university's connections with slavery and reporting to the campus, a marked contrast to the historians and professional researchers employed to create many of the other universities' reports. Though the methods by which they were created were different, those universities' reports provided insight into how this project could be organized and what areas of the past could be explored. This report is organized into three sections. Section 1 introduces the project and describes the methods of research. The second section speaks to the development of slavery in a larger framework. The third section covers the early history of the university and the role slavery played in its creation and development by focusing on three founders, before concluding with a brief survey of the way slavery shaped the university's subsequent development.

The goal of History 429 was not to apologize for the university's relationship to slavery, but to understand more fully how slavery's history shaped its founding and subsequent development. Ultimately it is up to the university and the campus community—students, faculty and staff—to decide what to do with the findings of this report. The university's history is intimately tied to the institution of slavery. The Maryland Agricultural College was founded amid a great debate about slavery in a state where the institution's future was in doubt. While the founders' wealth derived from slave labor and the first students, many of whom were the sons of slaveholders, were expected to apply the knowledge they gained to administering their own farms and plantations, the university's first president was a powerful opponent of slavery. He took office only after being assured that no slaves would be allowed to work on campus. Both the slaveowning founder and the abolitionist president shared a commitment to improving agriculture. While their focus was on new methods, stock, seeds and the like, the question of labor—who would work the land—was not far from their minds. On the eve of the Civil War, the university, like most of Maryland, was caught between slavery and freedom, and both played important roles in its development.

Methods

In order to research such a vast topic, History 429 drew upon a variety of sources. With the help of numerous librarians and archivists, the students made a preliminary estimate of the types of sources they would need to examine, including archival records, legislative and judicial documents, laws, censuses, magazines and newspapers, oral histories, diaries and published compilations. Their search into slavery's history at the University of Maryland took them to a number of repositories, including the Maryland State Archives, the Maryland Room in the university's Hornbake Library, Swarthmore College in Philadelphia, the National Archives, the Prince George's County Historical Society, the Sandy Spring Historical Society, the Maryland Historical Society, the Smithsonian Institution and the Riversdale House Museum. The State Archives holds the Prince George's County land, tax, manumission and probate records, which helped provide insight into life in Prince George's County when the Maryland Agricultural College was founded. The Archives at the university holds several master's and doctoral theses focusing on university history, as well as periodicals such as *The Planter's Advocate* and *The American Farmer*. Swarthmore College and the Sandy Spring Historical Society hold the records of the Hallowell family, located at the Smithsonian's Anacostia Museum, including correspondence relating to the Maryland Agricultural College's first president, Benjamin Hallowell.

Ancestry.com, an online archive of census records and other genealogical records, was also useful. These records helped reconstruct the Bladensburg-Vansville District of Prince George's County, as well as the family trees of important university figures. The students also examined the diary and oral histories of the Plummer family. Adam Plummer was one of Charles Calvert's most trusted slaves and, after gaining his freedom, became a manager on one of Calvert's plantations. One of his descendents, the Rev. L. Jerome Fowler, has traced the history of the Plummer family in Prince George's County. Using Plummer's diary, the class was able to get a glimpse into both slave life in Prince George's County and life on one of the Calvert plantations. Students also consulted several historical works, including Professor George Callcott's "A History of the University of Maryland and Mistress of Riversdale," edited by Margaret Law Callcott. The former provides an in-depth look at the history of the university and its origins as an agricultural college, while the latter is a collection of letters written by Rosalie Stier Calvert, Charles Benedict Calvert's mother.

THE DEVELOPMENT OF SLAVERY

Slavery and Race in the Modern World; 1200–1600

The plantation slavery system that thrived in the United States until the Civil War took centuries to develop. Its origins can be traced to the discovery of cane sugar by European merchants following the 11th-century Crusades to the eastern end of the Mediterranean. Europeans, who had previously known no such source of sweetness, adapted this crop that was originally cultivated commercially in the Muslim world. They used it to enrich their cuisine, creating an enormous market for the new sweetener. By the 13th century, a new class of planters—mostly

Italian but backed by capital from all over Europe—had adopted Muslim techniques to grow sugar on the eastern Mediterranean island of Cyprus. In the centuries that followed, sugar production spread west to other Mediterranean islands and became a source of European wealth.[11]

Cultivating sugar was highly profitable, but also extremely labor intensive. Although Mediterranean sugar planters used black slaves carried across the Sahara, they relied principally on the labor of enslaved Slavic peoples purchased from the area surrounding the Black Sea. The word "slave," derived from "Slav," came to designate those forced to grow cane sugar and other crops under the most dismal of conditions. But in 1463, the Ottomans captured Constantinople and cut off the sugar planters' access to Slavic labor, forcing them to look elsewhere.[12]

Deprived of their usual labor force and reluctant to abandon the lucrative plantation system, European planters turned more fully to Africans. The Portuguese pioneered this shift when they carried the Mediterranean plantation system into the Atlantic and established sugar plantations on small islands like Cape Verde and Sao Tome with their convenient proximity to the West African coast. When the Portuguese carried the plantation system across the Atlantic to Brazil, they initiated a system that took millions of Africans from their homelands. Africans were separated from their families and forced to traverse the vast expanse of the continent on foot. Frightened and confused, African captives were inspected on the coast by slavers and then packed into slave ships designed to cram as many slaves as possible into a tiny space. Slaves were treated as cargo, not as humans. Millions died, some choosing to end their own lives as a result of their deplorable treatment. As the demand for sugar grew, the number of Africans transported to the Americas increased dramatically and Atlantic slavery became identified with blackness. Slavery, originally an economic system, became a racial system.[13]

Upon arriving in the New World, slave traders sold Africans like cattle. In New World ports, enslaved Africans were exposed to a myriad of new diseases as a result of the new climate and surroundings; again they died in large numbers. Many more Africans died when they were put to work on plantations in the Americas. After being sold, the lives of African slaves varied. Historians have presented numerous reasons for the diverse treatment of slaves, including the religion of their owners, the nature of the crops they grew and the demographic balance of New World populations. As the number of African slaves increased, Europeans came to see Africans as natural slaves.[14]

Slavery and Race in Mainland North America and the Chesapeake

The first black people to arrive in North America were not slaves. In the 17th-century Atlantic world, blackness did not necessarily mean enslavement and whiteness did not necessarily mean freedom. Many peoples, white and black, were held in various forms of bondage, of which chattel slavery was just one. Others were sold into servitude as punishment for debt or crime. Among the people of African descent to arrive in America were so-called Atlantic Creoles, people with a mixed ancestry who traced their beginnings to the historic encounter of Europeans and Africans on the west coast of Africa. They spoke a variety of languages and had a physical appearance that differed from those of the phenotypical African or European. They were able to maneuver through the Atlantic world as skilled laborers and polylingual translators. They often possessed Portuguese names and practiced a combination of European and African cultures. "Familiar with the commerce of the Atlantic, fluent in its new languages, and intimate with its trade and cultures, they were cosmopolitan in the fullest sense."[15] Their mixed race, however, made them outcasts within both the African and European communities—"they were condemned as being haughty, proud, and overbearing." In mainland North America, many Atlantic Creoles gained their freedom, and some rose to prominence. In 1621, a black man identified as "Antonio a Negro" was sold to the English at Jamestown. He eventually attained his freedom, anglicized his name to Anthony Johnson, married, raised a family, purchased land and owned several slaves himself. Later, parts of his family migrated to Maryland. His story illustrates the fluidity of race relations in the 17th-century Chesapeake. Black people enjoyed a degree of social mobility—even those with the humblest of origins.[16]

The early 17th-century Chesapeake was not a slave society, but a society with slaves. Slavery existed, but it was not the only or primary form of labor. The black population was small, and indentured English and Irish servants outnumbered enslaved Africans until the 1690s. Black people made up less than 10 percent of the Maryland colony's population. Moreover, not all black people were slaves; many labored as indentured servants and others managed to gain their freedom. People of African, European and Native American descent often worked and played together. As there were no slave statutes in the 1620s and 1630s, blacks and whites mixed freely.[17]

In the late 17th century, however, Chesapeake society began to change, becoming a slave society—that is, a society in which all social relations were informed by slavery. Tobacco came to dominate the economy of Maryland and Virginia, and, as it did, the demand for labor increased. Planters, who controlled the best lands, at first desired to maintain a white servant labor force, but the decline of the English indentured servant trade made this impractical and expensive. They turned to Africa, which, after the end of the British-owned Royal Africa Company's monopoly over the slave trade, allowed them to import large numbers of slaves directly from the continent. The black population expanded, growing to between one-third and one-half of the population of the region. The growth of African slavery united the white population, which viewed black slaves as different and dangerous. The old pattern of racial mixing disappeared. In 1691, Maryland forbade marriages between blacks and whites. White men and women, from former servants to poor farmers to rich plantation owners, stood together, distinguishing themselves from black people, who were now consigned to slavery. In 1705, Virginia consolidated its previously piecemeal, ad hoc laws dealing with slavery into a slave code confirming the establishment of a new pattern of race relations.[18]

Disdained and disparaged by whites, black people—most of them newly arrived Africans—began to create their own society. They married among themselves, promoting the development of an African American population. The black population of the Chesapeake increased so rapidly that by the middle of the 18th century, planters stopped importing Africans. Planters organized tobacco production according to the "quarter system"—a series of small units scattered across the countryside. Slaves moving from quarter to quarter enjoyed considerable mobility. Slaves expanded their kinship networks and their knowledge of the land, strengthening their hand when negotiating with their owners.[19]

The American Revolution struck a major blow to slavery. The chaos of the war created an opportunity for many slaves to procure freedom by running away and assuming the identity of free men and women. Slaves became central to both the British and American military operations, as laborers and eventually as soldiers. Although the British were the first to offer to exchange military service for freedom, the Patriots soon followed suit. In 1777, the Maryland legislature passed a substitution law that provided opportunities for slaveowners to escape military service by sending a slave in their place. In 1780, Maryland became so desperate for soldiers that the legislature allowed that "any able-bodied slave between 16 and 40 years of age, who voluntarily enters into service . . . with the consent and agreement of his master, may be accepted as a recruit." The legislature also required all slaveholders with six or more slaves between the ages of 15 and 45 to enlist a slave in the newly created slave regiment.

The claim in the Declaration of Independence that "all men are created equal" also undermined slavery. In states to the north, revolutionary egalitarianism put slavery on the road to destruction. Slavery survived in Maryland, but the legislature loosened its manumission laws, allowing slaveholders to free their slaves by will as well as by deed. Many did so, and others allowed their slaves to purchase their freedom. Quakers and Methodists, believing all people to be equal in the sight of God, also freed their slaves and allowed others to gain their liberty. As a result, the free black population grew rapidly. By the beginning of the 19th century, Maryland had the largest free black population among the slave states.[20]

Although free blacks enjoyed legal freedom, they were denied many of the rights of citizens. Free blacks could not vote, sit on juries, testify in court or serve in the militia. They were not allowed to own dogs, firearms or liquor, and could not sell pork, beef, mutton, corn, wheat or tobacco without a specific certification from three white neighbors who could vouch that they were "respectable citizens." By custom, they were either excluded from or segregated in many churches, schools, clubs and informal gathering places.[21] Still, the presence of so many free blacks distinguished Maryland from the slave states to the south.

Slavery and Race in Maryland and Prince George's County

Situated between the free states to the north and the slave states to the south, Maryland occupied a unique position in that its economy extensively employed both slave labor and free wage labor. In the northern part of the state, tobacco cultivation declined as farmers switched to grain production. Although slavery remained, farmers incorporated enslaved blacks into a mixed labor force of free white and free black wageworkers. In the southern part of the state, however, planters remained committed to tobacco and depended on enslaved workers. Between the two extremes was the Eastern Shore, where yet another mixed labor system developed. The historian Barbara Fields described the state as "two Marylands . . . . : one founded upon slavery and the other upon free labor."[22]

Sectional divisions within Maryland increased during the 19th century. Northern Maryland—Allegany, Baltimore, Carroll, Frederick, Harford and Washington counties—became increasingly tied to free wage labor and a mixed economy based on cereal farming and manufacturing. Between 1790 and 1850, the free population of northern Maryland increased such that nearly three-quarters of the state's whites and more than half of the state's free blacks could be found in that region. Much of the region's white population consisted of immigrants to the state, many of whom were foreign-born. As the region's free population grew, so did its wealth. Northern Maryland became the center of commerce and manufacture in the state.[23]

With its crowded docks, railroad yards and factories, Baltimore exemplified the economic dynamism of northern Maryland. Ships delivered cargo from all over the world and carried away America's agricultural bounty. Its railroad system, most particularly the B&O, connected Baltimore to the nation's agricultural interior, and manufacturing boomed. As it grew, Baltimore became less dependent upon slavery, and by 1860 only a handful of slaves remained. Instead, the city became identified with wage laborers, many of whom were Irish and German immigrants. At the same time, the city was home to the nation's largest urban free black population, creating a society whose economy and demography were in sharp contrast to the rest of the state.[24]

Southern Maryland—Anne Arundel, Calvert, Charles, Prince George's, Montgomery and St. Mary's counties—was characterized by its dependence on tobacco and slave labor. In 1850, the region produced 98 percent of the state's tobacco and grew little else. Yet its tobacco had difficulty competing with the crops from Kentucky and Missouri. Half of the state's enslaved population lived in southern Maryland, and it was the only region of the state where black people—overwhelmingly slaves—outnumbered their white counterparts. Unable to make a living in a region peopled by slaves, whites—particularly nonslaveholders—fled, migrating to Baltimore or to the West. At mid-century, only 12 percent of the state's white population resided in southern Maryland. Southern Maryland had become an agriculturally backward, declining region within the state.[25]

As northern Maryland grew in population and wealth, southern Maryland's slaveholders became more defensive, particularly about slavery. With sons and daughters seeking opportunities elsewhere, planters worried about the future of their region. At mid-century, southern Maryland's slaveholders joined with slaveowners from other parts of the state to revise Maryland's constitution. That revision, ratified in 1851, expanded the political power of the fading region by counting slaves for the purpose of representation, thus giving slaveholding districts additional weight in the state legislature. To ensure that their power would be maintained, slaveholding delegates also inserted a provision into the new Constitution preventing the legislature from abolishing slavery.[26]

The tension between the "two Marylands" hardly disappeared with the ratification of the new constitution. While slaveholders received new protection for slavery, the institution itself continued to decline as slaves were sold to the cotton South or ran away to the North. Meanwhile, the number of free blacks continued to increase. Between 1830 and 1860, free blacks grew from one-third to nearly one-half of the total black population. For many white Marylanders, the growing presence of free blacks signaled the eventual demise of slavery and challenged the future of white supremacy. It fed the anxiety of both slaveholders worried about losing their valuable property and nonslaveholders fearful of losing the privileges that accompanied a white skin. In contrast, these same changes cheered black people eager to see the expansion of freedom.[27]

Marylanders—whether free or slave, white or black, devoted to free labor or to slave labor—had a shared understanding of the changes that were reshaping their state and even their implications for the future, but they disagreed as to how to address these changes. Some slaveholders labored to find new ways to protect their right to human property, while others, though deeply committed to maintaining chattel bondage, conceded the eventual demise of slavery. Of the latter, some sought to rid the state of free blacks and create a white Maryland. The state itself supported various schemes to remove free blacks by subsidizing the Maryland Colonization Society, which had established its own colony within the borders of Liberia to house the state's black expatriates. But others were leery of this course, appreciating the importance of free black wageworkers to the labor force. Some urged the enslavement of free black people or at least the institution of a black code that would force free black people to work in conditions little better than slavery. Yet others, fearful that even the threat of enslavement would drive free black workers from the state, grudgingly accepted an uncomfortable status quo. Free blacks, for their part, steadfastly opposed the removal movement, frustrated the colonizationists and made it clear that enslavement would spark a mass exodus. Instead, they endeavored to expand freedom, helping slaves—many of whom were relatives and friends—escape bondage, sometimes with cash to purchase their liberty or directions to freedom in the North.[28] Each group pressed its own cause, but none fully gained its own way. The resulting stalemate created a sense of unease, which intensified with the growth of national conflict over slavery.

Prince George's County and the Bladensburg-Vansville District

The crisis was particularly intense in Prince George's County, nominally part of southern Maryland but deeply affected by its position between the cities of Baltimore and Washington. Tobacco remained at the center of the county's agricultural life. Its plantations and farms grew more tobacco than any other county in Maryland; at mid-century, it produced some 8 million pounds, almost double that of Anne Arundel County, the state's second-largest tobacco producer. But change was in the works. In 1850, Prince George's County also led all others in wool production. Other planters and farmers turned to cereals, dairying and truck farming for the Baltimore and Washington markets, revealing a shift toward a more mixed economy. Many planters and farmers had given up tobacco entirely, as they struggled to find the most profitable agricultural mix.[29]

The population of Prince George's County reflected its changing economy. In 1850, whites and free blacks composed 47 percent of the population, while slaves made up 53 percent. The population hardly increased during the next decade, and the division between free and enslaved people remained much the same. The free black population also held steady.[30] If the number of free blacks was growing—either by natural increase or manumission— newly freed black people probably were leaving for Baltimore, Washington or perhaps the free North. Unlike the northern portion of the state, with its booming free and declining slave populations, the signs of stagnation seemed to be everywhere. Prince George's was being left behind.

The changes were echoed in the Bladensburg-Vansville District of Prince George's County, home of the Calvert family and what would become the site of the Maryland Agricultural College. Like that of the county as a whole, the district's economy was dependent upon the cultivation of tobacco, and slaves composed nearly half the population.

Slavery was alive in the Bladensburg-Vansville District, and it affected all aspects of the lives of its inhabitants: whites, slaves and free blacks. But it was not well. The number of white slaveholders had been declining since the beginning of the century. While white non-slaveholders might participate in slavery by renting slaves annually, seasonally or for specific jobs, ownership of slaves was no longer economically feasible for most white men and women. Indeed, many white nonslaveholders had fallen out of the landed class, and some owned no property whatsoever. Likewise, the number of small holders—those who owned only a few slaves—also declined, although they continued to make up a majority of the district's slave-holding population.[31]

While most white men and women saw their position in society slip, some continued to prosper. The largest planters, who had long dominated the Bladensburg-Vansville District, consolidated their position after mid-century. In 1850, only eight planters were worth $10,000 or more. By 1860, that number had risen to 38. Although few in number, they continued to own the majority of slaves. Yet, even these men of great wealth worried about their future, as the profitability of slave plantations declined. Some sold slaves to the cotton and sugar fields of the Deep South to keep their enterprises in Maryland afloat. Others tried to maintain their wealth by experimenting with new crops and new agricultural methods. Neither option seemed to soothe their anxieties.

Whether they worked on plantations or farms, slaves in the Bladensburg-Vansville District labored at a variety of jobs. These changed with the season, as they moved from planting to harvest. But even during a single season, slaves could be found at a variety of tasks. They planted tobacco and grain, tended cows and sheep, cultivated gardens and repaired all manner of machinery. Although some skilled craftsmen found regular employment in shops or small manufactories, most slaves were jacks- and jills-of-all-trades. They were not assigned exclusively to the field or the house. Slaveowners assigned children and elderly men and women to duties around the house, but everyone, including the most skilled slaves, took turns in the field during planting and harvest.[32]

The slaves' various duties required mobility, and slaves moved about freely in the Bladensburg-Vansville District doing their owners' business or sometimes their own. Some ventured further afield, perhaps even visiting Baltimore or Washington. Cross-plantation courting and marriages created extended networks of kin that also kept slaves on the move. Black people of the Bladensburg-Vansville District had a good sense of the region's geography.

Knowledge of the world beyond the plantation or farmstead provided slaves with a deep appreciation for the changes that were reshaping Maryland and how they affected the Bladensburg-Vansville District. Most powerfully, the sale of slaves—generally young adults who were scarcely more than children—to the cotton South angered and saddened those left behind. From their own travels, slaves gathered scraps of information about Baltimore's large free black population with its numerous African churches and schools. Doubtless, they learned about the growing movement against slavery in the North and even in their own state. Such knowledge was reinforced by the handful of black people, slaves as well as free, who learned to read and write and could translate the strange markings in newspapers and journals that circulated surreptitiously.

Free black people provided another source of information for the enslaved. The district's free black population was a small minority—only 228 of 5,750 in 1850—and was not growing

(290 free blacks of 6,145 in 1860), but they lived independently and answered to no white master.[33] Many of these African Americans had obtained their freedom through an owner's bequest, and others had purchased themselves. Once free, they worked to liberate others with whom they lived, worked and intermarried. The slave and free black communities were closely connected. Where slaves received permission to live away from their owners, they frequently clustered together in small neighborhoods, sometimes with free blacks. For example, 12 free members of the Adams family—and probably some enslaved kin—lived within four separate households in the shadow of what would become the College Park campus.[34] But life remained hard. Free people of color worked as agricultural laborers, and very few, if any, owned land. Still, their ties with slaves, their ability to move about freely, their desire to improve themselves and their families and the example they provided that black people could attain freedom and work and live on their own worried many whites, especially slaveholders.

THE MARYLAND AGRICULTURAL COLLEGE

Charles Benedict Calvert: Founder

If planters dominated the Bladensburg-Vansville District, Charles Benedict Calvert—the principal founder of the Maryland Agricultural College—stood atop the district's planter class. "Founding" was a familiar avocation for the Calvert family, which could trace its ancestry in the New World to Cecilius Calvert, the Second Baron Baltimore, who established the colony of Maryland in 1632. In the centuries that followed, the Calvert family maintained its aristocratic lineage. Charles Benedict Calvert's father, George Calvert, was already a wealthy slave-owning planter when, in 1803, he married Rosalie Stier. The Stiers, Belgian royalists who had fled revolutionary France, had settled in Annapolis, and the marriage brought great wealth as well as another aristocratic connection to the Calvert line. George and Rosalie took up residence at George's Mount Albion plantation on the Patuxent River, but when Rosalie's family returned to Belgium in the wake of Napoleon's amnesty to royalist exiles, Rosalie gained possession of her family's Riversdale plantation in Prince George's County. Along with some 50 slaves inherited from the Stier estate and 70 of his own slaves, George moved his wife and their children to Riversdale.[35]

A shrewd businessman and an improving farmer, George Calvert quickly transformed Riversdale into a prosperous plantation. Drawing on Rosalie's fortune, he purchased land adjacent to the estate, greatly expanding its size. He introduced modern agricultural practices, such as crop rotation, "artificial grasses," hawthorn hedges and blooded stock. Although tobacco remained Riversdale's major crop, the Calvert estate also became known for its "fine breed of horses and cattle." As the Riversdale plantation grew, so did its slave population.[36]

Born in 1808, Charles Benedict Calvert was the fifth child of Rosalie and George. He enjoyed a privileged childhood on Riversdale plantation. Like his siblings, Charles Benedict was educated at private schools. He completed his secondary education at the Bladensburg Academy and subsequently enrolled at the University of Virginia. Calvert never graduated, but was awarded a certificate of completion.[37]

Upon leaving the university, Calvert returned home to assist his father in managing Riversdale and other family properties. He spent over a decade mastering the complicated operations
of the sprawling Calvert enterprises, gaining a deep interest in agriculture and an appreciation
of the new scientific methods that were transforming American farming in the 19th century.
When his father died in 1838, Calvert inherited Riversdale and took the leadership of the
Calvert family.

Charles inherited additional duties as executor of the Calvert estate, including responsibility
for his father's other family. Among George Calvert's slaves was Eleanor Beckett, with whom
George had a long-standing relationship and with whom he fathered at least two children, Caroline and Anne, prior to his marriage to Rosalie. Eleanor bore three other children after George
and Rosalie were married. Whether or not they too were George's children, he took responsibility for them. He freed Eleanor, Caroline and Anne, and, since Eleanor was free and under
Maryland law children followed the condition of the mother, the other children enjoyed freedom from birth. They all resided on one of Calvert's estates in nearby Montgomery County,
supported by Calvert.[38] In 1822, when a scheming neighbor challenged their right to freedom,
George returned to court to affirm Eleanor's and the children's liberty.[39] Meanwhile, Caroline
entered into a relationship with another neighboring planter, Thomas Cramphin Jr., that was
similar to her mother's relationship with George Calvert. Cramphin was a close friend of
George Calvert, and he made George the trustee of his estate, which he intended to leave to
Caroline and their children. When George died, Charles inherited that responsibility too.
Cramphin had feared that his white kin would challenge Caroline's right of inheritance, and
when the estate was probated, they did. Charles took up the cause of his black kin, defending the rights of his half-sister. Thanks to his efforts, Caroline kept her inheritance. Charles
adhered to a guiding principle of 19th-century American race relations, publicly denying his
black family but privately acknowledging them. When, like many slaveholders, Charles spoke
of his "family black and white," he knew of what he spoke.[40]

The same interests and responsibilities that required Charles to address such intimate family matters also elevated him in the public political arena. In 1838, the voters of the Bladensburg-
Vansville District elected Charles Calvert to the Maryland House of Delegates. Although they
refused him a second consecutive term, he returned to the legislature in 1843 and again in 1845.
While a member of the Maryland legislature, Calvert served on the House's Agriculture
Committee. There he began to address directly the state's growing economic crisis, which he
believed required a radical change in agricultural practice. Calvert spoke and wrote widely
about crop diversification, fertilizers, horticultural innovations and new technologies. He said
little about the matter of labor, and he remained almost totally silent on the question of slavery. In 1855, Frederick Law Olmsted, beginning his tour of the seaboard South, stopped at
Riversdale plantation and pointedly asked the great agricultural reformer about slavery. Calvert
informed his visitor he would rather not talk about it.[41]

What Calvert did not say to Olmsted, however, was far more telling than what he did. Most
slaveholders spoke freely about slavery, often voicing vociferous support for an institution
under abolitionist assault. They sought new ways to protect their property, denouncing people
of African descent as inferior to white people. Calvert may have chosen to hold his tongue
because of his position as the representative of a slaveholding district, or perhaps he understood

how his father's black mistress and his own black half-brothers and -sisters gave the lie to white racial pretenses. His own doubts about slavery's future may also have cautioned silence.

Calvert's actions spoke louder. He sent his sons to a school run by Benjamin Hallowell, a Quaker abolitionist whose own farms were a showcase for free labor, perhaps preparing them for the day when slavery would be no more.[42] In 1860, with the nation rushing toward civil war and Maryland divided, Calvert stood with the Union. While Abraham Lincoln received only 2 percent of the vote in Maryland, Calvert ran successfully for the U.S. House of Representatives on the Unionist ticket. He denounced Maryland secessionists, declaring, "If Maryland has a grievance under the General Government she should seek a remedy for them in and not out of the Union." Calvert liked to quote Henry Clay, who had declared, "I am for staying in the Union and fighting for my rights, if necessary, with the sword, within the bounds and under the safeguard of the Union."[43]

But if Calvert foresaw slavery's demise in some distant future, he defended its standing in the here and now. Once the war began and federal soldiers entered Maryland, Congressman Calvert demanded that soldiers who sheltered runaway slaves return them to their owners, continually calling upon President Lincoln and other Union officials to enforce the Fugitive Slave Law.[44]

Calvert's commitment to slavery waned as the war took its toll on the institution. Thousands of slaves found refuge with federal soldiers, and Union officials increasingly turned a deaf ear to Calvert's pleas. In April 1862, when Congress abolished slavery in the District of Columbia, thousands more Maryland slaves—many from nearby Prince George's County—decamped for freedom. Others gained their freedom when the Lincoln administration authorized slave men to enlist in the Union army, a freedom that was later extended to the immediate families of black soldiers. Whether Calvert freed his slaves directly or simply allowed them to take their freedom as slavery collapsed, at the time of his death in the spring of 1864, months before Maryland officially abolished slavery, an inventory of his estate listed no slave property.[45]

Calvert had preferred to say as little as possible about slavery, but he was a proponent of the reform of agriculture and used his time in Congress to further that agenda. He co-sponsored a bill creating a Bureau of Agriculture, which eventually became the federal Department of Agriculture, with a mandate to promote a national agricultural policy that did not include slavery.[46] Perhaps even more important, he began plans for an agricultural college that would help end the crisis weighing heavily upon his home state. The Maryland Agricultural College was a fitting culmination to a life committed to the remaking of Maryland agriculture.

Benjamin Hallowell: Founder

The Maryland Agricultural College had another founder, a man who shared Charles Calvert's passion for agricultural reform but whose origins, training and beliefs—particularly respecting slavery—differed greatly from those of Calvert. In 1858, when the trustees of the nascent Maryland Agricultural College sought a president for their new institution, they unanimously elected Benjamin Hallowell, a veteran educator who farmed in nearby Montgomery County. Hallowell was, in some ways, an ideal candidate. As a young man, he began teaching in Maryland schools. In time, he opened his own boarding school in Alexandria, Va., which drew students from all over the country and educated the sons of some of Maryland's leading families.[47] In 1842, Hallowell retired and settled into life on his farm, Rockland.[48] He enjoyed a reputation as a man of science and, like Calvert, was a leading advocate of agricultural reform. His interest in agricultural science, combined with a natural eloquence, led many local agricultural societies to invite Hallowell to speak at their annual fairs, elevating him to a position of prominence.[49] The trustees of the Maryland Agricultural College were so eager to bring this renowned educator and farmer to the new institution that they elected him to its presidency before he had been informed of his nomination.[50]

Despite his extraordinary credentials, Benjamin Hallowell was a surprising choice on the part of the trustees. As a member of the Society of Friends, or Quakers, Hallowell hated slavery, an institution that Quakers believed denied the spark of divinity that God had planted in every human being. Prior to the American Revolution, the Quakers had begun the process of ridding themselves of any connection to slavery, and by the 19th century opposition to the institution had become an article of faith within the sect.[51] But Hallowell, like many Quakers residing in the South, distinguished between the inhumanity of slave ownership and the humanity of slaveowners. He was careful to show the utmost respect for his slaveholding neighbors. While Hallowell had found a way to make peace with slaveholders, it did not mitigate his abhorrence of slavery or reduce his commitment to abolition.

Hallowell held a position of leadership in the small Quaker communities of southern Maryland and northern Virginia, whose religious and social identity rested on their opposition to slavery in a slave society.[52] During his years in Alexandria, Hallowell helped to found the Benevolent Society for Ameliorating and Improving the Condition of the People of Colour, whose aim was to assist enslaved African Americans in making legal claims to freedom in court. While members of the Benevolent Society carefully tempered their activities so as "not to interfere with slavery" or alarm local slaveholders, they did not conceal their purpose of securing slaves "their legal rights."[53] As secretary of the society, Hallowell traveled to the Maryland town of Upper Marlboro, where he secured freedom for a family of 13. Even in the face of their slaveholding neighbors, Quakers denounced slavery in the local press. Samuel M. Janney, another Alexandria Quaker and a cousin of Hallowell, blasted slavery in the *Alexandria Gazette*, in an essay so forceful that the editors of *Freedom's Journal*, the nation's first black newspaper, saw fit to publish it.[54] While cautious about confronting the powerful slaveholders among whom they lived, Hallowell and his Quaker brethren's opposition to slavery was unyielding. Years later, Edward Hallowell, a distant cousin who rose to the command of the famous Massachusetts 54th Colored Regiment during the Civil War, boasted of Benjamin's deep commitment to the destruction of slavery.[55]

Hallowell, like other Quaker farmers, also made the case against slavery by attempting to demonstrate that wage labor was more productive—and hence more profitable—than slave labor. In the 1850s, Moncure Conway, a Methodist preacher, passed through the Quaker settlement of Sandy Spring, Md., where Hallowell had taken up residence. When he asked a local farmer why the area was so prosperous, the man responded that it was partly due to the fact that Quakers paid their farmhands, rather than rely on slave labor. Conway later cited the Quakers' success as one of the reasons for his conversion to abolitionism.[56]

Hallowell boasted that the use of free, rather than slave, labor accounted for his own prosperity.[57] While many Marylanders disparaged the agricultural labor they identified with slavery, Hallowell celebrated the advantages, material and moral, of work on the land. He preached
that farming was the "occupation of occupations . . . the highest, the noblest that man can
engage in."[58] For Hallowell, labor promoted both prosperity and morality—the good society.

When the trustees elected Hallowell the first president of the Maryland Agricultural College, they knew they were choosing an abolitionist. Hallowell was aware that any agricultural
institution founded by planters such as Charles Calvert and Allen Bowie Davis would presumably employ slave labor. "I first wished to know whether free or slave labor was to be
employed," he wrote of the trustees' offer in his memoirs. "I was much gratified when informed
it was to be free labor only."[59] Given his lifelong abolitionist views and his determination not
to accept a position that he could not "conscientiously perform," Hallowell's presence at the
beginning of the Maryland Agricultural College indicates that the trustees of the early college
not only tolerated free-labor farming practices, but also actively sought to encourage them.

After only one month as president, however, Hallowell abruptly resigned. In his memoir
he diplomatically cited ill health as the reason, but his resignation was probably also due to
disagreements with the trustees on matters of administration. Hallowell had little patience
for the disorganized trustees and alluded to this frustration in his memoirs. A few months
after his resignation, Hallowell expressed similar views to his friend, Joseph Henry, the first secretary of the Smithsonian Institution. Hallowell "stated that the Trustees had commenced
before they were ready and that they had very crude ideas as to what was proper to be done,"
Henry later related.[60] Despite his resignation, Hallowell maintained an interest in the new
college. He told Henry that he intended to "continue his connection with it in the character
of a visitor" and proposed a commission to draw up a system of proper instruction and governance. In addition, Hallowell donated several scientific instruments to the school.[61]

Although Hallowell's time at the college was short, his selection affirmed the purposes of
the Maryland Agricultural College; Calvert and the trustees had sought out a man who was
known for his commitment to progressive agriculture and free labor. The short exchange that
Hallowell mentioned in his memoirs on the subject of slavery at the college is highly informative of the intentions of the trustees and the purpose of their new school. In an agricultural
district dominated by planters dependent on slave labor, the trustees of the college founded
an institution that conceded the efficacy—and perhaps the advantage—of free labor. Their
commitment to training students in the management of farms without using slave labor can
be seen in Hallowell's acceptance of the position. If Calvert represented a tepid commitment
to slavery, Benjamin Hallowell spoke to a deep commitment to freedom. This dual founding
in both slavery and freedom illustrates the conflicted origins of the Maryland Agricultural
College.

The Founding of the Maryland Agricultural College

The Maryland Agricultural College derived from the changes that roiled Maryland's economy and society in the middle of the 19th century. The crisis drew together men as different as the slaveholder Charles Benedict Calvert and the abolitionist Benjamin Hallowell.

Both men saw agricultural reform as critical to addressing the problems that weighed upon Maryland and threw the state's future into doubt. They envisioned the college as an engine of reform. It would train a new generation of farmers that would be knowledgeable in scientific farm management, familiar with advances in horticulture and animal husbandry and willing to embrace the newest technology. They, in turn, would bring prosperity and comity to Maryland.

Both Calvert and Hallowell had lectured widely on agricultural reform and its blessings at state and local agricultural societies. They joined their like-minded peers in presenting their views in *The American Farmer* and other agricultural journals. Thomas G. Clemson, who later gave his name to a similar college in South Carolina, followed the development of the Maryland Agricultural College closely. Writing in *The American Farmer*, he asserted that "the only hope we have for the advancement of agriculture is through the science . . . [The Maryland Agricultural College] will be the pride and ornament of the State; it will turn out annually persons well and properly educated. . . . Poor lands will be invigorated, and wealth and prosperity will prevail where desolation, want, and wretchedness now obtain."[62]

Chief among the founders' concerns was the issue of labor. Yet the new college's charter, like the founders themselves, said little directly about who would labor under the reformed regime. The founders made no mention of slavery, perhaps from fear of stirring sectional divisions and derailing the entire project. However, they spoke repeatedly of the "dignity of agricultural labor," a phrase of enormous portent in the ideological battles over slavery in the United States. For advocates of wage labor, slavery degraded agricultural labor and laborers by identifying work with slaves and thereby with black people. Calvert, Hallowell and the other leaders of the Maryland Agricultural College wanted to change that identification. "The vice of our educated young men, which lies at the foundation of all other vices, is contempt for agricultural, mechanical and all other physical labors," the trustees stated in their 1864 report to the legislature. "We are aware of no means, so effective, as to dignify labor by its connection with intellectual and moral culture."[63] The Maryland Agriculture College would transform the sons of Maryland into cultured gentlemen, knowledgeable about the classics and able to read Greek and Latin and to discuss the great events of history. Calvert and Hallowell were also determined to teach the collegians about the value of agriculture and the material and moral importance of work. At Hallowell's insistence and with Calvert's concurrence, no slaves would labor on the college's grounds; instead, the students themselves were required to work in the college's fields. They would learn firsthand the nobility of work; agricultural labor would no longer be denigrated. Elevating work in the eyes of white Marylanders would prepare for the day when slavery would be gone from the state.

Calvert's and Hallowell's vision found a good deal of popular support among Maryland's planters and farmers, who saw the college as an immensely valuable resource. As Calvert's dream neared fruition, they heaped praise upon him and his college. In 1856, as the legislature considered the college's charter, *The American Farmer* applauded the school as a "grand instrument of improvement" and an "institution of learning of the highest order."[64] John H. Sothoron, a large slaveholder and later a Confederate sympathizer, gave vocal support to Calvert's project and to Calvert himself in the state legislature, where he served as a senator.

"Need I name Chas. B. Calvert, Esq., the late President of the Maryland Agricultural Society, who in public and private life, has exhibited enlarged views on all questions affecting the public interest," Sothoron acclaimed. "For years past he had devoted his time, his energies, his means to the cultivation of this, the most important of all fields of labor; and having, step by step, progressed with other friends of the cause in the various paths leading to the consummation of their hopes."[65] Soon thereafter, the legislature passed an "act to establish and endow an Agricultural College in the State of Maryland," but made its opening contingent on the sale of $50,000 of stock to fund the college.[66] By the end of 1857, the required funds had been secured and a board of trustees that drew from Maryland's elite was in place.[67] Within a year, construction had begun on numerous buildings, including a "commodious Mansion house." As far as is known, no slaves labored to construct the buildings. Construction continued throughout the year, and on Aug. 24, 1858, the cornerstone was laid, an occasion marked by a speech from Calvert. The first students arrived a year later, on Oct. 5, 1859.[68]

But even as the college transformed from Calvert's dream to a reality, evidence of its dual origins was manifest. For if the college spoke to the nobility of free labor, the institution continued to rest upon slavery. At least 16 of the first 24 trustees held slaves. On average, they owned 25 slaves, putting most of the slaveholders in the planter class.[69] In 1860, the trustees held collectively nearly 400 slaves. Slavery underlay both the trustees' wealth and the political connections that made the college possible.

The connections between slavery and the college were also evident in the faculty and students, although here the records are more divided. Harry Dorsey Gough, who taught "exact science," farmed in Harford County with eight slaves—three adult women and five children. But Battista Lorino, who covered the courses in ancient and modern languages, apparently had no connections to slavery, as there are no records of his owning slaves.[70]

The student body was likewise divided between slaveholders and non-slaveholders. But most of the first students came from slaveholding families. Part of this circumstance was due to the planters' wealth, since only the wealthy could afford to educate their sons at the college. Indeed, when the college opened its doors in 1859, four of its first students were Charles Benedict Calvert's own sons—George H. Calvert Jr., who entered the school at age 19, Charles B. Calvert Jr., 16, William N. Calvert, 13, and Eugene S. Calvert, 12.[71] Nowhere were the dual origins of the Maryland Agricultural College more evident than in the men who filled the college's classrooms.

Adam Francis Plummer: Founder

Further complicating the origins was the historic role of the ubiquitous unpaid labor of enslaved black men and women that made—even the vision—possible. If barred from working on the campus by Hallowell's dictum, slaves labored everywhere around the campus. No enterprise in the Bladensburg-Vansville District existed without them, directly or indirectly. Maryland's slave-based economy formed the basis of the fortunes of Calvert, many of the trustees and stockholders and at least some of the teachers and students. Even as Maryland's slave-based economy declined, these founders maintained their positions by selling slaves to the South. Their labor and their persons thus made enslaved African Americans co-founders of the Maryland

Agricultural College. Their contribution was unpaid years of labor dating back to Maryland's founding.

Charles Benedict Calvert inherited slaves from his parents. One of those slaves was Adam Francis Plummer. Plummer's life and his family's history—although unique—reveals the intimate connections between the Maryland Agricultural College and the lives of black people who lived on and around the lands that would compose the campus. They provide a glimpse into the complex world in which African Americans of the Bladensburg-Vansville District lived. Calvert's slaves shaped that world as much as he shaped theirs. The slaves' stubborn refusal to accept the complete subordination that chattel bondage demanded and their determination to assert their humanity contributed to making slavery less and less profitable. Calvert experienced such defiance, which at times directly affected his life. In 1856, when Frederick Law Olmsted visited Riversdale plantation, he noted that Calvert's slave gateman refused to leave the entry hut and open the gate for him, even as Olmsted made his intentions known. Adam Francis Plummer, whom Calvert trusted and with whom Calvert had a close if complicated relationship, was much like that recalcitrant gatekeeper—a man determined to live life on his own terms.

The experience of Adam Plummer and his family was in many ways emblematic of the nature of slavery in Maryland. By the time the college was founded, almost half of the state's black population had gained its freedom. In nearby Baltimore and Washington, established free black communities provided examples of what black people free of slavery could accomplish. Throughout the Bladensburg-Vansville District, mobile slaves participated in the larger economy, owned property, attended church and, in some cases, learned to read and write. Like Adam Plummer, many black people shared a common ancestry with white people.

Adam Francis Plummer was born on George Calvert's plantation in 1819, the son of George's slaves William Barney Plummer and Sarah Norris. William Barney Plummer was the son of another Calvert slave, Milly, who was married to Cupid Plummer, the former slave of a Quaker woman named Jemimah Plummer (from whom he took his surname). Cupid Plummer, Adam Francis Plummer's grandfather, was one of the thousands of African Americans who fought in the American War of Independence and gained his freedom as a consequence.[72]

In 1781, when Cupid Plummer was discharged from military service, he was granted his freedom.[73] His wife and their children remained in slavery, since Maryland law required that children follow the status of their mother—that is, if their mother was a slave, they were slaves, even if their father was a free man. The entangled relations between the Calverts and the Plummers reveals the complications of race relations in Maryland. Cupid's and Milly's eldest son, William Barney Plummer, married Sarah Norris, one of George Calvert's slaves and the daughter of Calvert's mistress, Eleanor Beckett, by Beckett's husband. Caroline and Anne Calvert, George's children by Eleanor, thus became both Adam Francis Plummer's half-aunts as well as Charles Benedict Calvert's half-sisters. When Adam Francis Plummer was 10 years old, George Calvert took him to Riversdale to serve as Charles Benedict Calvert's personal servant. But the two were more than slave and master. Although Adam and Charles were not blood kin, family ties bound them together.

Perhaps it was those connections that allowed Adam to enjoy privileges accorded to few other slaves. While Adam was a slave at Riversdale, John Bowser, a black Methodist preacher, secretly taught him to read and write.[74] Many masters frowned upon slave literacy, and in some states—although not in Maryland—it was illegal to teach a slave to read or write. Charles Benedict Calvert never challenged Adam on this matter and indeed seemed to appreciate the benefits that Adam's literacy accorded him. In 1839, Adam began courting Emily Saunders, a slave from Three Sisters plantation, eight miles from Riversdale.[75] Two years later, they were married at the New York Avenue Presbyterian Church in Washington.[76] Their church ceremony allowed Adam and Emily to obtain an official certificate of marriage, an honor rarely extended to slaves. That document, like their courtship and church wedding, suggests the extent to which some Maryland slaves traveled on their own and enjoyed some of the privileges of free people. Such privileges extended only so far, however, even for the newly wedded Adam and Emily. After their marriage, Adam returned to Riversdale and Emily to Three Sisters. Adam made the eight-mile journey to Three Sisters nearly every weekend to visit his wife. In 1842, their first child, Sarah Miranda, was born, followed by Henry Vinton Plummer two years later. But the long journeys made it clear that privileged slavery was still slavery. Adam and Emily plotted an escape to the North or perhaps to Canada, using their marriage certificate as evidence that they were free. But, as they prepared to depart slavery forever, Emily confided the plan to an aunt, who disclosed it to her mistress. The marriage certificate was confiscated and Emily sent to labor in the field. Apparently Adam received no punishment from Charles Benedict Calvert. Adam continued to visit Emily, and their third and fourth children were born in 1846 and 1849, respectively.[77]

The difficulties of maintaining a family life in bondage and the omnipresent threat of sale to the South that induced Adam and Emily to risk all for freedom increased in the 1850s. The threat of sale weighed heavily on the Plummer family, and its reality was soon upon them. In 1851, the mistress of Three Sisters plantation died and willed Sarah Miranda to Mary Trueman Hilleary.[78] The following month, Emily and three of her children were sold at auction to Col. Livingston Gilbert Thompson of Meridian Hill in Washington.[79] Despite their relocation, Adam continued to visit his family on a regular basis, though Meridian Hill was farther from Riversdale than Three Sisters. After the birth of their seventh child, Adam was able to visit his wife less frequently because their separation became more extreme. Thompson willed Emily and her children to yet another distant slaveowner, this time near Ellicott Mills in Howard County, Md. Now Adam was able to visit his family only during the Easter and Christmas holidays.[80] Bad as this situation was, Adam's distress became more serious still. On the eve of the Civil War, Sarah Miranda's new master sold her. She was first sent to a slave pen in Alexandria and then transported to New Orleans.[81]

In 1862, when Congress abolished slavery in the District of Columbia, the Plummer family at last began to shake free of slavery. Adam's son, Elias Quincy, escaped to the nation's capital and freedom. Later that year, Adam's other son, Henry Vinton, escaped and joined the Union army.[82] The rest of the Plummers remained in slavery, unaffected by President Lincoln's Emancipation Proclamation, as it did not apply to Union slave states like Maryland. In October 1863, Emily made another bid for freedom, fleeing with her five remaining children. But the escape failed, and they were imprisoned in a Baltimore City jail as runaways.[83]

When Adam discovered that his wife and children had been jailed, he hurriedly applied to Charles Benedict Calvert, who gave him permission to visit them. In November 1863, he left Riversdale for Baltimore, where he secured a court order to release Emily and her children. The entire family returned to Riversdale where, for the first time, Adam and Emily were able to live together under the same roof. After the war, Henry traveled to New Orleans to find his sister, Sarah Miranda.[84] After a century of bondage, the Plummer family at last breathed free air.

Once free, Adam continued in Charles Calvert's employ and worked independently as well. By 1868, he had saved enough money to purchase 8 acres of land, which he named Mount Airy.[85] Freedom agreed with Adam Francis Plummer, and he lived to age 86, dying where he had lived, in the shadow of the newly renamed University of Maryland.[86]

Adam Plummer was never a student or teacher at the Maryland Agricultural College. Indeed, as far as is known, he never set foot on its campus. Yet his life—like that of many enslaved black men and women whose labor created the wealth that funded the college—was deeply connected to the history of the university. They, too, can be considered its founders. The failure to recognize the role that Plummer and other slaves played in creating the Maryland Agricultural College has had profound consequences.

EPILOGUE

The Long Shadow of Slavery

The noose hanging from a tree before the Nyumburu Cultural Center served as a chilling reminder of slavery's legacy and the system of racial exclusion and segregation that followed. Slavery cast a long shadow over the Maryland Agricultural College, and that shadow was extended to the college's successor, the University of Maryland.

With the coming of the Civil War, slavery was more than a shadow. Southern sympathies ran strong on campus. In the summer of 1864, when Confederate soldiers swept through central Maryland, they were welcomed to the campus of the Maryland Agricultural College by its Southern-leaning president, Henry Onderdonk, and celebrated by the students in a large ball. The Unionist state government never forgave the college for its apostasy. Soon thereafter, President Onderdonk resigned, and the college itself closed in 1866.

When the college reopened in 1867, little had changed for black people. Although slavery was gone, first by order of a new state Constitution in November 1864 and then by the ratification of the 13th Amendment to the United States Constitution in December of the following year, there were no black students or faculty. The Maryland Agricultural College remained an exclusively white institution.

By the end of the 19th century, the Maryland Agricultural College had become the University of Maryland, a federal land-grant college. In 1890, new congressional legislation, the second Morrill Act, stipulated that there be no "distinction of race or color" in the use of funds the federal government supplied. However, the school's trustees, deeply committed to maintaining a racially exclusive institution, refused to accept black students at the College

Park campus. Instead, they allocated one-fifth of the Morrill funds to the Princess Anne Academy on the Eastern Shore for the education of black students. Black students were no longer excluded from higher education in Maryland, but they were segregated and barred from the College Park campus.[87]

From then on, Maryland's public educational institutions at all levels maintained a policy of strict racial segregation until it was finally dismantled under the weight of legal challenges and other forms of protest. At the post-secondary level, African American students pursuing higher education were obliged to attend colleges set up specifically for blacks. Blacks who wanted to attend graduate and professional schools in areas where there were no black colleges were sometimes given exemptions. In a case that gained national attention, the university stopped black students from attending its law school in Baltimore.[88] School authorities, acting upon the petition of white students and faculty, denied readmission to the two black students who were already enrolled in the school. In 1930, the law school also denied admission to native Baltimorean Thurgood Marshall, who went on to become the nation's first black Supreme Court justice and one of the 20th century's leading legal luminaries. Five years later, however, after he received a law degree from Howard University School of Law, Marshall successfully represented African American Donald Murray in his attempt to gain admission to the University of Maryland Law School.

Despite court orders to desegregate, the University of Maryland continued to pursue a policy of segregation. One of the figures most closely associated with the Jim Crow policy of keeping the College Park student body all white was Harry Byrd, who served as president of the university from 1935 to 1954.[89] His prowess as a player and coach at the University of Maryland gave Byrd enormous authority, which he used to expand the College Park campus. The increase in funding and student enrollment, as well as the physical appearance of today's campus, stood side by side with his adamant pursuit of racist and segregationist policies. Byrd advocated separate colleges for African Americans and was a major force behind the establishment of the University of Maryland at Eastern Shore (formerly Princess Anne Academy), which was set aside for black students. After years of resistance, the College Park campus was forced to accept its first black undergraduate, Hiram Whittle, in 1951 and its first black female undergraduate, Elaine Johnson, in 1955. Despite the *Brown v. Board of Education* Supreme Court ruling in 1954, the university's student body remained largely devoid of black students and faculty through the early 1970s. However, the waves of student activism and social change that began in the 1960s as part of a larger national trend eventually led to a more diverse student body, the establishment and development of new university curricula, diverse centers of learning and organizations on campus committed to racial equality, in the process transforming and enriching the intellectual community of the College Park campus.

ACKNOWLEDGMENTS

All historians are indebted to the archivists, librarians, archaeologists and other experts who support their work. This was especially true for our class; for many of us, these two semesters were our introduction to archival research and truly tackling historical questions. We would like to thank all of the men and women who helped us throughout the project. We could not have succeeded without your knowledge, experience and support.

First, we give heartfelt thanks to our instructors, Professors Ira Berlin and Herbert Brewer. Without them, this class would not have existed. They taught us both by sharing their own knowledge and by stepping back and encouraging us to ask and seek answers to our own questions. They oversaw many heated class discussions about our findings and read countless drafts of our report. They have truly taught us the historian's craft, and have given us the passion and skills for many future research projects.

We would like to thank our university's president, C. D. Mote, Jr., for encouraging the development of this course and taking an active interest in our findings. President Mote supported the creation of this project to better understand our university's history, and we are proud to present this report to him. Teresa Flannery, now of American University, and Millree Williams, the university's senior director of public affairs strategy, appreciated the concern of many members of the College Park community for the historic relationship between slavery and the university and helped launch History 429. We appreciate their continuing concern.

Darlene King, Courtenay Lanier, Karen Rowe, Catalina Toala and Shayla Atkins of the History Department helped us with many practical aspects of our project. Without them, we could not have traveled to conduct our research or publish this report.

Professor George Callcott, our university's first historian, provided early direction for our research. He shared his knowledge, both of his own research and of the many resources to which we could turn to for more answers. Anne Turkos and Elizabeth McAllister of the Archives and Manuscripts Department, University of Maryland Libraries, provided guidance on the records of the Maryland Agricultural College.

We would especially like to thank Ms. McAllister for teaching our class about the basics of archival research. Edward Papenfuse, Chris Haley, Maya Davis and Michael McCormick at the Maryland State Archives shared their own research on the history and demography of slavery in Maryland, and their assistance was integral to the creation of several sections of this report.

Ed Day and Ann Wass at the Riversdale Historic Mansion gave us a wonderful introduction to Prince George's County history and provided encouragement throughout the project. Ann Wass also organized a forum where we were able to share our research with the Riverdale community. The Reverend Jerome Fowler, a direct descendent of Adam Plummer, spoke with our class and shared his family's history. As well as being highly informative, his engaging lecture brought his ancestors to life for us. Professor Leigh Ryan, director of the University Writing Center, who has a special knowledge of the Calvert and Plummer family at Riversdale, gladly shared her knowledge with us.

Archivists and librarians at various historical repositories throughout the state and beyond also provided critical assistance. At the Sandy Spring Museum, Margaret Mintz introduced us to the records of our first president, Benjamin Hallowell, and pointed us to the other repositories of his records. Susan Pearl played a similar role at the Prince George's Historical Society, as did Francis O'Neill at the Maryland Historical Society in Baltimore.

We would like to thank Patricia O'Donnell and Christopher Densmore at the Friends Historical Library at Swarthmore College for their patience and assistance as we worked our way through the Hallowell family papers, and also for explaining Quaker life in the 19th century.

Finally, we would like to thank Dennis Pogue, chief archaeologist at Mount Vernon, who gave us a direct feel for what life was like for slaves on an 18th-century Chesapeake plantation.

To all of these men and women and many others who helped each of us individually, we express our profound thanks.

Endnotes

1. Slave schedule for Bladensburg, Md., U.S. Manuscript Census, 1860, National Archives, Washington, D.C.

2. Kyle Goon, "On Slavery Question, No Definite Answers," *The Diamondback*, April 7, 2009.

3. Andrew Vanacore, "Campus' History of Slavery Overlooked," *The Diamondback*, Dec. 14, 2006, http://media.www.diamondbackonline.com/media/storage/paper873/news/2006/12/14/News/Campus .History.Of.Slavery.Overlooked-2551604.shtml [accessed April 26, 2009].

4. Ben Slivnick, "University Unveils Plan to Examine Slavery," *The Diamondback*, Feb. 7, 2008, http://media.www.diamondbackonline.com/media/storage/paper873/news/2008/02/07/News/Univ-Unveils.Plan.To.Examine.Slavery-3194219.shtml [accessed April 26, 2009].

5. Andrew Vanacore, "Police: Noose Found Outside Nyumburu," *The Diamondback*, Sept. 7, 2007, http://media.www.diamondbackonline.com/media/storage/paper873/news/2007/09/07/News/Police .Noose.Found.Outside.Nyumburu-2956644.shtml [accessed April 26, 2009].

6. The Maryland State Archives and the University of Maryland, *A Guide to the History of Slavery in Maryland* (Annapolis, Md., 2007), 1.

7. Deidre Walsh and Scott Anderson. "House Apologizes for Slavery, 'Jim Crow' Injustices," CNN, July 29, 2008, http://www.cnn.com/2008/POLITICS/07/29/house.slavery/ [accessed April 29, 2009].

8. *Slavery and Justice: The Report of the Brown University Steering Committee on Slavery and Justice*, http://www.brown.edu/Research/Slavery_Justice/report/; Yale, Slavery, and Abolition, http://www .yaleslavery.org/; "Slavery and the Making of the University" (University of North Carolina), http://www.lib.unc.edu/mss/exhibits/slavery/.

9. Brian Whitson. "The Lemon Project: A Journey of Reconciliation," The College of William and Mary, http://www.wm.edu/news/stories/2009/the-lemon-project-a-journey-of-reconciliation.php [accessed April 28, 2009].

10. "Group Shines Light on Slavery," *Wheel*, Oct. 29, 2007, http://www.emorywheel.com/detail .php?n=24571.

11. Phillip D. Curtin, *The Rise and Fall of the Plantation Complex: Essays in Atlantic History* (Cambridge, U.K., 1990), chaps. 1–2.

12. Ibid., chap. 2; David Brion Davis, "Sugar and Slavery from the Old to the New World," in *The Atlantic Slave Trade*, ed. David Northrup (Boston, 2002), 15–18.

13. Curtin, *Plantation Complex*, chaps. 2–3; Olaudah Equiano, "An African's Ordeal," in *The Atlantic Slave Trade*, ed. Northrup, 68; Thomas Fowell Buxton, "An Abolitionist's Evidence," in ibid., 71; Eric Williams, "Economics, Not Racism, as the Root of Slavery," in ibid., 2–7.

14. Curtin, *Plantation Complex*, chaps. 4–7.

15. "From Creole to African: Atlantic Creoles and the Origins of African-American Society in Mainland North America," *William and Mary Quarterly*, 53 (1996), 254.

16. Ira Berlin, *Generations of Captivity: A History of African-American Slaves* (Cambridge, Mass., 2003), chap. 1.

17. Berlin, *Generations*, chap. 1; Allan Kulikoff, *Tobacco and Slaves: The Development of Southern Cultures in the Chesapeake, 1680–1800* (Chapel Hill, N.C., 1986), chaps. 1–2, 8; *Guide to the History of Slavery in Maryland*, 3.

18. Berlin, *Generations*, chap. 2; Kulikoff, *Tobacco and Slaves*, chap. 8.

19. Berlin, *Generations*, chap. 2; Kulikoff, *Tobacco and Slaves*, chaps. 3–4, 8.

20. Berlin, *Generations*, chap. 3; Kulikoff, *Tobacco and Slaves*, 302–307, 417–420; Benjamin Quarles, *The Negro in the American Revolution* (New York, 1973), 56–58. See also Curtin, *Plantation Complex*, chap. 11.

21. Berlin, *Generations*, chap. 3; Barbara Jeanne Fields, *Slavery and Freedom on the Middle Ground: Maryland during the Nineteenth Century* (New Haven, Conn., 1985), 10, 34–35.

22. Fields, *Slavery and Freedom on the Middle Ground*, 1–6.

23. Ibid., 7, 19.

24. Ibid., 40–48.

25. Ibid., 10–14.

26. Ibid., 10–20.

27. Ibid., 70–84.

28. Ibid., 71.

29. J. D. B. DeBow, *Seventh Census of the United States* (Washington, D.C., 1853), 227.

30. DeBow, *Seventh Census of the United States*; Joseph C. G. Kennedy, *Preliminary Report on the Eighth Census: 1860* (Washington, D.C., 1862).

31. Free and slave population schedule for the Bladensburg-Vanville District, Prince George's County, U.S. Manuscript Census, 1850 and 1860, National Archives.

32. Kulikoff, *Tobacco and Slaves*, chaps., 8–10; Fields, *Slavery and Freedom on the Middle Ground; Guide to the History of Slavery in Maryland*, 11–14.

33. Free and slave population schedule for the Bladensburg-Vanville District, Prince George's County, U.S. Manuscript Census, 1850 and 1860, National Archives.

34. Ibid.

35. Margaret Law Callcott, ed., *Mistress of Riversdale: The Plantation Letters of Rosalie Stier Calvert, 1795–1821* (Baltimore, 1991), 2–17.

36. Callcott, ed., *Mistress of Riversdale*, 22; David Baillie Warden, *A Chorographical and Statistical Description of the District of Columbia* (Paris, 1816), 156.

37. John A. Garraty and Mark C. Carnes, eds., *American National Biography* (New York, 1999), 4: 246.

38. Callcott, ed., *Mistress of Riversdale,* 379.

39. Callcott, ed., *Mistress of Riversdale*; Prince George's County land records, Liber A. B. 2, folio 371, Maryland State Archives, Annapolis, Md.

40. Callcott, ed., *Mistress of Riversdale*, 378–384.

41. Frederick Law Olmsted, *A Journey in the Seaboard Slave States, with Remarks on Their Economy* (New York, 1856), 5–11.

42. Julia Wright Sublette, "The Letters of Anna Calhoun Clemson (1833–1873)" (Ph.D. dissertation, Florida State University, 1993).

43. Washington *Daily National Intelligencer*, Jan. 12, 1861; July 25, 1861.

44. Ira Berlin et al., eds., *Freedom: A Documentary History of Emancipation, 1861–1867*, Series 1, Volume 1: *The Destruction of Slavery* (New York, 1985), 336.

45. Prince George's County probate records, Maryland State Archives.

46. Garraty and Carnes, eds., *American National Biography*, 4:246.

47. Alexandria Boarding School circular, 1842, Benjamin Hallowell Papers, Box 240, Alexandria Library Special Collections, Alexandria, Va.

48. Benjamin Hallowell, March 9, 1843, "Hallowell Farm Book" folder, Sandy Spring Museum Collection, Sandy Spring, Md.

49. Address of Benjamin Hallowell (of Alexandria, Virginia) at the Meeting of the Agricultural Society of Montgomery County, Md., Sept. 9, 1852, Manuscript Collections, Maryland Historical Society, Baltimore.

50. Benjamin Hallowell, *Autobiography of Benjamin Hallowell* (Philadelphia: Friends Book Association, 1884), 163.

51. *The Old Discipline: Nineteenth Century Friends' Disciplines in America* (Glenside: Quaker Heritage Press, 1999), 290, Friends Historical Library, Swarthmore, Pa.

52. A. Glenn Crothers, "'I Felt Much Interest in their Welfare': Quaker Philanthropy and African Americans in Antebellum Northern Virginia," *The Southern Friend: Journal of the North Carolina Friends Historical Society* 29 (2007): 5.

53. Hallowell, *Autobiography*, 109.

54. Samuel M. Janney, "Of the Benevolent Society of Alexandria for Ameliorating and Improving the Condition of the People of Colour," *Freedom's Journal*, May 25, 1827, in Accessible Archives, http://www.accessible.com.proxy-um.researchport.umd.edu/accessible/docButton?AAWhat=built Page&AAWhere=FREEDOMSJOURNAL.FR1827052503.00198&AABeanName=toc3&AANext Page=/printBrowseBuiltPage.jsp [accessed March 20, 2009].

55. Edward Hallowell, "The Meaning of Memorial Day: An Address Delivered on Memorial Day, May 30, 1896, at a Meeting Called by the Graduating Class of Harvard University," 54, in volume printed privately by Quentin Davis, no. 66.

56. Moncure Conway, *Autobiography, Memories and Experiences of Moncure Daniel Conway*, 2 vols. (New York: Houghton, Mifflin and Co., 1904), 1:105–106.

57. Hallowell, *Autobiography*, 190.

58. Address of Benjamin Hallowell (of Alexandria, Va.) at the Meeting of the Agricultural Society of Montgomery County, Md., Sept. 9, 1852, Maryland Historical Society.

59. Hallowell, *Autobiography*, 162–163.

60. Joseph Henry to Alexander Dallas Bache, Dec. 22, 1859, Alexander Dallas Bache Papers, RU7053, box 4, Smithsonian Institution Archives, Washington, D.C.

61. Hallowell, *Autobiography*, 164–165.

62. "Maryland Agricultural College," *The American Farmer*, Sept. 1, 1856, p. 69.

63. *Report of the Trustees of the Maryland Agricultural College, to the Legislature of Maryland, January Session 1864* (Baltimore, 1864).

64. "Maryland Agricultural College," *The American Farmer*, Sept. 1, 1856, p. 69.

65. "Maryland Agricultural College," *The American Farmer*, June 1, 1856, p. 374.

66. "Maryland Agricultural College: An Act to Establish and Endow an Agricultural College in the State of Maryland," *The American Farmer*, April 1, 1856, p. 292.

67. George Callcott, *A History of the University of Maryland* (Baltimore, 1966), chap. 6.

68. Ibid., 80.

69. Slave schedule, U.S. Manuscript Census, 1850 and 1860, National Archives.

70. Records of the Office of Registration, Series I, Box 1, Student Register, 1859–1907, University of Maryland Archives.

71. Callcott, *History of the University of Maryland*, 147.

72. Bianca C. Floyd, *Records and Recollections: Early Black History in Prince George's County, Maryland* (Upper Marlboro, Md., 1989), 79.

73. Ibid., 80.

74. Ibid., 82.

75. Part of the Three Sisters plantation site is currently occupied by Charles Herbert Flowers High School, in the Prince George's County public school system.

76. Floyd, *Records and Recollections*, 82.

77. Ibid., 83–84.

78. Ibid., 83.

79. Nellie Arnold Plummer, ed., *Adam Francis Plummer's Diary*, 9, retrieved from http://anacostia.si.edu/Plummer/Plummer_Home.htm.

80. Floyd, *Records and Recollections*, 85.

81. Ibid., 86.

82. Henry Vinton Plummer subsequently became the first African American chaplain in the U.S. armed forces.

83. Floyd, *Records and Recollections*, 86.

84. Ibid., 88–89.

85. Ibid., 89.

86. Plummer, ed., *Adam Francis Plummer's Diary*, 27.

87. Callcott, *History of the University of Maryland*, 35–36.

88. *The New York Times*, Sept. 14, 1891.

89. Byrd remains the longest-serving president of the University of Maryland.

By Kyle Goon

The preliminary findings of a class created to research the university's involvement in slavery reveal no conclusive proof that slave labor was used to construct the campus, but the students involved hope they can offer a greater understanding of slavery in the region and time period the campus was built in.

The research, which the students of HIST 429I and HIST 429L, presented yesterday at a Black Student Union meeting, lacked a "smoking gun," or definitive evidence that the university's founders used slave labor to construct the campus. But their findings did show that at least 16 out of the university's original 24 trustees owned slaves, totaling to about 400 between them. Most university shareholders owned slaves as well, they said in their presentation.

Course leader and history professor Ira Berlin said his students have struggled to find the extent slavery was used on the campus in the absence of construction records. However, repeating a statement he has before stated in The Diamondback, Berlin said there is no question the university's origins are linked to slavery.

"If slaves didn't lay the brick, they made the bricks," Berlin said. "If they didn't make the bricks, they drove the wagon that brought the bricks. If they didn't drive the wagon, they built the wagon wheels."

Student Government Association President Jonathan Sachs, who is in the class, said it could recommend the university issue an apology for using slave labor depending on the information in their final report. University president Dan Mote declined to issue such an apology in 2007, citing existing records were too unclear to draw any conclusions.

The class was created in hopes of shedding more light on the issue, but they haven't made a definitive breakthrough. But that doesn't mean the time was wasted, students said.

BSU President Connie Iloh said she hoped their presentation would allow black students to both appreciate their opportunities and challenge the university to uncover more.

"Programs like this teach us history is important to learn," she said. "I wanted them to come so more people can have exposure to this information and appreciate what they can accomplish today when just 150 years ago, people at this university owned slaves.

"I also see people have a demand for more answers," Iloh added. "We want to know how we can learn more and how we can get involved."

One of the biggest questions the research has so far failed to answer is the reason the university's first president, Benjamin Hallowell, resigned only a month into his term. Hallowell was a Quaker and a radical abolitionist, and although the group cannot prove he resigned because the university was built by slaves, researchers think there is likely a connection.

A problem in resolving the issue is the lack of records from the time period. A 1912 fire destroyed the original construction records that could have shown slavery was used to construct the university, which forced the class to focus on determining the use and breadth of slavery in the surrounding area rather than the campus itself.

For example, 1850 census records of nearby Bladensburg and Vansville showed many white citizens owned at least one slave, and at least one citizen owned as many as 150. Slaves composed nearly half of Bladensburg's population in that time.

Other evidence uncovered includes records showing parts of the current campus were once owned by slaveowners. Slaveowner Israel Jackson lived in the area where the Clarice Smith Performing Arts Center was later built and is buried near Stadium Drive.

Researchers also delved into the human aspects of slavery. The diary of Adam Plummer, who served as a personal servant to Charles Calvert, revealed how Calvert allowed Plummer special privileges for slaves at the time. Also, the team explained George Calvert, Charles' father, had children with one of his slaves, Eleanor Beckett, and took care of his "other" family.

A highly anticipated and unusual study into the historical connection between the University of Maryland and African American slavery will be released and discussed at an event on Friday, Oct. 9 at 1 p.m.

Knowing Our History: African American Slavery and the University of Maryland, a new study conducted by UM distinguished university professor of history Ira Berlin and a class of top students, is the result of a year-long investigation.

The predecessor of the University, the Maryland Agricultural College, opened its doors in the fall of 1859.

With the encouragement of University of Maryland President C.D. Mote, Jr., Professor Berlin and his team sought to "explore, document and define the historic connections between African American slavery and the Maryland Agricultural College." They began by looking for what Berlin calls a "smoking gun," such as records showing that slaves constructed university buildings or were involved in campus operations. However, no such records were found.

"It was no secret that slavery had some relationship to the founding of the Maryland Agricultural College," Berlin says. "It could be no other way in Maryland, as slavery touched every aspect of life." But what precisely was that relationship? Prior research had been uncertain because campus records were lost in a catastrophic fire that destroyed much of the University over a hundred years ago.

Presentation of the research by Dr. Berlin and his students will be followed by remarks and comments from various experts and University officials, including President Mote.

Key Participants Include:

C.D. Mote, Jr., president, University of Maryland

Ira Berlin, distinguished university professor of history, University of Maryland, who has written extensively on U.S. slavery, including *Slaves Without Masters: The Free Negro in the Antebellum South* and *Many Thousands Gone: The First Two Centuries of Slavery in Mainland North America*

UM students from History 429—Berlin's research team, top undergraduate students

Rev. L. Jerome Fowler, great-great grandson of Adam Plummer, a slave in the household of University founder Charles, Benedict Calvert

Elizabeth McAllister, acting curator of historical manuscripts, University of Maryland

Dottie Chicquelo, assistant director, Office of Multi-Ethnic Student Education and director, UM Black Faculty and Staff Association

When:

Friday, Oct. 9, 1 p.m. to 2 p.m.

Where:

David C. Driskell Center for the Study of Visual Arts and Culture of African Americans and the African Diaspora

1214 Cole Student Activities Bldg

Directions and Parking online

Stops Short of Issuing an Explicit Apology
By Ben Slivnick

University President Dan Mote expressed regret on Friday for the university's early connections to slavery, but stopped short of issuing an apology.

His remarks came after students from an undergraduate research course released "Knowing Our History," a 40-page report showing an intimate relationship between slavery and the university's origins as an agriculture college.

Although the report found no definite proof that slaves built campus buildings or served the university's early students, it makes clear the university was a product of wealth built on slave labor and a society rooted in plantation culture. The report shows that 16 out of the university's original 24 trustees owned slaves, and Charles Calvert, the university's founder, owned 52 slaves.

After the students introduced their findings in a ceremony at the David C. Driskell Center, Mote repeatedly cast the university's founders as products of their time and did not formally apologize for the university's ties to slavery.

"As inheritors of a society in which slavery was practiced widely, we all share in the benefits and tragedies of that era," Mote said. "The University of Maryland is like many institutions founded in the era in which slavery was practiced in the United States. Because of this legacy, the university shares in the profound regret for the suffering and injustices."

The state of Maryland, the United States Congress and several other universities have issued such apologies.

Mote personally commissioned the research course last year after the university's 150th anniversary reignited a debate about slavery's role in building the Maryland Agriculture College, which later evolved into the university. But even after 18 undergraduates, a graduate student and history professor Ira Berlin investigated the matter for two semesters, the role slaves played in the university's founding is still not entirely clear.

The university's first president, Benjamin Hallowell, was an ardent abolitionist who accepted the position based on the condition that slaves wouldn't work the campus grounds. And the report notes that university's emphasis on agricultural science likely implied that even its slave-holding founders recognized the limitations of the state's struggling slave-based economy.

But Hallowell quit his job after one month at the institution, and it's unclear whether slaves worked on the campus after he left. Regardless, the report stresses the Maryland Agricultural College emerged from a slave-dependent economy.

Even if the slaves didn't lay a single brick on the campus, they likely delivered supplies and built its bricks and mortar, said junior history major Grace Waldron, who contributed to the report.

"In this economy, you're going to have slave labor involved in the building of this campus no matter what," Waldron said. "But whether they built the buildings, whether they labored on the campus, we just can't say with 100-percent certainty."

In light of their early findings, the students recommended the university study slavery further, issue a statement of regret and reassert its commitment to international fair-labor laws. They also urged Mote to honor Hallowell and the black laborers who contributed to the university by naming them as founders.

Mote said he would review the recommendations, but expressed reservations about adding to the list of the university's official founders.

"We're going to respond to the ones that we can respond to," Mote said. "We, of course, support those recommendations in general, but I think it's a bit difficult to change your founders. It's like trying to change the signers of the Declaration of Independence."

After the university's 150th anniversary, several black students and professors called on Mote to formally apologize for slavery's history on the campus. But the Rev. Jerome Fowler, the great-great-grandson of one of Calvert's slaves, balked at the idea on Friday.

"I believe the founders should be recognized, and of course, I am favorable to my ancestor being recognized as what they have called a founder of the school," he said. "My only concern, and the only hesitation that I have, would be the recommendation of a statement of apology coming from the university because none of us that are living were a part of that society. We are all of the present society. None of us are slaves. None of us are slaveholders."

THE "HURRIED" CHILD: MYTH VS. REALITY

Sandra L. Hofferth*
University of Maryland

David A. Kinney
Central Michigan University

Janet S. Dunn
Oakland Community College

ABSTRACT

Children's lives are increasingly structured with extracurricular activities. This research addressed three questions: (1) how active are American children; (2) are there differences by social class in extent of participation in these activities, either within or across communities; and (3) are children overscheduled to the extent that they experience stress symptoms? Data came from a nationally representative survey of children and their families and a qualitative study in two communities in the American Midwest. Only one-quarter of children were "hurried," half were focused on a single activity or balanced, and 15 percent had no activities. Children of mothers with more education and higher family incomes were busier. However, higher activity levels were not associated with greater stress symptoms. Instead, children who were uninvolved were the most withdrawn, socially immature, and had the lowest self-esteem. Children who were focused or balanced in their activities had the lowest levels of stress and highest self-esteem.

INTRODUCTION

Recent writings bemoan the loss of childhood. Children are not allowed to "be kids"—to play games at home with friends, siblings, and cousins, to visit family members, to play pickup ball games in the yard, and to ride bicycles around the neighborhood. Instead, because of their own busy schedules or a focus on enrichment, parents enroll their children in lessons, team sports, and other scheduled activities outside the neighborhood. The lifestyle in which parents spend their free time driving their children from a swim meet to gymnastics to a soccer match may not only cause adults stress, but also result in potential stress and strain for their children, a syndrome some have called "the hurried child" (Elkind, 2001). A recent report by the American

---

*All correspondence should go to the first author, Sandra L. Hofferth, 1210E Marie Mount Hall, Department of Family Science, University of Maryland, College Park, MD 20742. E-mail address is hofferth @umd.edu. Funding for this research was provided by the Alfred E. Sloan Foundation through the Center for the Ethnography of Everyday Life, University of Michigan.

Academy of Pediatrics reports that a "hurried lifestyle is a source of stress and anxiety and may even contribute to depression" (Ginsburg, 2006, pp. 10–11). Organizations such as "Putting Family First" have been formed to combat the perceived pressure to overschedule the lives of children and their families (Doherty & Carlson, 2002). In spite of these concerns, little is known about the proportion of children whose involvement in activities may be excessive.

Of course, not all families choose such a lifestyle; it has been suggested that scheduling varies by social class, with middle-class families being the most likely to overschedule children (Lareau, 2003). Social class can be defined by financial resources or by values and lifestyle. A focus on financial resources implies that families of every class have the same goals, but that they differ in their access to the resources needed to implement these goals. In contrast, a focus on values or knowledge motivating parental actions implies differences in objectives resulting from differences in education, occupation, or culture (Lesthaeghe & Surkyn, 1988; Thornton, 2004). Understanding how resources and values drive these changes in family lifestyles helps us evaluate their consequences and develop potential solutions to any problems we identify.

Finally, no existing research has systematically studied children's experience of stress, which, if prevalent, could imply long-term negative effects of this "hurried child" syndrome. We simply do not know whether children are thriving in their activity-rich lifestyle or buckling under the pressure to participate in after-school activities. Because activity decisions are not random, but are based upon parental objectives for children and children's own preferences (Dunn, Kinney & Hofferth, 2003; Lareau, 2002; Lareau, 2003), the relationship between activities and child stress symptoms may be spurious. Research has examined how families manage the new pressures of structured activities (Arendell, 2001) and adults' experience of time pressure (Jacobs & Gerson, 2004; Robinson & Godbey, 1997), however, there is little comparable research on children. Earlier research was illuminated primarily by conversations with parents as well as observations in the home. Lareau (2003) reported on conversations between children and parents or professionals in 12 families, but did not directly interview the children.

This paper addresses these gaps by focusing on the out-of-school activities in which elementary school-age children are involved, by examining the prevalence of the hurried child and hurried family in the United States today, and by exploring the extent of stress symptoms that children experience. The paper addresses three questions: (1) what proportion of American children are hurried?; (2) are there differences by social class and family structure in hurriedness, either within or across communities?; and (3) are the most hurried children likely to experience symptoms of stress? Multiple methods are used to make comparisons by social class in a nationally representative sample and in a qualitative data set collected within and across two communities in the upper Midwest. The quantitative data provide the national picture and the qualitative data provide information about how families experience their children's activities.

Are Children Participating in Too Many Activities?

That children participate in more before and after-school care and extracurricular activities, and experience increased structure in their lives is well-documented. What is not documented is that a large number of children have high levels of activity. Although several theorists (Elkind, 2001; Doherty & Carlson, 2002) argue that too many children have excessive demands placed upon them, there is no empirical evidence that this is the case. Lynott and Logue (1993) argue that, from an historical perspective, concern about "lost childhood" is a misreading of history, one that romanticizes an ideal-typical childhood that may have existed in only part of the twentieth century in the U.S.—the 1950s. Before it was made compulsory in the early 20th century, a minority of children attended school, and those who did attended for only a few years. Children participated actively in the business of the family, helping on the farm, providing labor to a family business, or working as indentured servants and apprentices (Mintz, 2004).

Between 1981 and 1997, two major changes in the lives of American children have been documented. First, the amount of free time, defined as time not spent in personal care, eating, sleeping, and school, declined about 7.5 hours per week, from 56.5 hours to 49 hours, from about 34 percent of a child's week to 30 percent (Hofferth & Sandberg, 2001b). Although seven and one-half hours in a week may not seem significant, it represents more than an entire school day. Second, children's time became more scheduled and organized, with structured activities such as sports, scouts, ballet, and music lessons taking up an increasing proportion of the after-school hours. For example, between 1981 and 1997, participation in sports rose 35 percent and participation in the arts (art, music, dance, drama) rose 145 percent for children between the ages of nine and twelve (Hofferth & Sandberg, 2001b). Thus, there is evidence of a significant increase in children's structured leisure activity over the past several decades. However, the data on hours in specific activities do not provide a sense of how individual children's lives are divided into time spent in extracurricular activities and whether they have too many activities or spend too much time in them.

Consequences of Increased Structured Time—Stress

In addition to having too many activities, hurriedness may be harmful to children's development (Elkind, 2001). One of the potential consequences of excessive expectations for children's future by parents and perfectionism on the part of children is stress (Luthar & Becker, 2002). From a physiological point of view, a stress reaction is the response of an organism to any aversive stimulus (Stefanello, 2004). According to Elkind, "stress is an unusual demand for adaptation that forces us to call upon our energy reserves over and beyond that which we ordinarily expend and replenish in the course of a 24-hour period" (Elkind, 2001, p. 166). In actuality, Elkind defines stress in terms of the *number of demands*, such that the greater the number of demands, the greater the stress (Elkind, 2001, p. 165). We add to this the *total amount of time*, not just the number of activities because some activities may be quite short. We also argue that control over one's time and activities may be protective against stress (Tansey, Mizelle, Ferrin, Tschopp & Frain, 2004), whereas pressure to become involved in activities in which parents have an interest may increase that stress. A final aspect of hurriedness is whether demands are age-appropriate. A narrow range of ages controls somewhat for this; of course, children differ in their ability to manage pressures by individual maturity and temperament. Although checklists to identify a number of stressors in a child's life have been developed, determining stress levels is problematic. In contrast, the literature seems to agree on a set of symptoms, which, if present, are a reasonable indicator of stress-induced psychological problems. These include internalizing problems such as depression, problems getting along with others, anxiety, crying, stuttering, and sleep problems (Band & Weisz, 1988; Reynolds, O'Koon, Papademetriou, Szczygiel & Grant, 2001; Stefanello, 2004, p. 294). The most common physical symptoms include stomach ache, diarrhea, nervous twitches, headache, hyperactivity, stutter, muscle tension, and bed-wetting (Stefanello, 2004, p. 294). If a child reports or is reported to have these symptoms, the child is said to be under stress.

Positive Consequences of Activity Participation

Children do not learn *only* in formal educational settings. At the beginning of the 20th century, social reformers promoted youth organizations, hobbies, and sports to foster development. Over the past century organizations such as the YMCA, Boy and Girl Scouts, and Little League have proliferated. They are believed to build character, discourage delinquency, and provide opportunities for growth (Larson, 1994). Two major arguments are that the activities promote integration of youth into the community, peer group, and family and that, in addition, activities promote individual personal growth and development, including improving self-concept. Prosocial behavior, social skills, and community involvement are part of the first objective and initiative, self-regulation, and self-esteem part of the second (Larson & Verma, 1999). Research demonstrates that participation in organized activities such as sports teams, lessons, and clubs is associated with lower rates of school failure, higher school achievement, including better grades, and higher rates of participation in college (Mahoney, Larson, Eccles & Lord, 2005). Studies also show that involvement in organized activities reduces problem behavior. Finally, organized activity participation is associated with psychosocial adjustment (Eccles & Gootman, 2002). It is linked to lower rates of anxiety and depression and higher self-efficacy and self-esteem.

Besides the social benefits of participation in activities, theory suggests that organized activities represent a context in which activities are highly valued and exciting, challenge is high and the opportunity for skill development is equally high. Research shows that the condition of high challenge and high skills (the flow) coincides with the most positive moods, self-esteem, high levels of concentration, and motivation and all these experiences are most likely to occur during structured leisure activities (Hektner, Schmidt & Csikszentmihalyi, 2007). Recent research also shows that one of the physiological indicators of stress, cortisol level, rather than being high, is lower under conditions of enjoyment, mastery and involvement (Adam, 2005). Cortisol increases under conditions in which challenges are beyond one's skill level (anxiety-producing) or when challenge is too low (boring). Adam (2005) states that challenges contribute to health and well-being and are necessary for daily functioning, growth and development. The proper balance between challenge and skill is key.

Involvement but Not Hurriedness: Balance

There is substantial research on the positive aspects of activity participation; there is almost no empirical evidence for the stress and strain part of the hurried child hypothesis. Work-family studies have focused upon adults; no studies have examined children's experiences.

In the lone book based upon their reports *(Ask the Children)*, children did not express dissatisfaction or unhappiness with their lives (Galinsky, 2002). Although coping skills develop with age, even children as young as 8 and 9 can express the methods they use to cope with everyday stressful events and circumstances (Band & Weisz, 1988; Pincus & Friedman, 2004). The present research makes a unique contribution in that it focuses upon the preteenage years, when excessive activity is least developmentally appropriate (Elkind, 2001) and children have the least developed coping skills (Pincus & Friedman, 2004). We ask whether more active children exhibit more symptoms of stress than less active children. However, we also examine whether activities benefit children's self-esteem, an important measure of psychological health.

Concerted Cultivation and Natural Growth Theories

Although early research was motivated by an interest in the fit between early socialization and adult personality and occupations in the 1950s and 1960s, recent ethnographic research has extended this socialization paradigm to contemporary childrearing. Concerned that children develop their potential skills, middle-class parents cultivate their children's verbal skills by spending time with them in extended discussions and negotiations and their extracurricular talents and social skills by enrolling them in sports, lessons, and youth organizations (Dunn et al., 2003; Lareau, 2003). Lareau called this the "concerted cultivation" model of parenting (Lareau, 2003). The result is the transmission of middle-class advantage from parents to their children because middle-class jobs require such skills. This model is consistent with the earlier socialization paradigm of middle-class parents fostering autonomy and self-direction in their children (Alwin, 2001; Schaefer & Edgerton, 1985; Kohn & Schooler, 1983; Kohn, 1977). The major issue is whether parents are pushing their children too much—pushing them into activities in which they are not interested.

Working-class parents, in contrast, are believed to take a more passive approach in caring for children, allowing them to develop through participation in normal family-based or neighborhood peer-based activities, with less structure and adult intrusion. This model of parenting Lareau called the "natural growth" model (Lareau, 2003). In communicating with children, working-class parents are said to be more directive, less skeptical of authority, and less interested in negotiation. As a result, children experience less control over their environments and have a sense of constraint rather than opportunity (Lareau, 2003). This is very much the obedient and conforming-to-authority set of traits discussed by Alwin (2001) and by Kohn & Schooler (1983) that working-class jobs both require and foster.

Additionally, parents are constrained by the settings in which they live and work, in particular by their personal resources and those of their communities. Compared to middle-class parents, working-class parents may be more constrained by their financial resources from making large investments in children's activities. They may depend more on free school-based activities than their middle-class counterparts, though the total number of activities may not vary. Previous research indicates that children of middle and working class parents have become increasingly involved in after-school activities over the past twenty-five years, but that the extent of children's participation still varies by social class.

Objectives of This Chapter

In this paper we develop a typology of the activity levels of 9–12-year-old children and examine its distribution using both a nationally representative sample of American children and two small qualitative samples. We then use statistical techniques to describe the association of social class, maternal employment and family structure with this activity typology, controlling for gender of the child. We hypothesize that children from middle class families, defined by education, occupation, income, or community, compared with working class families, are more likely to fall into the hurried category in terms of activity commitments. Children from two parent or dual earner families are also expected to be more likely to be hurried compared to children in single-parent families or single earner families. We examine evidence as to whether children are reported as experiencing more symptoms of stress as a consequence of being "hurried." We also examine levels of self-esteem across activity groups. Finally, returning to the qualitative data, we draw upon children's and parents' in-depth reports to enrich our understanding of the results found in the large-scale data.

DATA AND METHODS

The Child Development Supplement to the Panel Study of Income Dynamics

Children 9 to 12 years of age were drawn from the nationally representative 2002/3 *Child Development Supplement* (CDS) to the *Panel Study of Income Dynamics* (PSID); the CDS is a supplement to a thirty-four-year longitudinal survey of a representative sample of U.S. men, women, children, and the families in which they reside. With funding from the National Institute of Child Health and Human Development (NICHD), data were collected in 1997 about children under age 13 of PSID respondents, with up to two children per household randomly selected for inclusion in the supplement. Data were collected both from the primary caregivers and from the children themselves (for children over the age of eight). In 1997, interviews were completed with individuals in 2,380 households that contained a total of 3,563 children. The response rate was 88 percent. Interviews were conducted again over the fall and winter of 2002 to 2003, with a response rate of 91 percent. Only PSID-CDS non-Hispanic white children aged nine to twelve living with their mother and who had time diary information (79 percent) were included in the present study, a total of 331 children. To match the qualitative component we also examine a subset of children 9–12 living with a mother who has completed 12 years of schooling or more, 277 children. When post-stratification weights based upon the 2002 Current Population Survey were used, such as was done here, the PSID has been found to be representative of U.S. individuals and their families (Fitzgerald, Gottschalk & Moffitt, 1998a). Thus, weighted sample characteristics reflect the characteristics of the population of non-Hispanic white children age nine to twelve in the United States in late 2002 and early 2003.

Time Spent in Different Activities: Quantitative Data from the CDS

The 2002/3 Child Development Supplement collected a complete time diary for one weekday and one weekend day. The time diary, which was interviewer-administered either to the parent or to the parent and child, asked questions about the child's flow of activities over a twenty-four hour period beginning at midnight of a randomly designated day. These questions documented each activity that occurred, when it began and ended, and whether there was another activity at the same time. Children's activities were first assigned to one often general activity categories (e.g., sports and active leisure[1]) and then coded into three-digit subcategories (e.g., playing soccer). Coding was conducted by professional coders employed by the data collection organization; the level of reliability exceeded 90 percent. Time spent traveling for the purpose of engaging in a specific activity was included in that category. The distribution of the total time spent across these two days was examined to identify the proportion in the upper tail of the distribution. Eighty-two percent of children spent less than 4 hours in their activities across these two days; 4 hours served as the cut-off for low vs. high activity levels. Although we do not have data for all seven days of the week, comparisons across weekdays and weekend days show that weekdays are quite similar to each other in types and times of activities, and weekend days are similar to each other. Two days provide a reliable representation of a child's typical week.

Child Stress Symptoms

Symptoms of stress or distress are measured in the internalizing items of standard behavior problems measures (Luthar & Becker, 2002). Here children's stress symptoms were measured by a subset of items from the 30-item Behavior Problems Index, a standard instrument used in the PSID-CDS and NLSY-79 Child Study to obtain primary caregiver reports of the incidence and severity of child behavior problems for a wide age-range of children (Peterson & Zill, 1986; Baker, Keck, Mott & Quinlan, 1993; Hofferth, Davis-Kean, Davis & Finkelstein, 1999). In this scale the caregiver reported whether a statement was often true, sometimes true, or not true of their child's behavior. Several measures were created. Six items were selected as representing stress symptoms, according to the literature. He/she is: high strung and nervous; fearful or anxious; unhappy, sad or depressed; withdrawn; cries too much; or worries too much. Responses to items (1 = often true, 2 = sometimes true, and 3 = not true of child's behavior) were reverse-coded as (2 = often true, 1 = sometimes true, and 0 = not true) and summed so that a high value on the scale indicates more and more frequent stress symptoms and 0 means no reported stress symptoms. Means for the full scale averaged 1.9, with a standard deviation of 1.8, N = 331. The reliability for the scale, as measured by Cronbach's alpha, was .63. A confirmatory factor analysis was not able to reject the hypothesis that one factor fit the six items. We also used the complete internalizing scale that was constructed by NLSY staff based upon 13 items. Besides the items listed above, the complete scale includes items indicating the

---

[1] Included in sports are team sports such as football, basketball, baseball, volleyball, hockey, soccer, and field hockey; individual sports such as tennis, squash, and racquetball, golf, swimming, skiing, ice or roller skating, sledding, bowling, ping pong or pinball, judo, weight lifting, jogging or running, bicycling, gymnastics; and other activities such as playing Frisbee or catch, exercises such as yoga, and lessons in any of the above. Youth organizations include participation in Boy/Girl Scouts, Future Farmers of America, YMCA/YWCA, volunteer activities, and helping organizations/clubs in the community or school. Art activities include painting, drawing, sculpture, potting, creative writing, playing a musical instrument, singing, dancing, acting, and related lessons and rehearsals.

child has low self-esteem, has difficulty getting along with others, and is highly dependent. The reliability of the complete scale (.80), is higher than the stress subscale. We created two other subscales, an internalizing scale without the stress symptom measures (alpha = .74), and a child-self-esteem subscale (alpha = .66), which consisted of five mother-reported items.

To measure positive aspects of activity participation, we used a six-item scale of child-reported global self-esteem that was included in the PSID-CDS 2002/3 wave for children 8 and older. It includes items such as "I can do things as well as most people," I'm as good as most other people," and "when I do something I do it well." Scored from 1 = never to 5 = always, a higher score indicates greater self-esteem and has an alpha reliability of .78. Although not the stress construct specified in the literature, a decline in self-esteem is mentioned in the literature as a potential result from overactivity, and the advantage of using this scale is that it is self-reported by the child rather than the mother. The disadvantage is that only 225 of the 331 children answered this self-administered supplement.

Qualitative Studies in Riverview and Parkside

The qualitative data presented in this paper are based on personal interviews conducted with parents and 9–12 year old children from forty-three families living in two different Midwestern medium-sized communities. Each of these families included at least one school-age child who attended the local public school. Both communities are more than 93 percent white. Because we had several dimensions of families to examine (family structure, employment, and social class), we decided to include only non-Hispanic white families in this study.[2] Twenty families were interviewed in "Riverview" (fictional name) between November 1999 and May 2000 and twenty-three families were interviewed in "Parkside" (fictional name) between May 2000 and February 2001. For seasonal comparability, cross-data comparisons focus on the activities of the sixteen Parkside families interviewed in May and June 2000, during the 1999–2000 school year.[3]

We gained access to families through local public elementary and middle schools. Permission to use these schools as sites to recruit parents and children was granted by the superintendent of each public school district. With the assistance of the elementary school and middle school principals, we mailed recruitment letters and brief surveys to 125 families (25 each in grades 3–7) in Riverview and received responses from 42 parents interested in participating in the project, a response rate of about 34 percent. In Parkside, we mailed letters of information about the research project to parents of 131 children in grades 4–6 and received responses from 25 families, a response rate of 19 percent.[4] To obtain diversity on our major theoretical concepts (number of earners, education, income, family structure), we interviewed a subsample of 20 Riverview families, whereas we interviewed all but two of the Parkside respondents, for a sample of 23 families. Interviews were

---

[2] Most of the concern to date about hurried children has focused upon white middle class families.

[3] Five of the remaining seven families were interviewed in the summer, when children participated in fewer activities, one was interviewed in early September before activities had begun, and one was interviewed the following year, judged to be too long a time period after the other interviews to include.

[4] The sampling in Parkside was conducted towards the end of the school year, a busy time for families.

conducted by the authors with one parent (usually, but not exclusively, the mother) either at home or in a neutral location such as a coffee shop. Riverview children were interviewed in the school with no parent present. Parkside children were interviewed in the school with no parent present or in the home with parents out of earshot; three of the Parkside children were interviewed with at least one parent present during some of the interview. Interviews of children ranged in length from one-half hour to 45 minutes. Parent interviews averaged about an hour and a half, but a few lasted more than 2 hours. All interviews except one were taped and transcribed with the parent permission and child assent.

The first community, "Riverview," is a small city of approximately 40,000 residents (U.S. Census Bureau, 2005). The local economy is largely defined by the presence of several large corporations, a small private university, and a large hospital, all of which provide relatively equal numbers of white-collar and blue-collar jobs. These are linked to the relatively high educational level of its residents; almost 42 percent of the local population twenty-five years of age and over has a bachelor's degree or higher, compared to 24.4 percent for the U.S. adult population twenty-five years and older in 2000.

The second community, "Parkside," is smaller in population (30,000 residents) and geography than Riverview, and Parkside residents feel a strong sense of community in spite of being surrounded by other suburban communities with similar characteristics. The two communities differ most significantly in terms of their adult community members' educational achievement and types of occupation. Adults in the small city of Riverview are four times more likely than parents in the suburban community of Parkside to have completed at least a bachelor's degree. Similarly, Riverview adults are twice as likely to hold white-collar jobs compared to Parkside parents, who are more than twice as likely to hold blue-collar jobs as their Riverview counterparts. These significant differences are *not* reflected in the median family incomes of these two communities, which only differ by about $6,500 ($65,000 in Riverview vs. $58,500 in Parkside in 2000 dollars). We argue that although both of these communities can be considered middle class in terms of income, in terms of occupation and education, Riverview is "middle-middle" or "upper-middle" class, and Parkside is more characteristic of the "lower-middle" or "working class." In this paper we refer to it as "working class." Similar to Lareau (Lareau, 2003),[5] our definition of social class at the community level is based on the educational and occupational level of parents. At the family level it is based upon education and income.

Hurriedness and Stress in the Qualitative Data

The interviews were structured around a set of open-ended interview questions designed to elicit information about each child's daily activities and the family's weekly schedule. We obtained for each focal child a schedule of activities for the entire week in which the interview took place. We asked parents' about aspirations and goals for their children and what worked well in managing their schedules. Interviewing ended when the last parents interviewed added little new information. Parental interviews were transcribed and entered into ATLAS/ti. The interviews were initially coded using an open coding scheme based upon the questions used

---

[5] In Lareau's conceptualization, middle-class children had a parent who was employed in a managerial position or who used highly complex, educationally certified, college-level skills at work (Lareau, 2003). The

to structure the interview. It was during this coding that we identified the overall activity level of the child and any reports of stress in the present or past.

Axial coding was then conducted to compare the circumstances of families and children who reported experiencing stress symptoms. We attempted to link activity levels to stress symptoms and to identify family strategies for managing them. This led to our typology of hurriedness that included both number of activities and time. Finally, using selective coding we identified specific instances of hurriedness and stress as well as instances of inactivity and circumstances surrounding them. We thought that one of the potential sources of stress was extent of control over the activity—whether the child made the decision about participating in the activity or whether it was parent-imposed, so we examined responses to the question: "Whose idea was it to be in this activity (or go to this place)?" To gain information on the link between activities and stress from parents, we asked, "What activities that he/she does not now do would you like to see him/her do?" "How much does he/she like the activity and would he/she like to do something else?" From these questions we were able to determine whether parents and children were thinking of changing or dropping activities and why. To get at the question of how activities are managed, we asked, "Overall, what do you think has really worked well for you in terms of managing your work schedule and your child's school and activity schedule?" The last question was very useful in identifying families who had made changes based upon previous difficulties managing their and their children's schedules.

We were particularly careful about questions asked of children, not wanting to bias their responses with leading questions. Eight years appears to be a lower limit for children adequately and comfortably interacting with an interviewer about their activities, especially without a parent present. Research has demonstrated that, although 9–12 year old children are beginning to learn classification and temporal relations, they have problems with abstract concepts and are very literal in interpretation (Borgers, de Leeuw & Hox, 1999). They are also very suggestible, want to please the interviewer, and are reluctant to express opinions. We did not ask directly about stress because it was too abstract a concept. Instead, we asked a number of questions in which respondents could report any symptoms or concerns about their activities without us suggesting or implying they should feel stressed and strained. The following series of questions informed our conclusions about stress symptoms. After getting the complete list of children's weekly activities, we asked the child being interviewed, "Were there other things you wanted to do?," with a probe about how they felt about each activity. We then asked, "Would you have done it [the activity] if you didn't have to?" We also asked, "What are the things you enjoy doing the most outside of school?," "What kinds of things do you like to do with your friends?," "How about when you're by yourself, what do you like to do?," and "How about when you're with your family?" We also asked, "How much time do you have to do the things you want to do: a lot of time, some time, not very much, or hardly any time at all?" We coded instances of not wanting to go to an activity, being tired of the activity, being sore, preferring to do something else or nothing, crying, being overly tired out, and being worried, as symptoms of stress.[6] Child reports were also compared to

---

[6] Although being sore is not necessarily an indicator of stress, it was significant enough for the child to mention it and this occurred in the context of multiple overlapping activities in one particularly busy period.

parent reports in the selective coding phase. The strongest evidence for its existence were reports of stressful periods by both child and parent.

We also numerically coded the social and demographic characteristics of the thirty-six families in Riverview and Parkside who were interviewed during the 1999–2000 school year in order to compare their characteristics with those of the national sample of children in the PSID-CDS. Using the data from the two Midwest sites, we regressed (ordered logistic regression) our classification of activities in which the children were involved during the week of the interview on maternal education (in years), maternal education squared, maternal employment (employed part-time or employed full-time vs. not employed), family income, family structure (two parents versus one parent), and research site (Parkside vs. Riverview), controlling for the age and gender of the child. A comparable regression was conducted using the national PSID-CDS data without the "site" variable. Child age was never significant and was dropped. Part-time and full-time employment were also never statistically significant and were dropped from the analysis. Using the sample from Parkside and Riverview, additional quantitative analyses were conducted to determine whether the *type* of activity (sports, art activities, and youth groups) engaged in differed by these same variables.

RESULTS

Characteristics of Our Participants

According to the 2000 U.S. Bureau of the Census, 42 percent of the population of Riverview had completed a bachelor's degree, compared with 9 percent in Parkside (U.S. Census Bureau, 2005). Our qualitative samples were better educated than the overall population in these two communities. Of the sample we obtained in "middle class" Riverview, slightly more than half of children's mothers and three-quarters of their fathers had completed a college degree. In "working class" Parkside, 30 percent of mothers and no fathers had completed a four-year degree. Of the national sample of families in which a mother had completed 12 or more years of schooling, 40 percent of mothers and 50 percent of fathers had completed a college degree. The paternal education average of 14.5 years based on the PSID-CDS lies between the Riverview and Parkside averages (16.8 and 13.4 years, respectively), and the maternal average is similar to that of Parkside.

Community differences are reflected in occupational categories as well. More than two-thirds of mothers in both communities were employed. Forty percent of the Riverview mothers worked in professional occupations, 25 percent worked in administrative positions, and 5 percent were in blue-collar jobs. In Parkside (full sample), 17 percent worked in professional occupations, 39 percent worked in administrative positions, and 26 percent worked in blue-collar jobs. Fathers' occupations differed even more dramatically across the two sites. Three quarters of the Riverview fathers were employed in professional occupations, 5 percent were in administrative jobs, and only 15 percent were in blue-collar jobs. In Parkside, 9 percent were in professional occupations, 22 percent were in administrative jobs, and 52 percent of fathers were in blue-collar jobs. Based upon both education and occupation, Parkside is clearly a working class community and Riverview a middle class community.

Table 1: Descriptive Characteristics of Data Sources

	Riverview Proportion/ Mean	Parkside Proportion/ Mean	Parkside (school yr) Proportion/ Mean	PSID-CDS[a] Proportion/ Mean	PSID-CDS[b] Proportion/ Mean
Child age (yrs)	11.35	10.30	10.25	10.89	10.88
Child gender					
Boy	0.45	0.26	0.38	0.54	0.55
Girl	0.55	0.43	0.63	0.46	0.45
Family type					
Two parents	0.95	0.83	0.88	0.86	0.84
Single parent	0.05	0.17	0.13	0.14	0.16
Number of children	2.35	2.50	2.40	2.36	2.40
Maternal education (yrs)	15.65	14.45	14.34	14.38	13.67
High school (12 years of schooling)	0.10	0.09	0.00	0.26	0.34
Some college (13–15 years)	0.35	0.61	0.69	0.34	0.32
College degree or more	0.55	0.30	0.31	0.40	0.34
Paternal education (yrs)	16.84	13.40	13.00	14.53	14.23
High school or less	0.00	0.26	0.36	0.26	0.32
Some college	0.20	0.74	0.64	0.25	0.23
College degree or more	0.75	0.00	0.00	0.49	0.45
Maternal Occupation					
1 = Professional	0.40	0.17	0.00	na	na
2 = Administrative	0.25	0.39	0.56	na	na
3 = Blue collar	0.05	0.26	0.25	na	na
not employed	0.30	0.17	0.19	na	na
Maternal work schedule					
Full-time	0.45	0.39	0.38	0.50	0.49
Part time	0.20	0.43	0.38	0.31	0.31
Not employed	0.35	0.17	0.25	0.19	0.20
Paternal occupation					
1 = Professional	0.75	0.09	0.06	na	na
2 = Administrative	0.05	0.22	0.19	na	na
3 = Blue collar	0.15	0.52	0.63	na	na
4 = No dad/not employed	0.05	0.17	0.13	na	na
Paternal work schedule					
Full-time	0.95	0.83	0.88	0.79	0.79
Part-time	0.00	0.00	0.00	0.05	0.04
No dad/not employed	0.05	0.17	0.13	0.16	0.16
Income (dollars)	100,000	59,350	55,620	91,219	84,314
N	20	23	16	277	331

na—not available

[a] Children whose mother completed 12 or more years of school; [b] Full PSID-CDS sample

All children lived with their mother; not all lived with their father. In Riverview, 95 percent of the 20 families were two-parent families. Parkside families are similar to the national average for family structure: 83 percent of the full sample, 88 percent of the school-year sample of Parkside families, and 87 percent of the national sample were two-parent families. Based upon Table 1, the national sample falls in-between the two communities in social characteristics. Table 1, last column, shows the full PSID-CDS sample, not restricted by maternal education.

A Typology of Children's Activity Participation

Our activity groups are based upon both number of activities and time spent in them. Table 2 shows the distribution of the PSID-CDS national sample of children in six activity groups, for all white families and just for those in which the mother had completed 12 years of schooling or more. Focusing on the latter for comparison with the community samples, in 2002/3, 15.4 percent of non-Hispanic white children aged nine to twelve had no structured activities during the two days during the school year about which they filled out the diary, and these we refer to as "uninvolved." Almost 8 percent were involved only in youth organizations, 27.2 percent were involved only in sports, and 3.3 percent were involved only in art activities. Thirty-nine percent were involved in two of the three types of activities. The 7.3 percent who were involved in all three activities were defined as "hurried." Almost one-third of children who participated in a sport and only a small fraction of those in arts activities participated for 4 or more hours over 2 days. Our qualitative research showed that children involved for many hours in a sport were those whose families had the most time management problems. Thus children

Table 2: Percentage of Children Participating in Sports, Art, and Youth Organization Activities, One Weekday and One Weekend Day, 2002/3 PSID-CDS

Activity Category	Mom Ed 12+ years Percent	Full Sample Percent
No activities over two days	15.4	17.4
Youth organization only, <4 hours	7.5	7.4
Youth organization only, 4+ hours	0.0	0
Sports only, <4 hours	20.4	22.4
Sports only, 4+ hours	6.8	6.5
Art only, <4 hours	2.9	3
Art only, 4+ hours	0.4	0.3
Two types of activities, <4 hours	27.3	24.5
Two types of activities, 4+ hours	11.9	12.2
All three types of activities	7.3	6.2
Total	100	100
N	277	331

Source: 2002/3 PSID-CDS. Data are for non-Hispanic White children aged nine to twelve.

Table 3: Percentage of Children in Activity Categories, One Weekday and One Weekend Day

Activity Category	PSID-CDS[a]	PSID-CDS[b]	Parkside	Parkside[c]	Riverview
Uninvolved (no activities)	15	17	13	13	5
Focused (1 activity and <4 hours)	31	33	26	25	10
Balanced (2 activities and <4 hours)	27	25	30	31	40
Hurried (3+ activities or 4+ hours)	26	25	30	31	45
Total	100	100	99	100	100
N	277	331	23	16	20

[a] Includes only non-Hispanic White children aged 9 to 12, mother has 12+ years of schooling.

[b] Includes only non-Hispanic White children aged 9 to 12, all mothers.

[c] This subsample was interviewed during the 1999–2000 school year.

who participated in only one or two activities but who had high levels of involvement (four hours or more during the two survey days) were added to the "hurried" category. From this set of activities we developed a classification of children into four groups: Uninvolved, focused, balanced, and hurried.

Table 3 shows this typology of activities both for the national sample and for the two Midwest sites, Parkside and Riverview. As mentioned above, 15 percent of the children in the national sample had no activities and were classified as "uninvolved." Using the four-category typology described above, 31 percent of the children in the national sample had only one type of activity and spent fewer than four hours in this activity during the two survey days ("focused"), 27 percent of the children had two different types of activities and spent fewer than four hours in this activities during the two survey days ("balanced"), and 26 percent of the children either participated in all three types of activities or spent more than four hours in one or more activities during the two survey days ("hurried").

Of the sixteen Parkside children who were interviewed in the 1999–2000 school year, 13 percent were uninvolved, 25 percent were focused, 31 percent were balanced, and 31 percent were hurried. The distribution of children across the four categories is similar in the full Parkside group. Of the twenty Riverview children, 5 percent had no activities, 10 percent were focused, 40 percent were balanced, and 45 percent were hurried. The proportion of children with balanced and high levels of activity was greater in Riverview than in Parkside, and the proportion with no activities or a single activity was lower in Riverview compared to Parkside.

What Factors Are Associated with Hurriedness?

Table 4 presents the ordered logistic regression of our activity typology on education, family structure, site, income, family size and gender for children 9–12. In contrast to our hypothesis about community class differences, there is no difference in hurriedness between Riverview and Parkside; most of the variation is within rather than between communities. In all three data sets and both models, we see that *both* measures of family social class—education and income—are significantly associated with a greater chance of being in the high activity category.

Table 4: Ordered Logistic Regression of Activity Typology on Education, Family Structure, Site, Income, Family size, and Gender, Children 9–12

	Parkside/Riverview[a]		PSID-CDS, White only			
			Mother High School Grad plus[b]		Full Sample[b]	
	Model 1	Model 2	Model 1	Model 2	Model 1	Model 2
Variable	Coefficient	Coefficient	Coefficient	Coefficient	Coefficient	Coefficient
Intercept—Focused	61.248**	8.133	−7.848***	−6.373**	−6.962***	−5.042**
Intercept—Balanced	63.341**	9.939*	−6.585***	−5.105*	−5.8***	−3.876*
Intercept—Hurried	65.844**	12.345*	−4.877***	−3.389*	−4.074*	−2.159
Child Gender (male = 1, female = 0)	−1.745*	−1.325*	−0.05	−0.045	−0.004	0.007
Two parents	−3.455	−1.441	0.902*	0.946*	0.629*	0.806*
Mother's education (years)	7.044**	omitted	0.107*	omitted	0.122**	omitted
Mother's education squared	−0.208**	omitted	omitted	omitted	omitted	omitted
Mother completed 12 years	omitted	reference	omitted	reference	omitted	reference
Mother completed 13–15 years	omitted	reference	omitted	0.347	omitted	0.446*
Mother completed 16 years	omitted	2.85**	omitted	0.582*	omitted	0.818**
Mother completed 17+ years	omitted	1.178	omitted	0.601	omitted	0.794*
Log of family income	2.411*	2.961*	0.368*	0.339*	0.325*	0.256
Number of children	0.676	0.345	0.137	0.135	−0.009	−0.038
Site [Parkside = 2, Riverview = 1]	−0.233	0.388	na	na	na	na
N	36	36	277	277	331	331
−2 Log L			733.361	731.94	865.322	866.429

[a] Includes only families interviewed during the 1999–2000 school year.

[b] Mother's education was top-coded at 17 in the PSID-CDS

*p < .05, **p < .01, ***p < .001, one-tailed test

In the Parkside/Riverview data, we also see that the association between education and activity typology is curvilinear; children's chance of being hurried increases up to 16 years of schooling, after which it declines. In the PSID-CDS, the coefficient for the squared term was never significant (not shown), but this is because mother's education was top-coded at 17, resulting in no variation after 16 years of schooling. Children living with two parents are busier, according to the typology, than children who live with only one parent, but this is statistically significant only in the PSID-CDS. The number of children in the family is not linked to the extent of activity in either data set.

Parental Pressure on Children's Activity Participation

One source of stress is lack of control over one's time. How children initially become involved may affect their later willingness to participate and their experience of the activity. Based on our qualitative study, there appear to be three general ways children become involved in activities: (1) personal interest, (2) parental suggestion and pressure, and (3) the desire to be with friends. Schools send flyers home with the children announcing a variety of events and possible activities. Some flyers are discarded and others prompt action, depending on the child's interest. Parents also may suggest that the child try an activity. Probably the most common source of information and impetus for becoming involved in a particular activity is the desire to be with one's friends. We found all three routes into an activity reported by the families in our Midwest study.

A number of parents in our qualitative study were very explicit about their strategies of exposing children to a variety of activities in the hopes that their children could find something they liked and at which they could become skilled. Most seemed very sensitive to the expressed preferences of their children for activity involvement. As they explained:

> What I've tried to do is offer the kids a variety of things to try. And then if something is really what they want to do, then we go in that direction. (Billie, university teacher and mother of Tara [11]—Riverview—2 activities)

This middle-class Riverview parent clearly stated that she explicitly provided or sought out opportunities for her child to participate in activities, but then let the child make his or her own decision. In contrast, Ann's mother, Lynn, from working-class Parkside, did not seek out activities, but responded to flyers sent from the school if and only if the child showed an interest.

> [With softball] you get the flyers that come home with different activities. . . . She says that she's interested and if not, we don't worry about it. (Lynn, mother of Ann [12]—Parkside—5 activities)

Of course, this child was already highly active, with five activities. Lynn has a more passive approach than that of the previous Riverview parents, one which fits with the natural growth model, but with sensitivity to the child's preferences and interests, and in particular to Ann's tendency to try different activities.

Parents also provide pressure. This is particularly true for children who started in their activity at an early age. This pressure occurred in both communities. One Parkside child began dance classes in kindergarten and another began soccer at age five. One Riverview child also began soccer at age six. It is highly unlikely that these were child-initiated activities. Several children noted that one of their parents used to be involved in a particular activity and wanted them to try it for themselves.

One of the most common reasons we heard for being involved in an activity was to be with friends or because a sibling or other important person in the child's life (such as a father, sister, or cousin) was also involved. This was common in Parkside, the lower-middle class community, but not as common in Riverview. As this Parkside child explained:

> I used to follow my sister and do whatever she does. . . . So I wanted to try it [soccer] because she played. (Jen [11], daughter of Sally—Parkside—4 activities)

Hurriedness and Child Stress Symptoms—National Data

Table 5 shows means on the various measures of stress symptoms by the typology of hurriedness, using data from the National PSID-Child Development Supplement. Contrary to our expectations, stress symptoms were found to be highest for the *uninvolved* children, lowest for those involved in activities. *In no case did hurried children have the most symptoms.*

These results are supported by Table 6, which shows the results of regressing the different measures of stress symptoms on categories of the activity typology, controlling for social class, family structure, family size, and child gender. The activity typology categories are not associated with the first measure of stress symptoms (Measure A) based upon previous research. This provides the first quantitative evidence on a large national sample that increased child stress symptoms as reported by a parent are not "caused by" hurriedness. Nor is hurriedness linked to low self-esteem as reported by the child (Measure E). Contrary to our hypothesis, we found that *uninvolved* children are the ones who score highest on the internalizing measures. The largest effect was obtained using the total internalizing score. Uninvolved children scored

Table 5: Mean values on different measures of stress symptoms by activity typology[a]

Stress symptoms	Activity Typology				Total	
	Uninvolved	Focused	Balanced	Hurried	Mean	Stn dev
Parent reported:						
Stress symptoms	2.1	1.9	1.9	1.8	1.9	1.8
Internalizing (total)	4.4	3.4	3.0	3.2	3.4	3.3
Internalizing w/out stress	3.0	2.1	1.8	1.9	2.1	2.3
Low self esteem	1.9	1.3	1.1	1.2	1.3	1.5
N	62	108	77	84	331	
Child reported:						
Self-esteem	24.8	25.0	24.9	24.3	24.7	3.5
N	43	70	51	61	225	

[a]PSID-CDS Full Sample

Table 6: Ordinary Least Squares Regression of stress symptoms on social class, family structure and controls[a]

Variable	Measure A Stress symptoms		Measure B Internalizing total		Measure C Internal without Stress symp		Measure D Low self-esteem (parent)		Measure E High self-esteem (child)	
	Model 1 Coefficient	Model 2 Coefficient	Model 1 Coefficient	Model 2 Coefficient	Model 1 Coefficient	Model 2 Coefficient	Model 1 Coefficient	Model 2 Coefficient	Model 1 Coefficient	Model 2 Coefficient
Intercept	4.532**	3.473*	7.506**	4.544	4.557*	2.135	2.607	1.217	21.321***	19.489***
Uninvolved	0.055	0.067	0.928+	0.894+	0.855*	0.823*	0.647**	0.630**	-0.233	-0.150
Hurried	-0.069	-0.090	0.089	0.057	0.052	0.032	0.028	0.020	-0.538	-0.552
Child Gender (male = 1, female = 0)	0.178	0.172	0.183	0.168	0.028	0.017	0.062	0.057	-0.648	-0.640
Two parents	0.111	-0.046	0.164	-0.144	0.078	-0.128	0.281	0.190	0.234	-0.180
Mother's education (years)	-0.100**		-0.189**		-0.136**		-0.071*		-0.163+	
Mother completed <13 years		reference		reference		reference		reference		reference
Mother completed 13–15 years		-0.414		-0.935*		-0.631*		-0.276		-1.019+
Mother completed 16 years		-0.566+		-1.570**		-1.245***		-0.687**		-0.836
Mother completed 17+ years		-0.276		-0.493		-0.387		-0.227		-1.427
Log of family income	-0.140	-0.132	-0.156	-0.041	-0.053	0.056	-0.045	0.021	0.442	0.485
Number of children	0.050	0.071	-0.083	-0.030	-0.103	-0.060	-0.077	-0.054	0.433+	0.484+
Site (Parkside = 2, Riverview = 1)										
N	331	331	331	331	331	331	331	331	225	225
R square	0.037	0.0301	0.050	0.057	0.060	0.072	0.051	0.061	0.048	0.050

+ p < .10, *p < .05, **p < .01, ***p < .001, 2-tailed test

[a] PSID-CDS Full Sample

about 1 point higher on the total internalizing scale (Measure B), an effect size of 1/3 of a standard deviation, a substantial effect. The most highly significant association was between inactivity and low self-esteem (Measure D), which includes items such as no one loves him, seems to be in a fog, feels worthless or inferior, has difficulty getting his mind off certain thoughts, and feels others are out to get him.

We also found that children of mothers with more years of education were consistently less likely to show symptoms of stress than children of mothers with fewer years. If more educated mothers were unduly pressuring their children, the latter should show increased symptoms of stress, which was not the case. We explore this further using our qualitative data.

Hurriedness and Child Stress Symptoms—Qualitative Data

We found evidence in both Riverview and Parkside that children and parents were under occasional stress because of a large number of activities or the amount of time spent in them, but this did not appear to be continual or frequent. Six children out of forty-three (14 percent) expressed occasional stress or strain—not wanting to go to an activity, being tired of the activity, preferring to do something else or nothing, crying, being overly tired out, being worried, crying, showing symptoms of depression or anxiety, or having headaches or sore muscles.

For example, a nine-year-old girl in gymnastics three hours a day three days a week and with two other activities (ballet and ice skating) as well was pretty tired by Friday:

> Like usually on Fridays I'm like I don't want to be here . . . [but once I'm there] sometimes I just pep right up, (Serena [9], daughter of Judy—Riverview—hurried)

Another fourth-grader with five different activities (soccer, scouts, jump rope, recorder, and religious education) said:

> I just like to jump rope once in a while, but now I'm tired of it. . . . Every single time I do it for like five minutes and my feet are tired. (Laura [10], daughter of Jeannette (a medical billing clerk)—Parkside—hurried)

Given that the children seemed very compliant and only occasionally expressed dissatisfaction with their schedules and activities, we asked parents how they knew when children were doing too much. For example, one Riverview parent offered the following observation:

> I don't believe kids can really articulate that they're stressed. I think it comes about in other ways. . . . [M]y older one was, she seemed like she was tired and distracted, and distraught, and so we looked at our activity level and decided we had to cut back. (Cathy, homemaker and mother of Becca [10]—Riverview—balanced)

(Billie) said that she was very sensitive to her daughter Tara's stress symptoms, such as sleep disturbances, catching a cold, and crying. Tara stopped taking piano lessons because practice led to crying. Eventually they made a conscious decision to cut back to two activities.

There are three possible explanations for the lack of evidence of major problems in terms of child- and parent-reported stress: (1) children and parents under stress were not interviewed, (2) children and parents have gotten used to this lifestyle, and (3) most children are not overly scheduled or stressed.

Nonparticipation by Stressed Families

It is possible that parents who were currently under these stresses may not have agreed to be interviewed for the qualitative study. Many parents interviewed in Riverview indicated that they had been through a very busy period in the recent past when they felt as though they were overextended in terms of their daily and weekly schedules. This recurrent theme was most often articulated in answers regarding their current weekly schedules, when parents made unsolicited comparisons to how "overwhelmed" or "totally stressed out" they had been a year or two earlier when their children were involved in multiple activities. For example, "Billie" noted how she kept track of her daughter's and son's involvement in activities along with her husband's after-work commitments, and realized that, because her daughter was moving into the fifth grade with higher academic expectations, she would need "some down time in the evenings." So she discontinued her daughter's piano lessons, took her daughter out of Girl Scouts, and only let her continue basketball and ballet. In her words, Billie ". . . simplified [my family members'] lives" by limiting the number of activities her daughter (and son) were involved in.

However, there is little empirical evidence that our interviews captured a particularly low-activity group of families. National data suggest that, to the contrary, our qualitative studies captured more high-activity than low-activity families. Of all the children age nine to twelve in the nationally representative PSID-CDS, only 26 percent fell in the "hurried child" category, compared with 31 percent in Parkside (sixteen-case subsample) and 45 percent in Riverview. According to the PSID-CDS, 15.4 percent of the national sample had no activities, compared with 13 percent in Parkside and 5 percent in Riverview.

Families Accustomed to Lifestyle

A second possibility is that parents and children become used to the pace they set and do not evaluate it negatively. One strategy that parents use to justify and to help themselves feel satisfied with their own choices is to continually compare themselves to "other" families. Parents compare their parenting and time-use strategies to those of "other" families, who are often presented in negative terms. Parents seem to recognize that they could be doing "worse," and use this knowledge to achieve a sense of balance between the conflicting needs of various family members and the desires of parents and their children.

With regard to this second strategy, a number of the parents were asked how they see other families in the community coping with the time crunch. Invariably, the parents interviewed cogently stated that they frequently see other parents in the community "totally stressed out," rushing their children from school to one activity after another, and traveling out of town every weekend for yet another soccer or ice hockey tournament. For example, the following is a typical comment along these lines from a Riverview parent:

> I know some people . . . the parents really push the kids to get involved in not just school activities, but two or three other extracurricular activities at a real young age. And the kids end up being very burned out, and then don't want to do anything. And [the parents say]

"I've invested all this time and energy and money into dance lessons over the last four years and you will continue on." And then who is actually doing it? Is it the parents living through the child? Or is it because the kids want to learn a skill? (Erin, homemaker and mother of Judy [11]—Riverview—balanced)

It appears that parents draw on these vivid accounts of their harried neighbors to gain a sense of calm and contentment from their belief that, although they are busy, they are not "overdoing" it like some of the other parents in the community. Regardless of how hectic their lives were, every family could identify another family that was busier.

Children Not Over-Scheduled

Finally, a third possibility is that children are not all that busy. This interpretation is consistent with the results from the quantitative study. Children averaged 2 to 3 activities per week in both Riverview and Parkside. Most children were involved in a sport (or art activity) and one school or nonschool club. The third activity could be a second sport or an art activity. Riverview children were more likely than Parkside children to be in art activities, and Parkside children were significantly more likely than Riverview children to be involved in scouts and somewhat more likely to be enrolled in religious education. Although the average number of organized activities was the same across the two communities, the distribution of activity levels differed (Table 2). Riverview children were more likely to be hurried and less likely to be uninvolved than Parkside children and the national sample. This is because they spent more time in their activities. Riverview children were more likely than Parkside children to be involved in multiple sports during a week; the children involved in multiple sports activities were the ones most likely to complain of being tired.

Based on our qualitative study, we found little evidence that parental pressure was the major force leading to child participation in activities. There appear to be three general ways children become involved in activities: Desire to be with friends was the major factor leading to participation, followed by personal interest, and then by parental encouragement. Even when the latter was operative, it took child motivation to stick with the activity.

In fact, children with no activities caused considerable parent concern. Fifteen percent of the national sample, 13 percent of Parkside children interviewed during the school year, and 5 percent of Riverview children had no activities. For the most part, these children spent their after-school time riding their bicycles, playing with friends, reading, watching TV, playing basketball or pick-up hockey games, roller blading, and roller skating. Parents *worried* when children did not have *any* activities.

One child (David from Parkside) was in sixth grade and his only activity earlier during the school year was a church group. He played handheld video games (e.g., Playstation) a lot. David's father (Robert) was concerned that his sixth grade son did not want to do any organized activities. Robert commented that he was disappointed that his son had stopped taking guitar lessons, and thought his son would benefit from the social aspect of being involved in a team sport. Yet, he also was concerned about pushing his son:

I'm trying, you know, my wife and I fight back and forth a little bit about that nudge. . . . And I don't want to push him, then I think as soon as you push, they push back. (Robert, father of David [12]—Parkside—uninvolved)

Characteristic of several other children with low levels of activity was shyness or introversion. For example, Susan explained why her daughter, now involved in one after-school activity, stopped participating in gymnastics:

> Holly is really shy. And it's hard to get her involved in things, even with school, let alone outside of school. (Susan, mother of Holly [10]—Parkside—focused)

In both communities, parents whose children had many activities worked hard to keep them within limits, and parents whose children were participating in few or no extracurricular activities worried that their children might be missing something important.

DISCUSSION AND CONCLUSIONS

The structure of children's lives has increased over the past several decades. The number of after-school activities and weekend meets and games and the time spent in them have expanded greatly in the past two decades (Crosnoe, 2001; Hofferth & Sandberg, 2001b). As a result, many families wonder whether they are making the right decisions for their children and themselves. This research addressed, first, how active American children are; second, whether there is evidence that children from upper-middle class families are more active than those from lower-middle class families; and third, whether children are overscheduled to the extent that they exhibit stress symptoms.

The strength of this study is that we were able to use data from a large national sample of families and quantitative and qualitative data for the same age group of children from two different communities in the Midwest, one an upper-middle-class community and the other a working-class community. We had an unusually large sample size for qualitative interviews, 43 families. The different samples are similar in characteristics. This means that we could use the qualitative data from the community samples to provide more depth to data from quantitative analyses. The limited age range was useful in keeping variability by maturity relatively low and its effects insignificant; we were unable to directly adjust for differential maturity. The major limitation of the community samples is that they were restricted to white working-class and middle-class families. However, we argue that the "hurried child" is a white middle-class issue, and proposed solutions are focused on white, middle-class families, not minority or low-income families. In addition, low-income families are likely to be female-headed, which makes the resource constraints substantially unequal and confounds class with family structure, a problem for earlier research. This research avoids that pitfall.

The first question is whether a large proportion of children are overscheduled or "hurried." The current study found about 26 percent of American children 9–12 years old who had three or more activities or were involved in one or two activities for four or more hours on two days in the week. This group exemplifies what Elkind called "hurried children." The majority of children (58 percent) are either focused or balanced in their activities, and 15 percent are uninvolved.

Are activities a function of social class of the community or the family? Because of differences in parental education between our upper middle class and working class communities, we expected that there would be variations in the childrearing beliefs and values of parents across communities, and that these different beliefs would lead to differential involvement of their children in structured activities. However, our initial assumptions were wrong. Although children were definitely more hurried in the middle class community, children were active in both communities. Rather than activity differences being primarily *between* communities, we found that the major activity differences were *within* each community. Maternal education was more closely linked to the child's activities than any other factor, but it was not linear, rising and then falling as maternal education rose. There are two possible reasons for this nonlinearity. First, in highly educated families, such as the medical doctor married to a medical doctor, parents may be too busy to involve the children in multiple activities. Second, highly educated mothers may be more knowledgeable about professional concerns about the effects of excessive activities and limit their children's activities accordingly. This relationship between education and activities was similar in Riverview and Parkside. In both communities, parents saw education as key to the future. However, higher family income and having two parents were also linked to more activity. Besides education, financial and parental resources at home are critical to participation in activities. Both the national and community studies supported these conclusions.

The third question is whether children who are more hurried experience stress because of their schedules. We expected to find children with many activities to experience greater stress symptoms. However, we found little evidence for this hurried child hypothesis. In the national data set we did not find hurried children to be more likely to exhibit symptoms of stress or have low self-esteem. Instead, the *least active exhibited more symptoms* of withdrawal, inability to get along with others, and low self-esteem.

The results of the qualitative analyses support our conclusion that children are, for the most part, engaged voluntarily in healthy levels of activities and that their parents are wary and watchful for stress symptoms. Parents cut back their children's schedules when these occurred. The most interesting reports were that parents of children who did not participate in activities were quite concerned about it. Qualitative reports from parents and children suggest that children who have problems getting along with others, low self-esteem, or who are socially immature are those who rarely participate in extracurricular activities.

We argue that there are three reasons why we failed to find much evidence for excessive activities. First, those families whose children are overly hurried may not have participated in our studies. However, this explanation was not supported because both Riverview and Parkside children were *more*, not *less*, active than the average child aged nine to twelve in the national sample. Second, families may be used to a busy schedule or may have been through a busy time and subsequently cut back on their activities. As evidence, we found that some families reported that they had recently scaled back their activities; perhaps we were seeing families who had already gone through the overly stressed phase, and not those who were experiencing very busy times. In addition, families saw themselves as normal, whereas they could point out other families who had "too many" activities and seemed to be overly stressed.

However, the third possibility is that it is normal for healthy children to have lots of activities. The direction of causality is reversed; those who have adjustment problems are the ones who are uninvolved. Children today may be busier than they were in the recent past; however, that does not necessarily mean that this has caused them or their families excessive stress and strain.

Attaining Balance

The majority of children and their families in our study had attained a measure of "balance," meaning that they were involved in activities and organizations beyond the family, but within reasonable limits. Children's stresses were lowest in the "focused" and "balanced" categories. According to our definitions, such children had one or two activities, and the total weekly time in such activities was less than 4 hours over the two diary days. Such involvement appears to be both normal and valuable to child development; it was associated with lower stress and higher self-esteem on a variety of measures. Other research shows long-term benefits of organized activities as well (Mahoney et al., 2005).

What is important is that these activities not strain family members beyond their capacities. Besides each individual child's activities, parents need to balance the activities of other children and their own activities. Of the various strategies used, the most important we found was to reduce the mother's employment schedule from full-time to part-time, or, in some cases, to work at home. Mothers were most likely to alter their schedules, but fathers also made decisions to forgo promotions that would have increased their work time. Flexibility at work was helpful to both parents. The second major strategy was organization, including setting priorities and using technology, such as cell-phones. Communication among family members was critical. A third strategy was to enlist others as backup, including carpooling and getting help from relatives and neighbors. Siblings often attended each other's practices and lessons. The fourth strategy, involving the children in family routines and chores, facilitated the smooth running of the family. Finally, parents involved themselves in children's activities—as coach, den leader, PTO leader, and volunteer. Parents were aware of the dangers of too much activity and appeared relatively successful in managing their family's schedule. As one Parkside mother put it:

> I think we've got enough going on and all the right things going on . . . so I think we've got a pretty good balance on everything right now. (Joanne, mother of Michael [9]—working-class Parkside—hurried)

References

Adam, E. K. (2005). Momentary emotion and cortisol levels in the everyday lives of working parents. In B. Schneider & L. J. Waite (Eds.), *Being together, working apart: Dual-career families and the work-life balance* (pp. 105–133). Cambridge, England: Cambridge University Press.

Alwin, D. F. (2001). Parental Values, Beliefs, and Behavior: A Review and Promulga for Research into the New Century. In T. Owens & S. Hofferth (Eds.), *Children at the Millennium: Where did we come from, where are we going?* (pp. 97–139). New York: Elsevier Science.

Arendell, T. (2001). The new care work of middle class mothers: Managing childrearing, employment, and time. In K. Daly (Ed.), *Minding the time in family experience* (pp. 163–204). London: Elsevier Science.

Baker, P. C., Keck, C. K., Mott, F. L., & Quinlan, S. V. (1993). *NLSY Child Handbook, Revised Edition.* Columbus, Ohio: Center for Human Resource Research, Ohio State University.

Band, E. B., & Weisz, J. R. (1988). How to feel better when it feels bad: Children's perspectives on coping with everyday stress. *Developmental Psychology, 24*(2), 247–253.

Borgers, N., de Leeuw, E., & Hox, J. (1999). Surveying children: Cognitive development and response quality in questionnaire research. In A. Christianson, et al. (Ed.), *Official statistics in a changing world* (pp. 133–140). Stockholm: Statistics Sweden.

Crosnoe, R. (2001). The social world of male and female athletes in high school. In D. A. Kinney (Ed.), *Sociological Studies of Children and Youth* (pp. 89–110). Oxford, England: Elsevier.

Doherty, W. J., & Carlson, B. (2002). *Putting family first: Successful strategies for reclaiming family life in a hurry-up world.* Minneapolis, MN: University of Minnesota.

Dunn, J. S., Kinney, D. A., & Hofferth, S. L. (2003). Parental ideologies and children's after-school activities. *American Behavioral Scientist, 46*(10), 1359–1386.

Eccles, J., & Gootman, J. A. (2002). *Community Programs to promote Youth Development.* Washington, DC: National Academy Press.

Elkind, D. (2001). *The hurried child.* Cambridge, MA: Perseus.

Galinsky, E. (2002). *Ask the Children.* New York: Families and Work Institute.

Ginsburg, K. R. (2006). *The Importance of play in promoting healthy child development and maintaining strong parent-child bonds* (Clinical Report). Chicago, IL: American Academy of Pediatrics.

Hektner, J., Schmidt, J., & Csikszentmihalyi, M. (2007). *Experience Sampling Method.* Thousand Oaks, CA: Sage.

Hofferth, S. L., & Sandberg, J. F. (2001b). Changes in American Children's Time, 1981–1997. In S. Hofferth & T. Owens (Eds.), *Children at the Millennium: Where did we come from, where are we going?* (pp. 193–229). New York: Elsevier Science.

Hofferth, S., Davis-Kean, P., Davis, J., & Finkelstein, J. (1999). *1997 User Guide: The Child Development Supplement to the Panel Study of Income Dynamics.* Ann Arbor, MI: Institute for Social Research, The University of Michigan.

Jacobs, J. A., & Gerson, K. (2004). *The time divide: Work, family, and gender inequality.* Cambridge, MA: Harvard University Press.

Kohn, M. L. (1977). *Class and Conformity.* Chicago, IL: University of Chicago Press.

Kohn, M., & Schooler, C. (1983). *Work and personality: An inquiry into the impact of social stratification.* Norwood, NJ: Ablex.

Lareau, A. (2002). Invisible inequality: Social class and childrearing in black families and white families. *American Sociological Review, 67*(5), 747–776.

Lareau, A. (2003). *Unequal childhoods: Class, race, and family life.* Berkeley: University of California Press.

Larson, R. (1994). Youth organizations, hobbies, and sports as developmental contexts. In R. Silbereisen & E. Todt (Eds.), *Adolescence in context: The interplay of family, school, peers, and work in adjustment* (pp. 46–65). New York: Springer-Verlag.

Larson, R., & Verma, S. (1999). How Children and Adolescents Spend Time Across the World: Work, Play, and Developmental Opportunities. *Psychological Bulletin, 125*(6), 701–736.

Lesthaeghe, R., & Surkyn, J. (1988). Cultural dynamics and economic theories of fertility change. *Population and Development Review, 14*, 1–45.

Luthar, S. S., & Becker, B. E. (2002). Privileged but pressured? A study of affluent youth. *Child Development, 73*(5), 1593–1610.

Lynott, P. P., & Logue, B. J. (1993). The "hurried child": The myth of lost childhood in contemporary American society. *Sociological Forum, 8*(3), 471–491.

Mahoney, J. L., Larson, R. W., Eccles, J. S., & Lord, H. (2005). Organized activities as developmental contexts for children and adolescents. In J. L. Mahoney, R. W. Larson, & J. S. Eccles (Eds.), *Oganized activities as contexts of development* (pp. 3–22). Mahwah, NJ: Lawrence Erlbaum.

Mintz, S. (2004). *Huck's raft: A history of American childhood.* Cambridge, MA: Harvard University Press.

Peterson, J. L., & Zill, N. (1986). Marital disruption, parent-child relationships, and behavioral problems in children. *Journal of Marriage and the Family, 48*(2).

Pincus, D. B., & Friedman, A. G. (2004). Improving children's coping with everyday stress: Transporting treatment interventions to the school setting. *Clinical Child and Family Psychology Review, 7*(4), 223–240.

Reynolds, L. K., O'Koon, J. H., Papademetriou, E., Szczygiel, S., & Grant, K. E. (2001). Stress and somatic complaints in low-income urban adolescents. *Journal of Youth and Adolescence, 30*(4), 499–514.

Robinson, J. P., & Godbey, G. (1997). *Time for Life: The Surprising Ways Americans Use their Time.* University Park, PA: Pennsylvania State University Press.

Schaefer, E., & Edgerton, M. (1985). Parental and child correlates of parental modernity. In I. Sigel (Ed.), *Parental belief systems: The psychological consequences for children* (pp. 287–318). Hillsdale, NJ: L. Erlbaum Associates.

Stefanello, R. (2004). Short Communication: A preliminary study of stress symptoms and nutritional state in children. *Stress and Health, 20,* 293–299.

Tansey, T., Mizelle, N., Ferrin, J., Tschopp, M., & Frain, M. (2004). Work-related stress and the demand-control-support framework: Implications for the P × E fit model. *Journal of Rehabilitation, 70*(3), 34–41.

Thornton, A. (2004). *Reading history sideways: The fallacy and enduring impact of the developmental paradigm on family life.* Chicago, IL: University of Chicago.

U.S. Census Bureau. (2005). Retrieved February 25, 2005, from U.S. Census Bureau: http://factfinder.census.gov/home/saff/main.html?_lang=en.

Most Children Actually Thrive on Numerous Activities, Research Shows
By Joy Jernigan

No need to worry about frazzled kids cramming ballet lessons, soccer practice, Girl Scout meetings and piano recitals into their schedules come the new school year.

Turns out, most kids are fine. It's the parents, who bear the burden of shuttling kids from one activity to another and feel the pressure to see their children succeed, who might actually be the ones on overload.

Contrary to popular belief that many children today are stressed out by overscheduled lives, recent research suggests that a heavy load of structured activities is actually beneficial for children, according to Sandra L. Hofferth, director of the Maryland Population Research Center at the University of Maryland at College Park and author of a study titled "The 'Hurried' Child: Myth vs. Reality."

"We found that the very active children were thriving emotionally," said Hofferth, a family science professor. "In contrast, children who had the fewest activities were the most withdrawn, socially immature and had the lowest self-esteem."

Her research, published last month as a book chapter in "Life Balance: Multidisciplinary Theories and Research," followed children ages 9 to 12. Only one in four kids met the criteria of hurried—three or more activities or more than four hours devoted in a two-day period, Hofferth found. The vast majority of kids—58 percent—were balanced, meaning they were pursuing only one or two activities, and 17 percent were involved in no activities.

The research relied on nationally representative data as well as time diaries and interviews with parents and kids.

Although supported by additional studies that show most American youth lead balanced lives, Hofferth's findings are not without controversy. In the last two decades, many experts have lamented children's lack of time for free play. And in 2006, the American Academy of Pediatrics cautioned that a hurried lifestyle contributes to stress and anxiety in children and could lead to depression.

PARENTS NEED DOWN TIME, TOO

Kimberly Kauer said her busy kids are fine, but she's struggled with their full schedules.

The 38-year-old Redwood City, Calif., woman is the mother of Chloe, 6, and Beckett, 3. Last spring, her daughter was enrolled in gymnastics, swimming, Girl Scouts, Spanish class and softball.

"Once I started to get the second kid into the mix, I thought, each of the kids can handle what they're doing, but I can't handle what they're doing!" she said. "I really found myself getting really stressed."

What's significant isn't the number of activities but rather how much stress they cause for the kids and the parents, said William Doherty, professor of family social science at the University of Minnesota.

"A lot of parents feel under a tremendous time pressure from work and taking care of kids and taking care of the house," he said.

These days, everything revolves around kids and their schedules, but it's important to look at who else is affected by a child's activities, Doherty said. It's OK to keep your child off a traveling soccer team, for example, if you value family togetherness time on the weekends. Parents need down time, too.

"We live in an age of hyper-parenting when parents feel guilty about asking kids to make the smallest sacrifice for the good of the family," he said.

SETTING LIMITS

Heath Foster of Seattle likes the idea of exposing her three children—Sophia, 9, Kate, 7, and Gus, 4—to new experiences but tries to limit them to no more than two activities each at once.

"You have to talk these things through with your kids," she said. "But then you have to look at this on a piece of paper and think, do I want to be doing all of these activities at one time?"

Foster, 43, looks for activities close to home or tries to sign her kids up for programs at the same time. She used to drive several miles in heavy traffic to take her daughter to a gymnastics class until she decided that was "crazy." Now, instead of shuttling her children to piano lessons, a teacher comes to their house. Foster also tries to make sure her kids have a couple of days a week when they can come home from school and just hang out in their rooms.

"It's nice to keep things as simple as possible," she said.

Suzanne Strong of Redmond, Wash., cherishes the weeks when her kids have nothing going on. The 37-year-old mom limits her two children, Romeal, 12, and Paloma, 10, to just one activity at a time.

"We don't really enjoy running around in the evening after we're done with our day," said Strong, who works part time as a photographer and graphic designer.

Romeal, who will play soccer this fall, says the rule at his house is "school first, activity second."

While he says he sometimes thinks he might like to add another activity, he understands his parent's one-activity-at-a-time rule.

"Three would be too much," he said. "Two would be OK."

© 2010 msnbc.com

By Eric M. Uslaner

Does the Internet promote or impede social connections and trust? Using surveys from the Pew Center for the Internet and American Life, I show that Internet users are not social isolates. They tend to have slightly wider social circles than nonusers, but their Internet communications are largely with people they know. Consequently, it is hardly surprising that Internet users are no more trusting of strangers (but not less trusting either) than nonusers. However, trusting people are more likely to believe that they have little to fear from the Internet. They are more open to shopping on the Internet and are less likely to believe that their privacy will be violated on the Web; they are also less likely to use a false identity on the Web. The social connections that people make on the Internet do not promote trust—indeed, there is some evidence that chat rooms may bring together mistrusting people.

Keywords   Internet, social capital, trust

Alex Salcedo, a 13-year-old boy from Kensington, Maryland, was hit by a car near his home. He went into the intensive care unit at a local hospital, was put into an induced coma, and the prognosis was not good. His father created a Web page so that the family could keep apprised of his medical condition. Almost immediately, the family began getting messages of goodwill and prayers from as far away as Venezuela and Mozambique. The Web site received 66,000 hits, with 2,000 messages posted. Alex did not recover, but an online community formed, with a company providing a service to other families in crisis, http://www .medicalstatus.com; St. George, 1999). This is the good Net, a caring place where people give of themselves with no expectation of anything in return.

Kevin, a hospital security guard in Idaho, logged on to the Internet for the first time in 1995 in the hospital library. He accidentally discovered a pornography site and kept com-

Eric M. Uslaner is Professor of Government and Politics at the University of Maryland, College Park.

I am grateful to Ben Shneiderman and Peter Levine of the University of Maryland for sparking my interest in this topic and getting me to put my thoughts in order about it. I am also indebted to the people who attended my seminar—and who helped clarify my thinking—in the lecture series "The Internet and Its Impacts on Society" at the University of Maryland and to the editor and two anonymous reviewers for this journal. Thanks also to Andrew Kohut of the Pew Center for the People and the Press for providing me with the data from the 1998 Pew Technology Survey and to Lee Rainie of the Pew Internet and American Life Project for making the 2000 Trust and Privacy Survey available. Neither is responsible for my interpretations. And I am grateful to the General Research Board of the University of Maryland for a Distinguished University Research Fellowship that facilitated this research. A much shorter version of this article, using only the 1998 data, was published as Uslaner (2000). This article was originally prepared for the Joint Sessions of the European Consortium for Political Research, Workshop on Electronic Democracy: Mobilisation, Organisation, and Participation via New ICTs, University of Grenoble (France), April 6–11, 2000).

ing back to this and similar sites. "Eventually," *U.S. News and World Report* writer Joannie Fischer wrote, "the online sexual world came to take the place of any real-world contact with women." He eventually fell into a trap set by his employers and "now lives under the constant monitoring of his wife and his boss" (Fischer, 2000, p. 43). This is the bad Net, a place that denies reality and takes people away from whatever real-world social ties they have made.

Which is the real Internet, the good Net or the bad Net? This is a high stakes question because each side sees the World Wide Web as the possible solution or the villain in the drama of the decline of community. In many Western societies, and especially in the United States, there is a concern that citizens are becoming disconnected from each other. We no longer join groups, we don't socialize with each other, and, above all, we don't trust each other as much as we did in the past (Putnam, 2000). Supporters of the good Net approach see wired communications as bringing people back together in the spirit of those who helped the Salcedo family come to terms with its tragedy. Adherents of the bad Net theory see the Internet as accelerating the decline of civic engagement and good feelings.

Putnam (1993) referred to a "virtuous circle" of trust, group membership, and informal social ties that has become known as "social capital." Social capital helps make society and its government run more smoothly. But it is in shorter supply now than it used to be. During the 1960s, Americans began to withdraw from participation in all sorts of civic groups—from the traditional service organizations such as the Rotary Clubs, Kiwanis, and the League of Women Voters as well as bowling leagues and card-playing clubs. They socialized less with friends and neighbors and voted less often.

The "inevitable result" was that we became less trusting of one another (Putnam, 2000, chap. 8). In 1960, 58% of Americans believed that "most people can be trusted" (as opposed to saying that "you can't be too careful in dealing with people"). By the 1990s, barely more than a third of Americans trusted each other, according to national surveys such as the General Social Survey and the American National Election Study. Americans have lost their sense of community. We don't mix with each other as much as we used to, and we don't trust each other. We have become more balkanized, our public life has become more contentious, and our national institutions (especially the Congress) struggle to compromise on even the most basic public policy questions.

The principal villain in the decline of social capital is technology, especially television but perhaps also the Internet (Putnam, 2000, chap. 13).[1] I (and others) have exonerated television as the cause of the declines in civic engagement and trust elsewhere (Uslaner, 1998; see also Newton, 1999; Norris, 1996, 2000, 2001). I show in this article that the Internet is *not* to blame either (see also Norris, 2000, 2001; Shah, 1998). I shall examine the connection between the Internet, trust, and civic engagement, using a 1998 survey by the Pew Center for the People and the Press and a 2000 survey by the Pew Internet and American Life Project. Briefly, I find no evidence for the claim that people who have stronger social support networks in the "real world" avoid the Web. There is also little support for the argument that the Net is a haven for people who don't trust others. Nor is there any evidence that people who spend time online are less likely to trust others.

CIVIC LIFE IN THE NEW TECHNOLOGICAL ERA

The ultimate payoff of civic engagement is the trust it engenders with our fellow citizens. As Putnam (1993, p. 90) argues: "Participation in civic organizations inculcates skills of cooperation as well as a sense of shared responsibility for collective endeavors." Technology, especially television (but perhaps also the Internet), can lead us away from socializing into our private worlds. Watching a lot of television keeps us inside our homes and away from the civic organizations and social connections that generate trust. Heavy TV viewing also leads us to believe that the real world is as "mean" and violent as the programs we see on television, so it makes us less likely to trust strangers (Gerbner et al., 1980). Television produces misanthropes who see the world as a dark and threatening place and whose "Friends" are fictional characters whom you will never be asked to help out. The ultimate television viewer was Chauncy Gardner, the character in Jerzy Kosinski's novel, *Being There.* Gardner had no social ties and thought the television world *was* the real world.

That's the old technology. Today there are even more mistrusters, and civic engagement has dropped further. The new culprit seems to be the Internet. Even more so than television, the Internet may be a lonely place. We hear stories of people who become addicted to the Net, who spend their hours in front of a computer screen and ignore their families and dissociate themselves from friends. Television programs may make you think that the world is mean. The Internet will show you just how nasty folks can be.

When you enter an Internet chat room, you can hide your identity, "flame" other people, and "troll" first time visitors to a Web site. The Net can be a dangerous place, where "charities" solicit funds for nonexistent causes (Abelson, 1999), scoundrels feign love for lonely hearts, and unscrupulous hackers uncover your credit card numbers. The newsmagazine *U.S. News and World Report* (2000, p. 36) published a special investigative report suggesting that "the amount of bad stuff out there is truly staggering"—adoption scams, stalking complaints, rigged auctions, and even "the first Internet serial killer." We picture the Internet version of Chauncy Gardner as a loner sitting in front a keyboard, mouse, and monitor playing "Doom" (or whatever gamers do these days). This is the bad Net.

It would be easy to ignore these horror stories if there were not serious academic research supporting the view of the Internet as a haven for social isolates. At a minimum, Nie and Erbring (2000) report that heavy Internet users report that they have cut back on their social ties. Net use leads people away from social contacts and toward staring at their monitors in not-so-splendid isolation. Heavy Internet users *become* more depressed, lead more stressful lives, and have fewer friends, even though they may start out as well off psychologically as the rest of us (Kraut et al., 1998).

Yet, this is just one face of the Internet. Others see the Net as the great opportunity to rebuild our lost sense of community and trust. People come together on the Net through e-mail lists, affinity groups, support groups, and chat rooms. The Internet connects people from all over the world and may be, as Hauber and Hauben (1997, p. 5) argue, "a grand intellectual and social commune in the spirit of the collective nature present at the origins of human society."

The Internet also lets us connect with people with shared interests whom we otherwise would not meet. The Internet is the great leveller of class and race barriers, which have proven to be strong disincentives to effective participation in American society (Verba, Schlozman, & Brady, 1995). Our Net contacts may come from different backgrounds or live far away from us (Etzioni & Etzioni, 1997). All sorts of good things happen on the Net, including opportunities to volunteer (Maloney, 1999) and many different types of support groups. Some are simply outlets to share information. Others provide forums for people to connect with each other, such as USENET chat groups and the now-famous WELL, the Whole Earth 'Lectronic Link, which established itself as the counterculture on the Web (Rheingold, 1993). And others even serve as forums for people to help each other in times of crisis and grief (St. George, 1999). When people go online, they feel less restrained in interacting with strangers than they would in daily life (Tranvik, 2000, pp. 13–14).

Shah, Kwak, and Holbert (2001, pp. 150–152; see also Shah, 1998) argue that people who use the Internet for information (primarily exchanging e-mails) are slightly more likely to get involved in their communities and are significantly more likely to trust other people compared to people who use the Net for other reasons (ranging from chat rooms to buying goods to doing research to not connecting at all). Younger people who communicate with others are especially likely to trust others and to participate in their communities.

The Internet may well be the route to *restoring* our frayed social ties (Wellman & Gulia, 1999). While some studies see the Net as a mean place, others see it as a ray of hope. The Pew Internet and American Life Project reported survey results showing that Internet users have *wider* social networks than people who do not connect to the Web (Raney, 2000; Robinson et al., 2000). Moreover, these online connections often lead to "real-world" friendships (Blanchard & Horan, 2000; Parks & Floyd, 1996; Wellman & Gulia, 1999). As computer literacy and Internet access grow, Americans should reconnect with each other, thus forming the base for a new era of trust. This is the good Net. Which is the real Net?

THE NET: WHO GOES THERE?

I offer a third perspective: The Internet neither destroys nor creates social capital. There are both altruists and scoundrels on the Net, just as there are in everyday life (cf. Bimber, 2000; Wallace, 1999, p. 190). Indeed, the Internet, like television, mirrors everyday life. What people do online is pretty much what they do offline: They shop, they get sports news and weather, they plan their vacations, and, most of all, they contact people they already know through e-mail. At least one survey (Cole, 2000) and a time-diary study (Robinson et al., 2002) suggest that Net surfers socialize with others about the same amount as other people. The Net is not a threat. But it is not Nirvana either.

The major reason why the Internet is not the "new new thing" of trust and civic engagement is that much of the current discussion of the "virtuous circle" of trust, civic engagement, and socializing is misplaced. Trust in other people is trust in strangers, people who are different from yourself. Trust is essential for a civil and a cooperative society, but it does *not* depend upon your life experiences—whether you visit friends and relatives, join civic organizations, watch television, or surf the Internet. Instead, trust reflects an optimistic world view and a belief that others share your fundamental values. You learn trust from your parents, mostly when you are young, Elsewhere, I show how trust in others stems from an upbeat world view and is transmitted early in life from one's family rather than later in life from one's friends and civic groups (Uslaner, 2002, chaps. 4–5). If trust does not stem from social interactions—joining groups, participating in politics, and all sorts of informal socializing—there is little reason to presume that new technologies will fare any better in engendering faith in others.

You are not likely to become more trusting of people who are different from yourself by interacting in clubs or in coffee klatches with people like yourself (Uslaner, 2002, chap. 4). Nor are you likely to become more trusting through online communities. In each case, your social interactions occur with people who share your interests. There is no reason to presume that online support groups will do a better job of creating trusting attitudes than will choral societies or playing cards, two of Putnam's key civic associations.[2]

Similarly, there is little reason to presume that the Internet will make social butterflies out of homebodies. The Net does make communication easier, so it would hardly be surprising that people with lots of friends and large support networks will use the Internet more than loners. They have more people to talk to. However, these impacts should not be large. The Net is not transformative.

Much of the debate over whether "online communities" are really communities (cf. Etzioni & Etzioni, 1997; Galston, 1999; Rheingold, 1993) is misplaced—for two distinct reasons. First, we may expect too much of technology. Putnam's indictment of television may have been too hasty, as other research has shown (Newton, 1999; Norris, 1996, 2000, 2001; Uslaner, 1998). Bimber (1998) argues more broadly that there is little reason to expect a link between technology and civic engagement: With each new technology, from the post office to the telephone to television and the Internet, more and more people have access to information that would make it easier to participate in civic life. Yet, participation rates have contracted, not expanded, as information resources proliferate. The Internet can provide a forum for participation. It will not necessarily lead to more people getting involved. As Yogi Berra, the American baseball player and mangler of the English language, said: "If the people don't want to come out to the ballpark, nobody's going to stop them."[3] The same holds for the Internet: Joiners in the "real world" are the online activists. Whatever has happened to communities and trust—throughout the Western world, not just in the United States—is not likely the fault of the Internet or any other medium.

Second, communities, whether online or offline, generally don't build trust in strangers. They can't. Most of our group memberships and informal socializing take place with people very much like ourselves. And there is no way to get from trust in people like yourself to trust in strangers (Rosenblum, 1998, pp. 45, 48; Uslaner, 2002, chap. 5).

We may be more willing to make contact with "strangers" in online communities (Wellman & Gulia, 1999), but are these people we don't know, who may live in another part of the country or even the world, really "strangers"? From e-mail (the most widely used part of the Internet) to chat rooms to support groups, going online involves communicating with others. Trust develops between people of divergent backgrounds, whereas the Net excels in bringing together people who already have something in common—be it family ties, friendship, working in the same office, political views, or needing the same kind of medical information and/or psychological support. And many (most?) of these online communities are composed of transients—people who stop by to gain some information, get or give some moral support, and then go their own way (Galston, 1999, p. 52). They have little expectation of meeting the same people elsewhere in the wired world. What is perhaps the most widely visited *interactive* site, the auctioneer ebay, is based upon the premise of one-shot online meetings that are commercial transactions rather than social networks.[4]

Are you likely to meet different types of people in a USENET group discussing politics than you are in a "real life" group? Hill and Hughes (1997) suggest not. Online as well as offline, we are most likely to connect with people very much like ourselves. Preece's (1999) community of people with sports injuries are all interested in athletics. If we do make different types of connections online, it may well reflect an initial reservoir of trust rather than an acquired set of values. Stolle (1998) argues that trusting people may be more likely to get involved in their communities, reflecting a "self-selection" effect. The Net may consume trust, rather than produce it.

Trust is not irrelevant to the Internet. Far from it. Going online does not make people either more or less trusting, but trust shapes how people interact with each other. Trusting people are less likely to fear getting involved with strangers. In everyday life, trusters are less likely to lock their doors at night and to use guns to protect themselves. They are more likely to volunteer, give to charity, and invite strangers to their home (Uslaner, 2002, chaps. 2, 5). On the Net, trusting people should see others as nice folks who won't exploit them—so they should be less worried about violations of their privacy. They should be more likely to interact with strangers when there is no evidence of shared interests on the Net. And they should shun the "seamier" aspects of the Web, such as hiding their true identity. More generally, there is little reason to believe that people who trust others will be more or less likely to use the Internet.

Much of the "evidence" on the causes and effects of Internet use is anecdotal; this makes it easy for people to offer alternative accounts of who goes there. Yet, more and more of it is systematic. A small survey by Kraut et al. (1998) and a much larger one by Nie and Erbring (2000) found "mean world" effects. The subjects in each of these surveys were given computers *on the condition that they regularly logged on to the Web*. We don't know what effects the "forced" use of the Web had on people.[5] The Nie and Erbring (2000) study asked people whether their social interactions increased, decreased, or stayed the same but provided no baseline for the overall level of activity. If heavy Net users had less time for social interactions *but still were more active than the nonconnected*, there would be no way for us to know that from the Nie-Erbring study (from Stanford University).

The Cole (2000) study (from UCLA) shows no strong differences in social interactions between Net users and the unconnected, and these results are from a random sample of the American population, like the Pew surveys. This is more reasonable, but the published results from both studies so far have been bivariate. The studies by Shah and his colleagues (Shah, 1998; Shah et al., 2001) did use multivariate analyses. However, they used the DDB Needham Lifestyle Surveys, which are not random samples of the public. And their measure of "trust" was whether respondents see people as "honest." Honesty may *seem like* trust, but in the one survey that asked both questions (the 1972 American National Election Survey), the correlation between trust and honesty was just .345 (tau-b; see Uslaner, 2002, p. 72).

Thus, there is clearly the need for more systematic testing. And that is what I set out to do here.

WHAT THE DATA TELL US

What is the connection between trust, sociability, and Internet usage? I analyze data from two surveys: a 1998 survey of technology use by the Pew Center for the People and the Press and the 2000 Trust and Privacy Survey of the Pew Internet and American Life Project. The 1998 poll is the "gold standard" of surveys of Internet use. It includes many good questions about Web usage and social connections, as well as the generalized trust question. The 2000 survey has many more questions on Net usage, including a large number that might (and do) depend upon the sense of solidarity with others reflected in the generalized trust question. The 2000 survey, however, has no measures of social support networks. So the statistical models for the 2000 survey are not directly comparable to those for 1998. Each set of results is compelling in its own right to obviate the problems of comparability.

The linkage of Internet use with trust is the key question for determining whether the Net is good or bad (or neither). Questions of sociability are interesting in their own right—but it is unclear whether they are linked with generating trust. There is ample reason to be skeptical. Nonetheless, evidence for either sociability or social pathologies on the Web can at least alleviate or confirm the fears about the Internet. Does Internet use lead to social isolation, so that trust can never develop? Or might it lead to the creation of new communities that might provide more fertile grounds for trust?

The 1998 survey asked 2,000 Americans a variety of questions about going online, as well as about their social networks and their trust in others and in government. (Alas, neither survey asked questions on group membership, which is a key element of social capital.) I estimated 18 models using ordered probit analysis. These models allow me to determine which factors best predict different forms of Internet use. Each model contains many factors that might lead to more Internet usage,[6] but I focus on trust and measures of sociability ("How wide is your social support network?" "How often do you visit family members?" and "How frequently do you call friends?"). The results are presented in Table 1, which is split into four sections: frequency of use, sociability online, concerns about security, and what people do online. To save space, I only report the significance levels of the ordered probit coefficients. When a cell is blank, the coefficient is non-significant. A negative sign for significance level indicates that the coefficient is negative.

The results clearly show that the Internet is neither the tool of the devil nor the new Jerusalem—which heralds the renaissance of a national sense of community and trust in one another. For most types of general use of the Internet—using e-mail; getting information on health, business, sports, and stocks; expressing your views online; and buying goods online—trust either doesn't matter at all or doesn't matter much. Surprisingly, e-mail users are more likely to trust others, and people who get stock quotes online are ever so slightly more likely to trust others. These relationships are not strong. Beyond that, general use of the Internet is connected neither to trust nor to sociability. All sorts of people go online to seek information: the trusting and the misanthrope, the sociable and the recluse.

Table 1: Summary of Effects from 1998 Pew Technology Survey

	Trust	Support	Visit family	Call friends	Keep in touch	Paper	Watch TV	TV News	TV time	Trust government	Other significant variables
Frequency of use											
Use e-mail	.05	-.10	.10		.0001	.05					Age, student
Computer time			.05			-.05			.001		No religion
Online yesterday		.05									
Time online									.01		Male, student
Often online		.05			.0001					.01	Family income, age
Too much online		-.01									Male, single
E-mail: more communication									.01		Single
Sociability online											
Chat online	-.10				.01						Age
New friend	-.05						.10				
Give views online						.05					Student, not self-employed, single
Concerns about security											
Worry: privacy	-.0001				-.0001					-.01	
Worry: medical records insecure		-.01			-.05				.01		
Worry: virus	-.01				.01				Male		
What people do											
Health information					.0001		-.05			-.10	Male, single, no religion
Buy goods					.01						Age, male, income, single, no religion
Sports news					.05	.10			.05	-.10	Male, own home, single
Business news											Male
Stock quotes	.05						.05		.05		

325

There is little reason to expect that simply going online either taps or drains sociability (or trust). Kraut et al. (1998) and Nie and Erbring (2000) argue that people who spend a lot of time online are the misanthropes. But the Pew Center survey offers little support for this view. People who use their computers a lot, who spend a lot of time online (both in real time and how often they connect), and who *say that they spend too much time on the Net* are no less trusting than people who don't go online at all. Neither the Internet nor television remakes people's personalities (Uslaner, 1998).

The picture of heavy surfers as loners is also wrong: The heaviest users of the Internet have *wider* social circles and support networks. People with large support networks were more likely to be online yesterday, more likely to go online often, and less likely to say that they are online "too much." People who visit their family often are more likely to use e-mail (perhaps to contact the same family members) and to spend a lot of time on the computer. People who believe that the Internet helps them keep in touch (as opposed to isolating them) are significantly more likely to use e-mail, to go online often, to visit chat rooms, to get health information, to buy goods, and to seek out sports news. Much of the time, however, the size of support networks simply doesn't matter at all. The Internet, then, does not herald a new spirit of community. Rather, it is an additional outlet for people who already are connected to other people (Katz & Aspden, 1998).

Net usage is largely determined by demographics. The anecdotal profile of the Net surfer is a young male libertarian—and this is pretty much what we see in Table 1. Young male students, generally single and often with no religion (and sometimes distrusting government), are the heaviest users of the Net. In a few cases, such as how much time one spends online and whether one buys goods on the Internet, income matters. Overall, feeling comfortable with the Net (believing that it helps keep you in touch) and demographics overwhelm social ties and trust as predictors of Net use. There is little evidence in this survey that Internet users shut themselves off from other people—or from other forms of media, either. Net users are also generally more likely to spend a lot of time watching television and to read a newspaper regularly (cf. Norris, 2000, p. 117; Robinson et al., 2000, 2002).

There are two exceptions to this general pattern. First, a new innovation of the Internet—chat rooms—offers some hope that people of different backgrounds might get together and learn to trust one another. But here, of all places, we see some evidence of misanthropy. People who visit chat rooms or who make new friends online are no more or less sociable than anyone else. They don't have bigger or smaller support networks and are no more likely to visit relatives or call friends. Yet, they are *less trusting* than others (cf. Shah et al., 2001, p. 149). Perhaps people who make friends online, often anonymously, feel uncomfortable with meeting "real" strangers. And many, maybe most, chat rooms are marked by a dominant worldview or ideology—and dissidents often find out rather rudely that they are not welcome (Hill & Hughes, 1997; Wallace, 1999, pp. 101–102). People who frequent chat rooms seem to trust only people like themselves and fear people with different views.

Second, people who mistrust others fear the Internet much as they accept all sorts of other conspiracy theories. They worry about their privacy generally and in particular about the security of their medical records and downloading viruses. Trusters see the Internet as more benign. Trusting people believe that they can control the world and have faith that science will solve our problems (Uslaner, 2002, chap. 4). They see the Internet as an additional tool that gives them leverage over their world (Wallace, 1999, p. 173).

Overall, then, the 1998 Pew technology survey does not suggest a strong linkage between Internet usage and generalized trust. Misanthropes seem to worry about their security on the Web, as they do elsewhere (Uslaner, 2002, chap. 5). There is some evidence that people who socialize with friends and family connect to the Web more (and are likely to connect with many of the same people). And people who go to the Net for their social life—making new friends or visiting chat rooms—feel that most people are not trustworthy.

Overall, the 1998 Pew technology poll suggests that the Internet neither creates nor destroys social capital. Simply using the Internet does not distinguish trusters from mistrusters. There is some modest evidence that people with larger support networks go online more often, but they are not distinctive in their Internet usage otherwise. There are a few exceptions that seem to support the "bad Net" view: Mistrusters are more likely to make new friends online and ever so slightly more likely to go to chat rooms. This may reflect mistrusters' misanthropy—their willingness to make new connections when they can hide their own identity (see below) and to substitute vicarious friendships for real ones. Mistrusters are also more likely to worry that the Internet will intrude on their personal space. They are worried about privacy issues and even that their computers might become infected. Yet, none of these results imply that worrying about privacy or even getting a virus would make people *less trusting*. They only suggest that people who worry about others' motives offline also fear being tricked online.

THE EVIDENCE UPDATED: THE 2000 TRUST AND PRIVACY SURVEY

The 2000 Trust and Privacy Survey, with 2,117 respondents (Fox, 2000), has many more questions on Internet usage, but no questions on sociability. Here I focus on the connections between trust and 43 measures of Internet use in the survey. The models, which are more sparse than for the 1998 survey, are estimated by either ordered or simple probit analysis.[7]

The 43 measures are divided into four groups again: one for time online and using e-mail, a second for security concerns, a third for privacy issues, and a fourth for what people do on the Web. In Table 2, I summarize the results of the 43 probits, again focusing on significance levels of the coefficients. But this is too quick and unsure a method of investigating impacts. So in Tables 3 and 4, I report the probabilities derived from the probit analyses for the Internet variables that had significant coefficients for trust. Unlike regression analyses, the probit coefficients have no straightforward interpretations. The standard way of estimating impacts in probit is to estimate the probability that the dependent variable takes on a given value for both trusters and mistrusters, letting all other variables take their "natural" values.

Finally, in Table 5, I resolve an anomaly from Table 2. In Table 2, it seems that trusting people go online less than misanthropes. To see whether this finding is robust, I run a two-stage least squares regression, which permits reciprocal causation between frequency online and trust. This resolves the anomaly: Trust does not shape frequency online, nor does how often one surfs determine trust.

The easiest way to summarize Table 2 is that, once again, demographics are the key determinants of Internet use. Once more, most of the effects of time watching television are positive. But here the rationale isn't quite so compelling in all cases. Many of the most interesting questions in this table bear little relationship to media exposure. They do tap trust, and generally in predictable ways.

Table 2: Summary of Significant Predictors from 2000 Pew Trust and Privacy Survey

Dependent Variable	Trust	TV time	Significant Predictors
Time spent online		.10	Education, Black (−), male
Frequency online	−.10	.05	Male, retired, divorced/separated (−)
Read e-mail online		−.05	Age (−), education, female
Worry business gets personal info.	.0001	−.10	Black (−), age (−), divorced/separated
Worry others get credit card number			Black (−), single
Concerned hackers get credit card no.	−.001	.10	Female, single, age
Confident Web dealings private	.0001	−.05	Black (−), age (−)
Worry others read e-mail			Education (−)
Worry others know Web site visits	−.05		Unemployed (−), male, single (−)
OK for companies to track visits			Age (−), student, single (−), male
Companies must ask permission	.10	.05	Black (−), unemployed, female, single (−)
Worry download virus	−.01		Unemployed (−), Black
Concerned rumors on stock prices	−.05	−.10	Black
Concerned bad medical advice			Student, Black, female
Concerned others learn about you	−.10		
Concerned others use fake identity		.10	Female, single
Willing to use real name on Web site			Female
Have used real name on Web site	.10	.10	Age (−)
Ever used fake identity on Web	−.05		Education, male, age (−)
Ever used fake e-mail address	−.10		Age (−), read newspaper, male, education
Sent encrypted e-mail			Male, education, age (−)
Sign name on medical Web site		.10	Read newspaper, Black, male, retired (−),
Sign name on dating site		.05	Education, Black, male, single (−), unemployed
Use credit card for telephone orders	.001	.05	Read newspaper, Black (−), single (−), divorced (−)
Use credit card on Web		.05	Education, male, Black, read paper, retired (−)
Use online calendar for appointments		−.10	Education, female
Reply to e-mail from stranger	.05		Male, age (−)
Got offensive e-mail from stranger	−.05		Black (−), education
Made new friend on Internet			Age (−), single, divorced/separated
Visit chat rooms online		.10	Age (−), single, education (−)
Use online dating services			Single, divorced/separated
Participate in auction online			Black (−), male, retired (−), divorced/separated (−)
Use online banking	−.10		Student (−), age (−), read paper (−), male, single (−)
Ever clicked on ad on Web			Male, age (−), Black, read newspaper
Get news online			Student, education, male

(Table continues to next page)

Table 2: Summary of Significant Predictors from 2000 Pew Trust and Privacy Survey (*continued*)

Dependent Variable	Trust	TV time	Significant predictors
Get financial news online			Education, male, unemployed (−), retired, age (−)
Get product information online		.05	Single (−), male, read newspaper
Get travel information online			Education, female
Get medical information online		.05	Female, Black, single (−)
Get political information online			Education, retired (−), unemployed, divorced/separated
Get government information online			Education, retired (−), read newspaper, single (−), unemployed (−)
Go online for fun			Education
Ever buy product online		.05	

Note. Entries are significance levels from probits and ordered probits, with signs of probit coefficients.

The Pew Research Center for the People and the Press (1998, p. 1) reported that Internet users who had not made an online purchase were worried about credit card security. The Pew Trust and Privacy Survey in 2000 shows a high level of distrust of strangers: 61% of respondents say that you can't be too careful in dealing with people. And mistrusters are *very* concerned about the Internet. They see it as a threatening place where hackers might steal your credit card number, businesses will get personal information, Web dealings will not be private, others will know where you have been on the Web, you might download a virus, and others will learn private things about your life. In turn, they tend to limit their interactions. They don't respond to e-mail from strangers—even though they are *more* likely to say that they have received an offensive e-mail from a stranger. They respond in kind, being *less* likely to use their real name on the web and *more* likely to use fake identifications and e-mail addresses on the Web.

Trusting people show just the opposite profile. Offline, trusting people overall see the Web as a place occupied with many trustworthy people and companies. They have no desire to hide their identity. Trusting people are more tolerant of people of different races and religions and of minorities that have faced discrimination. They have more favorable attitudes toward immigrants and are more likely to favor open markets. Online, trusters respond to e-mails from strangers and receive fewer offensive missives from people they don't know (either because it takes more to offend them or they get on fewer lists with people who write nasty notes). They worry less about what others might learn about them and don't fear that others will invade their personal lives or spread lies. They are more likely to demand that companies ask permission to get personal information, but they will use their credit card numbers for phone orders (though, surprisingly, there is no difference for Internet orders).

On matters not related to privacy and security, there is little that separates trusters and mistrusters on the Net. Trusting people are no more likely to go online to get information of any sort, or even to buy products. They are no more prone to go to the Web for fun or to spend lots of time on it. There is one exception: how often people go online. There is a modest negative relationship between trust and how often people go online. I shall revisit this below.

Table 3: Simple Probit Probabilities for Trust: 2000 Pew Trust and Privacy Survey

Dependent Variable	Careful	Trust	Change in Probability
Use credit card on phone	.559	.647	.088
Use real name on Web site	.557	.631	.074
Ever used fake ID on Web	.308	.232	−.076
Replied to e-mail from stranger	.236	.307	.071
Received offensive e-mail from stranger	.329	.235	−.094
Companies on Internet should ask permission for personal information	.837	.874	.037
Used Internet banking	.178	.131	−.047

In Tables 3 and 4, I present the probabilities of some of the significant variables in Table 2 for trusters and mistrusters. For the simple probits in Table 3, the interpretations are straightforward: 63.1% of generalized trusters say that they use their real names on the Web, compared to 55.7% of mistrusters, for a difference of 7.4%. This percentage difference is called a probit "effect." We see similar effects for ever having used a fake ID on the Web and having replied to e-mails from strangers—and slightly larger ones for using a credit card on the phone and receiving an offensive e-mail from strangers. The effect is somewhat less for whether companies should ask permission for personal information on the Internet. This is not surprising, since the issue is more consensual and also less prone to personal worries. In Table 2, trusters are (perhaps surprisingly) less likely to use Internet banking. Here we see the difference is about 5%. Overall, on matters of privacy, trusters are between 7% and 10% more likely to give strangers (and companies) the benefit of the doubt.

The interpretations for Table 4 are somewhat more complicated, since each of the dependent variables is categorical. I have divided the table into four columns of data, since most of the Internet questions had four categories. Frequency online and time online have seven and eight categories respectively, so I report the extreme categories. A total of 18.5% of trusters *never* go online, compared to 14.9% of misanthropes; 18% of trusters, compared to 22.1% of misanthropes, go online several times daily. For time online, there are few significant differences.

We see more pronounced differences for privacy concerns. Mistrusters are 12.4% more likely to be *very* concerned that businesses have access to their personal information (and 4% less likely to be not at all concerned). They are almost 20% more worried that Web dealings are not private (combining the last two categories) and 8% less likely to dismiss a worry that someone might know which Web sites they have visited. Mistrusters are 8% more likely to worry a lot about downloading a virus and almost 15% more likely to be very worried about hackers getting their credit card number. The differences in concern for false rumors on stock prices and learning about people on auctions are smaller: 5% to 6%. These differences probably reflect lower participation rates in stock trading online (just 11% of the sample) and taking part in auctions (16%).

Perhaps people don't participate in these activities because they are concerned about security, though the data in Table 2 don't provide much support for this argument. Nevertheless, these findings suggest that people who already mistrust others will be particularly concerned

Table 4: Ordered Probit Probabilities for Trust: 2000 Pew Trust and Privacy Survey

Variable	Category			
Frequency online	Never	Rarely	Every day	Several times daily
Careful	.149	.024	.256	.221
Trust	.185	.028	.239	.180
Time online	None	Less than 15 min	3–4 hours	4 hours or more
Careful	.482	.028	.045	.058
Trust	.451	.028	.050	.067
Concerned business gets personal info.	Very	Somewhat	Not too	Not at all
Careful	.660	.242	.055	.043
Trust	.536	.298	.084	.082
How confident Web dealings private	Very	Somewhat	Not too	Not at all
Careful	.064	.427	.307	.203
Trust	.143	.525	.234	.098
Worry someone might know Web sites visited	A lot	Some	Not very much	Not at all
Careful	.094	.240	.274	.392
Trust	.063	.197	.264	.476
Worry about virus from downloading	A lot	Some	Not very much	Not at all
Careful	.201	.379	.263	.157
Trust	.126	.332	.300	.242
Worry hackers get credit card number	Very	Somewhat	Not too	Not at all
Careful	.503	.099	.099	.133
Trust	.357	.130	.130	.229
Concerned about false rumors on stock prices	Very	Somewhat	Not too	Not at all
Careful	.292	.218	.202	.288
Trust	.231	.204	.209	.356
Concerned others learn about you from online actions	Very	Somewhat	Not too	Not at all
Careful	.327	.281	.186	.205
Trust	.277	.275	.199	.249

about Internet security and privacy. Since most Americans don't trust each other, this is a potentially worrisome feature for the growth of online business and investing. While it seems at least a bit curious that people will do business on the Internet even as they worry about its security, it doesn't take much imagination to think what type of scare might drive people away from e-commerce, or perhaps Web sites more generally.

These findings suggest that many Americans see the Web as more threatening than welcoming. There is a reservoir of suspicion that technologies beyond our control, often beyond our comprehension, are intruding on our personal lives, with less than benign intentions. This makes sense when we realize that mistrust reflects a pessimistic world view and a feeling that things are beyond our control (Uslaner, 2002, chaps. 2, 4). And these worries go well beyond our own personal fears. Almost 60% of Americans worry that others might learn about them from online auctions, even though just 16% have ever taken part in such an auction."

The growing opportunities for socializing on the Web are not havens for caring people looking to bond with like-minded folk. Forty-three percent of people who have made new friends online have used a fake ID, compared to just 19% of people who have not made a new friend (phi = .232, Yule's Q = .511). Thirty-eight percent of folks with new online friends have used a fake e-mail address, compared to 15% without such friends (phi = .247, Yule's Q = .555). We see a similar dynamic for chat rooms, with almost identical percentages and measures of association.[8] This pattern even holds for using online dating services: 20% looking for love used fake e-mail addresses, compared to just 6% who did not seek a mate (phi = .185, Yule's Q = .560).

We should not mistake socializing with trusting. One is neither the cause nor the effect of the other. Misanthropes have friends and family too—and it seems that many of their friends are online. Deception is easy on the Internet. Recall the cartoon in *The New Yorker* where a canine sits in front of a computer and mumbles to another dog: "On the Internet, nobody knows you're a dog." The ability to hide your true identity gives mistrusters a defense mechanism on the Internet that is not so easily available in real life.

Some forms of Web use make us vulnerable to people who would deceive us. People visiting auctions are twice as likely to use a false e-mail address as those who don't visit auctions (phi = .142, Yule's Q = .388). If you are prone to mistrust others, the Internet will prove you right.

Yet, this is just a partial view of the Internet. Sixty percent of all respondents have never gone to chat rooms *or* made new friends online. Only 15% of all respondents have used a fake ID and have gone to chat rooms or made new friends online. Most people who use the Internet log on for such mundane reasons as getting e-mail (87%) or obtaining information on government (51%), travel (37%), or medical conditions (36%). We are most likely to exchange e-mail with people we already know well, so e-mail can help foster the "good Net." Going online for information doesn't involve two-way communication. So you can't be "exploited" by mistrusters (assuming that the information is correct).

Most of the time, then, the Net is neutral. It neither creates social bonds nor destroys them. It does not build up trust or destroy it. To make the point more clearly, I conducted a two-stage least squares analysis of trust and frequency of going online. Here I seek to determine whether trusting people go online less often or whether going online frequently makes people less trusting, as the "mean world" thesis would have us believe. I chose frequency of going online for this analysis because trust had a significant effect on it in Table 2. I report the two-stage least squares model in Table 5.

Table 5: Two-stage Least Squares Estimation for Trust and Frequency Online: 2000 Pew Trust and Privacy Survey

Independent Variable	Coefficient	T Ratio (significance)
Equation for trust in people		
Frequency online	−.054	−.919
Time online	−.001	−.045
Visit chat rooms	−.032	−.523
Make new friend online	−.009	−.126
Been cheated when buying online	.139	.908
Credit card ever stolen	.006	.093
Concerned others give fake ID	.022	1.031
Know what cookies are	.080	1.286*
Most people are fair	.359	6.320***
Satisfied with direction of country	.125	2.223**
Age	.001	.430
Education	−.015	−.813
Family income	.018	1.070
Black	.122	1.399*
Student	.028	.458
South	−.133	−2.169**
Midwest	−.114	−1.438
Time watching TV per day	−.035	−2.115**
Constant	.326	.203*
Equation for frequency online		
Trust in people	−.527	−.987
Read newspaper	−.269	−1.128
Time watching TV per day	.112	1.475*
Education	.055	.646
Student	−.046	−.163
Unemployed	.759	1.870**
Black	.178	.462
Gender	.052	.218
Retired	.893	1.640*
Single	−.188	−.592
Divorced/separated	−.255	−.360
Family income	.158	2.351**
Age	−.011	−.955
Ever buy at auction	1.160	3.988****
Ever buy stocks	.888	2.438**
Constant	.899	.96

$N = 327, R^2 = .050, \text{RMSE} = 2.759.$

*$p < .10$; **$p < .05$; ***$p < .01$; ****$p < .0001$.

The Pew Trust and Privacy Survey does not have the range of variables that I have generally included in models for trust. The survey is particularly lacking in measures of optimism and control. I thus include one measure of optimism (satisfied with the direction of the country) and a surrogate often used as part of a trust scale, whether one believes that most people are fair.[9] Aside from that, the model includes the standard demographics, dummies for region (we know that the southern states have lower levels of trust and many midwestern states are higher in trust), how much time the respondent watches television, and a series of measures of Internet use, including how often one goes online. Finally, I use a measure of whether the respondent knows what a "cookie" is as an additional measure of education. Some other models for trust (Brehm & Rahn, 1997; Gerbner et al., 1980; Putnam, 1995) have argued that people who watch a lot of television become less trusting. I have found that once measures of optimism and control are added to the mix, especially in simultaneous equation estimations, the effects of television viewing vanish (Uslaner, 1998). But the present survey has no good measures of optimism, so I include the amount of television respondents view in the equation. The equation for time online includes trust, other media consumption, demographics, and two key reasons why people go online: to go to auctions and to buy stocks.

The results of the two-stage least squares estimation are clear: Going online a lot does *not* make you less trusting. Nor does how much time you spend online, whether you visit chat rooms, make new friends, have been cheated when you bought something, have your credit card stolen, or are concerned that others will use fake identities. Internet usage does not destroy trust, but it doesn't create trust either. No matter what you do online, you don't become more (or less) trusting. The model suggests that the more you watch television, the less trusting you'll be—but this result is not sustained in other surveys with better measures of optimism and control. The two measures of optimism and control are by far the best predictors of trust. Of the other predictors, only the dummy variables for South and Black reach significance.

Trusting people are also no more or less likely to go online frequently than misanthropes. Indeed, the main reason why people go online frequently is to buy things, either at auctions or from stock brokers.[10] Some other demographics also matter: People who watch a lot of television also go online more frequently, as do the unemployed and retired (who have more free time at different hours of the day) and people with higher incomes.

GOOD NET, BAD NET

Overall, there are no grounds for proclaiming a "good Net" or a "bad Net." Most uses of the Internet are rather mundane. Most people don't go online looking to build a sense of community—or to destroy it. Yes, there are plenty of opportunities to deceive on the Web. The Internet is filled with pornography, but it didn't invent sex, and nobody is forcing folks to visit these sites (or others that sell Viagra to dogs or let children gamble). And yes, there are more opportunities on the Web to give to charities, to find volunteering opportunities, and to give solace to others. But that isn't the whole Internet either. Perhaps if the surveys had included questions on these activities, which *are linked to trust* (Uslaner, 2002, chap. 5), I might have found more evidence for the "good Net." The World Wide Web is very much like the world. It makes things better in some ways and worse in others. But it is not transform-ing. If you want to make a revolution, you have to go offline.

The Internet, then, is not a reservoir of social capital. As in everyday life, there are places where trust matters, and there are even more places where it doesn't. Trust matters most when people fear the unknown and worry that this new technology can come back to haunt them. And there is little evidence that the Internet will create new communities to make up for the decline in civic engagement that has occurred over the past four decades in the United States. Yet, there is even less evidence that the Internet is pushing people away from traditional social ties or making them less trusting. The following is a brief summary of what I have found regarding the Internet, trust, and social ties:

- Trusting people are generally not more likely to use the Internet than mistrusters.
- Mistrusters may substitute virtual friends on the Internet for "real-life friends" (although these relations are not strong).
- As trust makes people willing to take risks offline, trusters are more willing to take risks online (such as entering their credit card number or replying to e-mails from strangers). Mistrusters worry about their privacy from both businesses and people who might learn about them online. They are more likely to use fake names and phony e-mail addresses, and they worry about the quality of information they find online. However, all of this behavior online fits with what we know about the suspiciousness of mistrusters offline (Uslaner, 2002, chap. 5).
- Social ties have little effect on Internet usage overall. The major exception is that people with larger support networks spend more time online. This is hardly surprising, and it does not indicate that the Internet makes people more sociable. Rather, it shows that people use the Internet to connect with people they already know.
- Negative or positive experiences online have no effect on people's trust in others. Spend-ing a lot of time online neither increases nor decreases trust. Even people who have had bad experiences online—or who worry that others might try to exploit them—do not become less trusting. People who make new friends online don't become more trusting either. Experiences on the Internet, like most events in adult life, do not affect trust.
- The principal determinants of trust are demographic: Young, highly educated White males are the Americans most likely to use the Internet (in a variety of ways). While the impact of television viewing on Net usage is inconsistent, most of the time people who use the Internet are also plugged into their television sets (see also Norris, 2000).

The message of these findings is the Internet is not a threat to our society or its moral fiber. Regulating the Net won't solve our social problems or save our children from evil influ-ences. Children develop trust in others by learning from—and emulating—their parents, and not from what they (don't) see on television or on the Web. And how much one trusts others as a child largely determines how much one trusts others as an adult. Yes, the world *may* seem a more dangerous place on television or on the Web. And the Internet makes such mean sites more readily available than the everyday world (or even television). But this does not mean that the Net (or any other form of media) poses a real threat to most families. By itself, it is neither a threat to civil society and sociability nor a panacea.

Notes

1. Putnam (2000, pp. 170–171) is agnostic about the positive or negative effects of the Internet, even as he is convinced that television leads people away from social contact.

2. See Uslaner (2002, chap. 5) for evidence that neither of these activities, nor any other form of group membership or informal socializing, leads to more trusting attitudes.

3. Cited at http://www.yogi-berra.com/yogiisms.html. Accessed March 5, 2001.

4. If there were more frequent interactions, people could buy and sell without the need for an intermediary auctioneer.

5. Examining only those people who go online may lead to erroneous conclusions, especially since most people don't spend a lot of time on the Internet. The Kraut et al. (1998) survey only had 169 respondents, and most of the correlations were rather low.

6. I use other variables to ensure that the relationships between Internet usage, on the one hand, and trust and sociability, on the other hand, are not spurious. The other variables are age, gender, being a student, family income, owning your own home, being self-employed, being single, having no religion, how much time you watch television each day, how often you read a newspaper, whether you trust the federal government, and whether you believe that the Internet helps keep people in touch with one another.

7. There are more than 43 questions on the survey (as there were more than 18 in 1998). I selected those that were of greatest theoretical relevance to trust. The models included trust, time spent watching television, newspaper readership, education, student, unemployed, race, gender, retired, single, age, and a dummy variable for being either divorced or separated. The survey also asked about income, watching television news, and whether one watches television other than news at all. However, these variables were highly collinear with the others and were dropped from many analyses, so I excluded them from all models. I used simple probit analysis for dichotomous variables and ordered probit analysis for dependent variables with three or more categories.

8. The coefficient for trust in the probit analysis for the 2000 Pew Trust and Privacy Survey was not significant, while the coefficient for trust in the 1998 technology survey was significant at $p < .10$. This is *not* attributable to an attenuation of the relationship between going to chat rooms and trust-since the simple correlation was *higher* in 2000 than in 1998. It seems that the constellation of controls may be the reason for an insignificant coefficient in the 2000 data.

9. See Uslaner (2002, chap. 3) as to why the fairness question should *not* be part of a trust scale. It seems to be a workable substitute for a measure of optimism and control.

10. The variable frequency online is the *number of times a day you go online*, while the variable time online is *how much time each day you spend online*.

References

Abelson, R. (1999, November 17). As e-giving sites spring up, some say it's donor beware. *New York Times*, Washington edition, p. 21.

Bimber, B. (1998). The Internet and political transformation: Populism, community, and accelerated pluralism. *Polity, 31*, 133–160.

Bimber, B. (2000). Information, technology, and the organization of political engagement in the United States. Retrieved from *http://jsis.artsci.washington.edu/progrma/cwesuw/bimber.htm*

Blanchard, A., & Horan, T. (2000). *Can we surf together if we're bowling alone? An examination of virtual communities and social capital.* Unpublished manuscript, Claremont Graduate School.

Brehm, J., & Rahn, W. (1997). Individual level evidence for the causes and consequences of social capital, *American Journal of Political Science, 41*, 988–1023.

Cole, J. I. (2000). *Surveying the digital future.* Los Angeles: UCLA Center for Communication Policy.

Etzioni, A., & Etzioni, O. (1997). Communities: Virtual vs. Real. *Science, 277*, 295.

Fischer, J. (2000, August 28). Base instincts: Internet addiction. *U.S. News and World Report*, p. 43.

Fox, S. (2000). *Trust and privacy online: Why Americans want to rewrite the rules.* Washington: Pew Internet and American Life Project.

Galston, W. A. (1999). (How) does the Internet affect community? Some speculations in search of evidence. In E. C. Kamarck and J. S. Nye (Eds.), *Democracy.com?: Governance in a networked world.* Hollis, NH: Hollis Publishing Company.

Gerbner, G., Gross, L., Morgan, M., & Signorielli, N. (1980). The "mainstreaming" of America: Violence profile No. 11. *Journal of Communication, 30*, 10–29.

Hauber, M, & Hauben, R. (1997). *Netizens.* Los Alamitos, CA: IEEE Computer Society Press.

Hill, K. A., & Hughes, J. E. (1997). Computer-mediated political communication: The USENET and political communities. *Political Communication, 14*, 3–27.

Katz, J. E., & Aspden, P. (1998). Social and public policy Internet research: Goals and achievements. Retrieved from *http://www.communitytechnology.org/aspden/aspden_talk.html*

Kraut, R. E., Scherlis, W., Patterson, M., Kiesler, S., & Mukhopadhyay, T. (1998). Social impact of the Internet: What does it mean? *Communications of the ACM, 41*, 12.

Maloney, J. (1999, November 17). Volunteers log on, help out. *New York Times*, Washington edition, p. 20.

Newton, K. (1999). Mass media effects: Mobilization or media malaise? *British Journal of Political Science, 27*, 577–599.

Nie, N. H., & Erbring, L. (2000). *Internet and society: A preliminary report.* Stanford, CA: Stanford Institute for the Quantitative Study of Society, Stanford University.

Norris, P. (1996). Does television erode social capital? A reply to Putnam. *PS: Political Science and Politics, 29*, 474–480.

Norris, P. (2000). *A virtuous circle: Political communication in postindustrial societies.* Cambridge: Cambridge University Press.

Norris, P. (2001). *Digital divide? Civic engagement, information poverty & the Internet in democratic societies.* Cambridge: Cambridge University Press.

Parks, M. R., & Floyd, K. (1996). Making friends in cyberspace. *Journal of Computer-Mediated Communication,* 1. Retrieved from *http://www.acsuc.org/jcmc/vol11/issue4/parks.html*

Pew Research Center for the People and the Press. (1998). The Internet audience goes ordinary: Online newcomers more middle-brow, less work-oriented. Retrieved from *http://www.peoplepress.org/tech98sum.htm*

Preece, J. (1999). Empathic communities: Balancing emotional and factual communication, *Interacting with Computers, 12*, 63–77.

Putnam, R. D. (1993). *Making democracy work: Civic traditions in modern Italy.* Princeton, NJ: Princeton University Press.

Putnam, R. D. (1995). Tuning in, tuning out: The strange disappearance of social capital in America. *PS: Political Science and Politics*, pp. 664–683.

Putnam, R. D. (2000). *Bowling alone.* New York: Simon & Schuster.

Raney, R. F. (2000, May 11). Study finds Internet of social benefit to users. *New York Times*, Washington edition, p. E7.

Rheingold, H. (1993). *The virtual community: Homesteading on the electronic frontier.* Reading, MA: Addison-Wesley.

Robinson, J. P., Ketsnbaum, M., Neustadtl, A., & Alvarez, A. (2000). Mass media use and social life among Internet users. *Social Science Computer Review, 18,* 490–501.

Robinson, J. P., Ketsnbaum, M., Neustadtl, A., & Alvarez, A. (2002). Information technology, the Internet, and time displacement. Unpublished paper, University of Maryland—College Park.

Rosenblum, N. L. (1998). *Membership and morals.* Princeton: Princeton University Press.

Shah, D. V. (1998). Civic engagement, interpersonal trust, and television use: An individual-level assessment of social capital. *Political Communication, 19,* 469–496.

Shah, D. V., Kwak, N., & Holbert, R. L. (2001). "Connecting" and "disconnecting" with civic life: Patterns of Internet use and the production of social capital. *Political Communication, 18,* 141–162.

St. George, D. (1999, November 26). On the Web, a world of hope is spun for teen. *Washington Post,* pp. A1, A28.

Stolle, D. (1998). Bowling together, bowling alone: The development of generalized trust in voluntary associations. *Political Psychology, 19,* 497–526.

Tranvik, T. (2000). Surfing together and the rise of social capital? Unpublished manuscript, LOS Centre, University of Bergen, Bergen, Norway.

U.S. News and World Report. (2000, August 28). The Web's dark side, pp. 36–45.

Uslaner, E. M, (1998). Social capital, television, and the "mean world": Trust, optimism, and civic participation. *Political Psychology, 19,* 441–467.

Uslaner, E. M. (2000). Social capital and the Net. *Proceedings of the ACM, 43,* 60–64.

Uslaner, E. M. (2002). *The moral foundations of trust.* New York: Cambridge University Press.

Verba, S., Schlozman, K. L., & Brady, H. (1995). *Voice and equality: Civic voluntarism in American politics.* Cambridge, MA: Harvard University Press.

Wallace, P. (1999). *The psychology of the Internet.* New York: Cambridge University Press.

Wellman, B., & Gulia, M. (1999). Net surfers don't ride alone: Virtual communities as communities. In P. Kollock and M. Smith (Eds.), *Communities and cyberspace.* New York: Routledge.

Online Businesses Would Do Well to Cultivate Their Visitors' Adventurous,
Trusting, Optimistic, Risk-taking World Views.
By Eric M. Uslaner

Commercial Web sites have been making concerted efforts to reassure their customers that their transactions and personal information are safe. This site won't violate your privacy, we are told. This is all to the good, but Web site designers must also be concerned with something over which they have no control: Are people generally trusting? If not, they may steer away from risky activities, including Web commerce.

Over a recent lunch with a survey researcher who works at a nonprofit institution in Washington, D.C., we discussed my work on trust. I had just finished a talk at his organization where I distinguished between strategic trust, or the kind of trust that reflects our experience with particular people doing particular things, and moralistic (or generalized) trust, or a more general value we learn early in life. Strategic trust can help us decide whether a specific Web site is safe: Is our information secure there? Will it install spyware on our computers? Will it redirect us to places we don't want to go on the Internet? And if it's a commercial Web site, will it deliver what it promises? We can learn about these sites by reading about them or by our own direct experience.

Moralistic trust is not based upon everyday experience but instead on an optimistic world view we learn at an early age: The world is a good place; it is going to get better; I can make it better; and it is thus not so great a risk to agree that most people can be trusted. Moralistic trust won't tell us anything about a particular Web site or personalities on the Web. However, moralistic trust will give us sufficient faith to take risks on the Web in the first place. Mistrusters will simply stay away altogether.

My colleague asked: You say trust is not based upon experience, but what about the Internet? All sorts of danger lurks there; just to get online one must establish a firewall, because people are constantly trying to hack into your system. He runs a virus checker constantly and at least once a week uses a spyware search utility to see which companies are trying to track his every move. His email has a spam filter to isolate the dozens of daily invitations to pornographic Web sites and other attempts to sell him stuff he doesn't want. Then there is the teenager haven of instant messaging, which, we now learn, is a major source of identity theft online. So how can we expect people to suffer through all of this insecurity and still believe that most people can be trusted?

My colleague thinks the Internet is a source of trust and mistrust. But the Internet really depends upon trust rather than creates trust. People who trust each other are more likely to be comfortable with new technology, even if they don't trust particular Web sites. Most online retailers go to great lengths to demonstrate their trustworthiness. EBay's "Safe Harbor" promises a (limited) guarantee against online fraud, giving each seller a rating for integrity. Online merchants trade in strategic trust, the good reputation of sellers, and the company itself. The company that claims to ensure privacy online calls itself Truste. This is all to the good, but moralistic trust plays a more important role in shaping whether people view the Internet as a great new opportunity or as a threat.

Consider the optimists first: Michael and Ronda Hauben in their 1997 book *Netizens* called the Internet "a grand intellectual and social commune in the spirit of the collective nature present at the origins of human society." Others view new Web sites (such as friendster.com) as great hopes for getting people together in pursuit of common goals or just simple love. Meetup.com brought 150,000 Americans together to support Howard Dean, who set records for raising campaign funds on the Internet in 2003. Everett Ehrlich, a former U.S. Undersecretary of Commerce, wrote in The *Washington Post* that the days of political parties are over; citizens can now take politics away from the professionals and put it into their own hands.

Alex Salcedo, a 13-year-old boy from Kensington, MD, was hit by a car near his home in 1999. He was rushed to a local hospital and put into an induced coma; the prognosis was not good. His father created a Web page so the family could keep apprised of his medical condition; eventually Alex died. The Web site received 66,000 hits, with 2,000 messages posted.

Mistrusters bring us back to reality. Kaycee Nicole Swenson, a 19-year-old girl from Kansas suffering from leukemia, created a blog of her illness and remissions called Living Colours; thousands of people visited her site for almost a year. Many sent her gifts, and all were sad when the site announced her death May 15, 2003. It was all a hoax; there never was a Kaycee. The blogger was really a 40-year-old woman with two healthy children.

Back to reality again. Friendster has almost four million registered users, but nobody knows how many of them are real people. The *New York Times* (Nov. 27, 2003) reported 2,619 "pretendsters" have been terminated by the site, but it is still pretty easy to go on a cyberdate with someone who isn't really there.

Mistrusters would argue that Kaycee Swenson illustrates you can't be too careful dealing with people. It might do little harm to read her story, but don't send her gifts, and be very wary of sending anyone money on the Internet. Trusters would say miscreants are everywhere, and a handful of bad experiences should not cause us to withdraw from social connections, especially with people we don't know.

The Internet can seem a trusting or a mistrusting place. But it is largely a reflection, perhaps in bas relief, of the larger society. All around us we see both nice people and scoundrels. The Internet can scare away someone who already doesn't trust other people, as I showed in the *2000 Trust and Privacy Survey* of the Pew Internet and American Life Project. Mistrusters overestimate the amount of risk in their worlds. Hackers might steal their credit card number; businesses can get their personal information; their Web dealings might not be private; others will know where they have been on the Web; they might download viruses; and others will learn private things about their lives. Mistrusters are less likely to use their real names on the Web and more likely to use fake identifications and email addresses.

People who trust others underestimate the risks of daily life and are more likely to go online and give out personal information. They adapt more quickly to new technologies and dismiss the chance that their computers will be infected by viruses when they're online.

Before deciding whether to buy from an online retailer, we must first be comfortable with new technology. Moralistic trusters are risk takers and don't feel threatened by online transactions. Online retailers should pay as much attention to this type of trust as they do to their own trustworthiness. At a site like eBay, you can fall prey to sellers who manipulate their ratings or to people with no history at all but who offer deals too good to be true; I was taken in by both.

Strategic trust may lead people away from online commerce after bad experiences. Moralistic trusters look at a negative experience as just that and discount bad news. A new technology like the Internet needs more than just the strategic trust a retailer can provide. Its future may depend upon a more general faith in humanity, not just in machines.

By Herman Daly

I am very grateful to the National Council for Science and the Environment for magnanimously conferring on me their "lifetime achievement award." The achievement award is a great encouragement to me, even though the adjective "lifetime" inevitably evokes the preview of an obituary—a kindly intended yet sobering *memento mori*. More than an encouragement for my remaining years, however, I believe this award will be an encouragement to those younger people to whom the real work of building the green economy will fall.

There are many friends and collaborators with whom credit must be shared for any achievement that somehow gets credited to my account. First and foremost is my life partner and wife of 46 years, Marcia Damasceno Daly. Next my co-authors: Robert Costanza, John Cobb, Robert Goodland, Josh Farley, Brian Czech, and my colleagues Salah El Serafy, David Batker, Peter Victor, and Peter Brown. And thanks to Louisiana State University, the World Bank, and the University of Maryland for employment and support.

What I like best about this conference is that it focuses on important questions too often avoided. I'd like to take this occasion to say a few words about just one of the questions raised by the organizers, namely:

WHAT DOES ECONOMIC GROWTH MEAN IN A GREEN ECONOMY?

Let me first consider the meaning of "economic growth;" next the meaning of a "green economy"; and then try to put them together.

The term "economic growth" has two distinct meanings. Sometimes it refers to the growth of that thing we call the economy (the physical subsystem of our world made up of the stocks of population and wealth; and the flows of production and consumption). When the economy gets physically bigger we call that "economic growth." This is normal English usage. But the term has a second, very different meaning—if the growth of some thing or some activity causes benefits to increase faster than costs we also call that "economic growth"—that is to say, growth that is economic in the sense that it yields a net benefit or a profit. That too is accepted English usage.

Now, does "economic growth" in the first sense imply "economic growth" in the second sense? No, absolutely not! Economic growth in the first sense (an economy that gets physically bigger) is logically quite consistent with *uneconomic* growth in the second sense, namely growth that increases costs faster than benefits thereby making us poorer. Nevertheless, we assume that a bigger economy must always make us richer. This is pure confusion.

That economists should contribute to this confusion is puzzling because all of *micro*economics is devoted to finding the optimal scale of a given activity—the point beyond which marginal costs exceed marginal benefits and further growth would be uneconomic. Marginal Revenue = Marginal Cost is even called the "when to stop rule" for growth of a firm. Why does this simple logic of optimization disappear in *macro*economics? Why is the growth of the macroeconomy not subject to an analogous "when to stop rule"?

We recognize that all microeconomic activities are parts of the larger macroeconomic system, and their growth causes displacement and sacrifice of other parts of the system. But the macroeconomy itself is thought to be the whole shebang, and when it expands, presumably into the void, it displaces nothing, and therefore incurs no opportunity cost. But this is false of course. The macroeconomy too is a *part*, a subsystem of the biosphere, a part of the Greater Economy of the natural ecosystem. Growth of the macroeconomy too imposes a rising opportunity cost that at some point will constrain its growth.

But some say that if our empirical measure of growth is GDP, based on voluntary buying and selling of final goods and services in free markets, then that guarantees that growth consists of goods, not bads. This is because people will voluntarily buy only goods. If they in fact do buy a bad then we have to redefine it as a good. True enough as far as it goes, which is not very far. The free market does not price bads, true—but nevertheless bads are inevitably produced as joint products along with goods. Since bads are un-priced GDP accounting cannot subtract them—instead it registers the additional production of anti-bads, and counts them as goods. For example, we do not subtract the cost of pollution, but we do add the value of the pollution clean-up. This is asymmetric accounting. In addition we count the consumption of natural capital (depletion of mines, wells, aquifers, forests, fisheries, topsoil, etc.) as if it were income. Paradoxically, therefore, GDP, whatever else it may measure, is *also* the best statistical index we have of the aggregate of pollution, depletion, congestion, and loss of biodiversity. Economist Kenneth Boulding suggested, with tongue only a little bit in cheek, that we re-label it Gross Domestic *Cost*. At least we should put the costs and the benefits in separate accounts for comparison. Not surprisingly, economists and psychologists are now discovering that, beyond a sufficiency threshold, the positive correlation between GDP and self-evaluated happiness disappears.

In sum, economic growth in sense 1 can be, and in the US has become, *uneconomic* growth in sense 2. And it is sense 2 that matters.

Enough on economic growth. What then is a green economy? It is an economy that imitates green plants as far as possible. Plants use scarce terrestrial materials to capture abundant solar energy, and are careful to recycle the materials for reuse. Although humans are not able to photosynthesize we can imitate the strategy of maximizing use of the sun while economizing on terrestrial minerals, fossil fuels, and ecological services. Ever since the industrial revolution our strategy has been the opposite. Fortunately, as economist Georgescu-Roegen noted, we have not yet learned how to mine the sun and use up tomorrow's solar energy for today's growth. But we can mine the earth and use up tomorrow's fossil fuels, minerals, and waste absorption capacities today. We have eagerly done this to grow the economy, but have neglected the fact that at some point economic growth in sense 1 becomes *uneconomic* growth in sense 2.

In spite of the fact that green plants have no brains they have managed to avoid the error of becoming dependent on the less abundant source of available energy. A green economy must do likewise—seek to maximize use of the abundant flow of solar low entropy and economize on the scarce stock of terrestrial low entropy. Specifically, a green economy would invest scarce terrestrial minerals in things like windmills, photovoltaic cells, and plows (or seed drills)—not squander them on armaments, Cadillacs, and manned space stunts. A green economy can be sufficient, sustainable, and even wealthy—but it cannot be a growth-based economy. A green economy must seek to *develop* qualitatively without *growing* quantitatively—to get *better* without getting *bigger*.

There is another kind of green economy that seeks to be green after the manner of greenback dollars, rather than green plants. Green dollars, unlike green plants, cannot photosynthesize. But dollars can miraculously be created out of nothing and grow exponentially at compound interest in banks. However, Aristotle noted that this kind of growth is very suspect, because money has no reproductive organs. Unlike green plants, green money seeks to grow forever in the realm of abstract exchange value, even as we encounter limits to growth in the realm of the concrete use values for which money is supposed to be an honest token and symbol.

Recently we have grown, or rather "swollen," by expanding the symbolic realm of finance. Debt is a mere number (like negative pigs) and can easily grow faster than the real wealth (positive pigs), by which it is expected to be redeemed. Wall Street has bought and sold an astronomical number of negative pigs-in-a-poke—they have "sold bets on debts and called them assets," as Wendell Berry succinctly put it. We have recently experienced the failure of this fraudulent attempt to force expansion. Yet we have so far been unable to imagine any policy other than restarting the old growth economy for another round. After the next crisis we should try to avoid the Ponzi scheme of growth and build a steady-state economy—a green economy that is sustainable, just, and sufficient for a good life.

For more on that subject, and for serious intellectual and political efforts on its behalf, by people who I hope will be receiving your lifetime achievement award in the not too distant future, please Google the Center for the Advancement of the Steady State Economy, the US Society for Ecological Economics, and Solutions.org.—Thank you!

A REVIEW AND ASSESSMENT BY THE CENTER FOR INTEGRATIVE ENVIRONMENTAL RESEARCH (CIER) AT THE UNIVERSITY OF MARYLAND

Contributing Authors:

Sean Williamson, Research Assistant,
Center for Integrative Environmental Research

Colleen Horin, Research Assistant, Center for Integrative Environmental Research

Matthias Ruth, Director, Center for Integrative Environmental Research

Roy F. Weston, Chair for Natural Economics

Kim Ross, Executive Director, Center for Integrative Environmental Research

Daraius Irani, Director, Regional Economic Studies Institute (RESI)
of Towson University

INTRODUCTION

Climate Change and the Cost of Inaction

Policymakers across the country are now seeking solutions to curb greenhouse gas emissions and to help us adapt to the impending impacts triggered by past emissions. The debate to date has primarily focused on the perceived costs of alternative solutions, yet there can also be significant costs of inaction. Climate change will affect our water, energy, transportation, and public health systems, as well as state economies as climate change impacts a wide range of important economic sectors from agriculture to manufacturing to tourism. This Chapter highlights the economic impacts of climate change in Maryland and provides examples of additional ripple effects of climate impacts, such as impacts on reduced spending in other sectors and resulting losses of jobs, wages, and tax revenues.

It is a key premise of this Chapter that climate will continue to change even if emissions of greenhouse gases will be drastically reduced. This is because the interdependent physical, chemical and biological processes in the oceans, atmosphere and on land do not respond instantly to changes in greenhouse gas emissions and because those greenhouse gases have mean residence times in the atmosphere of decades to over a century. While it is imperative that humans reduce their disruptive impact on climate and ecosystems, they must begin to prepare themselves for the changes they have kicked off since the industrial revolution.

Responses to climate change in the public, private and nonprofit sectors typically are separated conceptually into mitigation and adaptation actions. These two kinds of responses have often been perceived as fundamentally different: mitigation reduces emissions of greenhouse gases with benefits to the larger global community, whereas adaptation reduces vulnerabilities of individual sectors or regions, without necessarily addressing the root causes of climate change. However, considerable overlap between climate change mitigation and adaptation actions exists (Pielke et al. 2007, Ruth et al. 2006), and spending on one can simultaneously advance the goals of the other. Furthermore, mitigation and adaptation can promote broader goals of social, economic and environmental resilience, which will be essential to preparing society for a wide range of future changes, including those associated with climate.

Past research and modeling have concentrated on the quantification of costs for specific mitigation measures and, to a much smaller extent, on cost of adaptation actions. The narrow focus on mitigation was prompted because mitigation is essential to address the root causes of human-induced climate change. The focus on mitigation cost was justified by the fact that benefits of mitigation efforts are frequently diffuse and hard to quantify. The discussion of adaptation strategies has long been relegated to the sidelines, largely because adaptation was perceived to simply provide local benefits without taking on global responsibilities. Similar to mitigation, quantification of adaptation costs concentrated on the up-front financial burden to those who take action.

Not all environmentally induced impacts on infrastructures, economy, society and ecosystems reported here can be directly related to climate change. However, historical as well as modeled future environmental conditions are consistent with a world experiencing changing climate (Ruth 2006).

Models illustrate what may happen if we do not act now to effectively address climate change and if adaptation efforts are inadequate. Estimates of the costs of adapting environmental and infrastructure goods and services to climate change can provide insight into the very real costs of inaction, or conversely, the benefits of maintaining and protecting societal goods and services through effective policies that avoid the most severe climate impacts. Since it is typically at the sector and local levels where those costs are borne and benefits are received, cost estimates can provide powerful means for galvanizing the discussion about climate change policy and investment decision-making.

These cost estimates may understate impacts on the economy and society to the extent that they simply cover what can be readily captured in monetary terms. The broader impacts on the social fabric, long-term economic competitiveness of the state nationally and internationally, changes in environmental quality and quality of life largely are outside the purview of the analysis, yet are not likely trivial at all. Together, the monetary and non-monetary, direct, indirect and induced costs on society and the economy provide a strong basis on which to justify actions to mitigate and adapt to climate change.

The remainder of the first section provides a primer on the science of climate change, the subsequent effects expected to manifest globally, in the Northern Hemisphere, and in Maryland, and the methodology used in this Chapter. The second section focuses specifically on Maryland and discusses the physical changes expected to play out in the state over the coming century. The third section suggests the impacts of climate change on Maryland's coastal infrastructure. The fourth section elaborates on economic costs and benefits expected to be incurred by Maryland tourism, agriculture, natural resources, and human health as a result of climate change. The fifth and final section assembles and recaps the expected economic costs, identifies specific data and knowledge gaps, and highlights the need for further understanding of the significant economic impacts of climate change.

A Primer on Climate Change

Earth's climate is regulated, in part, by the presence of gases and particles in the atmosphere which are penetrated by short-wave radiation from the sun and which trap the longer wave radiation that is reflecting back from Earth. Collectively, those gases are referred to as greenhouse gases (GHGs) because they can trap radiation on Earth in a manner analogous to that of the glass of a greenhouse and have a warming effect on the globe. Among the other most notable GHGs are carbon dioxide (CO_2), methane (CH_4), nitrous oxide (N_2O) and chlorofluorocarbons (CFCs). Their sources include fossil fuel combustion, agriculture, and industrial processes.

Each GHG has a different atmospheric concentration, mean residence time in the atmosphere, and different chemical and physical properties. As a consequence, each GHG has a different ability to upset the balance between incoming solar radiation and outgoing long-wave radiation. This ability to influence Earth's radiative budget is known as climate forcing. Climate forcing varies across chemical species in the atmosphere. Spatial patterns of radiative forcing are relatively uniform for CO_2, CH_4, N_2O and CFCs because these gases are relatively long-lived and as a consequence become more evenly distributed in the atmosphere.

Steep increases in atmospheric GHG concentrations have occurred since the industrial revolution. Those increases are unprecedented in Earth's history. As a result of higher GHG concentrations, global average surface temperature has risen by about 0.6°C over the twentieth century, with 10 of the last 12 years likely the warmest in the instrumental record since 1861 (IPCC 2007a).

A change in average temperatures may serve as a useful indicator of changes in climate, but it is only one of many ramifications of higher GHG concentrations. Since disruption of Earth's energy balance is neither seasonally nor geographically uniform, effects of climate disruption vary across space as well as time. For example, there has been a widespread retreat of mountain glaciers during the twentieth century. Scientific evidence also suggests that there has been a 40 percent decrease in Arctic sea ice thickness during late summer to early autumn in recent decades and considerably slower decline in winter sea ice thickness. The extent of Northern Hemisphere spring and summer ice sheets has decreased by about 10 to 15 percent since the 1950s (IPCC 2007a).

The net loss of snow and ice cover, combined with an increase in ocean temperatures and thermal expansion of the water mass in oceans, has resulted in a rise of global average sea level between 0.1 and 0.2 meters during the twentieth century, which is considerably higher than the average rate during the last several millennia (Barnett 1984; Douglas 2001; IPCC 2001).

Changes in heat fluxes through the atmosphere and oceans, combined with changes in reflectivity of the earth's surface may result in altered frequency and severity of climate extremes around the globe (Easterling, et al. 2000; Mehl, et al. 2000). For example, it is likely that there has been a 2 to 4 percent increase in the frequency of heavy precipitation events in the mid and high latitudes of the Northern Hemisphere over the latter half of the twentieth century, while in some regions, such as Asia and Africa, the frequency and intensity of droughts have increased in recent decades (IPCC 2001). Furthermore, the timing and magnitude of snowfall and snowmelt may be significantly affected (Frederick and Gleick 1999), influencing erosion rates, water quality agricultural productivity, and many other attributes of our biophysical environment. Since evaporation increases exponentially with water temperature, global climate change-induced sea surface temperature increases are likely to result in increased frequency and intensity of hurricanes and increased size of the regions affected.

The physical changes in Maryland resulting from climate change will generally be similar to changes in the Northern Hemisphere, but the local-scale changes that are tightly correlated to Maryland's geography, hydrology, and ecology will be of the utmost significance to the state's natural resources, economy and its people. Maryland can expect temperatures to be warmer during every season, with the largest deviations from average temperature occurring during the summer months. Annual precipitation will increase and more winter precipitation will fall as rain; there will also be more frequent and intense storms. Sea level rise will inundate and alter much of the Maryland coastline.

Impacts of Climate Change Throughout the United States and Maryland

This study on the economic impacts of climate change in the State of Maryland is intended to help inform the challenging decisions policymakers now face. It builds on a prior assessment by the Center for Integrative Environmental Research, entitled *US Economic Impacts of Climate Change and the Costs of Inaction*, which concluded that throughout the United States, individuals and communities depend on sectors and systems that are expected to be greatly affected by the impacts of continued climate change (Ruth et al. 2007).

- The agricultural sector is likely to experience uneven impacts throughout the country. Initial economic gains from altered growing conditions will likely be lost as temperatures continue to rise. Regional droughts, water shortages, as well as excess precipitation, and spread of pest and diseases will negatively impact agriculture in most regions. Storms and sea level rise threaten extensive coastal infrastructure—including transportation networks, coastal developments, and water and energy supply systems.
- Current energy supply and demand equilibria will be disrupted as electricity consumption climbs when demand grows in peak summer months. At the same time, delivering adequate supply of electricity may become more expensive because of extreme weather events.
- Increased incidence of asthma, heat-related diseases, and other respiratory ailments may result from climate change, affecting human health and well-being.
- More frequent and severe forest fires are expected, putting ecosystems and human settlements at peril.
- The reliability of water supply networks may be compromised, influencing agricultural production, as well as availability of water for household and industrial uses.

While climate impacts will vary on a regional scale, it is at the state and local levels where critical policy and investment decisions are made for the very systems most likely to be affected by climate change—water, energy, transportation and public health systems, as well as important economic sectors such as agriculture, fisheries, forestry, manufacturing, and tourism. Yet, much of the focus, to date, has been on the perceived high cost of reducing greenhouse gas emissions. The costs of inaction are frequently neglected and typically not calculated. These costs include such expenses as rebuilding or preparing infrastructure to meet new realities and the ripple economic impacts on the state's households, the agricultural, manufacturing, commercial and public service sectors.

The conclusions from our nation-wide study highlight the need for increased understanding of the economic impacts of climate change at the state, local and sector level:

- Economic impacts of climate change will occur throughout the country.
- Economic impacts will be unevenly distributed across regions and within the economy and society.
- Negative climate impacts will outweigh benefits for most sectors that provide essential goods and services to society.
- Climate change impacts will place immense strains on public sector budgets.
- Secondary effects of climate impacts can include higher prices, reduced income and job losses.

Methodology

This chapter identifies key economic sectors in Maryland, which are likely affected by climate change, and the main impacts to be expected. The chapter provides examples of the direct economic impacts that could be experienced in the state and presents calculations of indirect effects that are triggered as impacts on one sector in the economy ripple through to others. While we do not suggest that any of the past weather-related impacts on the state are, unequivocally, climate change induced, observations of past impacts can help illustrate the kinds of challenges to be faced in the future, and the kinds of costs to be incurred, should the state not adequately adapt to climate change.

The study reviews and analyzes existing studies such as the 2000 *Global Change Research Program National Assessment of the Potential Consequences of Climate Variability and Change*, which identifies potential regional impacts. Additional regional, state and local studies are used to expand on this work, as well as new calculations derived from federal, state and industry data sources. The economic data is then related to predicted impacts of climate change provided from climate models.

Since the early 1990s, and especially during the 21st century, significant progress has been made in understanding the impacts of climate change at national, regional, and local scales. The Canadian and Hadley climate change models are cited most frequently and we look first to these, yet there are many other valuable models used by some of the specialized studies we cite in this chapter. These models can, at coarse spatial and temporal scales, illustrate how climate change may manifest itself in Maryland. Combining the insights from these models with observations of impacts in the past helps illustrate the nature and magnitude of changes that may lie ahead. One particular issue of interest at the state level are economic ramifications of climate change, including often overlooked ripple economic effects on other sectors and the state economy. To calculate these, we employed a modified IMPLANTM model from the Regional Economic Studies Institute (RESI) of Towson University. This is a standard input/output model and the primary tool used by economists to measure the total economic impact by calculating spin-off impacts (indirect and induced impacts) based upon the direct impacts which are inputted into the model. Direct impacts are those impacts (jobs and output) generated directly by the project. Indirect economic impacts occur as the project (or business owners) purchase local goods and services. Both direct and indirect job creation increases area household income and results in increased local spending on the part of area households. The jobs, wages, output and tax revenues created by increased household spending are referred to as induced economic impacts.

CLIMATE CHANGE IN MARYLAND

In the last century, Maryland has experienced rising temperatures, increased precipitation, more severe weather events, and a rise in sea level. Average annual temperatures for the Mid-Atlantic region have increased by .5–1°F (.3–.6°C) since 1900, which is more than the global average, while Maryland's average annual temperature has increased about 2°F (1°C) (Fisher et al., 1997; US EPA 1998; NOAA 2008a). The average temperature of the Chesapeake Bay has warmed by 2°F over the same time period (MCCC 2008). The greatest temperature increases have occurred during the winter months and all other seasons have increased slightly less (NOAA 2008a). Average precipitation has increased by 10 percent throughout most of Maryland and the entire Mid-Atlantic region of the US has received 12–20 percent more major weather events relative to the previous century (US EPA 1998; NOAA 2008a; IPCC 2001). The sea level along the Maryland coastline has risen at a rate of 3–4 mm/year (.14 inch/year) over the last century—nearly twice the global average of 2 mm/year (.08 inch/year) (MDNR 2008; Oppenheimer et al. 2005).

These trends are predicted to continue or worsen if climate change progresses unchecked. Average yearly temperatures are expected to increase by 3–6°F (2–4°C) in the winter and by 4–8°F (2.2–4.4°C) in the summer (US EPA 1998; IPCC 2007b; MCCC—STWG 2008). Precipitation will increase by 20 percent in Maryland with more rainfall in the winter and less in the spring (US EPA 1997; Fisher et al. 1997; IPCC 2007b). As climate change raises ocean temperatures, alters weather patterns, and contributes to the melting of polar icecaps and subsequent sea level rise, Maryland can expect significant coastal impacts. Major coastal storms will be more intense and more frequent (EPA 1998, IPCC 2007b). By century's end, 5–15 percent more late-winter storms may develop in the Northeast as storm systems move further north in response to warmer ocean surface temperatures (Frumhoff et al. 2007). Perhaps most significant to Maryland, sea level rise will increase by .6–1.22 m (24–48 inches) over the next century along the coast (MCCC 2008; MDNR 2008; IPCC 2007b).

MAJOR ECONOMIC IMPACTS

The largest economic impact of climate change for Maryland will be on its coastal infrastructure and development. By the end of the century, expanding ocean water and melting polar ice caps will raise sea levels and expedite shoreline erosion; an estimated 6.1 percent of Maryland's 4,360 miles of coastline is vulnerable to inundation by 2100 (US EPA 1998; MCCC 2008). Further coastal impacts will come in the form of more frequent and intense storms as well as flooding. Considerable strain will be placed on Maryland's coastal infrastructure and development, not to mention the estimated 6.3 million people that will live in Maryland's counties by 2020 (MDNR 2002; USCB 2006).

Population and economic growth trends will likely place more people and infrastructure at risk of negative climate change impacts in Maryland in the coming decades. Maryland's state gross domestic product has increased nearly 70 percent from 1997–2007 and average per capita income has increased 60 percent in the same time period (US BEA, 2007). The population of Maryland grew 33 percent between 1980 and 2005, and Maryland Department of Planning projects another 20 percent increase in population between 2005 and 2030 (MDP, 2007). These growth trends will require commensurate increases in development of residential and commercial areas, utilities, roads, and public services, all of which increase the amount of assets in Maryland that are vulnerable to damage from climate change.

Development patterns in the Chesapeake Bay watershed show a trend towards higher population density and urban land use, which could exacerbate the effect of climate change on groundwater aquifers by increasing water runoff rates. There was a 21 percent increase in urban land use and a 5.6 percent increase in mixed land use in the Chesapeake Bay watershed from 1985 to 2002. Higher residential densities and associated commercial development raise the imperviousness of ground surfaces, increasing area runoff (Nelson, 2005).

Coastal areas are becoming more susceptible to the effects of climate change as developments and populations grow in those areas. The population density of Maryland's eastern shore increased 30 percent from 1985 to 2002. The total number of people living along the coastline in the United States is predicted to increase from 139 million in 1998 to 165 million in 2020 (Nelson, 2005). These developments put more properties at risk of flooding and storm damage from rising sea levels and more intense weather events.

Currently, Maryland's coastal counties and Baltimore City are home to 67 percent of the state's population in addition to hosting numerous tourist destinations, industrial sites, extensive commercial and residential development, and diverse ecosystems (MDNR 20028a). Because of the economic and geographic differences between Maryland's Baltimore–Washington corridor and its more rural and coastal regions, the effects of climate change will not be uniform across the state. Altogether, sea level rise, flooding, and major storm events will take an exacting toll on Maryland's multi-faceted and economically valuable coastal communities.

Industrial and Urban Coastal Impacts

Among all Baltimore–Washington corridor counties, only Calvert, Anne Arundel, Baltimore, Harford, and Charles counties are coastal, but because of the connectedness of the corridor, it is useful to consider the region in its entirety. The Baltimore–Washington corridor is the most economically valuable region in Maryland with 86 percent of the population and 90 percent of the wages (US EPA 2004). Climate change, and more specifically sea level rise and extreme weather events, will significantly impact *transportation and trade* in the corridor.

The trade, transportation, and utilities sector accounts for $3.4 billion (2007) in wage earnings in the Washington–Baltimore corridor region (US EPA 2004). At the end of FY 2007, the Maryland Department of Transportation calculated it had $13.2 billion (2007) in total assets; among the capital assets are critical arteries for transportation including the Baltimore Harbor Tunnel, the Port McHenry Tunnel, the Chesapeake Bay Bridges, and the Francis Scott Key Bridge (MDOT 2007). Although inundation in Baltimore and Annapolis is expected to be minimal, the increasing rate of shoreline erosion resulting from sea level rise could weaken bridge support systems, limit access for maintenance, and deteriorate low-lying roads (Titus and Richman 2000). Extreme weather events such as hurricanes and tropical storms have the potential to create drastic impacts for Maryland's urban transportation and commerce. For instance, 2003's Hurricane Isabel brought 4–12 inches of rain and storm surges of 6 to 8 feet to Baltimore and Annapolis (Bennett 2005; NOAA 2008b). Water flooded Baltimore's Pratt and Light Streets in addition to numerous local businesses and homes, and the Baltimore Harbor Tunnel was closed for a period of time; the ultimate toll throughout Maryland from Hurricane Isabel was $462 million (2007) (Bennett 2005; Roylance 2006). Such extreme weather events will likely be more intense under a scenario of undeterred greenhouse gas emissions (IPCC 2007).

As for coastal *shipping*, sea level rise poses a serious threat to accessing and operating Maryland ports. The Port of Baltimore produces $1.98 billion (2007) in annual economic benefits and provides for 127,000 maritime related jobs (US EPA 2004). Keeping the appropriate water depth is a critical aspect of port maintenance, and the Port of Baltimore dredges its waterway regularly to keep the flow of goods unimpeded. However, if increased levels of trash and sediment continue to deposit in Baltimore Harbor due to increased levels of runoff upstream from flooding, dredging operations could become both more costly and environmentally damaging (Moss et al. 2002). Low-lying access roads are at risk to flooding while shipping ports will have to adjust infrastructure to establish a working land-sea interface. Commercial fishing and crabbing in Maryland generates more than $207 million (2007) annually and manufacturing contributes $1.76 billion (2007) in wages—both of which are dependent on reliable access to ports from both land and sea (US EPA 2004; BEA 2007). Steadily rising sea levels as well as abrupt nonlinear sea level increases could create economic hardships for Maryland's shipping, fishing, and manufacturing industries. A 1 percent decrease in shipping activity at the Port of Baltimore between now and 2018 would result in an indirect economic impact of roughly $361 million on Maryland's GDP and a loss of more than 3,600 jobs (RESI 2008).

Residential and Rural Coastal Impacts

The economic impacts manifesting from climate change will be significant along the industrial and urbanized Baltimore—Washington corridor, but the most visible, and possibly more expensive economic impacts, will occur along the residential and rural portions of Maryland's coast. Sea level rise in Maryland is predicted to claim more land than the national average due to local conditions that make the shoreline particularly vulnerable to soil erosion and land subsidence. Maryland is the fourth most vulnerable state with an estimated 6.1 percent of its land likely to be inundated by a rise in sea level (MCCC 2008). Currently, an estimated 30 percent of the state's coastline undergoes erosion and an average of 260 acres are lost each year (EPA 2004). Maryland's Southeastern counties are most vulnerable to sea level rise and inundation due to their low-lying topography and exposure to the ocean.

In Maryland, much of the vulnerable land below 3.5 meters is undeveloped barrier island or tidal wetlands (USEPA 2007). Nonetheless, Ocean City and other developed areas along the Eastern shore are very susceptible to rising sea levels. Furthermore, although less than 10 percent of Maryland's population lives on the Eastern shore, the area is culturally significant for the state, it is growing rapidly (i.e., 32.9 percent in Dorchester County), and it is a popular destination for summer vacationers (USEPA 2004). An Environmental Protection Agency study (1985) on Ocean City beaches suggested that without preventative measures, a 15-inch increase in sea level would result in a 216–273 feet loss of shoreline (US EPA 2007). With an estimated 3,750 households in Ocean City and property values that likely exceed one million dollars, such a loss in shoreline and land availability would easily translate into a several billion-dollar loss (USCB 2000). Protecting coastal development from inundation, beach erosion, and salt-water intrusion will be costly and uncertain. Ocean City benefited from a beach replenishment project in the late 1980's, which cost $38 million (2007), but more replenishment will need to occur if Ocean City beaches are to endure increasing sea levels (US EPA 1998).

Rural Maryland will not only incur economic costs from a rise in sea level and increased flooding, but also from more intense storms. Once the wetlands and barrier islands that serve as a buffer between communities and the ocean are deteriorated, damage from extreme events will be enhanced. Hurricane damage along the Northeast US coast has cost an estimated $5 billion (2007) per year with much of this cost coming from single major storm events (Frumhoff et al. 2007). For example, Hurricane Floyd ravaged the Eastern shore of Maryland in 1999 when storm water discharge rates reached 100-year levels and total property damage totaled $17.76 million (2007) (Tallman and Fisher 2000). Last, the insurance sector will likely face unstable periods as property succumbs to flooding and shoreline inundation. For instance, flooding from heavy rains in June of 2006 cost insurers in the Baltimore–Washington region over $25 million (Cohn, 2006). Maryland's finance and insurance sector accounts for $8.5 billion (2007) in wages and salary and supplies 4.2 percent of the states employment base (USBEA 2007). It is predicted that by 2080, insurers' capital requirements to cover the cost of hurricane damage in the US will increase by 90 percent (Association of British Insurers 2005).

It should be noted, that the construction sector benefits from flooding or the destruction of infrastructure, as it will be involved in the rebuilding effort. But while jobs are created in the rebuilding effort, those construction workers are not available to build new buildings and infrastructures elsewhere. As a result, the state's infrastructure and building stock cannot expand to accommodate new economic growth. The insurance sector maybe impacted, but it would likely adjust its rates to reflect new probabilities of flooding and storm damage. This increase in rates would divert disposable income from consumption to that sector.

ADDITIONAL ECONOMIC IMPACTS

In addition to the economic hurdles that will impair Maryland's coastal development and transportation infrastructure, tourism, agriculture and health-related economic losses will likely transpire as a result of climate change.

Tourism

In 2006, Maryland's tourism generated roughly $11.72 billion (2007) in visitor spending, directly supported 116,000 jobs, and created $920 million (2007) in state and local tax revenue (MOTD 2008). Based on tourism-derived state tax revenue from each county, roughly 62 percent of tourist activity takes place in the state's coastal counties, renowned for the public beaches, beachfront real estate, and tourist hotspots, such as Ocean City (MOTD 2008). However, with a weakening coastal infrastructure, beach erosion, and the very real threat of seawater inundation in locations like Ocean City, tourism is likely to suffer in Maryland.

Increasing beach erosion and more major storms may render the Maryland coast a less attractive tourist destination. It is estimated that beaches will erode at a rate of 50 to 100 times faster than the rate of sea level elevation and that the cost of replenishing the coastline after a 20-inch rise in sea level would be between $35 and $200 million (Zhang 2002; US EPA 1998). As the cost of maintaining and protecting beaches from erosion increases, both residents and tourists may find locations like Ocean City are too expensive. As with coastal infrastructure and development, we can expect extreme weather events to be associated with a loss in economic activity in the tourism sector as well. Barrier islands and other tourist destinations around the Eastern Shore are major targets for hurricanes and tropical storms and as storms occur more often and are more intense, tourists may be less willing to risk their vacation.

Maryland is also an ideal location for eco-tourism because of the Chesapeake Bay, which harbors an estimated 2,700 species. In 2006, an estimated 166,000 non-Marylanders spent more than $30 million (2007) on wildlife watching in Maryland (USFWS 2006). However, losses in eco-tourism are likely to result as a 21 percent reduction in mid-Atlantic wetlands between now and 2100 hinders shorebird nesting and fish nurseries (Najjer et al. 2000). Hunting and fishing is also big business in Maryland. The US Fish and Wildlife Service (2006) estimated 43,000 people hunted waterfowl in Maryland in 2006, generating $26.23 million (2007) in economic activity (USFWS 2006). As a result of wetlands loss, the economic activity generated by waterfowl hunters will likely decrease. Climate change is a multidimensional problem for the Chesapeake Bay's aquatic life. Loss of wetlands will restrict species habitat locations, warmer and saltier water will restrict the range of cold, fresh-water species, and hypoxic conditions may be exacerbated, as a longer summer season will support more algae growth cycles (see Table 1) (Glick et al. 2007). In 2006, $308 million (2007) was spent on recreational saltwater fishing in Maryland (USFWS 2006). A 2 percent decrease in out-of-state wildlife watchers between now and 2018 would result in indirect losses to Maryland's GDP of $10 million and a loss of almost 100 jobs (RESI, 2008).

Agriculture

Agriculture is the second-largest land use category in the Mid-Atlantic region after forests (Alber, 2000). The total value of agricultural products in Maryland totaled nearly $1.5 billion (2007) in 2002, with crops accounting for 35 percent of that value (USDA 2002). Corn and soybeans make up the two largest volume crops by acreage (USDA 2002). While an increase in CO_2 concentrations could increase the yields of corn and soybeans, other climate changes will have a net negative effect on yields in the Appalachian region, which includes Maryland (see Table 2) (Abler 2000). As the values of production of corn and

Table 1: Projected Aquatic Species Changes as Result of Climate Change

Species	Likely Trend	Climate Change Impacts
Winter flounder	High Loss[1]	Temperatures could exceed habitable range
Soft-shelled clam	High Loss	Temperatures could exceed habitable range
Rockfish	Medium / Low Loss[2]	Water temperatures could reach near upper limit of habitable range; increased chance of mycobacterial infections
Atlantic Sturgeon	Medium / Low Loss	Water temperatures could reach near upper limit of habitable range
Blue crab	Medium / Low Loss	Declining eelgrass habitat with rising sea level and exacerbated eutrophication
Atlantic menhaden	Medium / Low Loss	Warmer water more conducive to mycobacterial infections
Eastern oyster	Medium / Low Loss	Warmer water more conducive to *Dermo* and *MSX*
Brown shrimp	Potential Gain[3]	Warmer water more favorable
Southern flounder	Potential Gain	Warmer water more favorable
Black Drum	Potential Gain	Warmer water more favorable
Grouper	Potential Gain	Warmer water more favorable
Spotted seatrout	Potential Gain	Warmer water more favorable

[1]Potential loss of species altogether in the Chesapeake Bay

[2]Likely decline in species range or viability in the Chesapeake Bay

[3]Likely expansion of species range or viability in the Chesapeake Bay

These probable effects were identified based on available information, but significant changes in key paramaters such as temperature and salinity are likely to have wide-ranging unpredictable effects on life cycles and food webs

Source: Glick et al. 2007

Table 2: Percent Changes in Regional Crop Yields Under Two Scenarios

Crop	50% increase in CO_2 (365 to 560 ppm)			Change from 1961–90 climate to 2025–34 climate		
	Northeast	Appalachian	Corn Belt	Northeast	Appalachian	Corn Belt
Unirrigated corn	10.5*	11.1*	9.0*	14.3*	−1.7	5.6*
Soybeans	18.6*	18.5*	17.0*	4.6	−7.0	−7.4*
Unirrigated alfalfa	—	—	19.2*	—	—	14.4*

Source: Abler, 2000

soybeans were $204 million and $108 million respectively in Maryland in 2007, future climate changes would have resulted in a loss of $11 million (USDA 2008).

Droughts caused by climate change could also take a severe toll on the agricultural sector. Although Maryland is expected to receive more precipitation, droughts may develop because warmer, more arid temperatures tend to draw moisture out of soil at a rate that offsets increased precipitation. Maryland has suffered through two regional droughts in the past ten years—one from 1998–1999, and another from 2001–2002. The first drought caused $800 million in crop losses throughout the mid-Atlantic region (Kunkle 1999). Consumers and livestock farmers feel the effects of crop loss in the form of higher food and feed prices. The price of a bushel of corn increased from $2.18 to $2.85/bushel, or 30 percent, in Maryland between 2001 and 2002 (USDA 2008).

Another detrimental effect of climate change on agriculture will be the northern expansion of *invasive species* due to higher temperatures, including warm-season weeds, nematodes, and insects (Abler 2000). Maryland farmers spent $39 million (2007) on pesticides in 2002 (USDA 2002) and that price will likely increase, but the cost of using more pesticide includes environmental degradation, as well. Runoff from pesticides contributes to degrading freshwater and coastal ecosystems (Rogers 2000). In addition to pesticide runoff, 64 percent of farms in Maryland have tested positive for cryptosporidiosis, which can reach shellfish populations in the Chesapeake Bay (Moss 2002).

In addition to invasive species, sea level rise due to climate change may cause saltwater intrusion into agricultural waterways and groundwater aquifers. Both rivers and the ocean feed water into the Chesapeake Bay, making it a body of brackish water. The level and extent of salinity in surrounding area groundwater and waterways is mostly a function of sea level (Heywood). Important Maryland crops such as corn and soybeans require very low salinity to grow (less than 2 parts per thousand for corn and less than 3/10 parts per thousand for soy) (Moss 2002). Also, groundwater aquifers that supply potable water might need to invest in desalination technology, which can increase the cost of water by over 50 percent (Kranhold 2008).

The composition of Maryland forests could change as a result of warmer temperatures. The hardwoods currently found in Western and Northern Maryland could be replaced by more heat tolerant southern pines and oaks (US EPA 2008). The threat of forest fires could also increase during the summer as a result of warmer temperatures, though this is dependent on annual precipitation fluctuations. The density of Maryland forests may change little or decrease by as much as 10 percent (US EPA 1998). Maryland's forest industry is the state's fifth largest providing for 18,000 jobs and $2.48 billion in economic activity (MDNR 2008b). Moreover, forestry is the number one industry in Western Maryland and the second largest industry after agriculture on the Eastern shore. With just a 1 percent decrease in harvestable trees as a result of decreased forest density between now and 2018, we can expect an indirect economic loss of over $263 million on Maryland's GDP and a loss of over 1,600 jobs (RESI 2008).

Health

Health impacts related to warmer temperatures and water quality will likely develop in Maryland over the coming century. Higher temperatures can have particularly acute respiratory health effects in cities, where heat islands develop because of concrete and asphalt cover and non-point source pollution causes poor air quality and high concentrations of ground level ozone (Moss, 2002). Maryland can also expect higher rates of heat-related deaths during the summer months. A study by the Johns Hopkins School of Public Health correlated daily mortality rates and temperatures for eleven east coast U.S. cities from 1973–1994 and found that there is a "Minimum mortality temperature" (MMT) above which heat-related deaths increase steadily. The study found that Baltimore ranks first among east coast cities for the rate of increased mortality at temperatures above the MMT (see Table 3) (Curriero et al. 2002). As summer days grow hotter due to climate change, Baltimore and other Maryland cities should be prepared to deal with higher rates of heat-related health effects.

Higher temperatures will also increase demand for water supplies used for both drinking and irrigation. To be sure, low quantities of water are a serious threat to human health, but perhaps more insidious is the problem of impaired water associated with a reduced supply and flooding. Reduced water supplies lead to a higher concentration of bacteria, pesticides and other unwanted biological organisms as well as chemical substances than would be present under normal conditions. Moreover, warmer water and longer seasons facilitate the growth of algae and harmful bacteria that lead to fish kills and generally poor water quality. Where warmer temperatures do not impair water quality, flooding from an elevated sea could potentially introduce bacteria, harmful chemicals and salt water into fresh drinking water sources (Frumhoff et al. 2007). In 1992, for example, salt water recharged the Potomac-Raritan-Magothy aquifer and the chloride concentrations increased from 10mg/liter to 70mg/liter; a higher than ideal amount of chloride for drinking water (Oppenheimer et al. 2005).

In addition to sea level rise, increased precipitation will take a toll on public health in Maryland. Another study from the Johns Hopkins School of Public Health shows a positive correlation between higher-than-average precipitation events and outbreaks of waterborne diseases (Curriero et al. 2001). Greater intensity runoff events can increase particulate and chemical concentrations in aquifers for drinking water, as well. Runoff can damage water and sewage treatment plants and cause septic tanks to fail, both of which increase the risk of drinking water contamination (Neff et al. 2000).

City	Minimum Mortality Temperature (MMT)[1]	Cold slope[2]	Hot slope[3]
Boston, Massachusetts	69.71	−4.34	5.83
Chicago, Illinois	65.17	−2.25	2.45
New York, New York	66.42	−3.59	6.28
Philadelphia, Pennsylvania	70.58	−4.37	6.11
Baltimore, Maryland	70.46	−2.65	6.56
Washington, D.C.	70.56	−3.13	3.67
Charlotte, North Carolina	90.38	−3.27	NA
Atlanta, Georgia	76.29	−2.91	5.41
Jacksonville, Florida	76.75	−3.76	3.71
Tampa, Florida	80.71	−7.12	1.43
Miami, Florida	80.92	−5.46	4.01

[1] Percentage change in mortality per degree centigrade

[2] Cold slope = average slope of the estimated relative risk curves at temperatures lower than MMT

[3] Hot slope = average slope of the estimated relative risk curves at temperatures hotter than MMT

CONCLUSION

Recap of Climate Change Impacts

The economic impacts of climate change on Maryland will depend on the exact physical changes that manifest. Although there is a degree of uncertainty, the consensus scientific literature agrees that annual average temperatures will increase by 3–8°F, annual average precipitation will increase by roughly 20 percent, there will be more frequent and intense late-winter storms, and sea levels will rise by 24–48 inches in Maryland, throughout this century (Fisher et al. 1997; US EPA 1998; NOAA 2008a). The physical changes that develop will significantly alter the State's coastline, beachfront, agricultural productivity, species biodiversity, weather patterns and other factors that are tightly correlated with economic conditions.

Another critical factor dictating how the economic impacts of climate change play in Maryland is population growth and development. As Maryland's population grows by 20 percent between now and 2020 and as the State's GDP grows at a rate between 60–70 percent, economic losses from climate change will run in parallel (US BEA 2007; MDP 2007). By becoming a more populated, developed, and economically interconnected State, there will be more avenues for direct and indirect effects of climate change to impact the State. The growing and interconnected nature of the State could potentially make it more vulnerable to the cascade effects of climate change if there isn't a strong effort now to stimulate a resilient and robust economy that can cope with the expected impacts of climate change.

Missing Information and Data Gaps

This study is subject to the uncertainties inherent in measuring global climate change impacts and climate change itself and attempts to reflect this as best as possible through use of scenarios and ranges of confidence. Additionally, quantifying the economic impacts of climate change deserves significantly more focus as this chapter and much of the literature on the topic primarily address the potential impacts from a qualitative perspective. Further, data gaps exist between the effects of climate change in one particular sector and the ripple effects that manifest in interconnected sectors. Analysis of this sort would be useful to policy-makers and businesses at all levels and sizes. Information that would be especially useful for policy makers would be more precise figures, e.g., for land and property along the highly threatened portions of Maryland's coast.

Recommendations and Considerations

Maryland's greatest challenge is likely to be in adapting to climate change along its expansive coast, as this is where the most significant economic and ecological impacts will occur. The State's economy is particularly vulnerable because of the scale of development along the coast and the high rate at which coastal erosion and subsequent water elevation will afflict its shoreline. Further development along the State's shoreline needs to be carried out with the understanding that the shoreline is not stationary and will steadily move inwards throughout the coming century. Lastly, legislators may want to consider legislation to circumvent health related impacts of climate change related to the urban heat island effect and decreases in fresh drinking water quality and quantity. The urban heat island effect can be mitigated through careful city planning and smart growth (e.g., incorporating more green space into development sites). One tactic for maintaining water quality is to encourage streamside tree planting and plant buffer strips as they absorb harmful pollutants as well as reduce water warming.

Lessons Learned

As we begin to quantify the potential impacts of climate change and the cost of inaction, the following five lessons are learned:

- First, there are already considerable costs to society associated with infrastructures, agricultural and silvicultural practices, land use choices, transportation and consumptive behaviors that are not in synch with past and current climatic conditions. These costs are likely to increase as climate change accelerates over the century to come.
- Second, while some of the benefits from climate change may accrue to individual farms or businesses, the cost of dealing with adverse climate impacts are typically borne by society as a whole. These costs to society will not be uniformly distributed but felt most among small businesses and farms, the elderly and socially marginalized groups.
- Third, benefits from climate change may be fleeting—for example, climate does not stop to change once a farm benefited from temporarily improved growing conditions. In contrast, costs of inaction are likely to stay and to increase.
- Fourth, climate models and impact assessments are becoming increasingly refined, generating information at higher spatial and temporal resolutions than previously possible.

Yet, little consistency exists among studies to enable "summing up" impacts and cost figures across sectors and regions to arrive at a comprehensive, statewide result.

- Fifth, to provide not just a comprehensive statewide assessment of impacts and cost, but to develop optimal portfolios for investment and policy strategies will require support for integrative environmental research that combines cutting-edge engineering solutions with environmental, economic and social analysis. The effort and resources required for an integrative approach likely pale in comparison to the cost of inaction.

Works Cited

Abler, D.G., and Shortle, J.S. 2000. Climate change and agriculture in the Mid-Atlantic region. *Climate Research* 14: 185–194.

Association of British Insurers. 2005. Financial Risks of Climate Change. Available online at http://www.abi.org.uk/Display/File/Child/506/Financial_Risks_of_Climate_Change.pdf

Barnett, T.P. 1984. The Estimation of "Global" Sea Level Change: A Problem of Uniqueness. *Journal of Geophysical Research* 89: 7980–7988.

Bennett, K. 2005. When Will the Bay Flood Again?: Understanding the Ups and the Downs of the Chesapeake Bay. BayWeekly.com (Vol. 13: Issue 36). Available Online: http://www.bayweekly.com/year05/issuexiii36/leadxiii36.html

Bureau of Economic Analysis (BEA). 2007. Available Online: www.bea.gov.

Bureau of Labor Statistics. 2008. Inflation Calculator. Available Online: http://data.bls.gov/cgibin/cpicalc.pl Cohn, Meredith. June 30, 2006. Storm claims likely to top $25 million: but the cost of damage is expected to be far more. The Baltimore Sun. Available online: http://www.accessmylibrary.com/coms2/summary_0286-16539716_ITM.

Curriero, F.C., Patz, J.A., Rose, J.B., Lele, S. 2001. The Association Between Extreme Precipitation and Waterborne Disease Outbreaks in the United States, 1948–1994. *American Journal of Public Health* 91(8): 1194–1199.

Curriero, F.C., Heiner, K.S., Samet, J.M., Zeger, S.L., Strug, L., Patz, J.A. 2002. Temperature and mortality in 11 cities of the eastern United States. *American Journal of Epidemiology* 155(1): 80–87.

Douglas, B.C. 2001. *An Introduction to Sea Level, in Sea level Rise: History and Consequences.* B.C. Douglas, M.S. Kirney, and S.P. Leatherman (eds), San Diego, CA: Academic Press, pp. 1–11.

Easterling, D. R., G. A. Mehl, et al. 2000. Climate Extremes: Observations, Modeling, and Impacts. *Science* 289: 2068–2074.

Fisher, A., Barron, E., Yarnal, B., Knight, C.G., and Shortle, J. 1997. Climate Change Impacts in the Mid-Atlantic Region—A Workshop Report. Pennsylvania State University. Available Online: http://www.usgcrp.gov/usgcrp/nacc/mara-workshop-report-1997.pdf

Frumhoff, P.C. et al. 2007. Confronting Climate Change in the US. Northeast: Science, Impacts and Solutions. Union of Concerned Scientists. Available online at http://www.climatechoicesorg/ne/resources_ne/nereport.html.

Glick, P., Staudt, A., and Inkley, D. 2007. The Chesapeake Bay and Global Warming: A Paradise Lost for Hunters, Anglers, and Outdoor Enthusiasts? National Wildlife Federation. Available Online: http://www.nwf.org/sealevelrise/chesapeake.cfm

Heywood, Charles. 2003. Influence of the Chesapeake Bay Impact Structure on Groundwater Flow and Salinity. U.S. Geological Survey. Available online at: http://va.water.usgs.gov/GLOBAL/vwwrc.pdf

Intergovernmental Panel on Climate Change (IPCC). 2001. The Scientific Basis. Contribution of Working Group 1 to the Third Assessment Report of the Intergovernmental Panel on Climate Change. Eds. J.T. Houghton. Y. Ding, D.J. Griggs, M. Noguer, P.J. van der Linden, X. Dai, K. Maskell and C.A. Johnson. Cambridge, England and New York, NY: Cambridge University Press. Available online at http://www.grida.no/climate/ipcc_tar/

IPCC. 2007a. Climate Change 2007: Synthesis Report for the Fourth Assessment Report of the Intergovernmental Panel on Climate Change. Available Online: http://www.ipcc.ch/ipccreports/ar4-syr.htm

IPCC. 2007b. Chapter 11: Regional Climate Projections; Section 11.5: North America. Working Group I: The physical science basis of Climate Change. Available Online: http://ipcc.wg1.ucar.edu/wg1/Report/AR4WG1_Print_Ch11.pdf

Kranhold, Kathryn. January 17, 2008. Water, Water Everywhere. *The Wall Street Journal.* Available online at: http://online.wsj.com/article/SB120053698876396483.html?mod=googlenews_wsj.

Kunkle, F. and Brown, K. Farmers in Mid-Atlantic Region Suffers Severe Crop Losses in Drought. Business Network online article. Available online at: http://findarticles.com/p/articles/mi_hb5553/is_199908/ai_n22420506?tag=rel.res4.

Maryland Commission on Climate Change (MCCC). 2008. Climate Action Plan: Interim Report to the Governor and the Maryland General Assembly. Available Online: http://www.mde.state.md.us/assets/document/air/Interim_Climate_Action_Plan.pdf

Maryland Commission on Climate Change, Scientific and Technical Working Group (MCCC—STWG). April 25, 2008. Progress Report. (Personal Communication).

Maryland Department of Natural Resources (MDNR). 2002. Maryland's Coastal Program: Coastal Facts. Available Online: http://www.dnr.state.md.us/bay/czm/coastal_facts.html

Maryland Department of Natural Resources (MDNR). 2008a. DNR Answers Questions About Sea Level Rise in Response to IPCC Report. Available Online: http://www.dnr.state.md.us/dnrnews/infocus/sealevel_rise.asp

Maryland Department of Natural Resources (MDNR). 2008b. Forest Facts of Maryland. Available Online: http://www.dnr.state.md.us/forests/forester/mdfacts.asp

Maryland Department of Planning (MDP). 2007. Available Online: http://www.mdp.state.md.us/msdc/dw_Popproj.htm.

Maryland Department of Transportation (MDOT). 2007. Comprehensive Annual Financial Report: FY 07. Available Online: http://www.mdot.state.md.us/Transportation_Revenues_and_Expenses/Documents/2007_CAFR.pdf

Maryland Office of Tourism Development (MOTD). 2008. Maryland Tourism Fast Facts. Available Online: http://www.mdisfun.org/resources/FastFacts2008Final3forWeb.pdf

Moss, R.H., Malone, E.L., Ramachander, S., Perez, M.R. July 2, 2002. Climate Change Impacts: Maryland Resources at Risk. Joint Global Change Research Institute.

Najjar, R.G. et al. 2000. The Potential Impacts of Climate Change on the Mid-Atlantic Coastal Region. *Climate Research Journal* (14) 219–233.

National Oceanic and Atmospheric Administration (NOAA). 2008a. Satellite and Information Service. Maryland. Available Online: http://www.ncdc.noaa.gov/oa/climate/research/cag3/md.html

National Oceanic and Atmospheric Administration (NOAA). 2008b. Billion Dollar U.S. Weather Disasters. Available Online: http://www.ncdc.noaa.gov/oa/reports/billionz.html

Neff, R., Chang, H., Knight, C.G., Najjar, R.G., Yarnal, B., and Walker, H.A. 2000. Impact of climate variation and change on Mid-Atlantic Region hydrology and water resources. *Climate Research* 14:207–218.

Nelson, R.H. August 2005. "A Bigger Bang for the Buck: Offsets and other Cost-Effective strategies for Nitrogen Reductions for the Chesapeake Bay." Maryland School of Public Policy.

Oppenheimer, M. et al. 2005. Future Sea Level Rise and The New Jersey Coast: Assessing Potential Impacts and Opportunities.

Pielke, R., G. Prins, S. Rayner and D. Sarewitz. 2007. Lifting the Taboo on Adaptation, *Nature,* Vol. 445, No. 8, pp. 597–598

Rogers, C.E., and McCarty, J.P. 2000. Climate change and ecosystems of the Mid-Atlantic region. *Climate Research* 14: 235–244.

Roylance, F.D. April 30, 2006. Perfect Storm, Awful Floods: New Models Show 20-ft. Surge Possible, Far Above Isabel's. Baltimore Sun. Available Online: http://www.baltimoresun.com/news/weather/hurricane/bal-te.slosh30apr30,1,4723475.story

Ruth, M., K. Donaghy and P.H. Kirshen (eds.) 2006. *Regional Climate Change and Variability: Impacts and Responses,* Edward Elgar Publishers, Cheltenham, England, 260 pp.

Ruth, M. (ed.) 2006. *Smart Growth and Climate Change,* Edward Elgar Publishers, Cheltenham, England, 403 pp.

Ruth, M., D. Coelho and D. Karetnikov. 2007. The US Economic Impacts of Climate Change and the Cost of Inaction, Center for Integrative Environmental Research, University of Maryland, College Park. (http://www.cier.umd.edu)

Tallman, A. J., and Fisher, G.T. 2000. Flooding in Delaware and the Eastern Shore of Maryland From Hurricane Floyd, September 1999. U.S. Geological Service (FS-073-01). Washington DC. Available Online: http://pubs.usgs.gov/fs/fs07301/

Titus, J.G., and Richman, C. 2000. Maps of Lands Vulnerable to Sea Level Rise: Modeled Elevations Along the U.S. Atlantic and Gulf Coasts. Climate Research (In Press). Available Online: http://www.epa.gov/climatechange/effects/downloads/maps.pdf

United States Bureau of Economic Statistics (USBEA). 2007. Regional Economic Accounts, Bearfacts 1996–2006: Maryland. Available Online: http://www.bea.gov/bea/regional/bearfacts/action.cfm

United States Census Bureau (USCB). 2006. State and County Quick Facts: Maryland. Available Online: http://quickfacts.census.gov/qfd/states/24000.html

USDA, National Agricultural Statistics Service. Maryland State Agriculture Overview: 2007.

USDA, National Agricultural Statistics Service. 2002 Census of Agriculture.

United States Environmental Protection Agency (US EPA). 1998. Climate Change and Maryland. U.S. EPA (236-F-98-0071). Washington DC. Available Online: http://yosemite.epa.gov/oar/globalwarming.nsf/UniqueKeyLookup/SHSU5BUSTE/$File/md_im pct.pdf

United States Environmental Protection Agency (US EPA). 2004. Appendix B Global Climate Change and Maryland. Available Online: http://www.epa.gov/climatechange/wycd/stateandlocalgov/downloads/MDAppendices.pdf

United States Environmental Protection Agency (US EPA). 2007. Potential Impacts of Sea Level Rise on the Beach at Ocean City, Maryland. Available Online: http://www.epa.gov/climatechange/effects/coastal/SLROcean_City.html

United States Fish & Wildlife Service (USFWS). 2006. National Survey of Fishing, Hunting, and Wildlife-Associated Recreation: Maryland. Available Online: http://www.census.gov/prod/2008pubs/fhw06-md.pdf

Zhang K. et al. 2004. Global Warming and Coastal Erosion. *Climate Change* (64) 41–58.

By Martin Luther King, Jr.

PUBLIC STATEMENT BY EIGHT ALABAMA CLERGYMEN

(April 12, 1963)

We the undersigned clergymen are among those who, in January, issued "An Appeal for Law and Order and Common Sense," in dealing with racial problems in Alabama. We expressed understanding that honest convictions in racial matters could properly be pursued in the courts, but urged that decisions of those courts should in the meantime be peacefully obeyed.

Since that time there had been some evidence of increased forbearance and a willingness to face facts. Responsible citizens have undertaken to work on various problems which cause racial friction and unrest. In Birmingham, recent public events have given indication that we all have opportunity for a new constructive and realistic approach to racial problems.

However, we are now confronted by a series of demonstrations by some of our Negro citizens, directed and led in part by outsiders. We recognize the natural impatience of people who feel that their hopes are slow in being realized. But we are convinced that these demonstrations are unwise and untimely.

We agree rather with certain local Negro leadership which has called for honest and open negotiation of racial issues in our area. And we believe this kind of facing of issues can best be accomplished by citizens of our own metropolitan area, white and Negro, meeting with their knowledge and experience of the local situation. All of us need to face that responsibility and find proper channels for its accomplishment.

Just as we formerly pointed out that "hatred and violence have no sanction in our religious and political traditions," we also point out that such actions as incite to hatred and violence, however technically peaceful those actions may be, have not contributed to the resolution of our local problems. We do not believe that these days of new hope are days when extreme measures are justified in Birmingham.

We commend the community as a whole, and the local news media and law enforcement officials in particular, on the calm manner in which these demonstrations have been handled. We urge the public to continue to show restraint should the demonstrations continue, and the law enforcement officials to remain calm and continue to protect our city from violence.

We further strongly urge our own Negro community to withdraw support from these demonstrations, and to unite locally in working peacefully for a better Birmingham. When rights are consistently denied, a cause should be pressed in the courts and in negotiations among local leaders, and not in the streets. We appeal to both our white and Negro citizenry to observe the principles of law and order and common sense.

Signed by:

C.C. J. CARPENTER, D.D., LL.D., *Bishop of Alabama*

JOSEPH A. DURICK, D.D., *Auxiliary Bishop, Diocese of Mobile, Birmingham*

RABBI MILTON L. GRAFMAN, *Temple Emanu-El, Birmingham, Alabama*

BISHOP PAUL HARDIN, *Bishop of the Alabama-West Florida Conference of the Methodist Church*

BISHOP NOLAN B. HARMON, *Bishop of the North Alabama Conference of the Methodist Church*

GEORGE M. MURRAY, D.D., LL.D., *Bishop Coadjutor, Episcopal Diocese of Alabama*

EDWARD V. RAMAGE, *Moderator, Synod of the Alabama Presbyterian Church in the United States*

EARL STALLINGS, *Pastor, First Baptist Church, Birmingham, Alabama*

LETTER FROM BIRMINGHAM JAIL

MARTIN LUTHER KING, JR.
Birmingham City Jail
April 16, 1963

Bishop C. C. J. Carpenter
Bishop Joseph A. Durick
Rabbi Milton L. Grafman
Bishop Paul Hardin
Bishop Nolan B. Harmon
The Rev. George M. Murray
The Rev. Edward V. Ramage
The Rev. Earl Stallings

My dear Fellow Clergymen,

While confined here in the Birmingham City Jail, I came across your recent statement calling our present activities "unwise and untimely." Seldom, if ever, do I pause to answer criticism of my work and ideas. If I sought to answer all of the criticisms that cross my desk, my secretaries would be engaged in little else in the course of the day and I would have no time for constructive work. But since I feel that you are men of genuine good will and your criticisms are sincerely set forth, I would like to answer your statement in what I hope will be patient and reasonable terms.

I think I should give the reason for my being in Birmingham, since you have been influenced by the argument of "outsiders coming in." I have the honor of serving as president of the Southern Christian Leadership Conference, an organization operating in every Southern state with headquarters in Atlanta, Georgia. We have some eighty-five affiliate organizations all across the South—one being the Alabama Christian Movement for Human Rights. Whenever necessary and possible we share staff, educational, and financial resources with our affiliates. Several months ago our local affiliate here in Birmingham invited us to be on call to engage in a nonviolent direct action program if such were deemed necessary. We readily consented and when the hour came we lived up to our promises. So I am here, along with several members of my staff, because we were invited here. I am here because I have basic organizational ties here. Beyond this, I am in Birmingham because injustice is here. Just as the eighth century prophets left their little villages and carried their "thus saith the Lord" far beyond the boundaries of their home town, and just as the Apostle Paul left his little village of Tarsus and carried the gospel of Jesus Christ to practically every hamlet and city of the Greco-Roman world, I too am compelled to carry the gospel of freedom beyond my particular home town. Like Paul, I must constantly respond to the Macedonian call for aid.

Moreover, I am cognizant of the interrelatedness of all communities and states. I cannot sit idly by in Atlanta and not be concerned about what happens in Birmingham. Injustice anywhere is a threat to justice everywhere. We are caught in an inescapable network of mutuality, tied in a single garment of destiny. Whatever affects one directly affects all indirectly. Never again can we afford to live with the narrow, provincial "outside agitator" idea. Anyone who lives inside the United States can never be considered an outsider anywhere in this country.

You deplore the demonstrations that are presently taking place in Birmingham. But I am sorry that your statement did not express a similar concern for the conditions that brought the demonstrations into being. I am sure that each of you would want to go beyond the superficial social analyst who looks merely at effects, and does not grapple with underlying causes. I would not hesitate to say that it is unfortunate that so-called demonstrations are taking place in Birmingham at this time, but I would say in more emphatic terms that it is even more unfortunate that the white power structure of this city left the Negro community with no other alternative.

In any nonviolent campaign there are four basic steps: (1) collection of the facts to determine whether injustices are alive; (2) negotiation; (3) self-purification; and (4) direct action. We have gone through all of these steps in Birmingham. There can be no gainsaying of the fact that racial injustice engulfs this community. Birmingham is probably the most thoroughly segregated city in the United States. Its ugly record of police brutality is known in every section of this country. Its unjust treatment of Negroes in the courts is a notorious reality. There have been more unsolved bombings of Negro homes and churches in Birmingham than any city in this nation. These are the hard, brutal, and unbelievable facts. On the basis of these conditions, Negro leaders sought to negotiate with the city fathers. But the political leaders consistently refused to engage in good faith negotiation.

Then came the opportunity last September to talk with some of the leaders of the economic community. In these negotiating sessions certain promises were made by the merchants—such as the promise to remove the humiliating racial signs from the stores. On the basis of these promises Rev. Shuttlesworth and the leaders of the Alabama Christian Movement for Human Rights agreed to call a moratorium on any type of demonstrations. As the weeks and months unfolded we realized that we were the victims of a broken promise. The signs remained. As in so many experiences of the past we were confronted with blasted hopes, and the dark shadow of a deep disappointment settled upon us. So we had no alternative except that of preparing for direct action, whereby we would present our very bodies as a means of laying our case before the conscience of the local and national community. We were not unmindful of the difficulties involved. So we decided to go through a process of self-purification. We started having workshops on nonviolence and repeatedly asked ourselves the questions, "Are you able to accept blows without retaliating?" "Are you able to endure the ordeals of jail?"

We decided to set our direct action program around the Easter season, realizing that with the exception of Christmas, this was the largest shopping period of the year. Knowing that a strong economic withdrawal program would be the by-product of direct action, we felt that this was the best time to bring pressure on the merchants for the needed changes. Then it occurred to us that the March election was ahead, and so we speedily decided to postpone action until after election day. When we discovered that Mr. Connor was in the run-off, we decided again to postpone so that the demonstrations could not be used to cloud the issues. At this time we agreed to begin our nonviolent witness the day after the run-off.

This reveals that we did not move irresponsibly into direct action. We too wanted to see Mr. Connor defeated; so we went through postponement after postponement to aid in this community need. After this we felt that direct action could be delayed no longer.

You may well ask, "Why direct action? Why sit-ins, marches, etc.? Isn't negotiation a better path?" You are exactly right in your call for negotiation. Indeed, this is the purpose of direct action. Nonviolent direct action seeks to create such a crisis and establish such creative tension that a community that has constantly refused to negotiate is forced to confront the issue. It seeks so to dramatize the issue that it can no longer be ignored. I just referred to the creation of tension as a part of the work of the nonviolent resister. This may sound rather shocking. But I must confess that I am not afraid of the word tension. I have earnestly worked and preached against violent tension, but there is a type of constructive nonviolent tension that is necessary for growth. Just as Socrates felt that it was necessary to create a tension in the mind so that individuals could rise from the bondage of myths and half-truths to the unfettered realm of creative analysis and objective appraisal, we must see the need of having nonviolent gadflies to create the kind of tension in society that will help men rise from the dark depths of prejudice and racism to the majestic heights of understanding and brotherhood. So the purpose of the direct action is to create a situation so crisis-packed that it will inevitably open the door to negotiation. We, therefore, concur with you in your call for negotiation. Too long has our beloved Southland been bogged down in the tragic attempt to live in monologue rather than dialogue.

One of the basic points in your statement is that our acts are untimely. Some have asked, "Why didn't you give the new administration time to act?" The only answer that I can give to this inquiry is that the new administration must be prodded about as much as the outgoing one before it acts. We will be sadly mistaken if we feel that the election of Mr. Boutwell will bring the millennium to Birmingham. While Mr. Boutwell is much more articulate and gentle than Mr. Connor, they are both segregationists dedicated to the task of maintaining the status quo. The hope I see in Mr. Boutwell is that he will be reasonable enough to see the futility of massive resistance to desegregation. But he will not see this without pressure from the devotees of civil rights. My friends, I must say to you that we have not made a single gain in civil rights without determined legal and non-violent pressure. History is the long and tragic story of the fact that privileged groups seldom give up their privileges voluntarily. Individuals may see the moral light and voluntarily give up their unjust posture; but as Reinhold Niebuhr has reminded us, groups are more immoral than individuals.

We know through painful experience that freedom is never voluntarily given by the oppressor; it must be demanded by the oppressed. Frankly I have never yet engaged in a direct action movement that was "well timed," according to the timetable of those who have not suffered unduly from the disease of segregation. For years now I have heard the word "Wait!" It rings in the ear of every Negro with a piercing familiarity. This "wait" has almost always meant "never." It has been a tranquilizing thalidomide, relieving the emotional stress for a moment, only to give birth to an ill-formed infant of frustration. We must come to see with the distinguished jurist of yesterday that "justice too long delayed is justice denied." We have waited for more than three hundred and forty years for our constitutional and God-given rights. The nations of Asia and Africa are moving with jet-like speed toward the goal of political independence, and we still creep at horse and buggy pace toward the gaining of a cup of coffee at a lunch counter.

I guess it is easy for those who have never felt the stinging darts of segregation to say wait. But when you have seen vicious mobs lynch your mothers and fathers at will and drown your sisters and brothers at whim; when you have seen hate filled policemen curse, kick, brutalize, and even kill your black brothers and sisters with impunity; when you see the vast majority of your twenty million Negro brothers smothering in an air-tight cage of poverty in the midst of an affluent society; when you suddenly find your tongue twisted and your speech stammering as you seek to explain to your six-year-old daughter why she can't go to the public amusement park that has just been advertised on television, and see tears welling up in her little eyes when she is told that Funtown is closed to colored children, and see the depressing clouds of inferiority begin to form in her little mental sky, and see her begin to distort her little personality by unconsciously developing a bitterness toward white people; when you have to concoct an answer for a five-year-old son asking in agonizing pathos: "Daddy, why do white people treat colored people so mean?"; when you take a cross country drive and find it necessary to sleep night after night in the uncomfortable corners of your automobile because no motel will accept you; when you are humiliated day in and day out by nagging signs reading "white" and "colored"; when your first name becomes "nigger" and your middle name becomes "boy" (however old you are) and your last name becomes "John," and when your wife and mother are never given the respected title "Mrs."; when you are harried by day and haunted by night by the fact that you are a Negro, living constantly at tip-toe stance never quite knowing what to expect next, and plagued with inner fears and outer resentments; when you are forever fighting a degenerating sense of "nobodiness";—then you will understand why we find it difficult to wait. There comes a time when the cup of endurance runs over, and men are no longer willing to be plunged into an abyss of injustice where they experience the bleakness of corroding despair. I hope, sirs, you can understand our legitimate and unavoidable impatience.

You express a great deal of anxiety over our willingness to break laws. This is certainly a legitimate concern. Since we so diligently urge people to obey the Supreme Court's decision of 1954 outlawing segregation in the public schools, it is rather strange and paradoxical to find us consciously breaking laws. One may well ask, "How can you advocate breaking some laws and obeying others?" The answer is found in the fact that there are two types of laws. There are *just* laws and there are *unjust* laws. I would be the first to advocate obeying just laws. One has not only a legal but moral responsibility to obey just laws. Conversely, one has a moral responsibility to disobey unjust laws. I would agree with Saint Augustine that "An unjust law is no law at all."

Now what is the difference between the two? How does one determine when a law is just or unjust? A just law is a man-made code that squares with the moral law or the law of God. An unjust law is a code that is out of harmony with the moral law. To put it in the terms of Saint Thomas Aquinas, an unjust law is a human law that is not rooted in eternal and natural law. Any law that uplifts human personality is just. Any law that degrades human personality is unjust. All segregation statutes are unjust because segregation distorts the soul and damages the personality. It gives the segregator a false sense of superiority and the segregated a false sense of inferiority. To use the words of Martin Buber, the great Jewish philosopher, segregation substitutes an "I-it" relationship for the "I-thou" relationship, and ends up relegating persons to the status of things. So segregation is not only politically, economically, and sociologically unsound, but it is morally wrong and sinful. Paul Tillich has said that sin is separation. Isn't segregation an existential expression of man's tragic separation, an expression of his awful estrangement, his terrible sinfulness? So I can urge men to obey the 1954 decision of the Supreme Court because it is morally right, and I can urge them to disobey segregation ordinances because they are morally wrong.

Let us turn to a more concrete example of just and unjust laws. An unjust law is a code that a majority inflicts on a minority that is not binding on itself. This is *difference* made legal. On the other hand a just law is a code that a majority compels a minority to follow that it is willing to follow itself. This is *sameness* made legal.

Let me give another explanation. An unjust law is a code inflicted upon a minority which that minority had no part in enacting or creating because they did not have the unhampered right to vote. Who can say the legislature of Alabama which set up the segregation laws was democratically elected? Throughout the state of Alabama all types of conniving methods are used to prevent Negroes from becoming registered voters and there are some counties without a single Negro registered to vote despite the fact that the Negro constitutes a majority of the population. Can any law set up in such a state be considered democratically structured?

These are just a few examples of unjust and just laws. There are some instances when a law is just on its face but unjust in its application. For instance, I was arrested Friday on a charge of parading without a permit. Now there is nothing wrong with an ordinance which requires a permit for a parade, but when the ordinance is used to preserve segregation and to deny citizens the First Amendment privilege of peaceful assembly and peaceful protest, then it becomes unjust.

I hope you can see the distinction I am trying to point out. In no sense do I advocate evading or defying the law as the rabid segregationist would do. This would lead to anarchy. One who breaks an unjust law must do it *openly, lovingly* (not hatefully as the white mothers did in New Orleans when they were seen on television screaming "nigger, nigger, nigger") and with a willingness to accept the penalty. I submit that an individual who breaks a law that conscience tells him is unjust, and willingly accepts the penalty by staying in jail to arouse the conscience of the community over its injustice, is in reality expressing the very highest respect for law.

Of course there is nothing new about this kind of civil disobedience. It was seen sublimely in the refusal of Shadrach, Meshach, and Abednego to obey the laws of Nebuchadnezzar because a higher moral law was involved. It was practiced superbly by the early Christians who were willing to face hungry lions and the excruciating pain of chopping blocks, before submitting to certain unjust laws of the Roman Empire. To a degree academic freedom is a reality today because Socrates practiced civil disobedience.

We can never forget that everything Hitler did in Germany was "legal" and everything the Hungarian freedom fighters did in Hungary was "illegal." It was "illegal" to aid and comfort a Jew in Hitler's Germany. But I am sure that, if I had lived in Germany during that time, I would have aided and comforted my Jewish brothers even though it was illegal. If I lived in a communist country today where certain principles dear to the Christian faith are suppressed, I believe I would openly advocate disobeying those antireligious laws.

I must make two honest confessions to you, my Christian and Jewish brothers. First I must confess that over the last few years I have been gravely disappointed with the white moderate. I have almost reached the regrettable conclusion that the Negroes' great stumbling block in the stride toward freedom is not the White Citizens' "Counciler" or the Ku Klux Klanner, but the white moderate who is more devoted to "order" than to justice; who prefers a negative peace which is the absence of tension to a positive peace which is the presence of justice; who constantly says "I agree with you in the goal you seek, but I can't agree with your methods of direct action;" who paternalistically feels that he can set the timetable for another man's freedom; who lives by the myth of time and who constantly advises the Negro to wait until a "more convenient season." Shallow understanding from people of good will is more frustrating than absolute misunderstanding from people of ill will. Lukewarm acceptance is much more bewildering than outright rejection.

I had hoped that the white moderate would understand that law and order exist for the purpose of establishing justice, and that when they fail to do this they become the dangerously structured dams that block the flow of social progress. I had hoped that the white moderate would understand that the present tension in the South is merely a necessary phase of the transition from an obnoxious negative peace, where the Negro passively accepted his unjust plight, to a substance-filled positive peace, where all men will respect the dignity and worth of human personality. Actually, we who engage in nonviolent direct action are not the creators of tension. We merely bring to the surface the hidden tension that is already alive. We bring it out in the open where it can be seen and dealt with. Like a boil that can never be cured as long as it is covered up but must be opened with all its pus-flowing ugliness to the natural medicines of air and light, injustice must like-wise be exposed, with all of the tension its exposing creates, to the light of human conscience and the air of national opinion before it can be cured.

In your statement you asserted that our actions, even though peaceful, must be condemned because they precipitate violence. But can this assertion be logically made? Isn't this like condemning the robbed man because his possession of money precipitated the evil act of robbery? Isn't this like condemning Socrates because his unswerving commitment to truth and his philosophical delvings precipitated the misguided popular mind to make him drink the hemlock? Isn't this like condemning Jesus because His unique God consciousness and never-ceasing devotion to His will precipitated the evil act of crucifixion? We must come to see, as federal courts have consistently affirmed, that it is immoral to urge an individual to withdraw his efforts to gain his basic constitutional rights because the quest precipitates violence. Society must protect the robbed and punish the robber.

I had also hoped that the white moderate would reject the myth of time. I received a letter this morning from a white brother in Texas which said: "All Christians know that the colored people will receive equal rights eventually, but is it possible that you are in too great of a religious hurry? It has taken Christianity almost 2,000 years to accomplish what it has. The teachings of Christ take time to come to earth." All that is said here grows out of a tragic misconception of time. It is the strangely irrational notion that there is something in the very flow of time that will inevitably cure all ills. Actually time is neutral. It can be used either destructively or constructively. I am coming to feel that the people of ill will have used time much more effectively than the people of good will. We will have to repent in this generation not merely for the vitriolic words and actions of the bad people, but for the appalling silence of the good people. We must come to see that human progress never rolls in on wheels of inevitability. It comes through the tireless efforts and persistent work of men willing to be co-workers with God, and without this hard work time itself becomes an ally of the forces of social stagnation.

We must use time creatively, and forever realize that the time is always ripe to do right. Now is the time to make real the promise of democracy, and transform our pending national elegy into a creative psalm of brotherhood. Now is the time to lift our national policy from the quicksand of racial injustice to the solid rock of human dignity.

You spoke of our activity in Birmingham as extreme. At first I was rather disappointed that fellow clergymen would see my nonviolent efforts as those of the extremist. I started thinking about the fact that I stand in the middle of two opposing forces in the Negro community. One is a force of complacency made up of Negroes who, as a result of long years of oppression, have been so completely drained of self-respect and a sense of "somebodiness" that they have adjusted to segregation, and of a few Negroes in the middle class who, because of a degree of academic and economic security, and because at points they profit by segregation, have unconsciously become insensitive to the problems of the masses. The other force is one of bitterness and hatred and comes perilously close to advocating violence. It is expressed in the various black nationalist groups that are springing up over the nation, the largest and best known being Elijah Muhammad's Muslim movement. This movement is nourished by the contemporary frustration over the continued existence of racial discrimination. It is made up of people who have lost faith in America, who have absolutely repudiated Christianity, and who have concluded that the white man is an incurable "devil." I have tried to stand between these two forces saying that we need not follow the "do-nothingism" of the complacent or the hatred and despair of the black nationalist. There is the more excellent way of love and nonviolent protest. I'm grateful to God that, through the Negro church, the dimension of nonviolence entered our struggle. If this philosophy had not emerged I am convinced that by now many streets of the South would be flowing with floods of blood. And I am further convinced that if our white brothers dismiss us as "rabble rousers" and "outside agitators"—those of us who are working through the channels of nonviolent direct action— and refuse to support our nonviolent efforts, millions of Negroes, out of frustration and despair, will seek solace and security in black nationalist ideologies, a development that will lead inevitably to a frightening racial nightmare.

Oppressed people cannot remain oppressed forever. The urge for freedom will eventually come. This is what has happened to the American Negro. Something within has reminded him of his birthright of freedom; something without has reminded him that he can gain it. Consciously and unconsciously, he has been swept in by what the Germans call the *Zeitgeist*, and with his black brothers of Africa, and his brown and yellow brothers of Asia, South America, and the Caribbean, he is moving with a sense of cosmic urgency toward the promised land of racial justice. Recognizing this vital urge that has engulfed the Negro community, one should readily understand public demonstrations. The Negro has many pent-up resentments and latent frustrations. He has to get them out. So let him march sometime; let him have his prayer pilgrimages to the city hall; understand why he must have sit-ins and freedom rides. If his repressed emotions do not come out in these nonviolent ways, they will come out in ominous expressions of violence. This is not a threat; it is a fact of history. So I have not said to my people, "Get rid of your discontent." But I have tried to say that this normal and healthy discontent can be channeled through the creative outlet of nonviolent direct action. Now this approach is being dismissed as extremist. I must admit that I was initially disappointed in being so categorized.

But as I continued to think about the matter I gradually gained a bit of satisfaction from being considered an extremist. Was not Jesus an extremist in love? "Love your enemies, bless them that curse you, pray for them that despitefully use you." Was not Amos an extremist for justice— "Let justice roll down like waters and righteousness like a mighty stream." Was not Paul an extremist for the gospel of Jesus Christ— "I bear in my body the marks of the Lord Jesus." Was not Martin Luther an extremist— "Here I stand; I can do none other so help me God." Was not John Bunyan an extremist— "I will stay in jail to the end of my days before I make a butchery of my conscience." Was not Abraham Lincoln an extremist— "This nation cannot survive half slave and half free." Was not Thomas Jefferson an extremist— "We hold these truths to be self evident that all men are created equal." So the question is not whether we will be extremist but what kind of extremist will we be. Will we be extremists for hate or will we be extremists for love? Will we be extremists for the preservation of injustice or will we be extremists for the cause of justice? In that dramatic scene on Calvary's hill three men were crucified. We must never forget that all three were crucified for the same crime—the crime of extremism. Two were extremists for immorality, and thus fell below their environment. The other, Jesus Christ, was an extremist for love, truth, and goodness, and thereby rose above His environment. So, after all, maybe the South, the nation, and the world are in dire need of creative extremists.

I had hoped that the white moderate would see this. Maybe I was too optimistic. Maybe I expected too much. I guess I should have realized that few members of a race that has oppressed another race can understand or appreciate the deep groans and passionate yearnings of those that have been oppressed, and still fewer have the vision to see that injustice must be rooted out by strong, persistent, and determined action. I am thankful, however, that some of our white brothers have grasped the meaning of this social revolution and committed themselves to it. They are still all too small in quantity, but they are big in quality. Some like Ralph McGill, Lillian Smith, Harry Golden, and James Dabbs have written about our struggle in eloquent, prophetic, and understanding terms. Others have marched with us down nameless streets of the South. They have languished in filthy, roach-infested jails, suffering the abuse and brutality of angry policemen who see them as "dirty nigger lovers." They, unlike so many of their moderate brothers and sisters, have recognized the urgency of the moment and sensed the need for powerful "action" antidotes to combat the disease of segregation.

Let me rush on to mention my other disappointment. I have been so greatly disappointed with the white Church and its leadership. Of course there are some notable exceptions. I am not unmindful of the fact that each of you has taken some significant stands on this issue. I commend you, Rev. Stallings, for your Christian stand on this past Sunday, in welcoming Negroes to your worship service on a nonsegregated basis. I commend the Catholic leaders of this state for integrating Springhill College several years ago.

But despite these notable exceptions I must honestly reiterate that I have been disappointed with the Church. I do not say that as one of those negative critics who can always find something wrong with the Church. I say it as a minister of the gospel, who loves the Church; who was nurtured in its bosom; who has been sustained by its spiritual blessings and who will remain true to it as long as the cord of life shall lengthen.

I had the strange feeling when I was suddenly catapulted into the leadership of the bus protest in Montgomery several years ago that we would have the support of the white Church. I felt that the white ministers, priests, and rabbis of the South would be some of our strongest allies. Instead, some have been outright opponents, refusing to understand the freedom movement and misrepresenting its leaders; all too many others have been more cautious than courageous and have remained silent behind the anesthetizing security of stained glass windows.

In spite of my shattered dreams of the past, I came to Birmingham with the hope that the white religious leadership of the community would see the justice of our cause and, with deep moral concern, serve as the channel through which our just grievances could get to the power structure. I had hoped that each of you would understand. But again I have been disappointed.

I have heard numerous religious leaders of the South call upon their worshippers to comply with a desegregation decision because it is the law, but I have longed to hear white ministers say follow this decree because integration is morally right and the Negro is your brother. In the midst of blatant injustices inflicted upon the Negro, I have watched white churches stand on the sideline and merely mouth pious irrelevancies and sanctimonious trivialities. In the midst of a mighty struggle to rid our nation of racial and economic injustice, I have heard so many ministers say, "Those are social issues with which the Gospel has no real concern," and I have watched so many churches commit themselves to a completely otherworldly religion which made a strange distinction between body and soul, the sacred and the secular.

So here we are moving toward the exit of the twentieth century with a religious community largely adjusted to the status quo, standing as a tail light behind other community agencies rather than a headlight leading men to higher levels of justice.

I have travelled the length and breadth of Alabama, Mississippi, and all the other Southern states. On sweltering summer days and crisp autumn mornings I have looked at her beautiful churches with their spires pointing heavenward. I have beheld the impressive outlay of her massive religious education buildings. Over and over again I have found myself asking: "Who worships here? Who is their God? Where were their voices when the lips of Governor Barnett dripped with words of interposition and nullification? Where were they when Governor Wallace gave the clarion call for defiance and hatred? Where were their voices of support when tired, bruised, and weary Negro men and women decided to rise from the dark dungeons of complacency to the bright hills of creative protest?"

Yes, these questions are still in my mind. In deep disappointment, I have wept over the laxity of the Church. But be assured that my tears have been tears of love. There can be no deep disappointment where there is not deep love. Yes, I love the Church; I love her sacred walls. How could I do otherwise? I am in the rather unique position of being the son, the grandson, and the great grandson of preachers. Yes, I see the Church as the body of Christ. But, oh! How we have blemished and scarred that body through social neglect and fear of being nonconformists.

There was a time when the Church was very powerful. It was during that period when the early Christians rejoiced when they were deemed worthy to suffer for what they believed. In those days the Church was not merely a thermometer that recorded the ideas and principles of popular opinion; it was a thermostat that transformed the mores of society. Wherever the early Christians entered a town the power structure got disturbed and immediately sought to convict them for being "disturbers of the peace" and "outside agitators." But they went on with the conviction that they were a "colony of heaven" and had to obey God rather than man. They were small in number but big in commitment. They were too God-intoxicated to be "astronomically intimidated." They brought an end to such ancient evils as infanticide and gladiatorial contest.

Things are different now. The contemporary Church is so often a weak, ineffectual voice with an uncertain sound. It is so often the arch-supporter of the status quo. Far from being disturbed by the presence of the Church, the power structure of the average community is consoled by the Church's silent and often vocal sanction of things as they are.

But the judgment of God is upon the Church as never before. If the Church of today does not recapture the sacrificial spirit of the early Church, it will lose its authentic ring, forfeit the loyalty of millions, and be dismissed as an irrelevant social club with no meaning for the twentieth century. I am meeting young people every day whose disappointment with the Church has risen to outright disgust.

Maybe again I have been too optimistic. Is organized religion too inextricably bound to the status quo to save our nation and the world? Maybe I must turn my faith to the inner spiritual Church, the church within the Church, as the true *ecclesia* and the hope of the world. But again I am thankful to God that some noble souls from the ranks of organized religion have broken loose from the paralyzing chains of conformity and joined us as active partners in the struggle for freedom. They have left their secure congregations and walked the streets of Albany, Georgia, with us. They have gone through the highways of the South on torturous rides for freedom. Yes, they have gone to jail with us. Some have been kicked out of their churches and lost the support of their bishops and fellow ministers. But they have gone with the faith that right defeated is stronger than evil triumphant. These men have been the leaven in the lump of the race. Their witness has been the spiritual salt that has preserved the true meaning of the Gospel in these troubled times. They have carved a tunnel of hope through the dark mountain of disappointment.

I hope the Church as a whole will meet the challenge of this decisive hour. But even if the Church does not come to the aid of justice, I have no despair about the future. I have no fear about the outcome of our struggle in Birmingham, even if our motives are presently misunderstood. We will reach the goal of freedom in Birmingham and all over the nation, because the goal of America is freedom. Abused and scorned though we may be, our destiny is tied up with the destiny of America. Before the pilgrims landed at Plymouth, we were here. Before the pen of Jefferson etched across the pages of history the majestic words of the Declaration of Independence, we were here. For more than two centuries our foreparents labored in this country without wages; they made cotton "king"; and they built the homes of their masters in the midst of brutal injustice and shameful humiliation—and yet out of a bottomless vitality they continued to thrive and develop. If the inexpressible cruelties of slavery could not stop us, the opposition we now face will surely fail. We will win our freedom because the sacred heritage of our nation and the eternal will of God are embodied in our echoing demands.

I must close now. But before closing I am impelled to mention one other point in your statement that troubled me profoundly. You warmly commended the Birmingham police force for keeping "order" and "preventing violence." I don't believe you would have so warmly commended the police force if you had seen its angry violent dogs literally biting six unarmed, nonviolent Negroes. I don't believe you would so quickly commend the policemen if you would observe their ugly and inhuman treatment of Negroes here in the city jail; if you would watch them push and curse old Negro women and young Negro girls; if you would see them slap and kick old Negro men and young Negro boys; if you will observe them, as they did on two occasions, refuse to give us food because we wanted to sing our grace together. I'm sorry that I can't join you in your praise for the police department.

It is true that they have been rather disciplined in their public handling of the demonstrators. In this sense they have been rather publicly "nonviolent." But for what purpose? To preserve the evil system of segregation. Over the last few years I have consistently preached that nonviolence demands that the means we use must be as pure as the ends we seek. So I have tried to make it clear that it is wrong to use immoral means to attain moral ends. But now I must affirm that it is just as wrong, or even more so, to use moral means to preserve immoral ends. Maybe Mr. Connor and his policemen have been rather publicly nonviolent, as Chief Pritchett was in Albany, Georgia, but they have used the moral means of nonviolence to maintain the immoral end of flagrant racial injustice. T. S. Eliot has said that there is no greater treason than to do the right deed for the wrong reason.

I wish you had commended the Negro sit-inners and demonstrators of Birmingham for their sublime courage, their willingness to suffer, and their amazing discipline in the midst of the most inhuman provocation. One day the South will recognize its real heroes. They will be the James Merediths, courageously and with a majestic sense of purpose, facing jeering and hostile mobs and the agonizing loneliness that characterizes the life of the pioneer. They will be old, oppressed, battered Negro women, symbolized in a seventy-two year old woman of Montgomery, Alabama, who rose up with a sense of dignity and with her people decided not to ride the segregated buses, and responded to one who inquired about her tiredness with ungrammatical profundity: "My feets is tired, but my soul is rested." They will be young high school and college students, young ministers of the gospel and a host of the elders, courageously and nonviolently sitting in at lunch counters and willingly going to jail for conscience sake. One day the South will know that when these disinherited children of God sat down at lunch counters they were in reality standing up for the best in the American dream and the most sacred values in our Judeo-Christian heritage, and thus carrying our whole nation back to great wells of democracy which were dug deep by the founding fathers in the formulation of the Constitution and the Declaration of Independence.

Never before have I written a letter this long (or should I say a book?). I'm afraid that it is much too long to take your precious time. I can assure you that it would have been much shorter if I had been writing from a comfortable desk, but what else is there to do when you are alone for days in the dull monotony of a narrow jail cell other than write long letters, think strange thoughts, and pray long prayers!

If I have said anything in this letter that is an overstatement of the truth and is indicative of an unreasonable impatience, I beg you to forgive me. If I have said anything in this letter that is an understatement of the truth and is indicative of my having a patience that makes me patient with anything less than brotherhood, I beg God to forgive me.

I hope this letter finds you strong in the faith. I also hope that circumstances will soon make it possible for me to meet each of you, not as an integrationist or a civil rights leader, but as a fellow clergyman and a Christian brother. Let us all hope that the dark clouds of racial prejudice will soon pass away and the deep fog of misunderstanding will be lifted from our fear-drenched communities and in some not too distant tomorrow the radiant stars of love and brotherhood will shine over our great nation with all of their scintillating beauty.

Yours for the cause of
Peace and Brotherhood
MARTIN LUTHER KING, JR.

IX

APPENDICES

THE A PAPER

1. It not only fulfills the assignment but does so in a fresh and mature way. The paper is exciting to read; it accommodates itself well to its intended audience.
2. The evidence is detailed and used persuasively and where appropriate; citations are used effectively where appropriate and are formatted correctly.
3. The organization gives the reader a sense of the necessary flow of the argument or explanation. Paragraphs are fully developed and follow naturally from what precedes them; the conclusion reinforces the reader's confidence in the writer's control of the argument. Organizational guides are used as appropriate.
4. The prose is clear, apt, and occasionally memorable. The paper contains few, if any, errors of grammar, mechanics, word choice or expression, none of which undermines the overall effectiveness of the paper.

THE B PAPER

1. The assignment has been followed and fulfilled at a better-than-average level. The paper appropriately addresses its intended audience.
2. The evidence is detailed and persuasive. The paper may sometimes rely too heavily on the obvious, though the writer does not consistently settle for the obvious. The reasoning is better than adequate: it is thoughtful, with awareness of other points of view.
3. The introduction and conclusion are clear, but perhaps not as forceful as they could be. Most paragraphs follow well and are appropriately divided, though one or two could be better placed and developed.
4. The expression is more than competent. Not only is sentence structure correct, but subordination, emphasis, sentence length, and variety are used effectively. Some sentences could be improved, but it would be surprising to find serious sentence errors, such as comma splices, fragments, or fused sentences, in a B paper. Punctuation, grammar, and spelling reveal proficient use of the conventions of edited American English.

THE C PAPER

1. The assignment has been followed at a satisfactory level. The paper presents an appropriate thesis. However, the thesis may be too broad or general, or its presentation may be problematic in some way—e.g., the intended audience may, for various reasons, have trouble immediately discerning the thesis.

2. For the most part, the argument is supported with evidence. However, while an effort has clearly been made to find and use the best sort of evidence, the evidence is likely to be obvious; the paper may even lack some pertinent information. The reasoning, while generally sound, is predictable; or the reasoning, while generally good, is occasionally flawed. There is some awareness of other points of view.

3. There is an implicit sense of organization, but several paragraphs and/or sentences within paragraphs are misplaced to the extent that the organizational structure is recognizable but disjointed.

4. Sentence structure is generally correct, although the writer may show limited competence with sentence effectiveness, failing to use such elements as subordination, sentence variety, and modifiers to achieve emphasis. A C paper may thus be characterized by a "wooden" style. Comma splices, unintentional fragments, and fused sentences—errors that betray inadequate understanding of sentence structure—may occasionally crop up. The vocabulary is fairly limited. The paper may contain errors in spelling, mechanics, and grammar that reveal unfamiliarity with conventions of edited American English. (While a C paper may differ from a B paper in containing some errors in mechanics, grammar, vocabulary or expression, note that too many errors of this sort will quickly change a C paper to a D or F paper.)

THE D PAPER

1. There is a poor sense of audience and a limited sense of purpose. The purpose or thesis cannot be discerned without significant work on the part of the reader.

2. Necessary evidence is out of order and/or missing; irrelevant evidence may instead be present. The reasoning will necessarily be flawed.

3. The organization is difficult to discern. The introduction is unclear or nonexistent, paragraphs are not well-developed or arranged, transitions are incorrect or missing.

4. There are numerous errors in grammar, spelling, and punctuation. The diction and/or syntax may be so weak that sentences are sometimes incomprehensible for the intended audience, although experienced readers can make sense of what is written. Lack of proofreading may turn an otherwise adequate paper into a D paper.

THE F PAPER

1. It is off the assignment. The thesis is unclear; the paper moves confusedly in several directions. It may even fall seriously short of minimum length requirements.

and/or

2. There is virtually no evidence, or the attribution of evidence is problematic or has been neglected.

and/or

3. The organization seems to a significant degree haphazard or arbitrary.

and/or

4. Numerous and consistent errors of grammar, spelling, punctuation, diction or syntax hinder clarity or even basic communication. Some sentences are incomprehensible.

PHILOSOPHY OF GRADING

There are two ways to approach the problem of defining grades. One is to take them linearly—to begin, for example, with A, define what an A grade is, and then move on to B, C, D, and F, showing how each falls short of the grade just before it. This is probably the most common system, the one students and teachers are both most accustomed to. But this system has one important disadvantage: the danger of presenting A as a norm, a standard from which work receiving other grades has not just deviated, but has fallen short. The problem with this approach is that A is not a standard in that sense; that is, work that merits A is not "normal" work, but rather work that is striking in its excellence, work that is superior in all respects. A-quality work is both exceptional and rare.

There is, however, another approach, one that more accurately reflects basic divisions between levels of quality. In this approach, we begin by thinking first about the most basic division—that between satisfactory work and unsatisfactory work. We start therefore by defining C work. This division serves as a more accurate guide to the assignment of grades, in that it makes it clear that C, B, and A represent different levels of achievement, given the basic stricture that the task was completed satisfactorily to begin with. D and F likewise represent different levels of falling short of fulfilling the assignment.

Note that both presentations, the linear sequence, and the organization that starts with a division between satisfactory and unsatisfactory work, say essentially the same things. Examining both should give a clear picture of what level a paper must achieve to receive a specific grade.

GRADING STANDARDS[1]

To get a grade of C, an essay must be adequate in each of the following four areas.

1. **Content**. The C paper fulfills the assignment. It meets all specified requirements as to length, subject, pattern of organization, etc. Moreover, it presents a sound central idea supported by relevant material. The central idea may be lacking in originality, and the support may achieve nothing greater than sufficiency, but everything is there and in place.
2. **Evidence and reasoning.** The argument is appropriately supported with evidence, and the reasoning used in the argument is clear and makes sense. Possibly the reasoning is predictable, or the evidence may occasionally be on the obvious side, but both are sound and clear. The paper shows awareness of other points of view.

---

[1]These grading standards have been adapted by permission from the standards used in the Hood College, Maryland, English Department.

3. **Organization.** The paper has a discernible and logical plan. The entire essay is unified in support of the central idea; individual paragraphs are similarly unified in support of subordinate points. The train of thought is generally clear. Failure to provide an effective introduction and conclusion, or, alternatively, to provide adequate transitions may occasionally make the organization seem a bit disjointed. (Note that if both of these occur, we are likely no longer dealing with a satisfactory paper—the reader will have to work too hard to make sense of it.) In contrast, the organization may be artificial, forced and labored. Essentially, however, logical order prevails, to the benefit of the intended audience.

4. **Expression and literacy.** Although the style need not be distinguished, the C paper is written in clear English. The C paper may commit a few of the errors listed below, but such lapses must not be serious enough or frequent enough to interfere significantly with the communication of ideas: loosely strung out sentences; choppy sentences; poor parallelism; illogical word order or subordination; unnecessary shifts in subject or verb; awkward use of the passive voice; wordiness; vague, trite or inappropriate diction; dangling or misplaced modifiers; subject-verb disagreements; pronoun-antecedent disagreements; unclear or problematic pronoun reference; incorrect verb forms; mixed constructions or any other ungrammatical constructions; run-on sentences; comma splices; sentence fragments; any misuse or omission of punctuation marks; misspellings; errors in capitalization and in hyphenation or compounding of words.

The C paper, then, is satisfactory. It may not display special competency, but it gets the job done.

The B paper goes beyond adequacy to excellence. The thesis may be more original or interesting, and the paper shows full awareness of its intended audience. The evidence is detailed and fully persuasive. The reasoning is thoughtful and shows clear awareness of other points of view. The organization is clear, and the presentation flows naturally from point to point—no misplaced paragraphs, no loose ends left dangling. The overall structure of the paper is well thought out and is appropriate to its audience and purpose. Sentence structure and diction are effective, requiring only minor improvements. There are at most only infrequent and minor errors in grammar, punctuation and spelling.

The A paper has all the virtues of the B paper, but in fuller measure and to an exceptional degree. It is particularly marked by originality in thought and elegance of style. The best evidence is used, and used effectively. The organization is carefully crafted to give a sense of the necessary flow of the argument. Audience accommodation is adeptly managed.

Work that falls below the C standard is inadequate in at least one of the four areas.

The D essay fulfills the assignment overall, but to an inadequate degree. A few, but not all, of the following problems may occur. The paper does not appeal to the intended audience or does not satisfactorily fulfill its stated purpose. Sometimes, the purpose cannot be discerned without some work on the reader's part. Evidence may be inappropriately obvious, out of order, or irrelevant; in some cases, important evidence may simply be missing. The reasoning is flawed or inadequately supported. It is difficult to keep track of the organizational structure. The paper may suffer from significant or numerous errors in grammar or mechanics, and the diction may be awkward or problematic for the intended audience.

The F paper shows more than one or two of the problems mentioned as typical of the D paper; or it is off the assignment or falls seriously short of length requirements (which almost invariably means insufficient depth of analysis or discussion); or the thesis is unclear; or evidence is missing or has been inappropriately attributed; or the organization is haphazard; or there are numerous and consistent errors in grammar, mechanics and diction.

DEPARTMENT OF ENGLISH
STATEMENT ON ACADEMIC DISHONESTY

All students are expected to have read and understood the University's statement on academic dishonesty found at the front of the schedule of classes. You will be held responsible for abiding by that statement. Cases of cheating (including borrowing or buying papers and using papers for more than one course), plagiarism, fabrication and facilitating academic dishonesty will be prosecuted.

A paper submitted in one course may *not* be submitted (even in a different version) to fulfill the requirements of another course. Violations of this rule constitute academic dishonesty; all exceptions must be approved in advance and in writing by the instructors of *both* courses.[1]

Pay particular attention to the following rules of citation:

I. Footnotes[2] were not invented only to prove authorship and give credit. They were meant *to help your readers find more information on your subject.* Recalling this point might help you understand that, although it is *not* common knowledge, it is not necessary to footnote the fact that Winnipeg is the capital of Manitoba. That information, although perhaps not commonly known, is easily found in many general reference books. No reader would need to go to a particular reference book to find that fact. The *general idea,* however, that the English-speaking Canadian provinces exhibit different cultural values from the French-speaking Canadian provinces *should* be footnoted, so that your reader knows (1) where you first learned of that difference, and (2) where he or she might find more information on this general point.

II. Remember these general rules:

(1) The actual words of any source must be enclosed in quotation marks and the source must be given.

(2) Footnotes indicate which *general ideas or points,* as well as facts and details, you have gotten from other writers or speakers. Ideas and general points—*not just exact words and small facts*—must be footnoted.

(3) Since the most important borrowing is of ideas, *the changing of wording, even substantial changing of wording, does not do away with the necessity to supply footnotes.*

---

[1]To streamline the process a bit, Freshman Writing's policy is that a student who wishes to use papers from another section of English 101 as the *basis* for work in her current section must first discuss the matter with her current teacher and provide him with a copy of the papers in question. The teacher will let her know whether she is permitted to use the papers, and if so, whether she needs to contact her previous teacher, or whether the teacher will do it for her.

[2]The term "footnote" is used here to indicate all forms of citation, whether at the bottom of the page, at the end of the paper, or within the text.

(4) When you *paraphrase* a point or statement of fact, you must supply a footnote. Paraphrasing means giving a general statement of a quotation in substantially different words. If you were to tell a fellow classmate about these points on "Academic Dishonesty," you would undoubtedly condense and paraphrase. Paraphrasing is sufficient for most uses. If you were debating the exact wording of one of these points, you would find it necessary to quote exactly. In either case, whether you paraphrase or quote directly, you need footnotes.

III. Remember too that a paper is more than a tissue of quotations and citations. The real paper is how you react to the problems of your subject and how you react to what you have read elsewhere. *If well-footnoted, a paper which is an accumulation of outside sources will never be plagiarism, BUT it might be a bad paper nonetheless.* Research and reading should be part of your preparation for a paper, but the heart of the paper is how *you* react to the primary and secondary texts you examine.

In general, failure to follow the above rules will be considered plagiarism.

X

INDEX